the Grace of God of Great Britaine France and Ireland King Defender

&ca

Whereas sundry of our Loyal Subjects, Inhabitants of a Tract of Land within the

d Newhampshire on the Westerly Side of Merrymack River, herein after Described, Have

Incorporated into a Township and Enfranchised with the Same Powers Authorities & Previlidges

And it appearing to us to be conducive to the General good of our Said Province, as

d Order and Encouraging the Culture of the Land, that the Same Should be done

Certaine knowledge, and for the Encouragment and promoting the good purposes and

ell beloved Benning Wentworth Esqr. our Governour and Commander in Chief

nd by these Presents for us our Heirs and Successors, Do will and Ordaine That the Inhabi-

ymack at the Northern Boundary Line of the Province of the Massachusets Bay, and runs from

iver, then by Said River to Flints Brook, then by Flints Brook into Flints Pond, then by a run

Brook to Merrymack River, then on the Westerly Side of Merrymack River to the place

ared and Ordained to be a Town Corporate, And are hereby Erected and Incorporated

Dunstable with all the Powers and Authorities, Previlidges Immunities and Franchises which

ve and To hold, the Said Powers and Authorities, Immunities and Franchises to

us our Heirs and Successors all White Pine Trees growing &

r Royal Navy, Reserving also the Power of Dividing the Said Town to us our Heirs &

s thereof, And as the Several Towns within our Said Province are by the Laws thereof

s as are mentioned in the Said Laws, We do by these Presents Nominate and appoint

Said Town at any time within thirty days from the Date hereof giving Legal Notice of the

ed the Seale of our Said Province to be hereunto affixed Witness Benning

first day of April, in the yeare of our Lord Christ 1746 and in the Nineteenth

orded the 4th Day of Aprile 1746

Pr Theodore Atkinson Se y

the Nashua experience

the Nashua experience

history in the making

1673/1978

by

THE NASHUA HISTORY COMMITTEE

published for the

NASHUA PUBLIC LIBRARY

by

PHOENIX PUBLISHING

Canaan, New Hampshire

Nashua History Committee.
    The Nashua experience.

    Bibliography: p. 262
    Includes index.
    1. Nashua, N. H.—History. I. Title.
F44.N2N27 1978   974.2'8   78-980
ISBN 0-914016-50-4
ISBN 0-914016-51-2 pbk.

Printed in the United States of America
by Courier Printing Company
Binding by New Hampshire Bindery
Design by A.L. Morris

Dedicated

to the memory of

ELIOT AVERY CARTER

First Citizen of Nashua

1886/1976

The Nashua History Committee, under the General Chairmanship of Clarke S. Davis, was composed of the following members who researched and wrote the history:

Florence C. Shepard, *Editor*

Robert C. Frost, *Assistant Editor*

Elizabeth C. Spring	Anne M. McWeeney
Robert W. Haven	Nyla Lipnick
Ruth M. West	Thomas Greenman

Virginia Nedved

Assistance in indexing was given by Carol A. Nelson, the manuscript typist was Margaret F. Green, and the following persons gave oral interviews on their recollections of Nashua events: John Sullivan, Dr. Luther March, Agnes Chesnulovich, Elizabeth Cole, and Bernice Pulsifer.

Contents

The cover illustration, Nashua Village from the South . . .painted by J. D. Crocker and lithographed by J. H. Sufford of Boston, was published circa 1840. The 200 year old house shown at the left is still standing, and was at one time the residence of Roscoe Milliken, Agent for the Nashua Manufacturing Company.

Acknowledgments

The Nashua History Committee gratefully acknowledges assistance given by the following persons and organizations:

Richard L. Cane, Nashua City Planner
Paul E. Newman of the City Planning Board
Lionel Guilbert, City Clerk of Nashua
Judge Robert F. Griffith, who read the manuscript for historical content
Rev. Soterios Alexopoulos for information on the Greek community
Samuel Tamposi for information on the Roumanian ethnic group
Alden W. Gould for material on the canals
Stuart H. Batchelder for the loan of letters
Robert Paine for the loan of his postcard collection
Edmund M. Keefe, President of the Nashua Historical Society
Mrs. Faith Flythe, Chairman of the Exhibits Committee of the Nashua Historical Society
The Nashua Chamber of Commerce
The Nashua-New Hampshire Foundation
The Nashua Historical Society
The New Hampshire Historical Society Library
The Massachusetts Historical Society Library
The New England Historic Genealogical Society Library
The Merrimack Valley Textile Museum

The Committee would like to extend a special word of thanks to the Finance Committee of the Board of Aldermen of the City of Nashua who recommended passage of an appropriation for the publication of the history.
The Editor and Assistant Editor wish to express their personal appreciation for the encouragement and helpfulness shown at all stages of publication by Al Morris and Lex Paradis of Phoenix Publishing.

Introduction

IT IS SIGNIFICANT that a new history of Nashua has been published. The previous history of our City, published in 1897, was written in the rather stiff, formal style of its day with heavy emphasis on the "great men" of that period. *The Nashua Experience* ambitiously attempts to review the early history of Nashua as well as pick up where the Parker history ended. Originally conceived as a bicentennial project of relatively brief scope, the project soon grew into a full-length book. Under the editorship of Florence Shepard, the History Committee wisely chose to expand the content of the book greatly, seizing an opportunity to break much new historical ground. The history documents the development of Nashua as we know it today with particular attention to the area's industrial development, municipal government, ethnic groups, labor history, women, the daily lives of ordinary people, transportation, education, and even a look into the future.

While a history may be written and read from various points of view, many town histories have provided their readers with little more than a quaintly nostalgic orientation to their area's past. This history seeks to portray accurately Nashua's past, without overly romanticizing it, by establishing a factual and graphic linkage of events and human experience.

It is hoped *The Nashua Experience* will help to provide a sense of perspective to a city which has experienced very rapid growth. As Nashua has become the focal point of development in New Hampshire, it is important that it retain a strong sense of its past as guidance for the future and that its people are able to maintain a strongly integrated sense of community.

A history seen from this point of view was colorfully expressed by that durable New Englander, Daniel Webster, who commented, "When the mariner has tossed for many days in thick weather, and on an unknown sea, he naturally avails himself of the first pause in the storm, the earliest glance of the sun, to take his latitude and ascertain how far the elements have driven him from his course."

Clarke S. Davis

Chairman, Nashua History Committee

Director, Nashua Public Library

The Ancient Township

to 1725

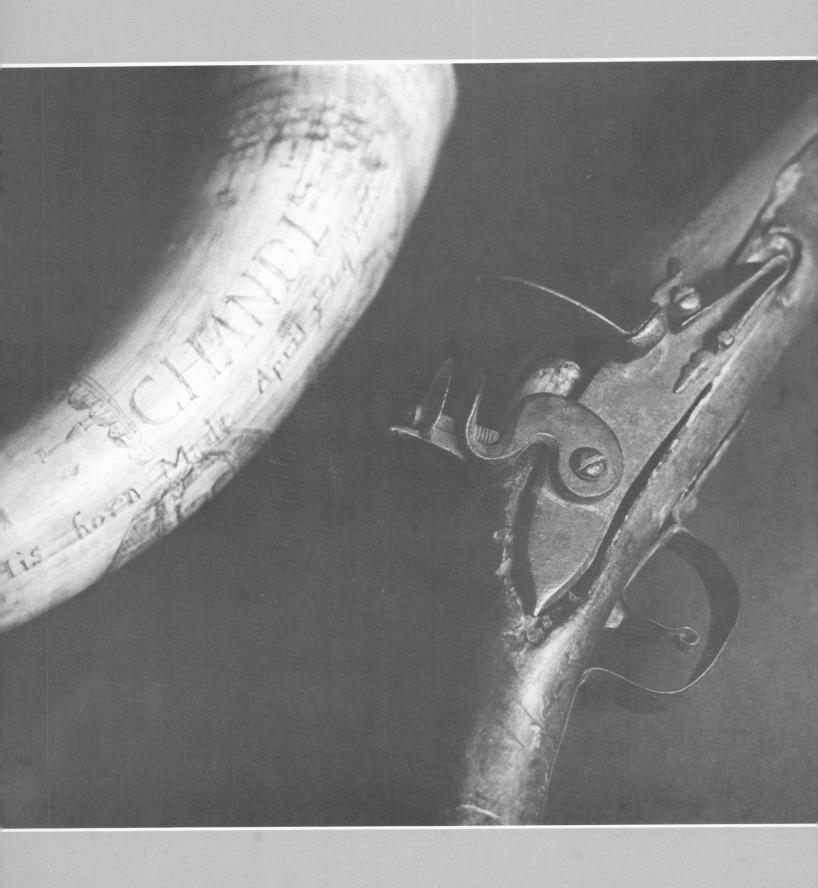

1

Before
the Charter

IN THE YEAR 1684 a young man named Samuel Whiting set out on a journey from Billerica to a place called Dunstable. It would take him several hours, so he would have to leave quite early in the day, a sturdy but very slow team of oxen pulling a wagonload of tools and supplies. No records tell us the exact time of year but it probably was spring, to allow for good weather to start his homestead.

Leaving Billerica, he crossed a bridge over the Concord River and followed a crude road that had been built through the wilderness to Chelmsford. Settled thirty years before, it was now a flourishing village of about sixty families, directly south of Dunstable. Here Samuel probably broke his journey to visit the Reverend Thomas Clarke, the local minister who was a friend of his father. Clarke, who also owned a small piece of land in Dunstable, would have the latest news of all of the families that had moved there from Chelmsford—the Blanchards, the Waldos, the Parkers, the Goulds.

The longest part of his journey still lay ahead, on the road that had been built recently to link Chelmsford and Dunstable. As the sun rose higher, he came to the place where the Merrimack River turns its course eastward to the sea. Trudging up its western bank, he soon found himself within that part of Dunstable that today is the town of Tyngsborough, Massachusetts. At the mansard-roofed house of Jonathan Tyng, overlooking the river, he undoubtedly stopped once more for rest, refreshment, and the latest news. He continued up a dusty trail that many years later was to become the Daniel Webster Highway. Near the spot where the Spit Brook Road crosses the highway, he came to the parsonage of his cousin, Dunstable's first minister, Thomas Weld. This home of a relative must have offered him temporary shelter until he had built his own dwelling. A mile or two beyond the parsonage awaited his family's grant on the southern bank of the Salmon Brook. Samuel Whiting had come home at last!

Whiting was twenty-two years old when he decided to pioneer on a grant of land that had been in his family for twenty-five years. Five years before this fateful journey, his father, the Reverend Samuel Whiting of Billerica, had inherited the land from his own father, the first Samuel Whiting, of Lynn. In the inventory of this estate, found in the probate records of Essex County, the value of all of the real estate is lumped together, so that it is not possible to determine the exact valuation placed on what he referred to in his will as "my farm at Dunstable."

Looking at the map on page 31, the exact location of the house that Samuel built for himself in the southwestern corner of his grant can be seen. Just south of the present Robinson Road, it was on the bank of an outlet of the Salmon Brook called Whiting Brook, long ago obliterated by the housing developments of later generations.

THE STORY of how the Whiting family had acquired four hundred acres of land in the heart of what is now the City of Nashua, New Hampshire, goes back to 1636 when the first Reverend Samuel Whiting had left England because he felt somewhat restricted in freedom of expression in the pulpit. On the long voyage, during which he suffered a bad case of seasickness, he was accompanied by his wife, Elizabeth St. John, and two children—their own son, Samuel, Jr., and Whiting's daughter by a former marriage, Dorothy. Samuel, Jr., later became pastor of the church in Billerica, while Dorothy married the Reverend Thomas Weld of Roxbury.

Role of the Whiting Family

Samuel left behind in England a brother, John Whiting, who served four terms as Mayor of Boston, the city that gave its name to Boston, Massachusetts. About two years after the minister and his family had arrived, John Whiting made a personal loan of fifty pounds to the Massachusetts Bay Colony, as a way of showing his support for a worthy common cause. Meanwhile, Samuel Whiting prospered and found the freedom that he sought—in fact, he was held in such high esteem by his parishioners that they named their town "Lynn" after his former home in England.

In 1659 he applied to the General Court of Massachusetts, on behalf of John Whiting, for a grant of land in repayment of the loan made twenty years before. The legislature, much richer in land than in money, was glad to discharge the debt in this way. The grant, duly recorded, described the land as being "on the western side of the Merrimack River, beginning at the mouth of the Salmon Brook and so extending upwards on the same brook about one mile and a half, being butted and bounded by the Merrimack River on the east and by the upland side on the north of the said brook." (This probably took in at least part of the present golf course of the Nashua Country Club.) When he received word of this grant, John Whiting immediately signed over the deed to his clergyman brother.

The third Samuel Whiting, who made the journey here in 1684 to live on the land that had originally belonged to his great-uncle, could trace a distinguished ancestral line on his grandmother's side. Elizabeth St. John Whiting, described by people who knew her as a beautiful and cultivated woman, was a direct descendant of ten royal houses of Europe, including William the Conqueror. To add further luster, she was related to Oliver Cromwell and England's most famous Chief Justice, Oliver St. John. It is also said that far more than mere wifely duty lay behind the willingness of this aristocratic lady to come to a strange and rough new land—personally she held very strong anti-royalist political views! For the rest of her life, she was quite content to be a parson's wife in Lynn.

With a similar feeling of contentment her grandson entered into the pioneer life of Dunstable. He was a town official in several capacities, married Elizabeth Read, daughter of a neighbor, and made a fortified garrison out of his house when the need arose. In 1704 he was taken prisoner by the Indians, but he escaped from Canada where he had been taken, made his way home, and later received a ten-pound award as compensation for his wounds and hardships. This would make an exciting adventure story in the history of Nashua except for the fact that there is no record of the circumstances under which he was captured or how he escaped.

When Samuel Whiting died in 1714, he was buried in his home town of Billerica. This family had a leading part in Dunstable's early history in other ways. A fourth Samuel, a son of the preceding, was badly wounded in the Fryeburg expedition of Lovewell's War. Another son, Leonard, was probably the first resident of the part of Nashua north of the Nashua River. It all happened because a mayor of Boston, England, made a fifty-pound loan when Massachusetts needed money.

The Whiting grant was only one of many made by Massachusetts around 1660 in the area that later became the township of Ancient Dunstable. Nashua, as we know it, was the central core of this township that was chartered in 1673. A 200-square-mile rectangle, on both sides of the Merrimack River and on both sides of the present Massachusetts-New Hampshire state line, was the mother of almost a dozen towns that are in existence today.

It may seem strange to try to visualize Massachusetts as having jurisdiction over the western part of New Hampshire all the way to Lake Winnipesaukee, but such was the case in the late seventeenth century and right up until 1741. Eastward, from the 40th to the 49th parallels, a huge territory had been granted to one man, John Mason. It was Mason who gave the name "New Hampshire" to an empire that he himself never had stepped foot on. He died as he was about to embark on a journey of inspection, and his heirs tried unsuccessfully for many years to hold on to the claim.

Exploration of the Merrimack Valley

In 1652, the Massachusetts General Court decided that the entire valley of the Merrimack should be explored to settle the question of where the river had its source. Up until that time, geographical confusion existed because of a theory that the river had its origin in New York State. Two famous military men of the time were the leaders of the party sent out on this mission: Captain Simon Willard and Captain Edward Johnson. Willard, a native of Concord, later settled in Groton where he built a comfortable and spacious home, Nonacoicus Farm, that was a mecca for colonial society until it was burned down in King Philip's War. Johnson was one of the founders of Woburn; he was also the author of one of the first histories of New England. Other members of the party were a professional surveyor and a young Harvard College student who assisted the surveyor.

The four explorers discovered that the Merrimack River emerged from Lake Winnipesaukee, and inscribed a rock to indicate that Massachusetts claimed as its territory all of the land up to three miles north of that point. The western boundary of the claim was the border of New York State. In 1833 the rock with the inscription was found in the river bed, and sixty years later a monument was erected over it. The Endicott Rock, so-called because John Endicott was the governor at the time of the survey, may be seen today on the shore of the lake, commemorating this claim once staked out by the Bay State.

The trip up the Merrimack to Winnipesaukee was only the first of several similar explorations undertaken by Willard and Johnson. In 1655 they came with a party of guides to investigate the various streams running into the Merrimack. The Pennichuck system interested them and they ventured inland to try to locate the source of this complex of ponds and brooks. Night came on and with it a heavy fog. The party became lost in the mists enshrouding the terrain and one member of the group commented that he felt that the place was "bewitched." This is how Witch Brook in Hollis got its name!

Massachusetts used some of the thousands of newly acquired acres to pay off its debts, compensate individuals and groups for services, and help some of its towns. The Whiting grant was one of the very few actually homesteaded by a member of the family receiving the grant. In most cases the land grants were regarded as investments, to be held until the tide of colonization reached the area and increased the value of the land.

The Hills Grant

One other grant that was developed by members of the family of the original grantee was that made to Joseph Hills, a founder and resident of Malden. In 1661 he was given five hundred acres in the area east of the Merrimack River, in what is now Hudson. While still living in Malden, England, where he was a woolen draper, Hills had advanced thirty-three pounds to the colony, and after he came over in 1638 he had done a valuable service by codifying the laws of Massachusetts. When the grant was first set up, it was in three different places and extended a long way beside the river. Hills himself requested that the land be laid out again so that it would be concentrated in one area, even if it extended further back from the river. Hills died in 1688 and his will mentions his land in Dunstable several times, as he parceled it out to various children and grandchildren, with the largest bequest going to his son, Samuel. In each case, the heir was given a small amount of the desirable meadow or riverside land in addition to a portion of the "upland." Hills also left fifty acres to a favored son-in-law, John Waite, who had come over with him in the same ship and helped him establish Malden. In the Old Dunstable Records the name of John Waite shows up as being a substantial landowner in the area in his own right as early as 1680.

The Hills grant was finally homesteaded by three grandsons of Joseph Hills, all sons of Samuel Hills, who moved here from Newbury. They are considered the first residents of what is now Hudson, traditionally supposed to have been settled around 1710.

Richard Dummer, a prominent citizen of Newbury, was another individual who had lent money to the colony in the late 1630s. He was now repaid with eight hundred acres of land along the Merrimack River. Dummer seems to have received a better deal than the Whitings, as he was awarded twice as much land for seventy-three pounds as they got for fifty pounds. The quality of the land, however, was a consideration in determining the value.

Other Early Grants

In November, 1659, a great many other grants were placed on record. Among the recipients were two of the passengers in John Winthrop's fleet that sailed here in 1630 and founded the City of Boston. One was John Wilson, Boston's first minister, who was given 1,000 acres, 700 on the Souhegan River and 300 "upon the head of Pennichuck Brook, being bounded by a great pond on the southwest called Pennichuck Pond." These two parcels of land were in compensation for his services as a chaplain in the war with the Pequot Indians. Wilson very soon turned the land into cash, selling it to Simon Lynde, another prominent Bostonian.

Another Winthrop passenger who received a grant was Samuel Cole, Boston's first innkeeper. His four hundred acres were rather irregularly distributed between "Little Nacook" and "Great Nacook" Brooks. *The History of Chelmsford* by Waters has a brief reference to this grant as having actually been made in May of 1658: "the neck of land desired, lying within a mile and a half of Nacooke, beyond the town of Chelmsford, granted to Samuel Cole by the General Court." Cole's name is listed as one of the "gentry" of Boston but there is no record as to why he was entitled to this gift. He was, however, a member of the Ancient and Honorable Artillery Company.

In the list of individuals benefiting from the land giveaway program of 1659, another person by the name of "Cole" is noted. This is a woman, Mrs. Anna Keayne Cole, who received a grant of five hundred acres, as did her granddaughter, Anna Keayne Lane. The older Anna was the widow of Robert Keayne, wealthy Boston merchant and first commander of the Ancient and Honorable Artillery Company. After his death, she married Samuel Cole, the Boston innkeeper. She had come from England with her first husband and a teenage son, Benjamin Keayne, in 1635. Benjamin later married Sarah Dudley, daughter of Governor Thomas Dudley, a marriage that was such a disaster that Benjamin fled back to England to escape a notoriously temperamental woman. The couple had one child, Anna, whom Robert Keayne wanted to leave well provided for financially. In one of the longest wills ever probated, Keayne, who started life as a tailor, bequeathed money to the Massachusetts colony on condition that his wife and granddaughter be given land grants. The money, incidentally, helped to build Boston's first city hall.

In the records of the General Court for 1659 we find the following evidence that Keayne's wishes were carried out:

In consideration of the late Captain Robert Keayne's liberal gift to the country in his will, the whole court met together voted that: Mrs. Anna Cole, the late relict of the said Captain Robert Keayne, and Anna Keayne, the grandchild, shall have five hundred acres of land apiece laid out to them and their heirs where it is to be found.

The land was "found" along the fertile banks of the Souhegan in what is now Milford and Amherst.

Documents preserved at the Massachusetts Historical Society reveal that Anna Cole was a strong-minded and intelligent woman. In 1657 the younger Anna became engaged to marry Edward

Lane, a new arrival in the colony, whom her grandmother suspected was a fortune-hunter. She had an ironclad prenuptial agreement drawn up to protect the girl's property. Within a few months after the wedding, the younger Anna tried to have her marriage annulled, apparently because of conflict over this agreement. The marriage continued, however, and the couple had two children before Lane died in 1663. Anna remarried, this time to a man named Nicholas Paige who was an executor of her grandfather's will. In references to these two women who owned land in the Greater Nashua area at this early date, we get glimpses of the character of each—the older Anna a level-headed and capable person, the younger Anna rather unstable and flighty, a woman who did not quite fulfill the hopes of her doting grandfather. The documents concerning them reveal that women in the seventeenth century not only had certain legal rights but were able to exercise considerable control over their property and money.

At least one grant traced to the eventual benefit of the heirs of the grantee was the one made to Phinehas Pratt. Pratt was a colonial adventurer who had been sent over as a member of a colonizing party by Thomas Weston, a supporter of the Plymouth Pilgrims. After a hazardous trip in a small boat down the coast of Maine, where their ship had originally landed, the party visited Plymouth and then went on to set up their own "plantation" near what is now the town of Weymouth. Pratt performed a famous feat of valor—a journey on foot, alone, through winter cold and snow, in constant fear of ambush, to warn the Plymouth people of an impending Indian attack. Many years later, old, sick, and in need, he wrote an account of his deeds and presented it to the General Court, as a hint that he felt he deserved some reward. In 1662 he was given a grant of three hundred acres of land in what is now Litchfield. Although this was of no real practical help to the aged Pratt, the land was finally sold in 1738 and the proceeds distributed among his grandchildren and great-grandchildren.

Billerica was a good example of a town that benefited from a land grant in the area that later became Dunstable. In 1657 it was involved in legal problems with its mother town of Cambridge, which had tied up many of the choicest plots of land within its boundaries. The people asked for additional territory and the Province of Massachusetts gave them a generous amount—no less than 8,000 acres straddling the Merrimack River, 6,300 in what is now Litchfield, and 1,700 in Merrimack, an area that was known as the "Naticook Lands." One year later, Billerica, having solved its Cambridge problems, decided to sell the grant to enrich the municipal treasury. In a transaction that is described in detail in Hazen's *History of Billerica,* a Boston man by the name of William Brenton purchased the entire grant for two hundred pounds. For many years this territory was called Brenton's Farm.

Land grants were made to some Massachusetts towns as a form of state aid to education. By provincial law it was compulsory that children be educated, but the towns often had a hard time financing schools and teachers' salaries. Land was given to them in some undeveloped area and these tracts were called "school farms," with the general idea that the eventual sale or leasing of the land would give them the funds they needed to support public schools. The town of Charlestown, for example, was given such a tract on the banks of the Souhegan River, near the place called "Dramcup Hill." It was not until 1743 that this Massachusetts town sold the property to a private individual.

The Rev. John Wilson, Sr., Boston's first minister.

The Ancient and Honorable Artillery Company

An example of an organization that received a land grant in this vicinity was the Ancient and Honorable Artillery Company, which could probably be best described as the National Guard of its day. (This company is still in existence as a ceremonial group.) The English parent company had existed for a hundred years when the American company was formed in 1638. Experience in this civilian military training corps paid off in fighting the Indians and, later, in the American Revolution. Recognition for its services was given when it was first organized; the province declared that it was entitled to one thousand acres of land at an unspecified place not already granted to anyone else. It was not, however, until September, 1673, that the grant was made specifically, taking in a large part of what is now Nashua's North End. When their "farm" was surveyed and laid out, they were given "1000 acres of upland and meadow . . . from a red oak tree . . . by a gully side on the bank of Merrimack River, on a straight line west by south." In the deed Spectacle Brook and Nashaway or "Watananock River" are mentioned.

This tract of land was part of the organization's real estate holdings. The company seems to have taken little interest in it until 1715 when the leadership decided to lease the land, at which time human habitation on the north side of the Nashua River was started on a modest scale. According to the official history of the company, the tenant was a member of the Whiting family, Leonard (one of Samuel Whiting's eight children), who fenced off fifty acres as a small farm and lived there for eleven years. A condition of the lease was that an apple orchard was to be planted, from the crop of which the company in Boston was to receive one barrel of cider a year.

In 1727 the Artillery Company sent a committee of seven members up to Dunstable to inspect this property. The committee took with them two local men, Henry Farwell and William Lund. Their detailed report states that they required this additional help to "gain a true knowledge of the waste thereon." They found many of the trees, including the red oak, used as markers fallen and decayed. Some of the abutting owners mentioned were Colonel Hutchinson, Colonel Tyng and Brenton's

Farm. The tone of the report implies that they did not find the "farm" especially promising, just a sandy pine forest; they noted that many of the best pines had been "bled," apparently the result of the turpentine-making operations of Dunstable residents. It also did not escape their notice that John Lovewell had been taking hay from the two patches of meadow and that someone had been cutting pine trees for lumber.

By 1731, the Artillery Company had decided this remote territory was not much good to them and voted to sell it, with the permission of the Massachusetts House of Representatives. In 1737 Colonel Joseph Blanchard, whose real estate transactions we shall hear more about later, bought the entire tract but there is no record of the price he paid. In 1789 his heirs finally paid off the mortgage after a law suit had been fought in the courts. Roberts' *History of the Ancient and Honorable Artillery Company* says only: "A mortgage was taken in security, and after the mortgagor's death long continued in dispute, until a suit thereon was commenced in the United States Court for the District of New Hampshire, and judgment rendered in the Company's favor."

Besides this grant bestowed on the Artillery Company itself, groups of officers were rewarded for special services. In May, 1659, seven were on record as having petitioned the Court to grant them "meete ffarmes"; each of the seven was to be given 250 acres, exact locations not specified at that time. In November of the same year, the Court records note that a specific piece of land "on the west side of the Merrimack River upon Salmon Brook," 1,000 acres altogether, had been surveyed and laid out to a group of four men, three of whom were among the seven listed in the May petition.

Three others of the seven were Peter Oliver, James Oliver, and John Evered. Along with another man, James Johnson, they were given a joint grant that is found in the Massachusetts archives. Dated June 7, 1659, it reads:

Laid out to Left. Peter Oliver, Capt. James Oliver, Capt. James Johnson and Ensigne John Evered: 1000 acres of land in the wilderness on the northern side of Merrimack River, lying about Nahamkeage, being bounded with Merrimack River on the south and on the west, the wilderness elsewhere surrounding according to marked trees, as by a plat taken of the same is demonstrated by Jonathan Danforth, Surveyor.

According to the *History of Chelmsford,* John Evered, a Chelmsford man who was also known by the alias of John Webb, bought out the interests of the other three officers. Evered was a maverick type of character, with considerable penchant for getting into trouble, but with a shrewd business sense. He died in 1668, and in settling his estate it was discovered that a Boston sea captain named Samuel Scarlet had bought the thousand-acre farm from Evered. The executor of Evered's estate insisted that the land should be surveyed again and the trees designated as boundary markers were marked with the letter "S." The deed confirming the purchase has been located in Liber VI of the *Suffolk Deeds,* dated April 27, 1670. This solves a long-standing mystery concerning how Captain Scarlet obtained this large tract of land on the eastern side of the Merrimack River, much of it in what is now the town of Dracut, Massachusetts. Incidentally, a document has also been found revealing that one week before his death Evered approached John Freake, Scarlet's business partner, with an offer to buy back the land for 120 pounds, which gives some indication of its value.

Scarlet, whose signature appears on the petition for a township charter in 1673, and who signed the minutes of the first town meeting in May, 1674, is an elusive person as far as personal information is concerned. The fragmentary facts about him that can be pieced together are that he was born in Kersey, England, was closely associated with a prominent shipping family, the Bendalls, and had one brother, John, who was the executor of his estate. He and Freake owned warehouses, docks, and wharves on the Boston waterfront. Scarlet was killed in a ship explosion in Boston Harbor in 1675. The name of John Scarlet occurs several times in the Old Dunstable Records as the person liable for payment of taxes on the land, which was not sold until 1711, when Lieutenant Joseph Butterfield and Joseph Perham purchased "the Scarlet farm, on the east side of the Merrimack River, next to Dracut line, now within the limits of Tyngsboro." Part of the one thousand acres was also located in what is now Hudson, according to ancient maps.

Two other individual members of the Artillery Company, each given five hundred acres of land on the Souhegan River, were Captain William Davis and Captain Isaac Johnson. The historian, Savage, in his monumental dictionary of New England genealogy, calls Davis "a man of wealth, enterprise, and discretion." In 1653 he was a commissioner appointed to undertake negotiations with the Dutch government of New York. Isaac Johnson was killed in the final episode in King Philip's War at Narragansett.

The Edward Tyng Purchase

Instances of land tracts changing hands by purchase reveal increased interest in this part of the frontier as the next stage for settlement. In 1660, Edward Tyng with great foresight had purchased a large acreage from James Parker of Chelmsford. Tyng was a Boston merchant, later a magistrate, who did not actually live on his estate in what is now the town of Tyngsborough until two years before his death. His son, Jonathan, started developing the property in 1668, building his house (which still stands) soon after. For the next forty-five years, the strong leadership of Jonathan Tyng was an important factor in the growth of Dunstable.

A grandnephew of Edward Tyng also purchased land in the Ancient Dunstable area. This was Thomas Brattle, grandson of Edward's brother, William, who had come from Dunstable, England, with him. Brattle's purchase was directly from an Indian chief, the head of the Massapoag group who once lived in what is now Dunstable, Massachusetts. This part of ancient Dunstable was called "Brattle's End."

The Bancroft Farm and Buried Treasure

The oldest farm (in the modern sense, not simply as a piece of wilderness land owned by an individual) is undoubtedly the Bancroft tract which straddled the present state line. It has a very interesting history. Its first owner was Edward Johnson, the Woburn explorer who was given land grants in recognition of his services as an explorer. Sometime in the 1650s Johnson sold this property to a rather colorful individual by the name of John Cromwell. Cromwell was a trader who made a fortune by bartering with the Indians for a commodity that was very important in colonial trade with Europe—luxurious furs. He was a squatter on the Naticook lands in what is now Merrimack, an independent and enterprising man who probably well deserves the title of first white inhabitant of this section of the Merrimack Valley. There are many legends and stories about Cromwell that have been passed down—he may or may not have cheated the Indians with whom he traded. Anyhow, he made enough money to acquire an extensive estate in Tyngsborough. After Cromwell's death in 1661, his widow was forced to mortgage the estate which was bought by Joseph Wheeler. It was later known as the Bancroft farm after it became the home of Colonel Ebenezer Bancroft who played an important role in the Battle of Bunker Hill.

The only story of the discovery of buried treasure in this area has its setting on the Bancroft farm. More than one owner after Cromwell accidentally found some of it. Present day descendants of Colonel Bancroft tell a story that has been passed down about a member of the family who turned up a large sum of money while plowing the fields. He hastily reburied the treasure in a secret place of his own choosing and, whenever he needed additional funds, would use some of this hidden supply. He told no member of his family where the hiding place was and, although he intended to make a deathbed disclosure, breathed his last before he was able to give the directions. His heirs were never able to locate it. Who originally buried the money and for what reason is a mystery to this day.

The First Nashua Resident

Joseph Wheeler, at whose house the first town meeting was held in 1674, has traditionally been called the first resident of Nashua proper. Wheeler was a lieutenant in the British Army and a member of a Concord family noted for military ability and exploits. His father, Captain Thomas Wheeler, once led an expedition to Brookfield in which he was ambushed by the Indians and severely wounded. Rescued by one of his sons, he managed to fortify a garrison for several days until help arrived. Simon Willard was one of those who came to his assistance, along with James Parker, later a Dunstable Selectman. When a provincial law was passed to regulate the fur trade, Thomas Wheeler was one of four men who bought the legal right to deal in furs in this area. The others were William Brenton, Simon Willard, and Thomas Henchman of Chelmsford. Because of this interest, the older

Wheeler lived for some time in the early 1670s with his son, Joseph. In fact, the main concern of the Wheelers, father and son, seems to have been the buying of furs from the local Indian trappers. They were undoubtedly living on what later was known as the Bancroft farm before 1673. An illuminating document in this regard is the text of an agreement, dated May 12, 1674, between Joseph Wheeler and a committee of four representing the new Township of Dunstable. This agreement is found on pages 144 and 145 of Volume I of the Dunstable Town Records, as copied by Joseph Blanchard in 1752. It spells out details of a land swap in which Wheeler surrendered one hundred acres of intervale land on the Merrimack River in return for a

tract of land beginning at a heap of stones being corner marker of said J. Wheeler's farm on Phillips Hill and so on thru the swamp near the place of passing over . . . to the upper end of Halfmoon Meadow, to the maple swamp, and so on thru the meadow . . . till it joins with Mr. Brattle's line at his northeast corner.

It is difficult to determine from this description if any of this land was in what is now Nashua proper. However, when the state line was drawn in 1741, part of the farm was on the New Hampshire side.

Nashua's first historian, Charles Fox, mentions the fact that there was evidence, such as full-grown apple orchards flourishing in 1673, that families had been living in the area for some time before the charter was granted. Who planted the apple trees? This is one of the unanswered questions in Dunstable-Nashua history. Their names are lost in the mists of time, because no records were kept and no personal recollections have been passed down concerning them. There were probably less than half a dozen families actually living here in the fall of 1673.

The people in Boston and other Massachusetts towns who were the owners of land grants or "farms" at the time constituted themselves the "Proprietors" of the area. This group had a genuine vested interest in setting up a town that would attract additional settlers. Twenty-six of these people got together, therefore, to draw up a petition to the Massachusetts General Court that the area be declared a township. The petition pointed out that "there [are] a considerable number of persons who are of a sober and orderly conversation, who do stand in great need of accommodations, who are willing and ready to make present improvements of the said vacant lands." In other words, they had confidence that, once a large area of the wilderness just north of Chelmsford and Groton had had boundaries defined and had been declared a legal entity, ambitious settlers would swarm in to take up homesteads.

One other document was also drawn up at this time—a contract which has been compared to the Mayflower Compact of the Plymouth Pilgrims, that laid down civic ground rules for the prospective residents. One of the clauses in the second document, called the Agreement, read "to the intent that we may live in love and peace together," sounding the keynote and expressing the spirit in which Ancient Dunstable was established. As the forest foliage blazed with autumn color in 1673, this organization of a new township took place. It was to remain in its original size and form for the next fifty years.

2

"That We May Live in Love and Peace Together"

THE AGREEMENT drawn up by the proprietors provided for minimal private property rights to be given to every family that came here to live. Each homesteader was responsible for improving his allotment of land so that his family could be self-supporting. This initial allotment for a personal house lot was an outright grant of ten acres. For every twenty pounds that an individual was worth, he was entitled to an additional free acre, up to a maximum of thirty acres. This meant that a settler who came to Dunstable with four hundred pounds in cash (over a thousand dollars) had a farm of thirty acres laid out to him, and the land itself actually cost him nothing.

Screening The Applicants

The Proprietors' group, who carefully screened the applicants for homestead lots, reasoned that a man had to have money to buy tools and equipment, farm animals, and seed in order to farm a very large tract of woodland and meadow. The man who had little or no money might not be able to fully exploit such a tract. They felt that he should start small and accumulate extra land when he could handle it. To judge from the transactions recorded in the Ancient Dunstable Records, many of the early arrivals were able to do this, and the most energetic bought hundreds of acres of additional land.

Setting forth as a general social aim the establishment of a community where everyone would "live in love and peace together," the agreement suggested that there should be respect for individual privacy. "Love thy neighbor and see that thy cows do not wander into his corn field" was an implied commandment. Besides specifying the size and type of fences and walls that should be erected along boundaries, the agreement provided for eminent domain. If a town meeting voted to build roads, a right of way through the lands of any owner could be claimed. If you were a land owner, you were also expected to pay taxes. The principal community expense was the support of the church and the minister, but roads, bridges, and the common grazing grounds were also important matters that involved all residents. What about schools for the education of the children? They were not even mentioned in any of the documents drawn up in connection with the organization of the town, nor were they mentioned for many years in town records.

The Charter Is Granted

In 1976, as the United States of America observed its two hundredth anniversary, Nashua marked the three hundred and third year of its founding. On October 26, 1673, the Massachusetts General Court granted a charter for the township. The area included the present towns of Dunstable and Tyngsborough, Massachusetts, plus parts of Dracut and Townsend, and the following places in the portion of the area ceded in 1741 to the State of New Hampshire: the City of Nashua and the towns of Hudson, Merrimack (as far as the Souhegan River), Litchfield, Pelham, Milford, Amherst, Hollis, and Brookline. Small sections of other present-day towns were also included in the chartered territory.

Portsmouth, Dover, Exeter, and Hampton were the four places in the Masonian Grant of New Hampshire that had already been established. Nashua can therefore rightfully claim to be the fifth place in present day New Hampshire that was chartered. The petition requesting township status had been signed on September 19, 1673, by the group of twenty-six men mentioned before. They were not the only ones having a vested interest in further settlement of the area, but were probably those who found it convenient to attend meetings. Whiting and Hills, for example, are two obvious names that are missing among the signatures. We have no information on the circumstances of the writing and signing of the petition or the drawing up of the agreement (there were no signatures on the agreement).

Background Of The Signers

The identities of twenty-four of the signers are known; nothing is known about Thomas Edwards and Samuel Combs. Edwards is listed as the owner of almost five hundred acres of land in the vicinity but the name of Combs is not found in any existing records. These were the twenty-four others, whose personal land holdings reveal the extent to which many of the original grants had been sold off between 1659 and 1673:

Thomas Brattle–his bold and flourishing signature leads all the others, giving the distinct impression that he was a leading advocate of the charter; he signed the minutes of the first town meeting.

Jonathan Tyng–undoubtedly another leader in the action; he represented the interest of the Tyng family, who owned well over ten thousand acres of land.

Joseph Wheeler–probably the first resident of Nashua proper; land owned by him is given in the proprietors' records as 322 acres.

Robert Gibbs–prominent Boston merchant who died a few weeks after he signed the petition; owned two hundred acres of Dunstable land, which was later bought by John Blanchard and Robert Fletcher.

John Turner–a Salem merchant; signed minutes of first town meeting; owned three hundred acres.

Sampson Sheafe–politically influential Bostonian who owned six hundred acres.

William Lakin–leading citizen of Groton; was on committee that arranged land swap for Joseph Wheeler mentioned in Chapter I.

James Knapp–also of Groton, a member of the committee that marked out Wheeler land swap.

Robert Proctor–of Concord, who, according to the oldest record books, owned over eight hundred acres of Dunstable land, later sold to the Harwoods.

Simon Willard, Jr.–son of the explorer and fur trader.

Thomas Wheeler–fur trader and father of Joseph Wheeler.

Peter Bulkeley–son of a famous clergyman of Concord, married Joseph Wheeler's daughter, Rebecca.

John Morse, Sr.–town clerk of Groton.

Robert Parris–soldier in King Philip's War, married John Cromwell's widow.

John Joliffe–wealthy and prominent Bostonian, owned over four hundred acres.

Zachariah Long–originally, like the Tyngs, from Dunstable, England, a resident of Charlestown; he owned five hundred acres here.

Six members of the Parker family–Abraham, the founder of Chelmsford, and four of his sons and one grandson: Joseph, John, Josiah, Captain James, and James, Jr.

Nathaniel Blood–a Parker son-in-law.

Samuel Scarlet–the sea captain who took advantage of an opportunity to invest in some wilderness real estate, in the southeastern corner of the area.

The charter itself consisted simply of a notation at the bottom of the petition, confirming the boundaries outlined in the request and stipulating that five hundred acres of the territory in question should be reserved for the use of the province, that

To the Honoured Govern.r Dep.t Gover.r with the Magis.
and Dep.ts now assembled in the Gen: Court at Boston Sep.t 1673

The Petition of the propriet.rs of the farmes that are laid out upon
Merrimak River and places adjacent; with others who desire to joyne
with them in the settlement of a plantation there

Humbly Sheweth that whereas there is a considerable tract of the Countrie
land that is enbironed with the propriaties of particular persons and townes
(viz) by the line of the towne of Cholmesford, and by Grauton line and by
Mr Brautons farme, by downham farmes: And beyond Merrimaks River
by the outermost line of Honour.d Rumbals farme and so to Cholmesford
line againe all which is in little Capacity of dooing the Countrie any servis
except the farmes bordering upon it, be adjoyned to the said land to make
a plantaton there: And there being a considerable number of persons who are
of a sober and orderly conbersation that doe stand in great need of accomodations who are willing and ready to make present improvement of the said
vacant Land: And the propriet.rs of the said farmes are therefore willing
to joyne with, and gibe incouragem.t to those that shall improve the said Land
the farmes of themselbes that are within the tract of Land before distin
containe about foure teene thousand acres at the least

Yo.r Petition.rs therefore humbly request the fabour of this honoured
Court that they will please to grant the said tract of Land to yo.r Petition.rs
and to such as shall joyne with them in the settlement of the land afore mentioned so that those who habe already improved their farmes there and
others also who speedyly intend to doo the like: may be in a way for the en
ioyment of the publiq ordinances of god: for with out which the greatest
part of the yeare they will be deprived of: the farmes being so far remoat
from any townes: And farther that this Honoured Court will please to grant
the like immunities to this plantaton as they in their fabours habe formerly
granted to other new plantatons; So shall yo.r Petition.rs be ever engaged
to pray &c//

The magists Judge it meet to   Tho: Brattle
grant the petitionrs request   Jonathan Tyng:
herein Provided that a farme of   Tho: Wheeler and Joseph wheeler
fibe hundred acres of upland & meadow Peter Buckley
be layd out of   John Parker   James Parker sen
this tract for the publick use that   John morse   Robert Gibbs
they so proceed in setling of plantation Samuell howe   John Turner
as to finish it and within three yeare James Parker eng Moses Pearle Samson Shee
& procure & maintaine an able ortheodox James Parker eng Samson Shee
minister amongst them: The magists hand Josiah parker
past this their brethren the deputys herto consenting Joseph fisher William fukim
Edward Rawson Secret   Nath Blood   Abraham foster
16 october 73   Robt Parris
The Deputies Consent herto   John fossike   James Knopp
William Torrey, Clerk   Zacharia Long: Robert Procter

the settlement be "finished" in three years, and that a minister be engaged and a church built as soon as possible.

The boundaries of the two hundred-square-mile township, fourteen thousand acres altogether, were defined in a general way in the petition. In May of the following year the famous Billerica surveyor, Jonathan Danforth, laid out the boundaries in more precise terms. A few names of landowners on the perimeters are mentioned: "Charlestown School Farm," "Mr. Brenton's land," "Henry Kimble's Farm at Jeremie's Hill," "Edward Colburn's Farm," "Captain Scarlet's Farm." The mystery name here is Henry Kimball, an individual who owned a piece of land on the Hudson-Pelham line but who has never been successfully identified. There were two or more men living at that time who bore this name, including a Boston blacksmith who was acquainted with Edward Tyng, but no documentary evidence has yet been uncovered as to exactly which Henry Kimball this landowner was or how he obtained the grant of land. It seems to be another unanswered question, probably because a clerk long ago lost or misfiled pertinent papers.

Choice Of Name

No name is given the proposed township in the petition or charter. In the copy of the text of the agreement in the Old Dunstable Records, the heading reads "the 15th of October, 1673, several town orders . . . drawn up . . . regulating of this town of Dunstable." We cannot, however, be sure that this is proof that the name had been decided at that time since this heading was probably composed some time afterward when the text was copied into the town records. Popular tradition attributes the choice of name to the influence of Mary Tyng, Edward's second wife. His first wife having died soon after their arrival in this country, he had returned to Dunstable, England, to remarry. It is quite possible that the second Mrs. Tyng suggested the name out of homesickness for her native town, or the people concerned may have felt close to it from hearing her description. Most of the settlers themselves were second or even third generation in America and had no personal memories of England.

The choice of name was certainly very closely related to the Tyng family and reveals the strength of their influence. The township is referred to as "Dunstable" in Danforth's surveying report. The name is, of course, still retained by Nashua's neighbor across the present state line, which recently celebrated the 1673 founding with festivities that included a visit from the Mayor of Dunstable, England.

Nashaway and Watananock were two Indian names connected with the area, and the question may well be asked as to why one of them was not chosen. Watananock, cited in various histories with several different spellings, was the word used by the local Indians in referring to the plain through which the Nashua River flowed. As late as 1702 the General Court in proposing to fortify the Salmon Brook settlement used the name "Watanuck." As for "Nashaway," this was the Indian name of a Massachusetts site, now Lancaster, at the source of the Nashua River near Mount Wachusett. The proprietors and settlers of our town apparently felt the need to give a strong English identity to the area. So it was called "Dunstable" and Dunstable remained the name of our part of the old township until 1837 when the name was finally changed to Nashua.

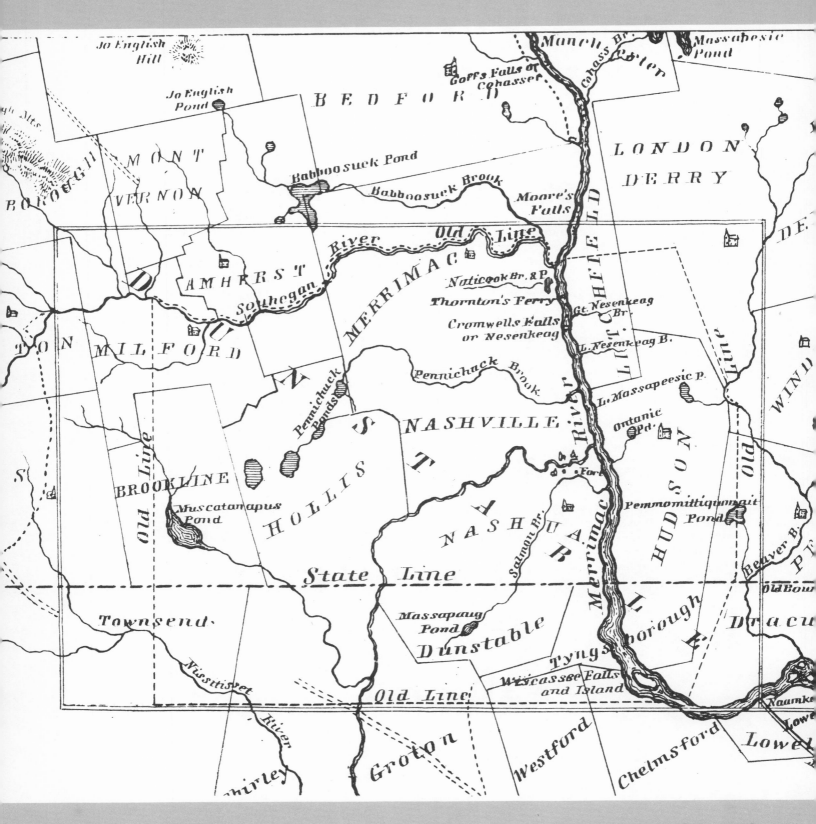

Map from Fox's "History of the Old Township of Dunstable" published in 1846. Dotted line is estimated boundary in 1673; rectangle shows boundary as surveyed by Jonathan Danforth.

3

Who Were the Thirty Families of 1680?

TRAFFIC on the Daniel Webster Highway moves heedlessly past an oasis of peace, the First Burying Ground sometimes referred to as the Old South. A visit to this historic site conveys a sense of being in two worlds, three hundred years apart. For it is here that many of the early pioneers are buried, as well as eighteenth century residents, including Revolutionary War veterans. It has been largely due to the efforts of the Daughters of the American Revolution that the cemetery has been preserved. An additional feature of interest is the old brick schoolhouse which has been completely restored to its original 1840 condition by the Kings Daughters Benevolent Association as a Bicentennial project. An attempt was made to reproduce a setting where Nashua school children studied up until 1921 when the school was closed. There is also a marker indicating the location of the second meeting house. Well shaded by beautiful old trees, bounded on one side by the flowing brook, it is a pleasant spot in which to spend a summer afternoon.

Thoreau Visits Nashua

Henry David Thoreau paid a visit here during his famous boat trip up the Concord and Merrimack Rivers in 1846. Here is how he described the burying ground:

It is a wild and antiquated looking graveyard, overgrown with bushes, on the highway, about a quarter of a mile from and overlooking the Merrimack, with a deserted millstream bounding it on one side, where lie the earthly remains of the ancient inhabitants of Dunstable . . . You may read there the names of Lovewell, Farwell, and many others whose families were distinguished in Indian warfare. We noticed there two large masses of granite more than a foot thick and rudely squared, lying flat on the ground over the remains of the first pastor and his wife.

In his book, *A Week on the Concord and Merrimack Rivers,* Thoreau's numerous other references to Nashua are well worth reading for a unique stranger's-eye-view of the village.

Elizabeth Wilson Weld

Unchanged since Thoreau's visit, the oldest stone, dated 1687, still lies level with the ground, marking the resting place of Elizabeth Wilson Weld. She was a granddaughter of the Reverend John

Wilson who was Boston's first minister and who received a grant of land at Pennichuck Pond. Anna Cole, another grantee, was her great-aunt, as Mrs. Cole and Mrs. John Wilson were sisters. On her maternal side, Mrs. Weld was a granddaughter of the Reverend Thomas Hooker, the first minister of Hartford, Connecticut.

She married Weld in 1681, coming to Dunstable from Medford where her father, the Reverend John Wilson, Jr., was the pastor. During the next five years she bore four children. The year 1686 must have been a tragic time for the couple, as they lost one child in April and another in July. Elizabeth's own death, at the age of only thirty-one, occurred a year later. Nothing more is known about the first Mrs. Weld, who typified the women who risked many hazards to make homes in the wilderness at this early date.

Weld remained a widower for several years before he remarried. His second wife was Mary Savage, a granddaughter of Edward Tyng (not his daughter, Hannah Savage, as stated by Fox). They had one son, Habijah, born after his father's death in 1702, who later became a prominent clergyman in Attleboro, Massachusetts. Thomas Weld's original flat gravestone was replaced by a substantial granite monument erected in 1875, which also memorializes the Reverend Nathaniel Prentice, his successor. The part of the inscription stating that Weld was killed by Indians is now considered inaccurate, as there was no Indian war taking place at that particular time.

The Thirty Families

The number of families living in Dunstable in 1680 is usually given as thirty, although some sources state that there were thirty-five families plus several single men, of whom Weld, who came here about 1678, would have been one. The total population was about 120. The map on page 31 gives an approximate idea of where some of these pioneering families had their homesteads.

Who were these people who cleared the fields, built the first roads and bridges, set up the first church, started town government? Some lived here for a few years, left when the threat of Indian attack frightened them away and never came back. Others had such a strong feeling of really belonging that they returned when the danger subsided and started all over again. A few remained through periods of war as well as peace. Many raised families whose descendants were still here at the time of the Revolution and well into the nineteenth century. There are a few people living in Nashua today who claim descent from these original families, most of them through female lines so that the original name has not been perpetuated.

At the first town meeting held after the end of King Philip's War, the limit of growth for the settlement was set at eighty families. This meeting was held on November 28, 1677, in Woburn, probably at the home of Elisha Hutchinson, who owned a considerable amount of land in Dunstable adjoining the Ancient & Honorable Artillery grant. The purpose of this meeting was joint planning by residents and non-resident proprietors on the resumption of settlement which had been interrupted by the war. They had not, for example, been able to meet the deadline for building a meeting house and hiring a minister.

At the town meeting in Woburn, only one of the five elected as Selectmen was an actual resident—Jonathan Tyng. The others were Thomas Brattle, Elisha Hutchinson, James Parker, and Abraham Parker. For many years such meetings of residents and non-resident landowners were held periodically in the Boston area. In 1694 the town records report a meeting held at the home of Josiah Parker in Woburn. In 1699 the meeting was held at the home "in the north end of Boston" of Jonathan Vial, an innkeeper whose name is often found listed as a taxpayer in the Dunstable records. Even in the early years of the eighteenth century out-of-town meetings were necessary for consultation on matters that concerned both residents and absentee owners. In fact, so many people in Boston or other places, such as Marblehead or Salem, owned land here that collecting the taxes from them was a major on-going problem. In what was known as a "second division," more and more people were purchasing land in the newly-opened-up territory from the old original grantees.

The Tyng Family

About two-thirds of the thirty families actually living here in 1680 can be accounted for. First and certainly foremost were the Tyngs. The first child born in Ancient Dunstable Township (of which there is any record) was Jonathan Tyng's sixth child, William. This birth occurred on April 22, 1679. In young manhood William became the leader of the "Snow Shoe Men," a band of scouts who patrolled the woods even in the winter during Queen Anne's War. He died of wounds and exposure in this service when he was thirty.

Old South Burying Ground.

The first recorded death in Dunstable took place in December, 1681, when the Honorable Edward Tyng passed away and was buried on his Tyngsborough estate. His tomb, covered by a slab bearing an inscription that is still legible, can be seen in the small cemetery near the Tyng home. It is believed that Mary Tyng, his wife, is buried in the same spot.

Historical weather records list the winter of 1680-1681 as one of the three most severe winters in New England in the entire seventeenth century. The deep snow, extreme cold, and howling winds meant that the people in isolated settlements such as Dunstable were almost totally occupied with sheer survival, trying to keep themselves and their farm animals warm and fed. For relief of illnesses they depended on home remedies and the nursing skills of the women.

April, 1682—the winter had not been quite as hard as the previous one, but the coming of this

Rachel Colburn's headstone in Old South Burying Ground.

month was welcome, as always, for it meant the end of snow and cold. In a few weeks the apple trees planted by the earliest anonymous inhabitants would be in full and fragrant bloom. On the fifteenth of this April the first baby girl was born in Dunstable. She was Sarah Sollendine, daughter of John and Elizabeth Usher Sollendine, a couple that was also living here in 1680.

The Sollendines

They had been married in August, 1680, in the first wedding to take place in Dunstable. He was a carpenter from somewhere around Boston, family origins completely unknown. She was a member of the prestigious Usher family and Mrs. Jonathan Tyng, Hezekiah Usher's daughter, Sarah, was her cousin. Elizabeth had been born in Stamford, Connecticut, where her father died when his children were all young, Hezekiah Usher becoming the guardian of his brother Robert's children. Usher was the enterprising Bostonian who obtained the rights to mineral deposits and excavated Mine Falls, hoping to find a rich vein of ore. Usher had other interests—he was Boston's first bookseller and imported printing machinery from England.

John Sollendine was exactly the type of settler the proprietors were looking for. Not only did the candidate have to be "of a sober and orderly conversation" and qualify as a good church member but he had to prove he possessed competence and experience in the various skills required for a self-sufficient pioneer way of life. A man who was a craftsman in a certain line of work was considered an especially desirable addition to the small community. Sollendine used his specialty, carpentry, to build things that the town needed—a sawmill, a bridge across the Salmon Brook, even the necessary meeting house. He moved up to Dunstable very soon after the charter was granted, probably in the spring of 1674.

John and Elizabeth Sollendine lived here for the rest of their lives and made their house into a fortified garrison during the Indian wars. They did not have the large family produced by most couples during this period (ten, twelve, or even fourteen children were not uncommon). They had just one other daughter besides Sarah and one son, John, Jr., who moved to Groton where the Usher family had acquired the property that formerly belonged

to Simon Willard. The Sollendines were, therefore, a one-generation family in Dunstable, but this was long enough for the name to become sort of a local symbol of the art of building. Nobody knows what happened to Sarah when she grew up.

We do not know when John Sollendine died. He probably is buried in the old Burying Ground but the gravestone has disappeared. His land was sold in 1729 to Hancock and Tyler, the Boston land speculators.

The Acres Family

One problem that threatened to disturb the ideal of "living in love and peace together" was hog-control. Hogs were an important farm animal but they did not understand the reasons for the walls and fences prescribed in the agreement drawn up by the proprietors. The fodder in the neighbors' yards always looked greener to them and they were experts at digging underneath obstructions and coming up on the other side. One of the earliest pieces of town legislation passed was what we might call a "hog-leash" law, under which every owner of hogs was supposed to keep his animals under control. The law proved unenforceable and hogs kept on running wild and doing damage all over town, just as before. The next step was the appointment of an official "hog constable," and in 1682 a man named John Acres was given this job and ordered to "pound, youke and ring the hogs of Dunstable." One of his duties was to place a device in the wandering hog's snout to prevent rooting under fences. The town did not pay for this service; each hog-owner had to pay the constable a yearly fee. By 1687, the hog population had increased to the point where two hog constables were required and it is noted in the records that John Gould had been appointed, in addition to the reappointment of Acres.

John Acres (sometimes spelled Akers) in 1679 left a place near Boston called Muddy River, which now has the more graceful name of Brookline. With him came his wife, whose first name was "Desire the Truth" (one daughter was also given this name), and five children. In Muddy River John had owned his own farm, so he certainly qualified as a likely settler on the basis of experience. The Acres lived here for about fifteen years and presumably returned to the safe haven of Muddy River during

King William's War. The land John had acquired was sold to Henry Farwell.

Acres probably came out of his Dunstable experience quite well financially, since the records show that he worked his original allotment into quite a large landholding.

The Blanchards

Deacon John Blanchard started the Blanchard dynasty which for several generations was noted for outstanding achievement, not only in Dunstable-Nashua, but in the State of New Hampshire. Various members of this brilliant family contributed to the political, military, and cultural life of both town and province/state. Intermarriages with other leading families, including the Ushers, the Farwells, the Hassels, the Cummingses, the Frenches, and the Lovewells, reinforced their position as leaders. In a colonial town, limitations of travel meant that children of neighbors tended to marry each other. Interlacing of blood lines was an important factor in cementing relationships within a given community.

John Blanchard moved with his large family from Chelmsford to Dunstable around 1680. There is some question concerning which early Massachusetts Blanchard family he belonged to. There is also a problem involving the identity of his first wife, as Ezra Stearns' assertion that she was Elizabeth, a daughter of Joseph Hills of Malden, is not borne out by the Hills family genealogy, in which Elizabeth is noted as having married a George Blanchard. John Blanchard's second wife was without a doubt the widow, Hannah Brackett Kinsley, the mother of most of his children. Her daughter by this former marriage was Elizabeth Kinsley who married John Cummings, Jr.; she was killed in an Indian attack of 1706.

An important historical document is John Blanchard's will, which was located several years ago in the Probate Records of Middlesex County. When Blanchard died in 1694, he left nine children, all of whom, including his daughters, were given bequests from the large amount of land that he had accumulated in the fourteen years he lived here. The ability of this family to acquire real estate was demonstrated from the very beginning. Some of the place designations mentioned in his will are: Danforth's Meadow, Buck Meadow, Huckleberry Hill, and Gilboa Hill (which Blanchard referred to as "Mount Gilbo"). The origin of this last place name is Biblical, from I Samuel: "Saul gathered all Israel together and they pitched in Gilboa."

Buck Meadow was not named for any early land owner. It was called that after the skeletons of two bucks were found there; they had died with horns interlocked while battling each other.

The Lunds

Another leading family that was here as early as 1680 was named Lund. There were still descendants of the name living in Nashua in the twentieth century. Charles Lund compiled a famous map in 1938 that is a primary source for knowledge of site locations in Ancient Dunstable. The very first Thomas Lund in this country was a trader and merchant of Boston who had only one child, a son, also named Thomas. After his father's death, having received a large inheritance, this second Thomas decided to move to Dunstable. He purchased land extensively, as did his two sons, a third Thomas Lund, and William.

Charles H. Lund, descendant of Thomas Lund who came to Dunstable around 1680.

Chelmsford Families

Chelmsford as Dunstable's next-door neighbor contributed a number of early settlers to the formation of the new town. The Parkers and the Waldos

Middlesex ss,

Pursuant to the within Warrant (or Order of Court) we the Subscribers have viewed several Tracts of Land in the Townships of Dunstable, Nottingham & Litchfield, being part of the Estate of Jn.o Clark Esq.r Dec.d five hundred Acres, part thereof in the Township of Nottingham: Two Hundred & twenty five Acres in the Township of Dunstable, & the Lands & Meadows yet to lay out to the Right Originally Jonas Clark's in the Common & undivided Lands in the Townships of Dunstable, Nottingham, & Litchfield, And sett off the one full & Equal Half for Quantity & Quality to M.r Jonas Clark being the Westerly part of the five hund.d Acres in Nottingham afores.d Containing four hundred and Forty Acres, the Divisional Line beginning in the North line of the s.d five hundred Acres, One hundred & twenty Rods from the Northesterly Corner thereof, from thence running South by Needle Eighty four Rods to the South line of the s.d 500 A.s so that the s.d four hundred & forty Acres lyeth on the Westerly side the s.d Line, And the remaining part of the Tracts as s.d we have Divided into Seven equal parts or Shares, for Quantity & Quality According to the direction of the within Warrant, which partition is as followeth Viz.t We have Divided & sett off to Jonas Clark a tract of Land Containing twenty two Acres being part of the forementioned five hundred Acres, & bounds thus, Westerly on the afore Described Divisionall line Northerly & Southerly by the line of the s.d five hundred Acres extending Easterly from the mentioned Divisionall line Forty four Rods, making the East & West lines thereof parrellell lines which is one equal seventh part in our Judgments.

Also have Divided & sett off unto Joseph Fitch in the right of Margaret his Wife the remaining part of the s.d five hund.
Acres

were two very prominent families. The interest of the Parkers is well demonstrated by the fact that no less than six of them signed the petition for the charter. The people of Chelmsford and Groton must have been greatly relieved when settlement got under way north of them, providing a buffer zone between their towns and the Indian-infested forests. The Parkers owned land along the boundary between these towns and Dunstable and some of their property fell on the Dunstable side of the line. Edward Tyng, it will be recalled, purchased his land from one of the Parker brothers. Fox definitely lists Joseph Parker as a "settler of Dunstable" and from 1675 to 1682 he served as Dunstable's first constable, which in a way could qualify him for the title of first policeman of the area. James and Abraham Parker were both elected Selectmen at the Woburn meeting in 1677, even though their family homesteads were actually in Chelmsford and Groton.

An equally influential Chelmsford family was that bearing the name of Waldo. In 1654 Deacon Cornelius Waldo, the immigrant ancestor, had moved from Ipswich to Chelmsford. He bought large tracts of land, some of which spilled over into the area that later became Ancient Dunstable. Three of his sons lived at one time or another on this property. Cornelius Waldo, Jr., was one of the seven founders of the first church of Dunstable. Cornelius, Jr., had married a woman from Boston named Faith Peck. After her husband's death, she returned to Boston and supported herself by operating a tavern or "pub," for which she had to take out a liquor license. This denoted unusual independence as widows in those days usually solved their problems by remarrying.

Another Waldo brother, Daniel, ran a grist mill in Chelmsford that reserved certain days for grinding the flour for the people of Dunstable. A Waldo sister married a schoolmaster by the name of Emerson and they became the great-grandparents of Ralph Waldo Emerson, the great Concord philosopher.

The Goulds, Samuel and John, were another pair of brothers who moved from Chelmsford in 1680. John died in 1689, but Samuel spent twenty years here before returning to Chelmsford where he died at the age of ninety. Samuel's chief claim to fame was his election to the post of "dog whipper." This apparently meant that he kept the local dogs from invading and disturbing Sunday services at the meeting house.

Obadiah Perry

Most sources agree that an Obadiah Perry, originally from Watertown, was probably living in Dunstable even before the signing of the charter. In 1667 he had married Esther Hassell, a girl from Cambridge, in a double wedding in which the other participants were his sister, Anna, and her brother, Joseph. The father of Esther and Joseph Hassell was Richard Hassell who, like many other Cambridge people, was given a homestead lot in Billerica when that town was first established. Later, about 1676, he and his wife, Joanna, finally moved to Billerica but stayed only three years; in 1679 they decided to join the Perrys in Dunstable. During King Philip's War Obadiah and Esther had taken refuge in Concord and Billerica, but had returned when the war was over. Soon after 1680 a young man from Concord, Christopher Temple, moved to Dunstable and in 1685 married Alice Hassell, a much younger sister of Joseph Hassell and Esther Hassell Perry. Meanwhile, Joseph and his wife, Anna Perry Hassell, had also moved to Dunstable. These families formed a closely knit group living on adjoining farms in the Salmon Brook area. The communal feeling in such close-knit groups was undoubtedly a source of strength that helped to lighten the burdens and hardships of life in the wilderness. In the case of the Hassell-Perry-Temple group, tragedy loomed in the future.

Other Early Families

Some of the other families who positively lived here in 1680 included Robert Parris, the associate of Jonathan Tyng; the Warners, the Cummings family from Rowley, Andrew Cook, the Frenches. Samuel Warner, originally from Ipswich, was one of the founders of Brookfield, Massachusetts. We have no record of exactly when he moved to Dunstable, but he was one of the seven founders of the church in 1685.

The Cummings family was very important in early Dunstable. John Cummings was the first Town Clerk and some of the handwriting in the early town records is undoubtedly his. Cummings was also one of the founders of the church in 1685.

Samuel French, another Dunstable pioneer, was a son of Lieutenant William French of Billerica. When quite young he had decided to try his luck in the new town "up north," just as a little later the young Samuel Whiting would decide to leave Billerica for Dunstable. The location of French's farm is described as "east of Nutting Hill." Samuel himself lived to be almost one hundred years of age. At least five generations of Frenches played prominent roles in Dunstable-Nashua.

Andrew Cook was another single man who arrived on the scene about this time. Apparently he started out in a modest way, receiving a homestead lot of fifteen acres. In June, 1681, his allotment was changed to thirty acres. He was later elected a fence viewer, married one of the Lovewell girls, and when the Indian threat became serious left town with his in-laws, never to return.

We have no exact date as to when Christopher Reade, Samuel Whiting's next-door neighbor and father-in-law, first came to Dunstable, but it probably was very early in the 1680s. Mrs. Whiting was his only child and inherited his estate.

Heads of some of the other families of 1680 were undoubtedly grown sons who had started their own farms. One was John Cummings, Jr. He and Elizabeth Kinsley, John Blanchard's stepdaughter, were married in September, 1680, making them the second pair of newlyweds. Isaac and Thomas Cummings are listed as having their own farms not long after.

The first Farwell in Dunstable was Henry who came from Chelmsford. The father of seven children, he was a leader in the affairs of the church and of the town. Active in military life, he was a lieutenant and later a captain. His home was one of the seven garrisons in the village, and at his death he was considered a wealthy man. Henry, Jr.'s wife was Esther, Captain Joseph Blanchard's daughter (her mother was Abiah Hassell, youngest daughter of Joseph and Anna Perry Hassell). The Farwells were good Indian fighters and respected citizens of the community. They, too, intermarried with the other prominent families including, in addition to the Blanchards, Lovewells, Frenches, and Cummingses.

All of the thirty or more families who had set up housekeeping here by 1680 enjoyed the advantage of coming in under the free land-allotment system which gave them a good start economically. They were high caliber people—sturdy, hardworking, capable of coping with hardship. Some were highly intelligent and talented, and reached for achievement beyond the limits of farm and town.

One unanswered question is exactly when the offer of free land ran out. Nowhere is there found any written record stating that the homestead award, of ten acres in outright grant, thirty acres to those who had some capital and a generous share in common land rights, no longer was valid. In the record books for the eighteenth century there are no long sections of "laying out" documents as in the seventeenth century records. Eventually there was automatic abandonment of the old system. All of the desirable land had been laid out to various individuals, large amounts had been reserved for "common land," extensive tracts had been bought up by settlers, and wealthy absentee owners held considerable property. Saturation was finally reached with newcomers obliged to purchase property from those who had come earlier.

4

A Town Starts to Grow

Oct. 16, 1736

"Laid out to William Tyler and Thomas Hancock, both of Boston, 200 . . . acres of land in Dunstable on the northwest part of Nissitissett, fifty acres thereof on the right of John Sollendine and fifty acres part thereof on the right of Thomas Clark, pewterer, in consequence of a grant made by the town of Dunstable in . . . 1682, to the proprietors of Watannock Neck."

Volume 1, Dunstable Records, page 100

The Dunstable Records

AN IMPORTANT primary source for happenings in early Dunstable consists of several volumes of original documents preserved in the City Clerk's office at Nashua's City Hall and at the Nashua Historical Society. It is most fortunate that these documents are still available even though the archaic handwriting is extremely difficult to decipher in many places and only fragments remain of some pages. Many more papers have undoubtedly disintegrated or become lost in the course of three hundred years.

To anyone with a sense of the drama of history, it is an exciting experience to pore over these volumes. Here are many details of town business—the laying out of allotments of land, the election of officials, checklists of taxpayers. Many unfamiliar names are encountered in these pages in addition to those that have always been part of Nashua's historic lore. Who, for example, was Captain Bartlett who was chosen moderator of the town meeting held on May 21, 1701? At this meeting exasperation over the number of persons in arrears on payment of the minister's rates apparently reached a peak and an ordinance was passed providing for forfeiture of their lands if they did not pay their assessments. A cryptic note is added to the effect that "this order is to continue from year to year hereafter till there be the full number of forty families settled in this town of Dunstable." With Indians still a hazard, the aim of building a community of eighty families had apparently been lowered.

Who were John Hubbard and Samuel Ledge, listed on a tax list as Boston men? Why did people from Marblehead buy land here in rather large numbers? We have heard of the Beale brothers from Marblehead, who actually did live here, but Samuel Morgan and John Loxman are unknowns. Who was "Mr. Rucko of Salem"? We know where Mr. Lynde's farm was, but where was "Mr. Devon's farm"? Why were one thousand acres laid out to Joseph Hills' son-in-law, John Waite, the location described as follows: "which land runs ENE on the north by Mr. Simon Lynde's farm . . . then it goeth over Pennichuck Pond"?

The unnumbered first volume of Dunstable Records contains an alphabetical list of proprietors in the first and second land divisions. According to

25

this list, the great Hezekiah Usher, the mineral hunter, owned only sixty acres of Dunstable land, not a large amount compared to many other holdings. Over a hundred pages of this volume contain the ancient land allotments and here again many unfamiliar names show up—E. McCarty (was he the first Irishman to own land in Nashua?), Thomas Webb, John or Jonathan Conners, John Woodman. Here also we find the earliest reference to "Gilbo Hill," dated 1679, mentioned in the laying out of land to Edward Tyng's daughter, Hannah Savage. Another female landowner was Elizabeth Sedgwick who was Hezekiah Usher's niece. And Mrs. Mary Tyng, it is discovered, owned many acres in her own right.

Many additional references are found to individuals cited only by passing mention in earlier histories. Fox, for instance, makes only one reference to Thomas Clark, the pewterer from Boston—an extract in which John Sollendine was commissioned "to build a sufficient cross bridge over Salmon Brook, near Mr. Thomas Clark's farm house." The town agreed to pay half the cost and Clark was to pay the other half. This man, always referred to as "pewterer" (in one place it is spelled "putier"), had actually quite a close connection with Dunstable, even though it does not appear that he was a regular resident. On August 1, 1682, he acquired four hundred acres, probably by purchase from a previous grantee, in the "Harbor" between the Nashua River and Salmon Brook. In the summer of 1684 there was a formal second division in that location and surveying was done to set the legal boundaries for new owners. Jonathan Danforth, the perennial surveyor, drew a rough map which is reproduced on the opposite page, indicating who these owners were. (In 1816, the New Hampshire antiquarian, John Farmer, presented the original of this map to the Massachusetts Historical Society which still owns it.) The four names involved were Christopher Temple, John Sollendine, Joseph Knight, and Thomas Clark.

The Mystery of Thomas Clark

Sollendine and Temple are well-known figures in Dunstable annals, but Knight and Clark are relatively obscure. In seeking the identity of Clark, the only clues are the words "of Boston the brazier" on the Danforth map and the word "pewterer" beside his name whenever listed in the records. Without this designation it would be impossible to determine who he was, since more Clarks migrated to America in the seventeenth century than persons with any other name; all Clarks had large families and named one of the sons "Thomas," with the result that by 1700 there were dozens of Thomas Clarks in New England.

The pewterers of Boston for the period of the late seventeenth and early eighteenth centuries have been fully accounted for by the historians of that craft, and there is only one by the name of Thomas Clark. His workshop was at the Town Dock from 1674 until his retirement in 1720. He was one of the most prosperous of all the pewterers, and was one of the twenty founders of the Brattle Square Church in 1700. He died in 1732 at an advanced age, leaving a very large estate, but there is no mention of any Dunstable land in its inventory. He had sold it in 1729 to William Tyler (Tyler Street in Nashua is named for him) and Thomas Hancock (an uncle of John Hancock), partners in real estate speculation, who, according to third division documents in Volume 1 of the *Dunstable Records,* bought up some of the land in the Harbor.

Did Thomas Clark ever make pewter in Dunstable? It is most unlikely, since the craft required about half a ton of equipment and materials and the market for the product was in the Boston area. The conclusion we inevitably come to is that Clark may have been Nashua's first "summer visitor," who enjoyed his "farm house" on the Salmon Brook as an escape from crowded city ways. Did Clark take orders for utensils from his Dunstable neighbors? He probably did but not a single piece, out of what must have been a tremendous production in a career of forty-six years, has survived. Even his touchmark is unknown. In fact none of the pewter made in Boston during this period is known to exist today.

Thomas Clark's name appears on several woodrate lists during the 1680s. In July, 1694, he is noted as being appointed one of a committee of four to collect delinquent non-resident taxes. Three of the committee were non-residents, Clark, Captain Jonathan Corwin, and Sampson Sheafe; the fourth was Jonathan Tyng, who was almost automatically placed on every committee set up to take care of various problems in Dunstable affairs. Clark's name

comes up again in the proprietors' committee reports as late as 1736 when they mention a "tract of land at Pennichuck Brook formerly laid out to Thomas Clark, pewterer, for 510 acres," showing that he had bought additional land.

Far less is known about Joseph Knight who also had a very common name. He probably was a member of the rather well-known Newbury family by that name. In 1682 he, too, bought land from one of the original grantees. There is no record, as in the case of Clark, of Knight building on the land or taking any part in local affairs. He appears to have been another absentee owner, of which there were an increasing number in the late seventeenth century.

During the peaceful interlude before the next Indian war caused another exodus, several newcomers took up residence in a second wave of migration after 1680. One of these was Samuel Searles, a nephew of Jonathan Tyng; his mother was Deliverance, Jonathan's sister, who had married Colonel Daniel Searles, for several years Governor of the West Indies island, Barbados. When both of his parents died on the island, young Samuel came to live with his uncle. (The big Tyng mansion seems to have sheltered from time to time various orphaned or homeless children of relatives.) Samuel eventually bought land of his own, married a girl from the Perham family, and lived here until his death in 1737. The Searles homestead on Searles Road was at one time used as a schoolhouse in the eighteenth century, when the schools were located in homes and moved semi-annually from one part of town to another. There are descendants of the Searles family still living in the area today.

The Lovewell Family

If any one name in Nashua history can be termed a "household word," it is probably John Lovewell. The Lovewell family moved here from Lynn in the early 1680s when the town was really starting to grow. It was one of the great Dunstable families, with descendants still living here in the middle of the nineteenth century. Their origins were obscured for many years because of a genealogical mix-up. As a result of this confusion, one of the John Lovewells was, according to folklore, supposed to have lived to the astronomical age of 120 years. Ezra Stearns, a professional genealogist and New Hampshire historian, patiently unraveled the twisted facts and found that two men of the same name had been mistaken for each other in the records. He proved that Nashua's famous patriarch was actually only about ninety-five when he died in 1755. This still stands as a remarkable instance of rugged old age, when the life expectancy at the time was around fifty. Stearns located a baptismal record showing that this man was born in 1660 in Massachusetts. The legend that he had fought as a very young boy in Cromwell's army was therefore disproved. Legends sometimes die hard and this one made Ripley's "Believe It or Not" at one time.

The father of this patriarch John Lovewell, the first John Lovewell, was a tanner from Lynn who moved to Dunstable, probably around 1683, with a grown family of five children, two sons and three daughters. Two of the daughters, Patience and Elizabeth, had married the Beale brothers from Marblehead. Samuel and William Beale decided to move here because their father, a thrifty miller who liked to invest in land, owned property in Dunstable. The third Lovewell sister, Phebe, married Andrew Cooke whose special town office was that of fence viewer. The two sons were John, who was a legend in his own time, and Joseph. After King William's War broke out this entire family group moved back to Massachusetts except for John, Jr. He and his wife, Anna Hassell, remained and raised a family that included Captain John Lovewell who gave his life at Fryeburg, Maine, in 1725 to stem the Indian threat to the northern frontier.

Lovewell was the owner of a sawmill on Salmon Brook. Fox says concerning the exact site:

. . . it is not improbable that it was on the spot where the 'Webb Mill' . . . now stands, since it is known that a mill stood there at a very early period, and it would probably be located as near the settlement as possible. There was originally a beaver dam at the place, and it required but little labor to prepare the site for the mill. Many years ago a mill crank was dug up near the spot, which must have come from its ruins.

Captain John Lovewell worked with his father in this business when he was not out chasing Indian scalps. It is a favorite Nashua tradition that Hannah Dustin, the Haverhill heroine, came for refuge to the home of the older John Lovewell after her famous exploit in escaping Indian captivity. A plaque on Allds Street marks the location of this dwelling, and commemorates the fact that Hannah Dustin slept there.

The Town Becomes Organized

Although Dunstable was a rather isolated settlement at this time, it took part in at least one important political event in the Massachusetts colony. When the towns were invited to send delegates to a convention in Boston to form a popular government after the English Revolution of 1688, Dunstable did send representatives. In June, 1689, John Waldo was the delegate; the following month his brother, Cornelius, attended, and later in the year Robert Parris went on this mission. This was the first serious attempt made by the colonists themselves to run their own political affairs instead of being ruled by a royal governor.

The growth and consolidation of the township during this period, the 1680s, were indicated by the fact that a need for a new meeting house was expressed only five years after the first small log structure had been built by John Sollendine. The original meeting house had been put up in 1678 to satisfy the requirement that the town must show signs of establishing a church within three years after the resumption of settlement in 1677. In 1682, according to Fox, thirty-five persons constituted themselves "proprietors." Twenty-one were nonresidents. The fourteen who lived here and held this place in the social hierarchy were: Jonathan Tyng, his mother, Mary Tyng; John Cummings, Sr., and his son, Thomas; John Blanchard, Abraham Parker, Joseph Wright (there is no record as to who he was), Samuel Warner, Joseph Parker, John Sollendine, Obadiah Perry, Thomas Lund, Joseph Hassell, and John Acres. Since we know that there were about thirty families here in 1680, this leaves sixteen or possibly a few more who were on a lower scale in the hierarchy—they farmed on their allotments, probably of minimum size, but were not wealthy or influential enough to be entitled proprietors.

By the 1680s, townspeople were elected as Selectmen and other officers and generally were in control of civic affairs. One of the projects undertaken was road building. In 1682 a committee was appointed "to lay out a Highway from Groton meeting house to Dunstable meeting house." The town was also under obligation to do its part in helping to build and then maintain the important bridge over the Concord River at Billerica. This was the only route to Boston, so all of the northern towns using it had to supply materials and labor whenever it needed repairs. Bridges as well as roads always needed work because of the ravages of winter weather and spring flooding.

No precise population figures are available for the end of the peaceful interval, 1690, when another Indian war had already started which would severely curtail the growth that had taken place. At the close of King William's War in 1699 Fox reports twenty families, based on the list of heads of households liable for payment of the minister's woodrate. There were four separate households by the name of Cummings and three Blanchards. Robert Usher, Elizabeth Usher Sollendine's brother, was now living in Dunstable. Two other additions to the list of names were William Harwood and Daniel Galusha. The Galushas were a Dutch family from Chelmsford. By 1701 there were 180 persons living here, distributed among twenty-five families. This new resurgence of growth was to be interrupted yet again, however, by Queen Anne's War which lasted for a long and agonizing ten years, from 1703 to 1713.

Although venturesome individuals had crossed the Merrimack and started farms soon after the Hills brothers had built their garrison, extension of settlement in the Brenton's Farm part of the township did not take place until after 1720. Continued fear and uncertainty concerning the Indian situation tended to confine the populated area to a tight cluster in the southern central part of the township.

The book of Ancient Dunstable records that is entitled *Volume I* concerns the continued efforts over a long period to trace land ownership in the area. At least one name famous in American history is mentioned in one of the reports of this perpetual committee that was called "the proprietors of the common and undivided lands in the Ancient Township of Dunstable." This particular report reads in part:

At a meeting of the proprietors of the common and undi-

vided land in the Ancient Township of Dunstable, held at the house of Mr. Thomas Harwood, innholder in Dunstable in the Province of New Hampshire, May 29, 1766, Honorable John Tyng, Esq., moderator by unanimous vote: Voted that John Hancock, Esq., of Boston be chosen agent for this propriety in the room of the Hon. Thomas Hancock, Esq., deceased.

John Hancock, first Governor of Massachusetts after the Revolution, inherited all of his uncle's business interests as well as his fortune. (Thomas Hancock was also John's guardian.) When Thomas Hancock died in 1764, the land he owned in Dunstable was part of his estate.

This volume of records is proof that for almost a century an organized group was in existence whose purpose was to keep track of who originally owned various tracts of land and who had bought or inherited it. Their task was not easy, to judge from another clause in the same report that makes note of John Hancock's membership on the committee. This clause mentions that "the state of this Propriety is much confused by reason of each proprietor's interest in the undivided land belonging to this propriety lying unknown and it being that some have got more than their proportion laid out." At this same time they placed an advertisement in the *Boston Gazette* so that persons having claims could come forward. In another report, several years later, there is a table giving the results of an attempt to ascertain who owned land originally and how much each had held. Some examples: John Lovewell, 780 acres; Elisha Hutchinson, 1,200 acres; the mysterious McCarty, 500 acres; John Waite, 1,200 acres; Robert Proctor, 829 acres; Sampson Sheafe, 600 acres; Hugh Woodbury, 878 acres; Joseph Wheeler, 322 acres.

The last record in the book is dated August 2, 1816, a report signed by Noah Lovewell, "proprietors' clerk," on the final meeting at the house of Captain Isaac Marsh. After that, the books were closed and the group disbanded, its work taken over by the usual legal machinery of deeds and probate records. For almost every year from 1729 until 1816, a succession of concerned Dunstable citizens had met formally to deal with these puzzling matters. The reports on their deliberations, in fading handwriting, form a strange link to the land grants, the first allotments to settlers, and the buying and

selling of tracts in the earliest beginnings of what is now Nashua.

One man who helped ensure that persons in the communities he served were able to live in love and peace together, free from boundary disputes, was Jonathan Danforth, the surveyor. In the complicated deed made out to Samuel Scarlet in order to settle Evered's estate, the land is described as "bounded as by a plott or draft taken thereof given under the hand of Jonathan Danforth, Surveyor." Danforth was a citizen of Billerica which he served as Town Clerk and Selectman. Among other talents, he was an excellent mathematician. He led a very busy life, spending a great deal of time, when weather permitted, tramping through the wilderness on surveying assignments for the provincial government or for towns requesting his services. The first big job he undertook in the Nashua area was the laying out of the Naticook lands.

Importance of the Surveyor

Since the basis for legal deeds was the surveying that determined the boundaries, how was this task performed in woodlands where there were no roads except Indian trails? What instruments were used to assure accuracy in measurements? The surveyor had to have a compass, of course, which he mounted on a wooden tripod or a support known as a "Jacob's staff." Since land was always measured in terms of rods, often called poles (16½ feet), the chain that was dragged over the territory was a certain number of rods long. The standard chain was four rods or 66 feet long, but in rough terrain a half-length was used.

In forging the iron-link chain, the special art of the blacksmith was required, as each link in the chain had to be exactly the same, slightly less than eight inches in length. The chainmen who measured out the chain under directions from the surveyor were the unsung heroes of the enterprise. Over hills and valleys, around rocks and other obstacles, through bushes, across streams, they put the chain down, picked it up, and put it down again. Corners of boundaries were indicated by landmarks that sound very impermanent and unstable to us today. Here is a sample from the old Dunstable record books, unfortunately undated:

Laid out to Andrew Cook on the east side of the Merrimack

River in Dunstable township, 120 acres of land, be it more or less, bounded by Samuel Beale's land beginning at a heap of stones and running by marked trees 40 pole north-easterly to a marked tree, the corner mark marked with A and C and running by Thomas Lund easterly one mile and a half to a heap of stones between two white oaks marked with C, running southerly to a pine tree marked to the corner and so running westerly by John Ackers to the first heap of stones.

Danforth, in making notations on his maps, used an early form of shorthand. An example can be seen on the 1684 "second division" map of the area between the Nashua River and the Salmon Brook, on page 27. When Danforth died in 1712, a poem written in tribute to his special genuis began:

*He rode the circuit, chained great towns and farms
     to good behavior; and, by well-marked stations,
He fixed their bounds for many generations.*

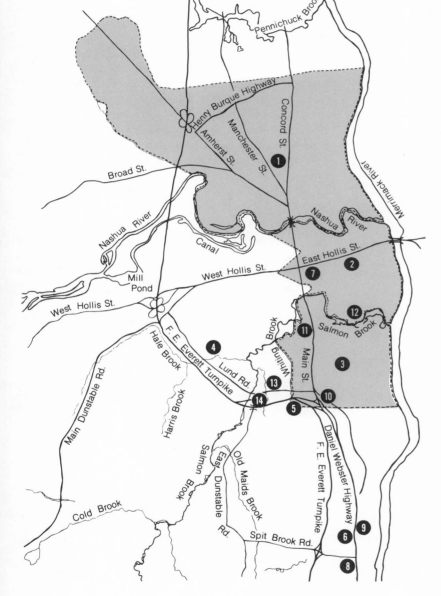

HISTORIC SITES IN NASHUA

1 Ancient and Honorable Artillery Company
2 1684 Second Division Survey
3 Whiting Grant (400 Acres)
4 Hassell House
5 Whiting House
6 Old South Burying Ground
7 Queen's Garrison
8 Weld Parsonage
9 Cummings Garrison
10 Meeting House Park
11 Bird Meeting House
12 Lovewell House
13 Lund House
14 Killicut-Blodgett House

5

Early Dunstable Was a Theocracy

IN 1885 when the First Congregational Church of Nashua celebrated its two hundredth anniversary, the main address was delivered by a native Nashuan who was a well-known teacher of oratory—John Wesley Churchill. Published several years later as a book, *Historic Sketch of Churches in Dunstable-Nashua, 1685-1885,* it included information about other denominations such as the Irish and French Catholic congregations.

The Church-State Form of Government

Churchill gave a simple explanation of theocracy, the church-state form of government under which the first few generations in Nashua lived. The Massachusetts Bay Colony was firmly based on this state-controlled religion of the Puritans, with towns obliged to support a minister and maintain a church. In a large territory, such as Ancient Dunstable, new towns were eventually formed because people living on the fringes or on the other side of a river found it a hardship to travel long distances to meeting every Sunday. Building their own church and setting up their own civic community were almost simultaneous.

Although Thomas Weld had joined the Dunstable settlement in 1678 or 1679, and from that time on had led Sunday services in the first little log meeting house, he was not formally ordained and the church itself was not organized as a parish until 1685.

Seven men formed the nucleus of the church: Jonathan Tyng, John Cummings, Sr., John Blanchard, Cornelius Waldo, Jr., Samuel Warner, Obadiah Perry, and Samuel French. The first deacons were Blanchard and Waldo. The date was December 16, 1685, when the members subscribed to a Covenant which in quite lengthy specifics spelled out their duties and listed the rules they were supposed to live up to as Christians. The preamble reads:

We covenant with our Lord and with one another, and we do bind ourselves in the presence of God, to walk together in all his ways according as he is pleased to reveal himself unto us, in his blessed word of truth, and do explicitly profess to walk as followeth, through the power and grace of our Lord Jesus Christ.

The minister was given an allotment of land or homestead lot and a salary of fifty dollars a year plus a supply of firewood, to which each household in the parish contributed. Since wood was the main source of energy for heating and cooking, this was an important part of his compensation. The assessment of a certain amount of wood to keep the parsonage fires burning was called the "wood-rate." One of the sources we have for knowledge of the families living in town at a given time is the checklist of those liable for their share of the minister's wood. The individuals concerned could not have dreamed that, almost three hundred years later, historical researchers would still note with interest that they were a little slow in delivering their share of cordwood to the parsonage! The reason in most cases was that the church member wanted to make sure he had enough wood for his own family. So much for the energy crisis in the late seventeenth century!

A further note on the central position of the church in the community is that it was desirable for a resident to be called a "freeman," a member in good standing in the church. This title was a basic requirement in order to vote or hold any public office. The non-conformist had no political power whatsoever.

In lean years, when the people could not pay all of the minister's salary, the Massachusetts General Court granted the town varying amounts toward this obligation. Several petitions have been preserved in which the Dunstable Selectmen humbly begged the authorities in Boston for a subsidy because a war with the Indians had decimated the population and cut off revenues. Incidentally, parishioners could pay part of their share of the ministerial salary in goods such as garden and dairy products but they were given only partial credit, usually fifty percent of what the goods were worth in money. The minister, who had spent several years training for this position, felt, as did most people with any standing in the town, that he had to have some cash income to provide for his family. His own kitchen garden, his cow, pigs, and hens supplied many of his food needs. The salary in English pounds, even in those days of self-sufficiency, purchased the few comforts that made wilderness life tolerable.

Mr. Weld, the first minister, was a graduate of Harvard College and came from a distinguished family of clergymen. The tiny settlement in the back woods considered itself fortunate that it was able to obtain the services of such an able man to care for its spiritual needs. The relationship between minister and parishioners took the form of a "settlement," meaning that the minister was assigned for life to the community.

Weld died in 1702, and until that time the church organization had been a cohesive one because of the strength of his personality and the love and respect felt for him by the people he served. Until 1720 the church was served by a succession of men, each staying only a short while. The unstable situation due to the threat of Indian violence was probably a factor in discouraging any minister from agreeing to "settle" in Dunstable. One transient pastor was the Reverend Samuel Parris, who stayed almost four years here after the Salem witchcraft trials in which he played a prominent part.

The second minister to be formally ordained and settled for life was Nathaniel Prentice. Mr. Prentice, who came to Dunstable in 1720, married Mary Tyng, a granddaughter of Jonathan Tyng. She was one of the three children of William Tyng (the first male child born here), and Lucy Clarke, daughter of the Reverend Thomas Clarke of Chelmsford. Mary's parents died while the children were very young. Mary and Nathaniel Prentice were married in 1723 in Woburn, Massachusetts, where the aged Jonathan Tyng spent his last years.

Mary Prentice emerges from the shadows surrounding women of the time as one of the most interesting female figures in Nashua history. She was apparently somewhat ahead of her times and is described as a vivacious and unusually spirited lady. She had a hobby that was certainly different from those of her feminine contemporaries—she was an excellent shot and enjoyed taking part in target-shooting contests. At one time she won a fowling piece offered as a prize in a competition. Although the women in the pioneer households were taught to load and shoot a gun as a matter of defense, this is one of the rare instances when a woman competed with men (and won) in marksmanship.

The Breakdown of Theocracy

Until 1737, when Nathaniel Prentice died, the Dunstable community was held together in reasonable harmony by his leadership and the lively pres-

ence of his remarkable wife. In the following year a new meeting house was built, followed by the settlement of a third minister, the Reverend Josiah Swan who married Jane Blanchard, a daughter of Captain Joseph Blanchard and Abiah Hassell Blanchard. It was at this point that theological friction began to tear the community apart. The 1740s, after the old township had been broken up into separate towns, while the part of Dunstable on the New Hampshire side of the new state line was trying to decide which state it belonged to, was also a period of intense religious dissension. A splinter party known as the "New Lights" had broken off from the established church. This reflected the influence of a man named Whitefield who wandered the countryside preaching a doctrine that interpreted the scripture differently from the Puritans. The New Lights were, of course, the forerunners of the Methodists.

In his history of the churches in Nashua, Churchill made the observation, "This union of Church and State was the fundamental error of the Colonists." He went on to say, "The theocratic system produced bigotry in the State and hypocrisy in the Church." Actually, the system worked quite well during a certain period to unify people *until* basic disagreements on points of theology began to emerge. Differences of opinion among strong-minded individuals produced a situation that can be compared to political shadings in today's world. New ways of thinking were accepted gladly by some, rigidly rejected by others. As a result, men who had felled the forests, plowed the fields, and fought off the Indians together in their youth often became enemies in old age.

The Reverend Josiah Swan himself was bitterly opposed to the New Light sect. The lay leader of the New Lights was Jonathan Lovewell, youngest son of John and Anna Hassell Lovewell, who later became an important political figure in the Province and State of New Hampshire. The leader of the orthodox group was Colonel Joseph Blanchard whose sister was the minister's wife. By 1747 Mr. Swan found himself unable to cope with the partisanship he encountered and gave up the position of pastor to return to his former home in Lancaster where he became a highly successful teacher.

His successor was the Reverend Samuel Bird, a

New Light, for whom a church was built that was called the "Bird Meeting House." The Blanchard sect resumed services in the meeting house that had been built in 1738 and started a movement to have the appointment of Mr. Bird declared illegal. At that time, although the town had been chartered as Dunstable, New Hampshire, in 1746, no provision had been made for calling an official town meeting under the new charter. When this was done by the State Legislature, the Blanchard forces won the battle and Mr. Bird left Dunstable.

Until 1767 the division in the church prevented settlement of a permanent minister. In 1761 a special town meeting had been held for the purpose of holding an open dialogue between the opposing groups (how we wish this could have been tape-recorded!). It ended in a reconciliation in which the "New England Confession of Faith" was adopted as a compromise doctrine. It was not until six years later, however, that the Reverend Josiah Kidder, a Yale graduate, accepted the pastorate of a reunited church, remaining in that position for the next half century. The Revolutionary War provided a common cause that swept away any remnants of the bitter controversy. The theocratic problem was resolved in 1796 when the connection between church and town was severed forever. Other religious groups established many churches in the next hundred years, and most of them have published their own histories which describe the role they played in the development of Nashua. A list of these will be found in the bibliography of this book.

In Dunstable's first sixty years, theocracy served, in spite of its flaws, to help the settlers maintain high morale in the face of hardships and danger. It was one of the reasons the first groundbreakers were able for a long while to "live in love and peace together." When its time had passed, other needs of the human spirit asserted themselves.

6

A Second Look at a Tragic Dilemma: The Indian Problem

A POEM, "The Last of the Nashaways," was a special feature of Parker's *History of Nashua.* It told of a band of wandering Indians who camped in Railroad Square on a summer day around 1842. They were welcomed by Daniel Abbot, Nashua's "great white father," and their chief replied:

From distant shores we hitherward are come
To view once more our fathers' ancient home;
To note again the streams they loved so well,
To mark the ground where in fierce strife they fell.
These have we seen, and to our children told
The wrongs ye did their sires in days of old.
Yet in our hearts we bear no thought of hate,
But only see the o'erruling hand of fate.

Could the violence that arose between the two races, white and Indian, have been avoided? There were certainly efforts on both sides to resolve the dilemma. On the Indian side, the conciliatory policies of Passaconaway and Wanalancet are too well known to require repetition. On the white side, dedicated missions were undertaken by religious leaders to educate and befriend the natives. John Eliot, who was a close associate of Thomas Weld's father in Roxbury, was tireless in his zeal to Christianize the Indians. Here in New Hampshire, it was Eleazar Wheelock's interest in educating Indian boys that laid the foundation for Dartmouth College.

The Indians of New England

In his *History of Hudson,* Kimball Webster told about excavations he had made near the Taylor Falls Bridge, in which he had uncovered Indian burial mounds, some containing skeleton remains in the typical flexed or sitting position. In 1835 a burial mound measuring 150 to 200 feet in diameter, six to eight feet high, was discovered in Manchester. There are undoubtedly many such mounds in wooded areas all over New Hampshire, but they have been worn down by the passing of time so that they are now indiscernible. Most thoughtful people feel that excavations, if done at all, should be left to the special skill of professional archeologists.

So little archeology has been done in the Merrimack Valley that first-hand information about the native Indians is sparse. A 1930 survey unfortunately did not include any "digs" in Nashua. All that we know is that a part of the Penacook tribe fished, hunted, and planted crops in this vicinity. One of their favorite places for cultivation was the alluvial land along the river banks; these plots had been so well tilled that the white settlers, coming after, were able to use them for their own vegetable gardens. Johnson and Willard, in their exploring trips up the Merrimack River, encountered several small Indian villages, one of them near the mouth of the Salmon Brook.

Large numbers of Indians lived in southern New Hampshire at one time in villages of about two hundred persons each. One of the stories that has been passed down by word of mouth concerns the remnant of the group that had inhabited the Nashua area. Reduced to about twenty-five members, they were camping on the north side of the Nashua River, approximately at the location of the present Main Street Bridge. Feeling that during the winter they would find more protection at Mine Falls, they asked for assistance from the white residents in moving their camp to that area. No date has ever been mentioned as to when this happened but it may have been during the peaceful interval between King Philip's War and King William's War, in the late 1680s.

There is almost nothing left now to remind us of the Indians who for thousands of years roamed this area—only a few arrowheads and hunting implements in museums and private collections, in somebody's dooryard a mortar that they used for grinding their corn. Probably the most lasting memorials to them, here as elsewhere, are the names of rivers, lakes, and hills.

The great Indian Family to which all New England Indians belonged was the Algonquian. As indicated on this map, two tribes predominated from northeastern Massachusetts to Maine: the Abnaki and the Penacook. The territory of the Penacooks included most of New Hampshire, northeastern Massachusetts and part of Vermont. The author of the poem bowed to tradition and referred to the local Indians as "Nashaways"; to have been strictly correct perhaps he should have used the name "Naticooks" or "Souhegans." Fox explained the divisions of the Penacooks as follows:

The Nashaways had their headquarters at Lancaster; the Nashobas at Littleton; the Pawtuckets at Pawtucket Falls; the Wamesits at Wamesit Falls, at the mouth of the Con-

Map showing location of Penacook Tribe in the seventeenth century.

cord River; the Naticooks in this vicinity; the Penacooks around Penacook, near Concord, N.H. Passaconaway was sachem of the Penacooks and held rule over all the Indians from the Piscataqua to the Connecticut, and all down the Merrimack; he resided at Penacook and the Naticooks, Pawtuckets, and Wamesits were subject to his power.

The Souhegans and Naticooks were the same group, according to Hodge's *Handbook of American Indians.* As for the Nashaways, they were definitely the group inhabiting the area around the source of the Nashua River, near Mount Wachusett. A scholarly study of the Penacooks is included in the famous work on Indian ethnology, Schoolcraft's *Indian Tribes of the United States.* According to Schoolcraft, the very first path for horseback riders from Nashua to Manchester was marked out so John Eliot could travel easily from one Indian group to another.

Whatever names the Indians in the Nashua area should be called, tangible facts about them are lacking. Even legends, genuinely known to have been passed down, and therefore providing us with important clues, are missing. An example of the tenuous nature of whatever legends we have is an article published in the *Nashua Daily Telegraph* in 1896 by a writer who claimed to have heard a legend connected with Old Maid's Brook, which flows through the southern part of Nashua. Since he revealed no source for his story, there is always the suspicion that it came out of his own imagination. For whatever it is worth, here is the plot:

The heroine was an Indian princess named Mooleewappa, daughter of the chief of the Massapoags, the group that occupied what is now Dunstable, Massachusetts. This group had been at war with the Otonics (a Hudson Indian group) and, to cement a peace treaty, the girl's father insisted on a marriage between his daughter and the son of the Otonic chief. Now, Mooleewappa found the young man quite repellent and begged her father to give up the whole idea. When he refused, she fled into the forest, pursued by the best archers of the neighboring tribes. She eluded her pursuers and lived in the wild until winter, when she slid under the ice of Old Maid's Brook. It goes without saying that her spirit haunts the area still!

Indians who became converted were referred to by the settlers as "praying Indians" and we detect a note of contempt in the use of this phrase by whites, some of whom felt cynically that it was enough that these had been vanquished without violence. A small number of these converted Indians was placed at one time on Wicasuck Island, in the middle of the Merrimack River, under the watchful eye of Jonathan Tyng, who was appointed their guardian. Robert Parris assisted him in this supervision of a sort of benevolent concentration camp for peaceable local Indians. The aim of the operation was to cut them off from communication with more warlike groups during King Philip's War. Fox says the group numbered only ten men and fifty women and children. In compensation for this caretaker duty, Tyng was given Wicasuck Island, today the site of the Tyngsborough Country Club.

King Philip's War

King Philip's War was the first of four distinct periods in Dunstable's first fifty years when growth of the settlement was interrupted by Indian wars. This first outbreak of violence occurred in the years 1675 and 1676. The second period was King William's War, 1689-1698. The third was Queen Anne's War, 1703-1713. The fourth period was one of renewed hostilities from around 1720 to the climactic event known as Lovewell's War in 1724-1725.

King Philip's War was led by the Chief of the Wampanoags, a son of the Pilgrims' friend, Massasoit. Philip earned the title "King" because of great personal charisma and political skill which enabled him to unify other Indian groups against the white invader. Philip's policies were the opposite of those of Passaconaway and Wanalancet. He felt that the Indians should put up a vigorous fight for their ancient rights. When open conflict resulted, pockets of white civilization such as Dunstable were in great danger because of their exposed positions. The entire village was evacuated as the families that had begun to clear land for farms returned hastily to former homes, many moving in temporarily with relatives.

Jonathan Tyng realized that it would not be wise for the village to be completely deserted. At least one person had to stay to keep watch and he chose to remain himself. Not by any means foolhardy, he dispatched a letter to the provincial authorities in Boston on February 3, 1676, asking for a contingent of soldiers to help him fortify his house. In addition to sending this guard, the Governor and Council also ordered a fort built at Pawtucket Falls near Lowell. The steps that lead to a secret lookout in the roof of Tyng's house can still be seen; here it is believed that he kept a lonely vigil watching for signs of Indian activity.

The war ended in August, 1676, when Philip was defeated and killed in the Narragansett Swamp fight. So savagely did the English destroy and humble the Indians that many of the survivors in Rhode Island were actually made slaves. An excellent and lively account of this entire conflict, which analyzes the motives of the Indians, is Clara Endicott Sears' book, *The Great Powwow*.

The growth of Dunstable continued after this interruption, as we have seen, and the next thirteen years saw slow but steady growth. As has been noted, the church was formally organized and a larger meeting house was built. About this time, the precaution was also taken of legally buying the land rights from the local Indians for a price of twenty pounds. Fox gives the value of the English pound as

$3.33 at that period. If this is correct, the Selectmen paid about sixty-five dollars or little more than thirty cents a square mile, a real estate transaction that can be well compared to the purchase of Manhattan Island by the Dutch in 1626.

The Lovewell Document

In their old age, John Lovewell and his wife, Anna, put on record an affidavit that might be considered Nashua's first oral history. Neither of the Lovewells could write and their "deposition" was dictated to a clerk and signed with their marks. Their intention was to pass down to posterity their personal account of how Dunstable had been affected by Indian violence. This amazing document is still on file in Concord, New Hampshire, at the State House.

From this document it can be estimated that about twenty-five inhabitants of Ancient Dunstable were massacred by Indians in the period between 1673 and 1724. This is a far lower percentage of the population than in many other New Hampshire and Massachusetts towns. In Dover almost the entire town was wiped out in a surprise attack on June 28, 1689. A similar attack was planned for Dunstable but was averted when two friendly Indians carried a warning to the commander of the Pawtucket Falls Fort. A military company was sent at once to Dunstable to guard the settlement.

Anna Hassell Lovewell had good reason to want to ensure that her memories would be preserved, as she was a woman who had suffered deeply from the deaths of relatives at the hands of the Indians. She was a member of the Hassell-Perry-Temple family group. In September, 1691, this group was traumatically assaulted and no less than five of its members were violently murdered. On September 2 her father, Joseph Hassell, her mother, Anna Perry Hassell, their son, Benjamin, and a young visitor, Mary Marks, were overwhelmed in a surprise attack. The Indians disappeared into the woods as swiftly as they had come. Mary Marks was a teen-ager, daughter of Patrick Marks who had moved to Dunstable the year before and who had served the town as surveyor of highways. The Marks family, not too surprisingly, moved away after this tragic episode. A boulder, with an inscription on a bronze plate, may be seen at the burial site

of the four victims in the field off Almont Street where they died.

Almost four weeks later, on September 28, the husbands of two of Anna Lovewell's aunts, Obadiah Perry and Christopher Temple, were suddenly killed in a similar attack on the bank of the Nashua River. A large boulder in the river was called "Temple's Rock" for a long time because it supposedly marked the spot where this second attack occurred.

The period of peace between England and France after the end of King William's War lasted only five years. Queen Anne's War, again between England and France, broke out in 1703 and, once more, the Indians were incited by the French in Canada to commit vicious attacks on the frontier towns of New England. During this period the "Snow Shoe Men" roamed the woods all year round, watching for Indian marauders. This was also the "garrison period," although many people had also fortified their homes during the previous war. As in 1675 and during the 1690s, many families simply left town. There had been no further settlement northward up the Merrimack Valley because of uneasiness over relations with the Indians, and Dunstable remained a frontier town. By 1711 there were only thirteen families left and these depended on a system of seven garrison houses for protection. One of these, Queen's Garrison, was built by the Massachusetts authorities to house the soldiers sent to the town as a guard. The location is described as "sixty rods easterly of Main Street . . . and about as far northerly of Salmon Brook." The other six garrisons were the houses of individuals which had been converted into strongly reinforced places of refuge and defense. The names of the owners were Jonathan Tyng, Henry Farwell, John Cummings, Samuel Whiting, Thomas Lund, and John Sollendine. In four of these houses, including Queen's Garrison, two and three families lived. The total population was eighty-six persons, compared with one hundred and eighty in 1701.

A Tragic Day

In 1706 a bitter lesson on the need for strict security measures had been learned. July 3 of that year had been another day of tragedy. Considerable confusion still exists concerning the exact details, as different sources vary in the telling of the story. It seems clear, however, that three different houses were the object of attack. A troop of soldiers, passing through town on their way back from a patrol mission, had stopped for rest at the Cummings Garrison. While partaking of liquid refreshments, they stacked their guns in a corner. A gay party was in progress when the Indians attacked. Mrs. John Cummings, Jr., was on her way with her husband to the barn to milk the cows. They were both shot, Mrs. Cummings dying instantly and her husband, wounded, managing to crawl into the woods. Meanwhile, the attackers had rushed the house through the gate left open by the couple and surprised the relaxing soldiers. At least four, unable to reach their guns, were killed.

On the same day a similar attack was made on the house of Nathaniel Blanchard. Mrs. Cummings' mother, John Blanchard's widow, was killed along with her son, his wife Lydia, and their daughter, Susannah. The third onslaught was on the house of the Galushas, which was burned down. Daniel Galusha's daughter, Rachel, aged twenty-three, was also killed. Five women lost their lives that day.

The story of Joe English illustrates the fact that many individual Indians became friends and helpers of the white people and quickly adapted themselves to the new society. Joe English was well known in Dunstable, spent a good deal of time here, and it was in Dunstable that he was killed. About three weeks after the massacre just described, Joe was escorting Lieutenant Butterfield and his wife, a Chelmsford couple. Near Holden's Brook they fell into an Indian ambush. The Indians, who regarded Joe as a traitor to his people, killed him instantly rather than by torture when he provoked them with an especially insulting remark. The Massachusetts General Assembly made a grant afterward to Joe's widow and children in recognition of his many services.

Local Indian Attacks

Even though this war, as far as European hostilities were concerned, ended with the Treaty of Utrecht in 1713, it was an uneasy peace on this side of the ocean. The conflict between Indians and whites was not really settled until the signing of the treaty at Casco Bay, Maine, in 1725. A local incident that rates as Nashua's favorite Indian story involved Nathan Cross, Thomas Blanchard, and nine men who tried to rescue them when they were kidnaped

by Indians. Cross was an early resident of Hudson. Blanchard was a grandson of Deacon John Blanchard. On a September day in 1724 the two men had gone to the area north of the Nashua River to make turpentine from the pine trees that grew so plentifully there. They had planned to spend the night at Lovewell's sawmill, since this task, probably an annual one, would take more than a day. While they were working, a party of hostile Indians suddenly appeared and seized both of them. Cross had time only to thrust his gun into the hollow of a tree and mark another tree hastily with a message indicating that they had been taken alive.

When Cross and Blanchard did not appear at the sawmill that evening, an alarm was spread and a party of nine men, five Dunstable residents, reinforced by four others from outside, set out to learn what had happened to them. Near the place later called Thornton's Ferry this search party was ambushed by Indians and all except one man, Josiah Farwell, were killed. The four from Dunstable—Thomas Lund, Ebenezer French, Oliver Farwell, and Ebenezer Cummings—were buried in a common grave at the Burial Ground, along with the four from other towns, Daniel Baldwin, John Burbank, a Mr. Johnson, and Benjamin Carter. Lund, son of the first Thomas Lund to come to Dunstable, was only forty-two years old when he died on that fatal day, September 5, 1724, leaving five children under twelve years of age. Visitors to the old Burying Ground may still read the inscription on the stone marking the common grave. It is Nashua's most famous epitaph and has been mused over by many passing by, including famous historians, one of whom remarked that it reminded him of a line from Gray's "Elegy":

This man with seven more that lies in this grave was slew all in a day by the Indiens.

What happened to Cross and Blanchard? Their abductors carried them off to Canada where they earned their freedom by building a sawmill for the French. After they returned home, Cross returned to the pine grove and retrieved his gun, and that very same gun can be seen today at the Nashua Historical Society.

Another incident of this period of warfare involved Thomas Lund's brother, William, who in this same year of 1724 was captured and taken to Canada. As often happened, a ransom was demanded for his release and his wife, Rachel, sold some of her own property and managed to collect the required sum, supposed to have amounted to five hundred French livres. A souvenir that was in the possession of the Lund family for a long time was her receipt from the Boston man who acted as go-between in the transaction. Lund returned safely and lived to an old age, and his wife forever after teased him by telling people: "He is now mine, for I have bought him."

Lovewell's Fight

The really decisive contribution to the solution of the Indian problem was made by Captain John Lovewell and his company, who were determined to stop this threat to the safety of the English settlements. The Province of Massachusetts offered a bounty for Indian scalps and Lovewell's company collected a large sum for scalps that they brought to Boston, as a result of forays they made on several occasions. Finally, Lovewell and his officers decided that the only way to end the Indian danger was to meet the enemy on their home territory in Maine. In the spring of 1725 they planned the raid and during the first week of May the company started out from Dunstable. Tradition has it that they stopped for breakfast at the Hills Garrison on the other side of the Merrimack. An old ballad, called "Lovewell's Fight," begins:

> *What time the noble Lovewell came*
> *With Fifty men from Dunstable . . .*

The actual number that started out was forty-seven, ten of whom were Dunstable natives: Lovewell himself, his brother-in-law, Josiah Farwell; his cousin, Benjamin Hassell; Jonathan Robbins, John Harwood, Noah Johnson, Robert Usher, William Cummings, Samuel Whiting, and Toby, a friendly Mohawk Indian. The rest of the band were from various Massachusetts towns and there was one man from newly-settled Londonderry, New Hampshire. Two of the party, William Cummings and Toby (of whom we have no further knowledge), became lame on the long march and turned back, reducing the group to forty-five.

Arriving at Ossipee Pond, they built a crude temporary fort on its western side and there were left the company doctor, one sick man, and eight who served as guards. The rest of the company pressed on toward the territory of Chief Paugus, leader of the Pigwacket Indians. (A fascinating fact about Paugus is that he was originally a Penacook, the son of Kancamagus and the great-grandson of Passaconaway.) Spotting a single Indian standing on a promontory, they decided that the rest of the Indians were somewhere in front of them. They removed their packs, left them on the ground, and continued to advance. Unfortunately, the Indians under Paugus were not ahead of them but were behind them, having just come from scouting down the Saco River. When the Indians came upon the pile of soldiers' packs, they counted them and realized that they outnumbered the whites more than two to one. Lovewell and his men were ambushed, the valiant captain and eight of his company dying in the first volley. With Lieutenant Seth Wyman of Woburn taking over the command, the rest of the company retreated to the shore of a pond that is now known as Lovewell's Pond. There they fought stubbornly all day, killing many of the enemy. The terrible battle did not end until Chief Paugus himself was killed when he went to a brook to clean his fouled gun. One of the white soldiers, a man named Chamberlain (some of the ballads say Wyman) also went to the brook to clean his gun, a truce being declared while they completed this chore. Each knew that it was one man or the other and Chamberlain is said to have won by striking his gun on the ground so that it primed itself. The bullet pierced Paugus' heart and Paugus' shot grazed Chamberlain's hair. The battle was over, the Indians collecting their dead and wounded, not bothering to scalp the dead among the whites. Some experts on firearms have questioned the story, but this is how it has been passed down.

After the battle, the survivors began the arduous trek back to civilization. One man rolled into a canoe on the river bank and, although wounded and exhausted, reached Saco in this way. The small fort in Ossipee was deserted when some of the others came to it. It seems that there had been a deserter in the company who, after Lovewell had fallen, had fled the scene in panic to rush back crying defeat, so the men remaining at the fort had immediately departed for home. A very special hero of this grim battle was the Chaplain, a young man named Jonathan Frye from Andover, Massachusetts. He died of his wounds three days after the battle, and the town that was settled later near the scene of the incident was named Fryeburg after him. The only two Dunstable men to survive were Noah Johnson and Samuel Whiting.

The saga of this battle beside a lonely pond in Maine passed into folklore and many songs and ballads were written about it. "Lovewell's Fight" ends thus:

> With footsteps slow shall travellers go
> Where Lovewell's Pond shines clear and bright,
> And mark the place where those are laid
> Who fell in Lovewell's bloody fight.

> Old men shall shake their heads and say
> "Sad was the hour and terrible,
> When Lovewell brave 'gainst Paugus went
> With fifty men from Dunstable."

Henry Wadsworth Longfellow, when a young boy growing up in Portland, Maine, wrote his first poem about this event:

Cold, cold is the north wind and rude is the blast
That sweeps like a hurricane loudly and fast,
As it moans through the tall waving pines lone and drear,
Sighs a requiem sad o'er the warrior's bier.

The war-whoop is still, and the savage's yell
Has sunk into silence along the wild dell;
The din of the battle, the tumult, is o'er,
And the war-clarion's voice is now heard no more.

Samuel Penhallow, a Portsmouth jurist, was writing a book about the Indian wars in 1725. He added a chapter about the Lovewell battle, in which he paid tribute to the warriors in a sonorous style:

In I Samuel, xxxI, 11, 12, 13, it is recorded to the immortal honor of the men of Jabesh Gilead, that when some of their renowned heroes fell by the hand of the Philistines, that they prepared a decent burial for their bodies. Now so soon as the report came of Capt. Lovewell's defeat, about fifty men from New Hampshire, well equipped, marched unto Pigwacket for the like end, but were not so happy as to find them; but Col. Tyng, from Dunstable, with Capt. White who went afterwards, buried twelve.

The name of the one deserter from the battle was not mentioned in any of the printed accounts for a long time; it was felt that he was not worthy to be listed in connection with those who stood firm. We now know who he was—twenty-three year old Benjamin Hassell, John Lovewell's own cousin. Afterward he seems to have lived it down somewhat, as he became, according to Stearns, a "useful and respected citizen of Merrimack," of which he was one of the first settlers. His sons served valiantly in the Revolution.

John Lovewell's wife, Hannah, whose maiden name is not known, gave birth to a son eight months after the battle. Later she remarried and lived in Merrimack with her second husband, Benjamin Smith, one of the first settlers of the Narragansett 5 part of that town. Pembroke, New Hampshire, was founded when grants of land in that area were awarded to the survivors and heirs of Lovewell's company, in gratitude for their heroic services. When Hannah Lovewell, Captain John's daughter, grew up, she married a Captain Baker from Roxbury and they decided to homestead on the share of the Pembroke grant that she had inherited. This couple became the great-great-grandparents of Mary Baker Eddy, founder of the Christian Science Church.

Fourteen out of the thirty-five who had engaged the enemy had died in the battle. The sorrow in Dunstable was very great when news of the outcome of the expedition reached the town. There was increased fear that, with so many men killed and so many others placed on ranger duty to guard against retaliation, the town was more defenseless than ever. The Selectmen and leading citizens sent an urgent petition to Boston on May 20, pointing out the discouraging situation. An extra guard was sent to Dunstable and all that summer and autumn an alert was maintained, but it finally became quite evident that the Indians had drawn off permanently after the Fryeburg battle. Dunstable was never in danger again.

Perhaps one of the best commentaries on the dilemma of Indian-White relations was made by the widow of a slain Indian warrior. Samuel Butterfield of Chelmsford had killed the warrior in self-defense and was captured by other members of the tribe. The chief told the dead man's widow that she could determine the manner by which Butterfield would be executed. The woman retired to her tent to think it over, emerged, and said: "Torturing and killing this man is not going to bring back my husband. This whole affair is just part of the fortunes of war, anyway. Let him live." In some versions of this story, the woman, having learned French in Canada, is supposed to have said, "C'est la guerre."

The Colonial, Revolutionary and Pastoral Periods

1725 - 1820

7

The Ancient Township Breaks Up

IN THE FALL of 1730, Peter Powers, working entirely by himself in a tract of land on the western side of the Nashua River, cut trees, built a log cabin and prepared a clearing for planting the following spring. He was twenty-three years old, strong and ambitious and not afraid to be the first white person to live in that part of Dunstable. There was land available nearer other farms, but it was too expensive for him. Powers had now lived in Dunstable about five years and had made many good friends, including the Blanchards, but he was still poor. There are no records showing just where he had lived at first; he may have leased a farm or been given a small free grant that was not large enough for a man with his prodigious energies. In 1728 he had married a Chelmsford girl, Anna Keyes, and they now had two sons, one a two-year-old, the other an infant, and family responsibilities had stirred him to decisive action. He had gone to Joseph Blanchard and obtained from the Propriety, which had just voted a third division of the common and undivided lands, a grant of thirty-seven and one-half acres in the wild area west of the Nashua River, where it turns northeastward on its final course to the Merrimack. To the people of Dunstable this area was known only by its Indian name— Nissitissit.

Samuel T. Worcester, the author of *The History Of Hollis,* searched the records carefully and found that no grant or sale of land in Nissitissit had ever been made before. Its seventy thousand acres were simply part of those "common and undivided lands" over which the Proprietors' association had jurisdiction. The transaction by which Powers acquired his thirty-seven and one-half acres is found in Volume I of the old Dunstable Records described in Chapter 4. His biographer states that, since no purchase price is given, "perhaps the Proprietors, in order to encourage him to open the land to the west, made it a free grant."

Peter Powers–Pioneer

Peter Powers, founder of Hollis, was born and raised in Littleton, Massachusetts. When he was seventeen or eighteen the Indian-fighting exploits of Captain John Lovewell were being discussed and Lovewell became a hero to young Powers. His biography, *Peter Powers, Pioneer,* written in 1930 for the two-hundredth anniversary of his settling in Nissitissit, describes the decisive moment when he left home to join this scouting group:

. . . when Peter strapped blankets, powder and a sack of corn meal on his back, pulled his fur cap down over his ears, fastened the thongs of his snowshoes and said goodbye to his father . . ., he little knew what the future had in store for him.

Although Powers actually did not see much real action with Lovewell's company, he came to Dunstable because of his associations with the local men who were part of the company.

Having built his cabin in the wilderness, ten miles away from the village of Dunstable itself, he did not want to wait even until spring to move his family into it. On a cold morning in January, 1731, Peter and Anna and their small sons set out to become the very first residents of what is now Hollis. Soon they were joined by other adventurous couples and a small settlement was established which in a few years required its own minister and church, and then demanded autonomy as a separate town. The Powers family prospered and Peter himself, having learned a great deal about real estate values from his friend Joseph Blanchard, became a dealer in land all over southern New Hampshire. Unfortunately, he died at the age of fifty before he had had time to consolidate his estate and debts ate up most of the money he left. Anna, the wife who had to draw on her own brand of courage to go with him into this uninhabited territory, lived to be ninety years old. A story that has been passed down in the family tells about an adventure she had on one occasion when, leaving her husband to babysit, she went on horseback, alone, to visit friends in the village. She was almost drowned in the Nashua River when a storm came up as she was returning to the cabin.

Early Hardships

Peter Powers is an example of the new generation of pioneers who now forged into the previously uninhabited forest lands in other parts of the old township. For fifty years wars had been going on. Belknap, New Hampshire's first historian, says: "Every man who was forty years old had seen twenty years of war." In 1725, for a while there was to be peace. Gradually those able-bodied men who had been assigned by the Massachusetts General Court to hunt out and destroy the "savage Indians" came home. The discouragement of their families, trying alone to carry on the planting and farm duties, as well as the businesses, was lifted. Families and friends, who, through fear, had removed to safer townships, gradually returned to Dunstable. In many cases they built their new homes on the fringes of the town, instead of near the center which, when they left, had been the safest place to live. New people, including young Powers, began to arrive. The frontiers were now beyond them and the settlement of the town began to increase rapidly. "Soon the wilderness was alive with population," Fox tells us. But some of this "wilderness," such as the Nissitissit area, was soon to be breaking away from Dunstable to become full-fledged towns.

Those inhabitants who had borne the economic as well as physical burden of the wars were very poor. Heavy public taxes were levied by the General Assembly of Massachusetts, for the wars had been not only long but expensive, and the ransoms had had to be paid for the release of captive citizens. Money was scarce. To confuse the conditions even further, the General Assembly of Massachusetts had issued bills of credit in 1721. They proved so popular that in 1727 it issued another sixty thousand pounds. In that year the share belonging to this town was received, and loaned to Rev. Mr. Prentice—the minister in those days was hired, fired and paid by the town—to be "applied in payment of his *future* salary as it should become due." "Thus early and easily," continues Fox, "did men discover and adopt the practice of throwing their debts upon posterity." Soon those bills of credit depreciated "ruinously." By 1750 the bills were worth but 12 percent of their original value.

The Town Experiences Difficulties

The amount of taxes raised from 1726-1733 for the general expenses of the town, including the support of the minister, varied from $250-$400. This was aside from the heavy taxes paid to the General Assembly of Massachusetts. The poverty of the township dictated action—or lack of action—on two important matters. The first: No representative was sent to the General Assembly. Although directed to do so, from 1693-1733 the town voted "not to send." The town would have had to pay the expenses and compensation of the representative.

The second: The delay in establishing schools. Although the settlers and their descendants felt that Education (with a capital E) was important, it was not easy to establish common schools. Fear of the Indians and the fact that in this large tract of land some of the houses of the settlement were far apart meant that no school was kept in the town.

In 1730 the town was indicted by the Grand Jury for having neglected to provide a teacher, which the law said must be done when a town increased to "fifty householders." On November 3, 1730, it was voted that it "be left with the selectmen to provide and agree with a person to keep a writing school in the town *directly.*" There is no record of any vote to raise money, choose a school committee, build a schoolhouse or any allusion to the subject of schools for many years. The selectmen may have counted the "householders" differently from the Grand Jury.

Before March, 1727, the town had raised "eight pounds for building a boat" which was probably a ferry boat over the Merrimack River from the Blanchard Farm, south of the mouth of the Salmon Brook, to that part of Dunstable where a few settlers had located themselves on the east side. Six years later that settlement was to become what is now Hudson.

In 1729 there was a vote, "that Lut. Henry Farwell shall Gine with the committye appointed to keep the Grait Bridge in Billerica in Good Repare." This "Grait Bridge" was over the Concord River on the main road to Boston so it was of importance. Besides having to supply a carpenter, each of the towns using it, Dracut, Billerica, Groton, Chelmsford, and Dunstable, was annually assessed pounds, shillings and pence for planks and nails as well as manpower. Every year that Bridge needed "reparing."

Breakup Of The Township

Hollis was not the only part of the old township to break away as a separate entity in the 1730s and 1740s. Merrimack and Nottingham West (later Hudson) became independent in 1733, Litchfield in 1734. What is now Amherst was granted in 1730 to the soldiers and heirs of soldiers who had fought in King Philip's War. It was one of several townships laid out to fulfill this long-delayed obligation; they were called the Narragansett townships and

Amherst was Number Four. In 1760 Amherst was incorporated by the Province of New Hampshire and named after Sir Jeffrey Amherst, Commander-in-Chief of the British Forces in North America. Milford was not incorporated until 1794, being formed out of parts of Amherst and Hollis.

In Hollis, as we have noted, the people eventually set up their own church. Hollis for several years was called the West Parish of Dunstable because this was what it was—a second parish established so that the people would not have to ford the Nashua River and go ten miles to attend meeting. In 1739 they were given a charter permitting them to tax the non-resident proprietors to help support their church but they were still not completely autonomous. One of the several boundary disputes which came up around this time involved a plan for the West Parish and the northern part of Groton to be joined into a single town. Finally, on April 3, 1746, Hollis was given its present name and chartered by the Province of New Hampshire.

On the reverse of the Charter of Dunstable, New Hampshire, signed by Benning Wentworth on April 5, 1746, there is a map showing the new boundaries of four towns: Dunstable itself, Hollis, Merrimack, and a place directly north of Hollis called Monson. Monson was a town that was born in April, 1746, struggled to survive for twenty-four years and failed in its efforts to maintain its identity. By 1753 it had only twenty-one houses and the people were so poor they could not pay their province taxes. The only public building they ever erected was a pound. In 1770 the New Hampshire authorities mercifully performed an act of geographical surgery, slicing Monson into sections and incorporating them into Milford, Brookline, Amherst and Hollis. A left-over slice of land a mile wide was disputed for a while and this is where the name "Mile Slip" originated. Another place name no longer used was Raby. This was the first name of a town that was incorporated in 1769, later changed to Brookline.

The period around 1740 was a time of upheaval, with the vast acres of the original Township of Ancient Dunstable slipping away in sections, like children tearing free of their mother's apron strings. Moreover, the settling of the boundary line between Massachusetts and New Hampshire was now coming to a crisis. Massachusetts was about to lose the rich Merrimack Valley, an event which was to affect the people of Dunstable by further dismemberment. The southern section of their town also would now become separate towns, one to become a second Dunstable, another to become Tyngsborough, with corners of the old grant to be swallowed up by other Massachusetts places such as Dracut and Townsend. What was left, in the center of the old territory, would be Dunstable, New Hampshire, which, with a few pieces snipped from time to time by legislative action, would become Nashua about a hundred years later.

The Boundary Dispute Settled

In 1741, "after a long and violent controversy and against the wishes of the inhabitants," as Fox tells us, the boundary between Massachusetts and New Hampshire was run. *The old New Hampshire-Massachusetts boundary line of 1741. A Controversy which lasted approximately two centuries,* is an excellent account written by City Engineer Fred L. Clark and read before the Nashua Historical Society on January 13, 1941. It is in their files and can be consulted there. This goes very fully into the whole involved question, for the story of the controversy of the bounds of the province began in the reign of His Majesty King James I, and carried through those of Charles I, William and Mary, and George II.

The towns in the southeastern section of the Province of New Hampshire were even more affected than Dunstable by the long delay in running the boundary. For these were being claimed by Massachusetts but "the people along the disputed line," says Mr. Clark, "were being forced to pay taxes to both Provinces, which did not help the goodwill toward a friendly settlement." Agents, committees and commissions were appointed by each province, met, quarrelled and disbanded.

In 1732-33, writes Clark, *Governor Belcher, upon his return from England, reported to the Lords of Trade, that he had taken all care and pains to have the long contested boundary dispute adjusted according to His Majesties Royal Orders, but there seemed to be no prospect of this being accomplished, and that "in the meanwhile the poor borderers were forced to live like toads under a harrow, being run into jail of the one side or the other because they so frequently quarrelled,–they pulled down one anothers*

houses, often wounded each other and bloodshed was feared unless the bounds were fixed."

Finally in 1741, Governor Belcher appointed George Mitchell, Esq. "to turn and mark out—such part of the boundary—beginning at the Atlantic Ocean and ending at a point due north of Pawtucket Falls—." In the same year the Governor appointed Richard Hazzen—"to run the portion of the line beginning at a point 3 miles due north of Pawtucket Falls in the Merrimack River, thence running due West until it met his Majesties other Governments." He was instructed

to take special care in spotting trees in the line and to leave the best monuments possible, also to note all hills, mountains, rivers, ponds, lakes and anything else of importance, recording same in his journal, a copy of which was to be returned with his survey plan.

On March 23, 1741, he

crost Merrimack River against Bancrofts lott and ran up through the house of the late Reverend Nathaniel Prentice of Dunstable–. Capt. Fletcher gave us a good dinner, the morning was cloudy and about one o'clock afternoon it began to snow and snowed fast all the remainder of the day, which hindered our moving further, here Caleb Swan and Ebenezer Shaw were sworn chairman . . . We lodged at Dunstable this night, some of us at the house of Joseph Blanchard, Esq, who generously entertained us, and the rest of the Company at French's Tavern.

The next day continuing snow kept them at Dunstable. On Wednesday the 25th by ten o'clock "it cleared up and we immediately set forward and measured to Nashua River—and at night lodged at James Blood's fire."

This boundary split what was left of Dunstable in two. It was confusing to the part in New Hampshire, whose citizens felt they must still appeal to Massachusetts for help in solving their problems. "Controversies gave rise to an excitement, intense and protracted," goes on Fox. Finally the town, on April 5, 1746, was incorporated by the State of New Hampshire, having right up to that date acted under the charter of 1673, obtained from Massachusetts.

We find this vote at a meeting of the Proprietors of the Common and Undivided Lands on April 30, 1746,—

that 30 pounds old tenor be raised and assessed on this

town and then the same be paid to Col. Joseph Blanchard for his paying for the Charter of this town and paying the Committee the charge of this town's being erected and incorporated into a Town and for his own time in getting the Charter.

The original copy of this charter is owned by the Nashua Public Library, having been purchased in 1903 from the estate of Dr. Israel Hunt of Boston. It is on exhibition in the library's local history room.

Peace it may have been from wars, but there was controversy in the frequent meetings of the Proprietors of the Common and Undivided Lands in the Township of Dunstable. Laying out the land, in the hands of a committee and Captain Joseph Blanchard and later his son, Colonel Joseph Blanchard, also a surveyor, was not a quiet nor a peaceful accomplishment.

Then, later, the confusion of how much in these years 1741-1746, Dunstable, New Hampshire should now send to Massachusetts, and how much Dunstable, Massachusetts and the other towns owed from the dates of their breaking away, for the minister's salary in Dunstable, New Hampshire were only two of the headaches for the inhabitants.

As we have seen, continuing disputes and differences over church matters finally in 1747 brought about two strong schools of thought led by Jonathan Lovewell and Colonel Blanchard, two distinguished men who had been much in public life. Following is part of Colonel Blanchard's long protest and petition to the Legislature, in his effort to prove that a town meeting held on September 29, 1746, was illegal:

Province of New Hampshire. I the Subscriber one of the Inhabitants of Dunstable and Quallified by law to vote in town affairs being present at the Meeting of the Inhabitants the 29th of Sept–1746 here by enter my Protest against the s'd meeting as Illegal and as to their Proceeding–first that the Place appointed for the Meeting House is not Just and Equall and ought not to be in that place, that sum of the Inhabitants were by the moderator [Jonathan Lovewell] admitted to vote who were not Quallified voters, also against that vote viz the Refusal of payment to Swan's Sallery. Also against removing of the meeting house untill such time as the Inhabitants of this side the Province line has settled the Interest there of with the Inhabitants of the south side. To Mr. Jonathan Lovewell Town Clerk I desire this my Protest may be entered. Joseph Blanchard.

Not only did this irate man protest—but he asked the legislature of New Hampshire "to investigate." Many months later there was an answering appeal to the legislature signed by Jonathan Lovewell, "respectfully" but in firm language, saying:

when the truth of the matter is That the Petitioners in a very Disorderly uncivil manner . . . Gathered a Party together, some qualified Voters, Some not so, and acted like a mobb of madmen in Such a manner as never was done in the Province Since it was a Government.

That was on May 10, 1748. On May 13, 1748, Blanchard's Petition was granted and "meetings and Votes mentioned hereby are declared illegal null and void." A new meeting "must be held with a moderator from another town who should be paid by the town." "Madman" Joseph truly *must* have been close to the Governor!

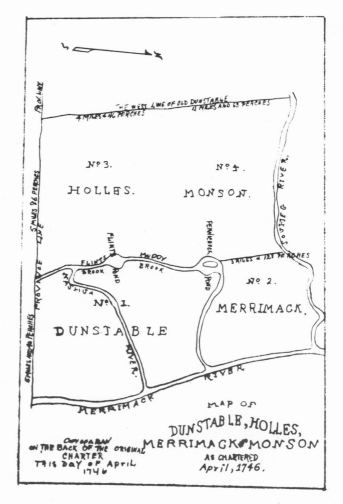

Tracing of map on reverse side of 1746 Charter of Dunstable.

8

Dunstable, New Hampshire, Before the Revolution

ROADS OF DIFFERENT WIDTHS were being laid out in all directions, many of them coming into the "Great Boston Road." That important "Grait Bridge" over the Concord River at the fordway in Billerica, on the Great Boston Road, which had been kept in annual "repare," was now seeing much travel. Passing over it were horses ridden by travelers, postriders, and town officials; and cattle being driven in the spring to better grazing grounds and back home, or fat and sleek to one of the big towns for barter in the fall. Small wagons of farmers and merchants, and ox teams with heavier loads, went over it; and once in a while a woman on horseback or in a carriage, going to the next town to visit friends or relatives, perhaps with her flaxwheel or basket of handwork. Quilting bees and a day of helping friends in need or sharing sewing or knitting chores—these were the only diversions the housewives had to break the awful monotony of their long, hard days.

Tradesmen began setting up stores in town. In the absence of money the housewife might exchange her goods for the merchant's. Farm products were still being taken to the wealthier towns and cities at least once a year for barter. Dunstable chose most often to take goods to the flourishing seaports of Salem and Newburyport for trading. The itinerant peddler, the sides of his patient horse bumped by the bulky saddlebags filled with the needles, pins, cloth, thread, pans, spices, salt, and many other needs of the women in the wilderness, still rode down the narrow sandy roads, but now deeper into the new "wilderness."

What was life like in this town of Dunstable from 1725 until the Revolution? We wish we could tell you factually. We know it was a time of little money and very hard work by every member of the family; it was a time of sadness, too, when almost every family buried some children before they became five years old, and most of the adults were elderly at forty-five or fifty.

Nature was kind to the hardy inhabitants. The Merrimack and Nashua Rivers and the wide and busy Salmon Brook, as well as Spit Brook, Old Maids, Pennichuck, and Naticook Brooks, afforded abundant fish for the men and water for the animals. By harnessing these streams, sawmills were run and later gristmills. Much later, by damming and further harnessing, bigger mills were supplied with power.

There were hills where the cattle, sheep, and horses could graze and, after all the trees had been felled, corn could be grown. Planks for their houses and barns, and firewood for their fireplaces were cut from those trees.

Money there was little of, but food was plentiful with the women's "kitchen" or "sallet" (salad) garden near the house, enough corn, wheat, and rye raised by each family for its needs, and the netting of fish and the shooting of game. On one day a week the grist mill in Chelmsford was open to Dunstable people for their grinding until the town built its own. Men clearing the land took their logs to early sawmills, either piled on ox sleds or by floating them down the rivers.

The settlers worked very hard at their land clearing, fence building, plowing, farming, animal care, their house and barn building and other heavy duties, plus their civic commitments. Every man was a farmer first. The parson, the merchant, the miller, the master carpenter, the blacksmith, the politician—whatever his work was—his chores on the farm had to come first.

Each woman accomplished an unbelievable amount of work every day. To feed her family she had a kitchen or sallet garden with common vegetables and herbs. She would fill bins in whatever cool cellar her house offered with "apples, potatoes, turnips, beets, carrots, and parsnips and have a hogshead of corned beefes, a barrel of salt pork, tubs of hams being salted in brine, tonnekins of salt fish, firkins of butter, barrels of applesauce, kegs of pigs' feet, . . ."

From the kitchen ceiling, or in the loft or attic, she hung strings of drying pumpkin chunks, slices of apple, and other fruits on strong linen thread.

All the work of caring for the milch cows fell to her lot. She milked them, separated the cream, churned the butter, made the cheeses—a laborious task—which were used not only by her family but for bartering, and made cooling drink for the children from the whey of the buttermilk. The housewife filled vast jars with preserves, pickled both garden and wild vegetables, fruit from the orchards, berries and herbs, as well as fish. Salt and spices for her food preservation would be all she needed to buy or procure by barter. In the late fall when the men had butchered the pigs, sheep, and cattle, or brought home a deer, the women took over the task of trying out the lard and saving the

tallow—it was also their lot to put the meat in the pickle or smoke it; the chickens, turkeys, ducks, and geese were in their care and they had the awful business of plucking the live geese twice a year for filling the feather beds.

In the spring the woman of the house made soap, a long day's messy, smelly job. The lye was made of wood ashes carefully hoarded during the year from the big fireplaces, leached by water which slowly seeped through the small cracks in the big wooden container, a process lasting several days. Out in the yard a great kettle was hung, or stood on a tripod, over fire kept burning constantly in a shallow pit. In it were melted many scraps of fat, carefully kept

Colonial foot warmer.

since the last soapmaking; and with that mess the prepared lye was boiled for hours. The result was soft soap that was then kept in a barrel outside, near the kitchen door. Gourds were used to scoop up the soap the housewife needed for her laundry. In those days this monthly chore was done outside, in great buckets. Lucky was the woman living near a brook where the rinsing could be done in the moving water.

The candle making was done in the late fall, using enough of the fresh tallow of the slaughtered animals to supply light for the coming year.

The women also did the carding of the wool,

spinning it, dyeing it—with dyes they had made from bark, berries, and the shells of nuts—weaving it, and then from that cloth cutting out garments for every member of the family and sewing them by hand. Then, too, the women grew the flax, prepared it in the various difficult stages to spin into linen thread for the weaving of linen cloth for shirts and summer clothing. Knitting of stockings was done by both girls and boys.

Brooms were fashioned from birch twigs by the children. After the family was supplied the child might be allowed to sell at the barter session for a few pennies. Pin money for the boys was also earned in the spring by cutting hoop-poles from black ash and hickory and selling these to the cooper for encircling his barrels, buckets, and pails.

Ayers' Mill on Pennichuck Pond was known as a spice mill.

The furniture, as well as the buildings, were made by the men and boys, simple at first but firm and long lasting. Craftsmanship and care were put into everything they made, for these things had to last. Their tools were hand-made, most often by the man who would use them until the more sophisticated mills, which would become foundries, came into being. Mortices and tenons (the interlocking units that joined timber together) meant fewer wooden pegs, or iron nails to rust. The only nails used were home-made until machine-made nails came in the nineteenth century.

Quill pens for the scholars were fashioned later by the schoolmaster, who also was responsible for making the ink by boiling bark and berries. It was carried in horns as the gunpowder was.

The First Schools

Joseph Dix became the schoolmaster for the town in 1772 and the records tell us served in that capacity for a good many years. He must have exerted a strong influence. When he came, the town was still not building any proper schoolhouses, as they were legally bound to do. For his first two years, Mr. Dix taught in two ends of the town for a few months at a time, at Mr. Searles' house in the south end, and in Mr. Gordon's house, almost to Merrimack, in the north. An ox-sled pulled the desks, benches, master's desk and stool, and his belongings through the dense growth of trees—mostly scrub pines—for the ten or so miles.

At the annual meeting of the "freeholders and other inhabitants of Dunstable Legally assembled at the meeting house" on March 2, 1772, the last item recorded in the clerk's report—"Proposal to See if the Town would raise money to Build School Houses in the Town and passed in the negative." But above that item we learn that it was "Voted that fifteen pounds of Lawfull money be raised for keeping school in Dunstable."

On March 1, 1773, and again on March 7, 1774, the vote had raised "the Lawfull money" for the school to "Twenty pounds." The teacher's salary was about one dollar a week and the town paid for his room and board, such as it was.

Finally in the record of the meeting of March 6, 1775, we find inside a very long and wordy paragraph reporting that they voted "their be a school house built in each of the Several school Districts in the Town of Dunstable—and that there be a committee in each of said Districts to fix a place—etc." And it was voted that eighty pounds lawful money be raised for building school houses in the several districts in Dunstable. It is nice to read that they also "voted that twenty pounds be raised to keep a school in the town for the current year."

The stipulation that the schools must be built by November of that same year would have been an incentive to "Schoolmaster" Dix to push things. Could it have been he who instigated this right-about-face in the thinking of the stubborn and in many cases illiterate townspeople, using the excitement of impending war to press for better education? In records we find that Joseph Dix served in the Army of the Revolution, 1775-1783. That could have meant that he was on call when needed. In

December, 1776, we find Captain Walker of this town raising a company from Dunstable and vicinity. Among those who enlisted were four from here, one of them being Joseph Dix.

The site of the first schoolhouse to be presided over by Mr. Dix was northwest of the old burying ground on the Lowell Road not far from the state line. It was a small one-room building with little windows high up on two sides. There was a great fireplace at one end to heat the building. Desks were wooden slabs laid over stakes driven into holes in the walls; their benches were rough planks supported by uneven stake legs. The schoolmaster's desk and tall stool sat in the middle of the room.

The Old Testament was used for reading and spelling; birch bark and sharpened lead bullets served as paper and pencil to be followed by charcoal and shingle and then by a slate for each child. The quill pens were fashioned for the pupils by the teacher, who also made the ink when paper came into use.

Formal education was not insisted upon and most parents had little interest in school attendance. The children found the school a relief from the drudgery at home. However, all chores had to be done before and after school, so many children who could not cope dropped out. It must have been especially difficult during the war years when the children were so badly needed at home.

Many interesting rules and regulations are to be found in the town records during this period. We learn one way the town avoided the welfare problem. In the records of 1743 we read that the constable was ordered to "warn" people,

all of them poor persons and neither Freeholders or Inhabitants of this town by law having come into this town to House Keeping and to Dwell and at present are Resident in a House of Mr. James Gordons without any consent of this town or Approbation from the selectmen & have resided for Twenty four days last past in this Town which they have no Legall Right to do. Now therefore that they might not become chargeable to this Town you [the constable] are here by commanded in his Majestys name forthwith to notifie and warn the said persons and every [one] of them that they and each of them Depart out of this Town with in fourteen days next coming at their Perrill.

The old problem of restraining livestock still required laws. Here are some samples taken from the Provincial Papers: "In Feb. 21, 1760, An act TO

PREVENT CATTLE AND HORSES GRAIZING ON THE UNFENCED LANDS IN SEVERAL TOWNS [one of them Dunstable] WHOSE OWNERS HAVE NO INTEREST THERE & FOR TAXING SUCH AS RUN THERE."

The Governor's Council and Assembly were asked to make "rules, etc." because "cattle and horses whose owners have no land in the same [towns] were sent to graize and were so unruly that a lawfull fence will not turn them and by reason there the Inhabitants often lose both their corn and grass."

In January, 1766, it was necessary for the Governor, Council, and Representatives, convened in General Assembly, to pass an act for regulating weights and measures. Every town had a Sealer of Weights and Measures and now he was authorized to warn those whom he suspected of having two sets of weights and measures, one legal, the other one he "secretes" and uses to weigh out materials for "innocent buyers." There were standards set up for building materials such as lumber and bricks, and even "the price and Assize of Bread." Dunstable must have had bakers, too, in those days and consumer protection was in action even then. Early fish and game laws were necessary also when it became apparent that the fish in the rivers and the game in the forests would soon disappear if fishing and hunting were not regulated. In 1758, an act was passed establishing a season for hunting deer, and eight years later another act to preserve the fish in the Merrimack River from "unnecessary Destruction" by "uninterrupted fishing" by seines, drag nets and "Wears." Another act of March 26, 1757, read: "No ram shall be suffered to go at Large within this Province from the 10th day of August to 15th day of November." The reason for this rule was to prevent lambing by the ewes during the coldest time of the year.

That was what life was probably like for the Dunstable people before 1775. They were very busy but they were content, healthy, and probably happier than many people nowadays.

9

The Revolutionary War

PEACE LASTED for some thirty years. Then the French and Indian Wars broke out. An expedition under General Sir William Johnson was planned in 1755 against Crown Point, then in possession of the French. A regiment of five hundred men was raised in New Hampshire and put under the command of Colonel Joseph Blanchard of Dunstable. One of the companies in this regiment was the famous Rangers, of which Robert Rogers was captain and John Stark (afterward general) was lieutenant. The regiment, stationed at Fort Edward, "was employed in scouting, a species of service which none could perform so successfully as the Rangers of New Hampshire." Another Dunstable officer was Jonathan Lovewell, commissary. After a few months the forces were disbanded. But the war continued.

In 1759 another regiment, of one thousand men this time, was ordered out from the State. Colonel Blanchard having died the year before, the command was given to Colonel Zaccheus Lovewell of this town, a brother of Captain John Lovewell.

The Idea of Rebellion

Loyal to the Crown through Great Britain's troubles with the French, the idea of rebellion must have begun to form in many minds even then. So little can be found in the records of Dunstable, New Hampshire about the Revolutionary period that we must use broader sources. We believe all the towns had similar experiences. Back in 1741 when the state line severed our town from Massachusetts no right to send a representative was granted us for many years. This right was then a favor granted by his majesty through "the governor of his Majesty's Province of New Hampshire bestowed only upon the loyal and obedient."

Fox tells us:

In 1774, however, when a collision with England began to be very generally expected, the General Assembly of New Hampshire claimed for itself the exercise of this right, and allowed certain representatives from towns not heretofore represented a seat and a voice in their councils. Immediately a petition was presented from this town, asking the privilege of representation, which was granted.

The New Hampshire Convention

To the Convention, meeting at Exeter in September, 1774, for the purpose of choosing delegates to the First Continental Congress, Jonathan Lovewell was sent as the delegate from Dunstable, New Hampshire by a vote of the Town Meeting. It was also voted to raise money "to purchase a supply of ammunition." Another vote at the same meeting was to pay their proportion of the "expenses of the Delegate [from New Hampshire] to the Grand Continental Congress," which met at Philadelphia the same month, and which published a Declaration of Rights, and formed an "association not to import or use British goods." From this time every movement toward liberty met with a hearty response from the citizens of Dunstable, New Hampshire.

From Fox again:

January 9, 1775, Joseph Ayers and Noah Lovewell were chosen to represent the town in the Convention which met at Exeter, April 25, 1775, for the purpose of appointing delegates, to act for this State in the Grand Continental Congress, to be held at Philadelphia, May 10, 1775. At this meeting, with a spirit characteristic of the times, and evidently anticipating a Declaration of Independence, they chose "Saml. Roby, Jona. Lovewell, Joseph Eayers, Benjamin Smith, John Wright, Benjamin French, James Blanchard and John Searle, a Committee of Inspection to see that the Result of the late Continental Congress be carried into practice, and that all persons in this town conform themselves thereto."

The Convention met again at Exeter on May 17, 1775, with the same delegates attending. Then it was that a Constitution for the government of the State was written. Finally, dated January 5, 1776, this Constitution was adopted. Ours was the first state to adopt its own. (In 1784 New Hampshire adopted the present Constitution.) Our State Constitution of 1776 made no provision for a governor or any chief executive officer of the State. The legislature was itself the executive, and upon every adjournment it was necessary to give somebody the power of acting in the case of an emergency. Of the responsible committee of safety "varying in number from 6-16, composed of the wisest, best and most active men in the different sections of the State— who had shown themselves the truest friends of their country, two members belonged to this town." Jonathan Lovewell was a member from June 20, 1777, to January 5, 1779, and Jonathan Blanchard from January 6, 1778.

This New Hampshire Constitution, adopted at the suggestion of the Continental Congress of May, 1775, was a bold step because it was a denial of England's right to rule over us, and a virtual Declaration of Independence. There was a House of Representatives and a Council of twelve men to be chosen by the people. Jonathan Blanchard was a member of the Council in 1776.

Dunstable and The Revolution

New Hampshire was "desirous and prepared for a collision; and no sooner did the news of the fight at Lexington on the 19th of April reach the State, than the whole population rushed to arms," the "most zealous" being the citizens of Dunstable. Fox goes on:

. . . nearly one-half the able-bodied inhabitants must have been in the army at the first call of liberty, a month before the battle of Bunker Hill. From no other town in New Hampshire was there so large a number in the army, as appears by the returns, and we record, a fact so honorable to their patriotism and courage, with a feeling of no little pride.

A few statistics show the population trends between 1725 and 1820. In 1730 there were 50 families and about 250 inhabitants. In 1767 there were 520 inhabitants broken down into 258 females and 262 males. Of the males there were 32 unmarried between sixteen and sixty, and 69 married. Under sixteen there were 151, and over sixty, 10. Lots of little boys and very few old men!

Eight years later, in 1775, at the beginning of the war, all the inhabitants of Dunstable, New Hampshire, numbered 705—329 females and 376 males. In 1775, Hollis had 1,255 persons!

In 1775, Captain (later Major) William Walker, a resident of this town, organized a company of sixty-six men. Here is Fox's account of their involvement in the Battle of Bunker Hill:

As soon as the British forces landed at Charlestown, the New Hampshire regiments were ordered to join the other forces on Breed's Hill. A part were detached to throw up a work on Bunker Hill, and the residue, under Stark and Reed, joined the Connecticut forces, under Gen. Putnam, and the regiment of Col. Prescott, at the rail fence. This was the very point of the British attack, the key of the American position. Here Captain Walker's company was formed, awaiting the attack. To be stationed there, in the post of danger, was a high honor, and well did the New Hampshire troops merit it, although not a few paid for the distinction with their lives.

None of Captain Walker's company, however, were among the immediate fatalities. Two Dunstable men were wounded, Joseph Greeley and Paul Clogstone, the latter dying of his wounds somewhat later. Another Dunstable man, not in Walker's company, who was killed was William Lund.

Although Captain William Walker is one of the most important military figures in our Revolutionary story, almost nothing is known about the man himself. We know that he was born in 1742 and died in 1825 and was married twice. He also served after the war as a Captain in the New Hampshire Militia. Why he came to Dunstable to live and how long he stayed here are mysteries.

A week before Walker organized his company, many citizens of Dunstable had "hurried to Concord to avenge the blood of their fellow citizens" arriving, of course, too late for the 19th of April itself. Forty of Walker's company, including the officers, were from Dunstable. The Company Roll can be found in Fox's *History of the Old Township of Dunstable,* page 172. On page 254, Appendix No. 11, is a "List of soldiers from that part of Dunstable which is now in New Hampshire in the Army of the Revolution, from 1775-1783." The list in a quick count numbers 163, fifteen of whom died in the War. Many on the list are Blanchards, Butterfields, Honeys, Harrises, Lunds, Lovewells, and Robys.

Early in 1776 New Hampshire raised three regiments of two thousand men placed under Colonels Stark, Reed, and Hale, which were sent to New York to join the army under General Sullivan for the invasion of Canada. A number of Dunstable men were among them. Other companies were formed in which Dunstable men enlisted. Many losses were sustained in consequence of which Jonathan Blanchard was sent by the legislature to Ticonderoga in October, 1776, to recruit the army. In every levy of two thousand men, the proportion to be furnished by this town was about 16. More than twice this number, however, must have been constantly in the army. In March, 1777, the town offered a bounty of one hundred dollars to every

soldier who would enlist and a large number joined the army then. Taxes, of course, rose to meet the demands of the war.

These Dunstable men were welcomed by every captain and colonel. Excellent marksmen from boyhood, they had been taught to hunt both "savages and wild beasts" in their frontier life, and to hunt the game birds and animals for food to feed their families. Clad in nondescript garments, they carried firearms of such variety and difference of calibers that the loose powder and balls distributed

by their officers had to be altered to fit.

Two names that had been prominent in the first fifty-year period continued to command attention in the Revolutionary period: Blanchard and Lovewell. Deacon John Blanchard's son, Joseph, married Abiah Hassell whose parents, it will be recalled, had died in the Indian Massacre of 1691. Called "Captain" Blanchard because he led a company scouting up and down the Nashua River looking for Indians, he was an innkeeper at the time of his death in 1727, at the age of fifty. He was one of

Detail of scrimshaw on 1773 powder horn shown on page 2.

the Proprietors and worked for them as a surveyor, "to run and stake the bounds" between towns. Earlier he had shared many responsible duties of trusteeship for the town with Lieutenant Henry Farwell. A skillful boat builder, he was given the job in 1726 of building the first ferry boat "to be finished within the year." No further mention is made of his work on the boat, and we can only assume it was delivered to the town before his death. Father of nine children, his only son to reach manhood was his namesake, Colonel Joseph.

In the Old South Burying Ground on the Lowell Road, not far from where the Blanchard house stood three hundred rods north of the state line, is an ancient stone bearing these words:

Here Lyes Buried
the Body of the Honble
JOSEPH BLANCHARD Esq
who departed this Life
April the 7th 1758
Aged 55 years

This Joseph was the colorful "Colonel" Blanchard mentioned in Chapter Seven. Stearns tells us "... he was an educated man of superior intelligence and capacity. He served the town of Dunstable with ability and credit. Commissioned "a Colonel of the regiment of militia in 1744—and maintaining intimate relations with Governor Benning Wentworth"—he was given command of a regiment of five hundred men in the expedition to Crown Point. One of the companies forming part of his regiment was the famous "Rogers Rangers" commanded by Robert Rogers and John Stark, later to become our famous New Hampshire General. When the state line divided New Hampshire from Massachusetts, Blanchard received the appointment of "Counsellor of State by Mandamus from the Crown. An office of great dignity and authority it was next to that of Governor the most honorable and responsible in the Colonies and was a gift of the King." He held this office probably until his death. On the death of Chief Justice Jaffrey, he was appointed judge of the superior court of judicature of the State, which he held for life.

In August, 1729, he had been named surveyor at a meeting of "free Holders and other Inhabitants of said Dunstable that are Quallified to vote in Town affiairs." His assignment was to lay out "ye Common and undivided Lands of Dunstable, for the Proprietors."

In 1776, Jonathan Blanchard, son of Colonel Joseph, was chosen for the Council of twelve, similar to our present Senate, provided for by the new Constitution of New Hampshire of January 5, 1776. For three years he was elected annually. In October, 1776, he was sent by the Legislature to recruit our regiments. In 1777 he was appointed Attorney General of the state and in 1778 he was made a member of the responsible and powerful Committee of Safety, serving for a long time. In 1784 he was raised from Major in the Militia to Brigadier-General. He was appointed Judge of Probate for Hillsborough County, an office he held up to the time of his death at the age of fifty. Fox describes Jonathan Blanchard as a man "who had not the advantages of a collegiate education, but was early initiated, by his father, into the active business of life." It would appear that this son of Colonel Blanchard was not nearly as controversial and bombastic as his father!

Joseph Blanchard, oldest son of Colonel Joseph, was one of the compilers of the first published map of New Hampshire which came out in 1761. He became a Merrimack resident and was in the Provincial Assembly 1762-1765. A skillful surveyor, he set the boundaries of many new townships. His associate in the production of the New Hampshire map was the Reverend Samuel Langdon of Portsmouth, a President of Harvard College.

Colonel Joseph Blanchard had thirteen children and died at the age of fifty-four, while Jonathan Lovewell, a widower since his early youth, was childless and lived to be almost eighty. Fox tells us that because "before 1800 there was no regular bred attorney in town, Judge Jonathan Lovewell and Judge Joseph Blanchard acted in that capacity whenever necessity required." They were friends in spite of their great differences of opinion. In 1754 they petitioned the General Assembly jointly for an act to raise money by extra taxes for rebuilding and maintaining a bridge over the Nashua River, probably the Runnells Bridge in Hollis.

Jonathan Lovewell was a representative in the Provincial House of Representatives from September, 1752 to September, 1755 "where his record was conspicuous," says Stearns. During the Revolution he was delegate from Dunstable in the first, second, fourth and fifth Provincial Congresses. The

Fifth Congress adopted a temporary constitution and by resolution became the first House of Representatives of the State of New Hampshire. Jonathan was twice elected one of the members of the State Committee of Safety. He was later appointed Chief Justice of the Court of Common Pleas for Hillsborough County. Stearns concludes his account of his life in his book, *Early Generations of the Founders of Old Dunstable,* with the following comment: "He died in 1792 and sleeps in an unmarked grave, but his name lives and his memory abides in the annals of Dunstable and New Hampshire."

Colonel Zaccheus Lovewell was a brother of Jonathan and of John, the hero of Pigwacket. He was also a military man who was a moderator and Selectman in Nottingham West (later Hudson) where he lived for several years. In the later years of his life he was once more a Dunstable resident. His wife was Esther Hassell, granddaughter of the massacre victims.

Before leaving this period in history, a note should be made concerning slavery before the Revolution. When the Revolution started, there were 87 Negroes and "slaves for life" in Hillsborough County. There is actual record of only one slave in Dunstable, a female owned by Paul Clogstone, who married a free black named Castor Dickinson; some time before the war he bought her freedom and that of her children. It is unfortunate that her name has not been passed down, as a woman who during part of her life played a unique role.

10

The Pastoral Period

THE TAVERN was an important part of the early life of Dunstable and indeed of all the growing towns. It was there that politics, crops, and religion were discussed, and there the hardy, rough, high-principled men could rest from their farm labors and quench their thirst with the good strong cider and imported rum from the great kegs in the tavern cellar. It was a welcome haven, and a place of cheer.

These taverns served the traveler on foot and on horseback. The post riders brought the mail, did errands, carried news, paid and collected bills. They were eager to stop at the tavern and be greeted heartily by the news-hungry inhabitants of Dunstable.

The roads at this time and for some years after had plain earth surfaces which were very dusty in dry times and deep in mud and almost impassable in wet. When stagecoaches came it was well that many taverns were ready, and that the "Grait Bridge" was strong enough to bear the weight of more and more of the coaches. Then, too, came the freighting teams, large wagons drawn by four, six, or eight horses, passing through the town constantly until the railroads were built.

Added to these were the smaller teams, owned and driven by farmers, carrying their own produce once or twice a year to the bigger wealthier towns and returning with supplies for themselves. And there were the country store-keepers, either being supplied by the merchants bringing through needed goods or going themselves to the bigger places to replenish their supplies. All this activity created a demand for taverns, which were numerous and busy, fully up to the needed requirements.

At the death of Captain Joseph Blanchard, an innkeeper, in the fall of 1727, Henry Farwell, Jr., hastened to ask the General Assembly of Massachusetts to issue him a license—which was granted—to become a taverner. One of the earliest in the town was Deacon Samuel French, whose tavern was close to the state line. It was at the home of Jonathan Lovewell, innkeeper (and bachelor), that the first of many town meetings was held on April 14, 1746, in Dunstable, New Hampshire. This house was "at the crotch of the roads about two miles below Nashua Village, and the meeting house was built upon the little triangular green in front of it."

At this first meeting after the charter was given

them, town officers were chosen, but at the second meeting it was voted "to build a new pound as near the Inn as a place could be found." It was located at the northeast corner of the road now going into the Country Club. Wandering animals could be a danger in many ways. Thomas Lund, also sexton of the meetinghouse and a grave digger, was paid eleven pounds "old tenor" for its construction. Many years later those great stones forming its high walls were used to build a house across the road which is still standing.

As early as 1769 five taverns were named, kept by the following persons: Benjamin French, Thomas Harwood, William Hunt, Jonathan Lovewell, Esq., and Widow Mary Butterfield. In 1792 the New Hampshire General Court passed an act authorizing the Selectmen of the towns to "grant licenses to keep tavern to suitable persons having accomodations, who might make application," giving them the right to retail rum, brandy, gin, wine, and other spiritous liquors.

The Cummings Tavern was in its day one of the favorite stopping places on the road.

In later years a floor was laid resting on the wide spreading branches of the large elm tree standing near the house; it was reached by a flight of stairs and guarded by a railing. It was quite a resort for driving parties from Lowell as well as Nashua; although it is not remembered that any serious accident ever happened from its elevated situation, still the descent must have been at times rather hazardous, considering the nature of the refreshment served to the exhalted guest!!!

Timothy Taylor, called the pioneer of the North Side, was licensed in 1801. He probably built later the tavern called the Indian Head Coffee House, which was at first of one story only. It was leased in 1813 to Phineas Whiting, Jr., who greatly enlarged it and added another story; but he failed and the lease was taken by Willard Marshall. Later it was included in the two hundred acres bought by the Nashua Manufacturing Co. from Benjamin J. French, on September 1, 1824, subject to the lease. On April 4, 1828, the Nashua Company sold it to Moses Tyler, who by report was a most admirable landlord. For the next fifty years its reputation was sustained and popularity increased with such jovial, hearty, attentive landlords as O. Bristol, P.O. Richmond, Mark Gillis, Gilman Scripture, and

others, who made this house noted all over New England for hospitality and cheer.

Parker tells us:

. . . The stagecoach was for many years an enlivening distinctive feature of Nashua and added interest and excitement to the daily life of the people. The stage driver was a prominent man and occupied a place both unique and of great responsibility. Packages confided to his care were promptly delivered; relying on his unfailing honesty he was often entrusted with large sums of money for the settlement of accounts between separated parties, often including bank exchanges; he was the active, energetic, living means of communication between the hamlet and the town, or the town and the city; with a lively dash and a sharp pull-up at the door of the tavern, while the horses were being changed, the eager crowd caught from his willing lips the news or gossip from the outer world above or below. In a twinkling, with a merry blast of the bugle he was off, leaving behind him a pleasurable sensation only appreciable to those who experienced it.

The first stage of which we have any account was a two-horse covered affair, owned and driven by Joseph Wheat, in 1796, from Amherst to Boston once a week and returning without a change of horses, stopping overnight at Billerica.

This route was later extended to Concord, connecting there with other routes beyond, and still later through Amherst into Vermont, keeping relays of horses along the routes. Where the Bank of New Hampshire now sits on the northwest corner of the intersection of West Pearl and Main Streets, the Francestown Stage Company had a large stable—later the Tremont House stable—which opened out into High Street. When the Lowell and Nashua Railway started, the staging interest was on the highest wave of its prosperity, more than thirty stages a day leaving or passing through the town.

The Merrimack River was used not only for fishing, and for floating logs in great numbers to sawmills lower down, but, too, for transportation. About one hundred years before the building of the Taylor Falls Toll Bridge in 1827 there were ferries straight across the river to Hudson and Litchfield—the earliest, established in 1729 and the busiest, was Cummings Ferry, which ran from the Cummings Farm in Hudson to near the mouth of the Nashua River. In 1742, this was relocated, landing at the end of Crown Street, and later operated by Hamblett and others. The Hills Ferry in the

Indian Head Coffee House, circa 1865.

northern part of the town was another, and Little's at South Nashua was a third.

There were a few pleasure boats and then there were the barges carrying freight. From the New Hampshire forests lumber and ship building materials as well as many other goods were carried to Newburyport. In rapidly growing Boston, badly needing the same materials, "influential capitalists and far-seeing investors" secured from the state a charter in 1793 to build the Middlesex Canal. "A narrow ditch, it ran like a silver ribbon for twenty-seven and a quarter miles from Middlesex Village, about a mile above present day Lowell, to the Charlestown Mill Pond near Boston," says Alex Ingraham in the April, 1969, issue of *Towpath Topics,* published by the Middlesex Canal Association. Falls and rapids in the Merrimack River had to be detoured around and that meant that locks had to be built—a great engineering feat for those days. On December 31, 1803, the canal was finally finished. The water route from the Charlestown Mill Pond (Boston) to Concord, New Hampshire, was 80 miles. From Boston to Manchester the trip up river took three days, and longer by half a day to Concord.

"Granite for the Quincy Market was transported from Concord; bricks were common merchandise for construction of mills at Lowell. Lumber for spars on sailing vessels at the Navy Yards and other ship building yards were down river cargo, usually in booms or 'shots' so-called,—" from Win-

nipesaukee and along the Merrimack. Other goods barged to Boston were "ashes, butter, cheese, beef, pork, cider and grains." The up-river cargoes on the return trip were "English goods, groceries, cod fish, macherell, salt, lime and plaster." During a busy season one report tells us there might be "about 50 boats in operation on both water-ways."

Steamboats had been tried and found impractical, one problem being that a steam boat could hardly make her way against the rapids at the mouth of the Nashua River, and the churning of the water was disastrous for the destructible walls of the locks and canals.

The main propulsion of these barges was manpower. The cargo was placed in the center to allow the two polemen to walk freely on either side of the boat. A square sail was hoisted when going down the river if there was a wind. Work usually had to stop around December 1 and started again at the beginning of April because of the ice and cold. These flat-bottomed barges were generally no more than seventy-five by nine feet, with both ends turned up. They could carry fifteen tons in high water, five to seven tons in low, and used a three-man crew. Besides the two polemen, the third crew member sat in the stern wielding an oak steering oar about twenty feet long. On the narrow canals horses were used to tow the boats. Even Nashua used to have a tow-path as shown in old pictures. Freight rates in the year 1815 between Boston and Concord, New Hampshire, were thirteen dollars per ton north, and eight dollars south.

As Lock and Canal Streets can testify, Nashua had for several years what was called in one book, "the Barge Canal." It was Nashua Manufacturing Company's boat canal running from Main Street at the bridge to the Merrimack River. Somehow the troublesome rapids at the mouth of the Nashua River had been overcome so that a landing for boats could be built there and a store near it. Later the barges coming up to the Main Street bridge pulled over to the northeast corner of the building still standing, where there can even now be seen the archway under which the barge pulled. Then the goods on it could be raised by a derrick into the storehouse owned by Ziba Gay. "It was mostly Hhds [hogs heads] of Rum and molasses," says one manuscript written in 1870 by Thomas Chase, a very old man then. "A lock was built just above the Nashua River on the Concord Road to connect with the Merrimack River. This lock was about 300 feet from the river." Now that the canal and locks named here have been so completely filled in, it is hard to imagine there ever was a canal there. That part of the canal to the west of the bridge toward Mine Falls, built by James F. Baldwin and whose architect was William Boardman, is still recognizable.

The canal from the bridge east to the Merrimack River was for transportation. That section to the west of the bridge and built first was for the purpose of supplying water power for the new mills which were being planned and established. Both parts were the work of the Nashua Manufacturing Company which needed a canal to deliver products to the metropolitan markets—by water from Nashua via the Merrimack River to the Middlesex Canal at Middlesex Village (now Lowell) and on to the port of Boston.

An older resident recalls that the canal beside Canal Street was not filled in until the First World War period (1919). She can remember her father reporting "another deer in the canal" when she was a child. The filling was done prior to an expansion of the mills on that street. When the coming of electric power eliminated the need for water power, the Nashua Manufacturing Co. surrendered the charter—stone blocks were removed from the locks and used as foundation for the mills. The Mine Falls Park development is the present day use put to that area once devoted to the advance of industry in the early nineteenth century. Good information can be found in the files at the Nashua Public Library on the Middlesex and other canals and locks on the Merrimack River.

By 1800 the population of Dunstable had increased to 826. The first national census in 1790 listed 115 *Heads of Families* of whom ten were women. The census of 1800 listed 135 *Heads of Families* of whom only four were women. The year 1803 was an important one for the town. A canal boat was built by Robert Fletcher with "sides 5 or 6 feet in height all around, and doors, and was looked upon as a 'wonder'—first one built here for regular transportation of goods." Thomas Chase's manuscript calls it "a canal boat of queer appearance which people said reminded them of Noah's Ark—." On July 4, 1803, this creation was launched from the landing on the Merrimack which was also used by pleasure boats to Lowell, "with a great gathering of the people and great rejoicing. The boat was christened *The Nashua* and the village, or that part of it near the joining of the Rivers which had been known as 'Indian Head,' received the name of NASHUA VILLAGE."

An oration by the new, young lawyer, Daniel Abbot—to be known because of it as "the father of Nashua"—given on that great day, can be found in several books and manuscripts in the library.

Going back to our canals: Mr. Ingraham's article states that two competitive types of transportation caused the short life span of the Middlesex Canal—the teamsters and the railroad. With regard to the teamsters, whose competition was felt most during the 1820s—with the rapid growth of the country, the roads and the turnpikes had become steadily more numerous and better. Now the "back" country further from the upper Merrimack River had to be tapped for timber and granite since the supplies nearer had been exhausted. The teamster could penetrate far into the country. "Once a load had been placed on a wagon, the improved roads naturally lent themselves to the idea of carrying the load the whole distance rather than to the canal where it would have to be unloaded from the wagon, reloaded on the canal boat, unloaded again at Boston (or wherever) and reloaded on teams again for its final destination." It was better for everyone to carry the load the whole distance, and the teams could also travel in the winter. "But the railroad caused the final death knell of the canal." Ironically, their roadbeds were often laid in the old canal towpaths.

From Parker's history and others we learn *how* the town was growing. The largest village in this town of Dunstable was at the "harbor," with taverns, shops, and dwellings. "Dunstable Plains," land still covered with its native growth of pines, lay between the "Harbor" and the Nashua River. The area north of the River was being built up. "Then only the Amherst and Concord with Main Street, and a road down the northern bank of the Nashua River to the boating house and ferries, were all the highways then existing."

We will quote from a few of the records to fill in our picture of the life of those times. From Parker, in 1803

a large one story dwelling house stood at the site of the Indian Head Coffee House and was kept as a tavern by Timothy Taylor, Esq. A large store owned and conducted by Robert Fletcher, who lived in Amherst, stood where Kendrick and Tuttle's store stood later, where Amherst Street leaves Main. Daniel Abbot and Charles Fox's office was a dwelling house occupied by "Uncle" John Lund, his brother and sisters, probably the Spalding house. Mr. Fletcher had started erecting a dwelling house, 3 stories in front and two in rear on the north-east corner of Main and Franklin Streets.

In September 1803, the Old Tontine, a long, low building at the head of Main Street was built and soon occupied by Mr. Abbot, Dr. Elias Maynard, Dea. James Patterson, bookbinder and a Mr. Clements, saddler.

Another report concerns Dunstable in 1822:

Dam across the Nashua River west of the bridge at its north end stood the grist mill of James Patterson, at its south stood Wm. Marshall's saw mill. At the Harbor, and on the west side of the road and north of the brook, we find the saw and grist mill of Israel Hunt, Sr., where his sons John and Israel were workmen. On the south side of the brook stood quite a pretentious 3-story shop occupied by E.F. Ingalls as a blacksmith and iron-worker. This shop had a trip hammer, and he made axes, hatches, hammers, the old-fashioned heavy hoe with a ring for a handle, and such other iron work as was called for by the community. The scythe shop of Isaac March [Marsh?] stood where the east mill now stands, and upon what was known as Dickerman's Location, just below the old Allds road bridge, was to be found the carding, fulling, pressing and dyeing shop of Enock Dickerman. There was also a dam and shop below

Dickerman's occupied by Daniel Ingalls as a blacksmith shop, where he had a trip hammer and lathe.

The First Post Office

Sometime between April 1 and July 1 of 1803 the Post Office was established in the town. This was opened in the tavern of Cummings Pollard not far north of the state line. General Noah Lovewell was named Postmaster. This was probably only an honorary title out of respect for his age and accomplishments, as the Assistant Postmaster, Pollard, was in charge of the office until 1811. Since "the first quarterly balance of postage acknowledges the sum of twenty cents," the work could not have been too taxing, although the next quarter the receipts had increased to the sum of two dollars, eighty-seven cents. Before 1803, the mail was brought into town by the stage coach or, as it was sometimes called, "old Wheat's mail stage" and earlier by post riders. Before this, mail had to be picked up at the Tyngsborough Post Office. In 1810, a history of the Post Office says, "the net rec'ts to the General Post Office were $31.86: the gross $46.00."

In 1811 the office was moved to the Harbor, to the dwelling house of Israel Hunt who had been appointed Assistant Postmaster. It was now located nearer the residence of General Lovewell who continued to superintend the duties of the office until his death in May, 1820. The next month John M. Hunt, Esq., a young man of 23 and son of Israel, was appointed Postmaster. He moved the Post Office from Israel's house across the road to the office of I. and John M. Hunt (their general store) where it remained for six years. These buildings were at 428 and 429 Main Street where two buildings of Rivier College now stand. After the erection of the cotton mills, the Post Office was moved to Nashua Village. John M. Hunt remained Postmaster until 1841.

In 1898 the two Hunt houses were finally torn down, in spite of some feeling that they were historic landmarks that should have been preserved.

Early Physicians

The first doctor practicing in Dunstable before, during, and after the Revolution was Dr. Nathan Cutler. In the Old Burying Ground is a stone on which we can read his name and the fact that he died on February 22, 1830, "Aet. 91."

At the time of the Revolution, Dr. Ebenezer Starr came here from Dedham and on April 21, 1776, married Hannah, daughter of Colonel Joseph Blanchard. He lived to be only 52 but his son, Dr. Augustus Starr, followed him and became the husband of Rebecca Blanchard, daughter and eldest child of Jonathan Blanchard. It is not known if this Dr. Starr stayed very long in Dunstable.

There were three other doctors here at the turn of the century: Dr. Elias Maynard occupied the old "Tontine" building as home and office in 1803 and 1804. He had been in Dunstable several years but soon afterward moved to Boston. Dr. Peter Howe was here from 1800 to 1837 or 1838. The third and the only physician before 1820 we can read about was Dr. Micah Eldredge, not a learned man but having "the gentlest of dispositions and most magnanimous heart." His practice was a large one.

All these physicians made their miles of rounds on horseback carrying their medicines and surgical instruments in saddlebags. Later they rode in their two-wheeled gigs, a tippy vehicle but suited to the narrow, rough, and often muddy roads, as well as to the open fields with ruts and rocks they were forced to cross. The leather curtains of the gig kept the inside relatively dry in rainy weather. There were many disadvantages and hardships a doctor had to face back then.

The woods and gardens supplied the physician of that day with many of his medicines. The more important drugs consisted of opium, iron, various barks and roots, as well as herbs, ground in the doctor's own mortar with his wooden pestle. Bloodletting was considered of great value, too. Nature herself was a great help in pulling the person through his illness. It was well that the inhabitants of New England were as hardy as they were.

In those days some of the physicians who were more dedicated and not as content as Dr. Eldredge to learn only from their patients, would ride their horses periodically to Boston to visit medical schools and hospitals to find what new methods and medicines were being used in the cities and larger towns. They brought back not only medical information but supplies of old and new medicines in their saddlebags.

These trips offered both refreshment of mind and body to the hard working doctor and opportunities to do errands in the city for many of his patients in Dunstable. He also brought back news and gossip of happenings in the world which the infrequent newspaper brought by the post rider might not mention in detail. For weeks afterward this "traveler" was sought out to liven taverns and homes with his tales of the outside world.

Daniel Abbot by 1820 had already established his image as "The Father of Nashua." Although his picture, as taken from Parker's History, shows him as an old man, it is easy to imagine him as a young, attractive lawyer who came from Andover, Massachusetts, in 1802. He was to spend fifty active and fruitful years here. "Mr. Abbot," says Parker, "was a good deal more to Nashua . . . than a resident and distinguished attorney." He was interested in every civic advancement and a leader in most of them. The Middlesex Canal had Mr. Abbot's endorse-ment and it was his spirited oration, at the Fourth of July launching of *The Nashua,* which gave the town its name. The house he bought in 1803 at the corner of Abbot and Nashville Streets, built earlier by John Lund, was his residence throughout his life in Nashua. The books in the Register of Deeds Office of those days list page after page of purchases of land and sales of land under the name Daniel Abbot. At his death he must have been a very wealthy man. His religious affiliation was with the Unitarian Church where he was very active, and he lies buried in the Nashua Cemetery just behind that church, among many other influential Dunstable and Nashua people.

When Abbot was a young man, he had studied with a second lawyer in Salisbury, New Hampshire, at the same time that another law student, named Daniel Webster, was there. It is said that Webster in later years was a frequent guest at the Abbot home. As we move into another period in Nashua's history, it will be seen how the dynamic influence of both of these men changed a pastoral village into an industrial mini-metropolis.

Carved woodblock used for stamping Nashua
manufactured yard goods. As described on page 103,
the Indian Head has been a Nashua symbol for two
hundred and fifty years.

From Country Village
to City

1820 - 1900

11

Introductory Review of Dunstable - Nashua in the Nineteenth Century

W HILE VISITING FRIENDS in Dunstable in the winter of 1826, Sally Belknap, a young lady from Framingham, Massachusetts, came down with a minor illness and consulted a local doctor, Elijah Colburn. Love at first sight resulted in an "understanding" by the time she returned home in February. They became engaged when he visited her in April and the wedding took place in June. This fast-moving romance was carried on by correspondence which has been preserved by their descendants. The courtship followed the rather formal ritual expected of young people of their class. In writing to his future wife, the doctor addressed her as "Dear Friend," for example. The depth of his feeling, however, comes through strongly in such sentences as this, at the end of his first letter: "And now from this time henceforth and forever may Heaven's best blessing attend and rest upon my beloved Sarah. Yours with much esteem, Elijah Colburn." What girl in any age would not be flattered by such a sentiment!

The marriage, which lasted for fifty-five years, was a very happy one, in spite of misfortunes such as the early deaths of several of their children. Sally Belknap Colburn's life as a Dunstable-Nashua resident spanned the rest of the nineteenth century. Her husband was the first physician to make house calls in a horse and buggy; he was assisted in a busy practice later in life by his son, Edwin.

As the date for his marriage approached, the young doctor became concerned about the many details involved in setting up a household. He went shopping for furniture in local stores and was disappointed in the quality available. The couple decided to buy the basic pieces they needed from a custom cabinetmaker in Framingham and have them shipped by way of the Middlesex Canal.

Dr. Colburn's shopping trip showed that Dunstable was not large enough yet to support retail establishments catering to a wide variety of tastes. The goods that were available were intended to supply an immediate need for inexpensive furnishings for the fifty new tenement houses that had been erected in 1825 to house the influx of workers for the cotton mills.

Dunstable In The Early 1800s

Between 1820 and 1830 Dunstable's population rose from 1,100 to 2,400. The year 1820, in fact, is a

date that marks a dividing line between two worlds, that of the rather sleepy agricultural village waiting for the next stagecoach to come through and that of a fast-growing industrial center. In 1820 the total extent of business in town consisted of five stores, six taverns, three grist mills, one clothing mill, one carding machine, two bark mills, and three tanneries. In the next decade Dunstable left behind forever this old era and moved rapidly into a mill town way of life. In June, 1823, the Nashua Manufacturing Company, formed under the leadership of Daniel Abbot, was incorporated by the State of New Hampshire. By the time Sally Colburn came here as a bride, the first mill had already gone into operation, producing cotton fabric. Sixty years later, an article was written for the *Telegraph*, reminiscing about the period from the mid-twenties to the mid-thirties, referring to it as a time of feverish activity that created an atmosphere similar to that of a western frontier town.

Another mill was started on the other side of the Nashua River at about the same time. It was the Indian Head Company and was originally built to make woolen cloth, a venture destined for early

bankruptcy. Wool was a much harder material to handle than cotton and the company did not have the necessary technical skill to meet competition. In 1830 the Jackson Company was to take over and convert it into another cotton mill, using the symbol of the Indian Head to mark its products. A dam built to provide the factory with power raised the water level so high that a new bridge at the Main Street crossing was necessary. The Nashua Manufacturing Company provided money and materials for the first adequate structure at this critical

Miniatures of Elijah Colburn and Sarah Belknap, painted before their wedding in 1826.

junction. This, too, required many repairs in subsequent years because of heavy traffic and spring washouts.

The big achievement of 1826-1827 was the building of the first Taylor Falls Bridge across the Merrimack River by a group of private proprietors who invested twelve thousand dollars in the project. Passage between Dunstable and Nottingham West (soon to be renamed Hudson) was made much easier by the opening of this bridge, a wooden, covered structure with three spans. Tolls were charged according to the type of traffic. It was not until 1854 that the bridge became a public right-of-way, owned jointly by the two towns.

Nineteenth Century Journalism

A sure sign of Dunstable's emerging importance as a business and trade center was establishment of the first newspaper. Late in 1826 two young men from out of town set up a printing press and started putting out *The Constellation and Nashua Advertiser*. The partnership soon broke up and one partner named Brown kept it going a few months, before the paper was taken over by Andrew E. Thayer, owner of a bookstore that included the first circulating library. Thayer's efforts at journalism ran aground on political shoals and in 1832 he sold the paper, which he had renamed *The Nashua Gazette and Hillsborough County Advertiser,* to Israel Hunt, Jr. Hunt built it into a leading voice of the Democratic Party which supported the principles of Andrew Jackson. In the same year, a second paper, *The New Hampshire Telegraph,* was started by Alfred Beard, a young man from Nelson, New Hampshire. Beard supported the Democrat Republicans or Whigs, the

party of Henry Clay. This paper was the ancestor of our present *Nashua Telegraph.* Both papers were weeklies for many years.

In 1835 Andrew Jackson was in the middle of his second term as President of the United States; William Badger of Gilmanton was Governor of New Hampshire. Issues of the *Gazette* for that year tell a great deal about how people lived and what they were concerned about. The paper consisted of only four pages, combining in this space the functions performed today by the TV newscast, the gossip tabloid, the opinion magazine, and the local shopper. It had its limitations, however, as a source of local news, as events happening in town had already been circulated by word of mouth by the time the next weekly edition came off the press.

The editor gave his readers what they really needed—a column of foreign news that had come over on the packet ships that plied the Atlantic; news on the state and national levels; items clipped from other newspapers to enliven the publication and satisfy the public's thirst for sensationalism. These latter were reprinted without headlines, preceded by exclamatory leads such as "Ghastly Accident," "Awful Calamity," "Strange Disappearance," "Violent Murder in New York," "Amazing Coincidence," etc. To take care of the requirements for "culture" each issue printed on the front page a sentimental poem and a short piece of sad and romantic fiction.

The advertisements in these old newspapers tell a story all their own. Isaac Spalding, who had gone into the retail business in Dunstable after an apprenticeship in Amherst, advertised profusely in both papers. He sold everything he could buy cheaply and his latest shipment might include nails, pots and pans, patent medicines, pantaloons. An example of the merchandise that he exhorted his customers to buy was "Mrs. Gardner's genuine Indian balsam of liverwort and hoarhound, prepared from a receipt originally procured from an Indian family, for complaints of the lungs." Spalding became in a few decades the wealthiest man in town by buying and selling such concoctions, along with groceries, clothing, and hardware.

There is evidence that quite a few women earned their own living, advertising their services as milliners, dressmakers, or private teachers. The forms of entertainment offered in the course of the year are indicated in the many announcements of traveling troupes such as theatrical companies and circuses, as well as ventriloquists and musicians. A menagerie and aviary entered town with a grand flourish, including a band in their cavalcade, and was recommended by the editor of the paper as very educational for children.

Besides the slavery question, other matters of controversy in 1835 were capital punishment, a proposed state insane asylum, and the coming of the railroad. In May, the Lowell and Boston Railroad went into operation, running between the two cities in the amazing time of one hour, fifteen minutes. In Dunstable there were now seven tri-weekly stage lines, one coach that ran daily, and four steamboats a day. Both newspapers argued that this traffic justified an extension of the railroad northward. Many citizens signed petitions asking that railroad service be made available in New Hampshire.

On December 23, 1838, Nashua got an exciting Christmas present when the first railroad train ran all the way to Main Street. One more revolution in transportation had taken place and the railroad from that day on would dominate. By 1850 the stagecoach and the Middlesex Canal system would be almost entirely phased out.

In the personals and legal ads in the paper, fathers often placed notices that sons, although under twenty-one, were on their own and could retain their earnings. Occasionally such a notice was inserted concerning a daughter who had probably gone to work in the mills. Although men frequently advertised that they would no longer pay the bills of errant wives who had left "bed and board," there was only one lady who used such a notice against her husband, specifically warning the tavern keepers

that she would not be responsible for his liquor tabs.

Nashua's growth profile shows periods of very rapid increase in population, punctuated by periods of slow increase or stagnation. The highest percentage of increase in the city's entire history was in the 1830s—in 1840 there were 150 percent more inhabitants than in 1830. This was at a time when the State showed an increase in population of less than 6 percent. Most of the newcomers were women and girls who came from small country places to work in the mills. However, many future business and professional men were also attracted to the lively and bustling town. One of these was Archibald Harris Dunlap, a member of the famous family of cabinetmakers. He was born in Antrim where his father made furniture and worked on inventions. In 1831, when he was fourteen years old, he and an older brother walked the thirty-five miles to Dunstable. Each carried a bundle of belongings in true Dick Whittington style, as they set out to seek their fortunes. Archibald eventually established a very successful garden seed business in Nashua and performed many services for his city, as well as for the state. He was noted for his conciliatory ability and helped resolve such conflicts as the location to be chosen for the Soldiers' and Sailors' Monument.

Dunstable Becomes Nashua

On January 1, 1837, Dunstable officially became Nashua. The change of name had been discussed for some time and was a logical move because of the accelerated growth of Nashua Village. It had become very confusing to have two towns with the same name next door to each other and mixups in mail happened quite often. Dunstable, Massachusetts, showed little inclination to be the one to make the change.

During the winter of 1838-1839, the need for a town hall was the chief subject of conversation, with disagreement over its location coming to a boil. At the Town Meeting of March, 1839, acrimonious debate took place, as the people who lived in the fast-growing area north of the Nashua River advanced arguments for putting up the proposed building in their territory. In 1842, the matter came to a vote, with the south side residents outpolling their neighbors. They went ahead with plans to build the Town Hall on the east side of Main Street.

EX · LIBRIS
KATE · SHURTLEFF · GROVER

There was a mass eruption of wrath north of the river and within a very few days the north siders had applied to the State Legislature to be incorporated as a separate town. On June 23, 1842, the town of Nashville came into existence and governed itself for the next eleven years. Franklin Pierce, who later became New Hampshire's only contribution to the presidency, represented Nashville as legal counsel in the establishment of the new town.

A leading member of the Nashville community was a brilliant young lawyer named Charles J. Fox. After attending Dartmouth and Yale Law School, he came to Dunstable to study law with Daniel Abbot, became his partner, and in 1840 married Abbot's daughter, Catherine. He became a member of the State Legislature, helping to publish the Revised Statutes, and was the co-editor of one of the first anthologies of New Hampshire literature. Fox was the author of Nashua's first chronicle, *History of the Old Township of Dunstable,* which was published after his premature death in 1846. The book was a labor of love for his adopted city and was considered a literary classic among New England town histories. It still stands as the foundation work for all historical writing about Dunstable-Nashua.

Ordinary citizens were less affected than business and professional people by the split in the community. Church attendance, for example, remained much the same as it had before, no matter which section the churches were in. Concerns of daily life went on as usual. A typical middle class householder was Daniel Spalding who lived in Nashville. Some recently discovered letters written by Daniel to a cousin, Benjamin Batchelder of Whitefield, reveal the patience and quiet endurance practiced by the average family in living from day to day.

Observations of Daniel Spalding

One letter indicates that Daniel Spalding, although still a young man, is in poor health. At one point he exclaims, Job-like: "My lameness holds on like poison to me yet." Although he can no longer work as hard as in former days, he keeps fairly busy—"I have a horse and pig to take care of and woods to saw." Daniel and his wife are still grieving over the loss of their only child. He comments:

Children are no trouble to wait upon compared with the troubled feelings of parents come to lose one by death. We had one, as interesting a child as any of its age, but his health was such that he worried us a great deal and was what folks would call trouble the first two months of his life, but he lived and was well afterwards till he was 7 months and 20 days old and he was snatched from us in blooming health, as it were, taken sick in the morn and died at midnight that night with inflammation of the brain. If he had lived he would have been a great deal of company now; he would have been 3 years old yesterday.

Nashua and Nashville Unite

The absurdity as well as impracticality of the two towns coexisting, one on either side of the river, became very clear after 1850. Leaders of both communities met for private talks on how the unfortunate division could be resolved. In June, 1853, Nashua was incorporated by the State of New Hampshire. The first mayor elected under the new city charter was Josephus Baldwin, a bobbin manufacturer whose home was almost directly across the street from City Hall. The new municipal government went into operation with a smoothness that reflected the general joy and spirit of harmony resulting from the reunion.

Among the many who worked hard to make Nashua once more a united community, Albin Beard, editor of the *Telegraph,* was especially articulate. He had taken over the paper when his twin brother, Alfred, had died in 1839. Although active in the affairs of Nashville, he always insisted that the ill feeling should be dispelled and actively advanced consolidation during his two terms as Mayor in 1858 and 1859. Beard's death in 1862, while in the prime of life, was felt as a great loss to everyone.

In December, 1853, the "Father" of Nashua, Daniel Abbot, passed away "full of years." Shortly before, Senator Charles Gordon Atherton had died suddenly at the age of only forty-nine. Atherton took a leading role in influencing Nashville to rejoin Nashua. In the United States Congress, where he served both as Representative and Senator, he was a strong debater. Atherton was one of several local men who were close personal friends of President Franklin Pierce.

As the Civil War period approached, other leaders came forward to replace those who had been influential in the first half of the century. Aaron Worcester Sawyer was Mayor in 1860 and later became City Solicitor; he was a fine lawyer, although not a graduate of any college or law school. Edward

Spalding was the first doctor to be elected Mayor, in 1864. A man of many interests, Spalding was President of the Pennichuck Water Works, a member of the School Board, and—on the side—specialized in settling large estates. He also found time to go fishing, a hobby which led to chairmanship of the original state body set up to supervise fish and game resources.

Virgil C. Gilman succeeded Spalding as Mayor and was always a popular and respected figure in Nashua. He was an expert bookkeeper and participated in various enterprises, including the small paper company that later grew into the present Nashua Corporation. He was also an effective public relations agent for Nashua, contributing numerous articles about the city to newspapers and magazines. Gilman was agriculturally-minded and was one of the first to breed the Plymouth Rock fowl. He and Dr. Spalding worked together to set up a fish hatchery that was the beginning of the one we have today.

After the Civil War, changes in Nashua followed in quick succession. New status was bestowed on the city in 1866 when it became the County Seat of Hillsborough County. A new building was required to house the county records and what better location than next door to City Hall? The following year, in 1867, when the Nashua Public Library was started, space for it was readily available in an unused section of the second floor of this County Records Building.

Organization of the Library

The Nashua Public Library was formed because of the determination of a group of young women who had organized during the Civil War to raise money for soldiers' benefits. Lucy and Kate Thayer, the lively and energetic daughters of Andrew Thayer, were members of this group, as well as Mary Hunt, who twenty-five years later would be personally involved in building a permanent home for the library. In 1851 the Union Atheneum, a private reading club, had been formed by a group of ninety persons from both Nashua and Nashville.

To encourage a public library this organization had agreed to donate its entire holdings if the city was willing to support one. The Nashua Manufacturing Company also donated its company library to the new institution.

Nashua's first City Hall in the 1870s with coach and one-horse shay in foreground.

Charles Gordon Atherton

Miss Emily Towne was the first of a succession of women who served as librarians until the 1950s. She had moved to Nashua with the county records, as her job was supervising clerical work on these documents. After the library was established, she decided to change jobs. Later on in her career she worked for the Registrar of Deeds. She was a good example of the unmarried woman who even then found ways to be financially independent while leading a fairly interesting life.

Post Civil War Developments

In 1868 one list was compiled of persons in Hillsborough County who were worth forty thousand dollars or more, and another was published showing more than two hundred persons in Nashua with incomes exceeding one thousand dollars a year. Isaac Spalding was the wealthiest man in the county, having multiplied profits from patent medicines and other necessaries into a fortune of $225,000. In the Nashua list, there were only nine men who counted annual income in five figures. Some of the best-known citizens, such as Dr. Elijah Colburn ($3,000 after forty-five years in his profession) reported incomes in the $1,500-$3,000 bracket. Luther Roby, whose business specialty was ship's timbers, made about fourteen thousand dollars, as did George Stark, manager of the Boston and Lowell Railroad.

On March 1, 1869, a daily newspaper made its appearance. *The New Hampshire Telegraph* became the *Nashua Daily Telegraph* under the editorship of Orren C. Moore who succeeded Albin Beard. After

Moore, one of Nashua's greatest journalists, died in 1893, his wife, Nancy, ran the paper for a period of about six years. The *Gazette* also became a daily in 1872 and continued publication until 1895. A successor, *The Nashua Daily Press,* published until 1905.

Probably the single phenomenon most responsible for change after 1870 was the French-Canadian migration. Within a few short years, the ethnic makeup of the population lost its previous homogeneity. The Irish in the 1850s had been the first to inject a new culture and, most striking of all, a different religious viewpoint. Their numbers were small, however, compared to the influx by the thousands of people from Quebec who surged in to work for a steady weekly wage in the cotton mills. From a population that remained on a plateau of ten thousand during the sixties, the census returns for 1880 showed almost a 30 percent increase. The 1890 figures represented a startling increase of 45 percent over 1880. Before 1900 the number of people living in Nashua was to go over the twenty thousand mark.

The 1870s was a time of expansion geographically, with residential building in many areas outside the industrial and commercial center of the city. Crown Hill particularly developed rapidly at this time. The public school system required an extensive building program during which the Mount Pleasant School, the Harbor School on Lake Street, and a new high school on Spring Street appeared. Another civic building that aroused much pride was the Central Fire Station on Court Street, built in 1870 and converted in 1970 into an Arts and Science Center.

In 1872 a second Catholic Church was built, known as St. Aloysius, to serve the French community. Another well-loved priest of this faith, Father Milette, came to Nashua in that year and immediately achieved his first objective, the building of this church, now known as St. Louis de Gonzague, which suffered a disastrous fire in July of 1976. Father Milette is one of Nashua's great legendary figures; many stories are still told about his self-sacrificing devotion to his church and its parishioners. If a friend offered to pay a trolley car fare for the good father so that they could both ride rather than walk to a destination, Milette would take the money and say "Fine, that is ten cents more for my church; we will both walk and enjoy the healthful exercise."

Nashua in the Mid-1870s

The Nashua directory for 1875 reveals many facts that add up to a profile of daily life at that time. All the cotton mills were going strong, with Nashua Manufacturing running eighteen hundred looms and seventy-six thousand spindles. There were about forty grocery stores, all clustered in the downtown area. Twenty-two dressmakers were listed, of whom about half were married women and half single; some of these undoubtedly did enough business to employ other women as seamstresses. Out of twelve music teachers, seven were women. Eight out of eleven milliners listed were women, pointing up the importance attached to that Victorian status symbol, milady's bonnet!

There were ten saloons, three of them on Factory Street, in spite of a state prohibition law and frantic temperance crusades. One restaurant took the precaution of announcing in its ad that it served "the best quality wines and liquors for medicinal purposes." Several establishments were listed under that peculiar eighteenth century heading "oyster and ice cream saloons." These were popular gathering places where groups of friends met for light refreshments, including presumably oysters.

The New Hampshire Gazeteer for 1874 notes that,

Virgil Gilman

Horse-drawn trolleys ran from
1885 to 1894, when electric
trolleys were introduced.

out of a total Nashua population of twelve thousand, over one-fourth were steadily employed, including fourteen hundred females. A third of the employed group were engaged in professional business and trade. Almost one thousand persons earned their living working for eight or nine non-textile manufacturing firms. Although textiles dominated the industrial picture, they by no means controlled it.

In 1876, the Centennial celebration of the Declaration of Independence took place, with chief attention focused on the great Philadelphia Exposition which was attended by many Nashuans. At home the streets on July 4 teemed with crowds in holiday mood, finding vantage points along the parade route. A feature of the program was a whimsical procession by a fun group known as the "Roaring Rattlers" who staged a take-off on pompous military units and civic organizations that took themselves a bit too seriously. Some of the groups in a mock line of march were "The Improved Order of White Men," "The Ancient and Dis Honorable Artillery from Dunstable," "The Franklin St. Infantry." There were also a formal parade, a speech by the Mayor, sports events, and fireworks.

In 1877 a presidential visit was the highlight. President Rutherford B. Hayes attended a banquet at the Tremont House, that famous hotel that until 1922 stood on the corner of Main and West Pearl Streets. In 1880, there were thirty-six telephones in Nashua, most of them in business offices. In 1881

it was time for a new Taylor Falls Bridge and a "modern" iron structure took the place of the old covered one, at a cost, for Nashua's share, of ten thousand dollars. The year 1886 saw the end of the gaslight era, as electric lights for the streets were cautiously installed on a "trial basis" at no cost to the city. The following year a contract was signed for these lights, so apparently the trial was successful.

First Women Physicians and Dentist

In 1888, the first woman physician, Dr. Ella Blaylock, a Canadian, started a practice here. She later married Henry B. Atherton and continued to practice for many years. In 1889 another woman physician, Dr. Katherine Prichard Hoyt, opened an office in Nashua, after working at the Women's Reformatory in Sherborn, Massachusetts. Dr. Hoyt had wanted to become a doctor from an early age and was encouraged in her ambition by her stepfather. Her specialties were obstetrics and gynecology. Dr. Atherton specialized in women's and children's problems.

The first woman dentist was Dr. C. Gertrude Locke, a daughter of Dr. Luther F. Locke, himself a well known dental practitioner in Nashua. She had three sisters in active professional life, two being practicing physicians and a third engaged in a still more novel field for a woman—that of architecture. Dr. Locke was graduated from the Boston Dental College (now Tufts) in 1895, and immediately commenced practice in her native city, fitting up a finely appointed office in the family residence at 11 Amherst Street.

In 1889 the Soldiers' and Sailors' Monument to the men who served the city in the Civil War was dedicated. Another presidential visit occurred in this year when Benjamin Harrison stopped off and was given a parade and luncheon.

Continued Growth

In 1891 the Police Station on Court Street, now the home of the American Legion, was opened. This eased crowded conditions at City Hall and enabled the Police Department to operate much more efficiently. In 1893, an Emergency Hospital was set up in a house on Temple Street. From this modest beginning, arising out of a desperate need to take emergency medical services out of the basement of City Hall, has grown the present Memorial Hospital.

It was also the year 1892 that marked a fifty thousand dollar gift to the city. Mrs. Mary A. Hunt and her daughter, Mary E. Hunt, decided to erect a library building in memory of husband and father, John M. Hunt.

In 1894, the old Indian Head Coffee House— where the stagecoaches once pulled up and the scene of many gay social affairs—was torn down and the new First Congregational Church erected on the Lowell Street site. This was the most distinguished building in terms of size and architectural detail that had ever been put up in Nashua. It made an impressive companion to the Hunt Memorial Library building when the latter finally was completed in 1903. Much of the financial support for the building of this fine church came from Mrs. Lucy Kendall Spalding, Isaac's widow.

Publication of Parker's History

In 1897 was published a second full-length history of Nashua, *History of the City of Nashua, N.H., from the Earliest Settlement of Old Dunstable to the Year 1895*, compiled by a committee of seventeen leading citizens under the editorship of Judge Edward E. Parker of the Probate Court. Judge Parker was a great-grandson of Prudence Wright, the Revolutionary War heroine who led a group of women in Pepperell "dressed in men's clothes and armed with pitchforks and scythes," in guarding a bridge over which a Tory spy was expected to pass.

The presentation of nineteenth century industrial and commercial history is an outstanding feature of this book. Short biographies of over one hundred citizens who had made solid contributions to the development of Nashua form a valuable source of information. Unfortunately, these are all men, with one token exception. The many capable women who helped make Nashua a pleasant and progressive city are given scant attention.

The life stories in Parker seem to us today to be over-laudatory, the subjects emerging as incredibly upright and flawless. We cannot help wondering which ones were in reality "gay blades" or whether a certain individual was as honest throughout his career as the editors say he was. Nevertheless, the energy and wide range of interests of these people come through impressively. Several offer real-life Horatio Alger stories, proving that Nashua offered good opportunities for poor men with brains and abilities to make their way to the top. Charles Holman, for example (father of the donor of Holman Stadium), was a penniless traveling salesman when

Dr. Katherine Prichard Hoyt.

he came here; he built a large confectionery business and was elected Mayor in 1878.

The Versatility of Thomas Sands

Versatility was characteristic of these people, enabling them to try out various careers. An exceptionally creative person and a good example of this ability to do many things well was Thomas Sands. He was a born inventor who was busy working out various ideas all his life. Inventiveness was at a high peak in the 1800s and Nashua had a great many people interested in the perfection of mechanical devices. Elias Howe is, of course, the most famous name in this regard; while living in Nashua he began his experiments on the sewing machine, working in a tiny shop at the Vale Mills.

Thomas Sands had little formal education because his childhood was spent at a remote site where his father was a construction supervisor. As a young man working in Boston, Sands once put into action his firm abolitionist principles by taking part in an armed attempt to free a Negro fugitive from jail. Among Sands' inventions were the roller skate, a brick-making machine (the patent for which he sold for twenty-five thousand dollars), a pipe organ, a card printing press that was the forerunner of the proof press, a spring needle for hosiery-making, and the White Mountain ice cream freezer.

Sands was engaged in so many different businesses (he sometimes opened up his own company to produce what he had invented) that his doctors told him he was shortening his life unless he slowed down. After supposedly retiring, he opened up two more businesses. He then topped off his career by winning the 1893 mayoralty campaign by seven votes, after several unsuccessful attempts (in one of which he lost by only eleven votes). Tom Sands—just one of the many remarkable people who lived in Nashua during the nineteenth century!

The canvas of nineteenth century Nashua is studded with men and women who made Nashua a better community. Although this period is now receding in memory into a dim and shadowy past, the more we know about the people who lived out their lives the more we can identify with them. In spite of differences in life styles, their ambitions and drives were much the same as ours today. We can be grateful for the foundation of today's Nashua that was laid by these citizens of another era.

As the twentieth century dawned, Nashua was the second largest city in New Hampshire. It had come a long way from the quiet village of 1820. In November of 1900, a brief obituary in the *Telegraph* announced the death at the age of ninety-four of Mrs. Sarah Belknap Colburn. Her husband and all of her five children had long since died when Sally, the girl from Framingham, went to rest. The final tribute paid to her was one that fitted many a woman of her time—they said that she was greatly loved by a large circle of friends.

12

Trade and Commerce

Within the memory of men now living a tonnage of vast proportions passed through this locality by canal, baggage wagons, and sleds from the northern and western part of the state, from the entire state of Vermont, and a considerable portion of Canada. Until the extension of the railroad system through the section referred to, many of the lines of passenger and freight traffic centered here. A large proportion of the merchandise from Boston was received in large invoices and distribution made to points north and west. Mercantile and financial business which began to develop in the early settlement of the neighborhood, in the gathering and sale of peltry of every kind, afterwards appeared fully developed in the handling at this point of a vast tonnage of the products of the sea and land. For these reasons men of the requisite business ability and financial resources were from time to time attracted to this place, and have at all times in its history been found in unusual numbers.

GEORGE A. RAMSDELL (only resident of Nashua to be elected Governor of New Hampshire during the nineteenth century), in Chapter on *Finance and Banking* in Parker's *History*.

THE DIARY of a Dunstable, Mass., girl named Almy Wilder (Nashua Historical Society collections) tells how she taught school in Nashua for a short period, boarding at the home of the Lunds on Robinson Road. The diary also gives some hints of what a shopping trip to Nashua in the 1850s was like for a farming family. The Wilder family had always been in the habit of making frequent trips to the "village" to do their trading. On March 5, 1854, an entry reads: "Brother and I go over to Nashua shopping . . . It was a hard afternoon's work . . . bad walking." In the absence of paved roads, an afternoon of trudging through the muddy streets must have been somewhat less than an enjoyable pastime, as shopping in those days was hardly a one-stop operation. On August 19th of the same year she wrote: "Mother and I go over to the village of Nashua. We got some crockery." The unpaved streets by then must have been very dusty under the heat of the summer day.

Nashua–An Early Trading Center

As the town exploded in population after 1830 the farmers in the surrounding agricultural area found Dunstable/Nashua a ready market for produce as well as a convenient place to buy most of the goods they needed. A parking lot for horses and wagons was maintained near Factory and Main Streets, with hitching posts to which were attached mangers for feeding the horses.

As late as 1845 it was still possible for a farmer to exchange farm produce such as eggs, butter, vegetables, fruit, and poultry for merchandise such as tools, hardware, and clothing by the barter system. At least two dry goods stores advertised this service. E.S. Newton, located at Walnut and Cedar Streets, stated in an ad that he offered the best variety of dry goods "at reasonable terms for cash or country produce." A Tenney and Hubbard ad stated that country produce was taken in exchange for dry goods at their store. Two other dry goods stores advertising at the same time, however, made it very clear that they were "cash stores." Soon after this time currency became the only accepted medium of exchange in larger towns.

Dry goods stores were by far the most common specialty retail business and several of these were run by women proprietors. The mill girls were steady customers as they often were given shopping assignments for their mothers back home on remote farms and tiny villages. Another type of store that specialized in a particular line of goods was that devoted to bakery and confectionary foods. The establishment of Harvey Johnson at 27 Factory Street dealt in confectionary, fruits, and—in addition—German-made toys. This odd combination of merchandise must have made it a popular gathering place for juveniles who had a few pennies to spend. In addition to a full stock of hard and soft bread the Nashua Bakery operated by Charles Taylor also offered a variety of pies, cakes, soda, and sweet or oyster crackers. Their ad suggested that people "wishing to bring in beans on Saturday evening shall not be disappointed in having a good Sunday dinner." It was not uncommon for bakeries to offer the use of their ovens to bake beans. On Sunday mornings the aroma of baked beans and fresh bread and rolls must have been nothing short of overwhelming! Presumably this service was for those who still followed the custom of doing no work, not even cooking, on the Sabbath. For the less religious, bakeries also received the beanpots for the traditional Saturday night supper.

In contrast to the specialty stores the firm of Munroe and Taylor was a typical general store where the shopper could choose from a vast array of goods—domestic and foreign hardware, cast German steel mill saws, lead pipe, iron wire, brass kettles, West India goods, molasses, sugar, coffee, salt, the most delicious teas, prime bleached sperm oil, flour. This emporium also offered a complete assortment of family groceries which they would deliver to any part of the village free. Their ad closed with the motto: "Large sales, Small Profits for cash on delivery or approved credit."

Catering to the Female Trade

By the 1840s, instead of going to Amherst, ladies could find all of their dressmaking needs well taken care of right in town. An example was the establishment of George T. Wheeler on Canal Street which offered the discriminating lady a complete line of the finest quality fabrics, the choices including cassimeres, satinets, plain and figured merinos, and highland plaids. At the same time she could select the perfect lace, ribbons, gloves, hosiery, and other accessories to complement her planned ensemble.

George A. Ramsdell of Nashua, elected Governor of New Hampshire in 1896 by the largest majority up to that time.

Millinery stores catered to men as well as women. E.B. Hines not only sold caps and hats but also paid cash for what were called "shipping furs." Men's tall hats were made of treated and shaved beaver fur. The pelts were shipped from this country to Europe and then imported as hats.

Women either made their own clothing or depended on dressmakers. Men's clothing was tailor-made. Among the many ads for tailors appears one by J.W. Winders who stated "all garments made by men." However, other tailors often had help-wanted ads placed for female seamstresses. Several women, such as Rebecca Wheeler who had a shop at 38 Factory Street, advertised as tailoresses, meaning probably that they made coats and suits for female customers. As early as the 1840s ready-made clothing was beginning to appear on the retail scene and in Nashua one could scrutinize the garments at the Boston Clothing Store.

One previously common and disagreeable farm chore, making soap, was beginning to be aban-

doned for the convenience of being able to purchase the item in a store in town. The City Directory for 1845 lists an advertisement for McLaren and McGilvary and Co. as dealers in "hard, soft and fancy soaps." They also carried a good stock of tallow, potash, and candles. Candles were still used a great deal for illumination since whale oil for lamps was quite expensive. They must have done a good business in their specialties as they had two stores, one near the Jackson Co. on Canal Street and the other near Nashua Manufacturing on Pine Street. Their business success was undoubtedly due largely to the fortuitous choice of locations, as hundreds of mill workers passed either store on the way to and from work daily.

Importance of the Horse

In the days of genuine horse power, the local livery stables were a vital part of every community. The forerunner of the contemporary service station, the livery stable provided many services for a horse-borne public, including boarding, renting, selling and buying, plus shoeing of horses. Many stables also carried various types of carriages and hacks for fair weather mobility and also sleighs for winter needs.

In conjunction with the livery stables the harness makers also figured prominently in the business community. Although they specialized in harnesses, the durability of their craftsmanship almost forced them into carrying also a full line of other leather products. Levi Hodge of Main Street advertised that in addition to harnesses, he offered trunks, valises, carpet bags and, of course, saddles for equestrians. Throughout the century horse trading and its related businesses flourished. Most owners took immense pride in their horses and rightly so, as they provided the only means of personal transportation until Henry Ford had a better idea.

Protecting Nashua's Health

The practice of medicine, though considered advanced by the standards of the times, was by today's standards almost like something out of the Dark Ages. Nashua Village had a generous number of chemist and apothecary shops where one could purchase numerous nostrums to cure all problems and ailments. Very much in vogue at one time was "Thompsonian medicine" and Nashua had several practitioners, such as N.P. Carter who was listed as a "Botanic Physician." Herbal treatments were used by them and at the apothecary of Albert Gilchrist one could purchase such medicines. Some of these remedies were rheumatic hot drops, wine bitters, dysentery syrup, balsam of life, pulmonary balsam, gum myrrh, slippery elm, and nerve powders.

An ad for the Nashua Medicine Store operated by Edward Lerned offered a line of drugs, medicines, perfumery, and English and French chemicals. Part of his ad seems to have been aimed at doctors rather than the general consumer. This was an announcement that German leeches were always on hand: "Physicians are respectfully invited to call and examine."

Incidentally the physicians, like merchants and other professionals, had no qualms about advertising their services and specialties. Their ads though discreetly worded nevertheless gave an idea as to who was practicing medicine, as well as areas of special expertise and, in some cases, self-imposed titles. Dr. J.S. Ball for example was listed as a surgeon dentist. The practice of dentistry was only beginning to be established as a profession in its own right.

An example of a woman health professional was Mrs. William W. Judd who operated the Anidrosis Sanitarium at 356 Main Street for many years toward the end of the century. This institution was described in a newspaper article as "combining the seclusion of a retreat and all the comforts of home for its patrons." Vapor baths and magnetic treatment were two methods used to relieve all kinds of ailments, including rheumatism, asthma, and hay fever. Mrs. Judd herself was "a kindly, motherly woman and experienced nurse of many years standing . . . She has filled important positions in noted hospitals and private sanitariums until she has become an expert." The article concluded with the note: "Nashua is proud of Mrs. Judd and the Anidrosis Sanitarium."

Other Business Enterprises

The village was also the location for many miscel-laneous entrepreneurs who provided a variety of services. Some of these were S. Palten, advertised as a silk, cotton, linen, and fur dyer; Wm. S. Gaskin, who was an accomplished carriage, sign and fancy painter; E.M. Hines, "Daguerro Artist," who would take your picture in his studios across from the Town Hall.

The first photographer (actually a Daguer-rotypist) in Nashua was a Mr. Lane from Boston who opened a studio in 1846 in the Long Block at Factory and Main Streets, later the site of the Beasom Block. S.B. Richardson, who took over this studio, went one step further in the Daguerrotype business. He offered instruction in the art and also had on sale instruments and all types of apparatus for those who wanted to experiment on their own in the new art of photography. He also announced that he had means for faking pictures, no matter what the weather.

One type of business which was always embroiled in controversy, yet always survived, was the barroom or saloon. It was not always actually called a saloon—in fact one owned by John Osborn was whimsically named the Factory Street Restorator. In contrast, another eating place called itself the Temperance Restorator, meaning that a patron could enjoy the bill of fare without being in the presence of beer or other alcoholic beverages.

· The saloons were an added attraction for the farmers bringing loads of produce into town. One story relates how two brothers enjoyed a surreptitious visit to one of them. The two farm boys sat down and ordered a single glass of beer which they shared between them. They then bought a very long cigar (it has been described as a "nine-incher") that was available at that time. Breaking it in two, each enjoyed his half. Finally a silence was broken as one brother leaned over and remarked to the other: "Hey, Joe, what do you 'spose Mother would say if she could see us spreein' it?"

A business building that has had a very long and varied history is the Tavern Hotel, hidden away on Clinton Street behind the Hunt Memorial Building. According to an article in the *Nashua Daily Press* for June 19, 1901, this brick building was erected in 1833 on the south end of the Railroad Square lot. The builders were the three Greeleys—Joseph, Ezekiel, and Albert—who had a produce store at the north end of the triangular lot now occupied by the Hunt Building. Hugh Jameson, a leading com-

petitor of Isaac Spalding, was proprietor of the ground floor store for many years. Jameson did a brisk business in rum or "Medford," as it was called. A forthright and plain-talking man, he disliked hypocrisy and noted that there were two kinds of customers who came to buy rum. One boldly brought in the large stoneware jug that was the appropriate receptacle and asked to have it filled. The other type came in carrying a large coffee pot, hoping to make the transaction less conspicuous. This latter type infuriated Jameson who was quoted as exploding in anger at one of these latter type customers: "If, sir, you want rum, sir, bring your jug, sir; pots, sir, don't go in my store, sir."

In 1901, when the article was written, the city of Nashua had put the building now on Clinton Street up for sale to clear the lot for erection of the Hunt library. The building was moved across the street to its present site. While in its original location, several different businesses were conducted in it, including a hardware store, a harness maker's shop, and a yeast-making enterprise. In an upstairs hall the Universalist Church organization held its first meetings. This hall was also the first meeting place for the Masonic Lodge and until the depot building was

built the town of Nashville used it as a town hall. An ironic fact about this building is that when it was first put up a special compass was imported from Boston to ensure that the side lines of the building ran truly north and south. Now, of course, they run east and west.

The Post Civil War Period

The steady growth and expansion of the business community was interrupted by the outbreak of the Civil War. When it ended Nashuans breathed a sigh of relief and attempted to rebuild their pre-war simplicity but—as after all wars—the general lifestyle was never to be the same again. One institution that came into its own was the grocery store where nothing but food was sold. Before the war the shopper bought various staples needed in the home at what were called "West India Goods" stores or even at places dealing principally in dry goods. In season fruits, vegetables, and dairy products were available not only in various types of stores but directly from the farmers' wagons that drove to all parts of town. By the 1870s the grocery store dealing exclusively in food products had become a solid part of the business scene.

An old account book used to list and value a grocery store inventory when the business was being sold has been preserved and gives an abundance of information regarding prices around 1870. Levi Barker, proprietor of Barker and Spoffard Groceries on Main Street, was in the process of turning over his entire inventory to Harvey Courser and H. Greenleaf, with the total value of the stock and presumably the selling price amounting to $1752.20. A random sampling of some of the products and their prices, figured to the unit cost, includes a bar of cold water soap for .13, laundry starch for .11 per pound, powdered sugar for .14 a pound, "Valley Mill" flour for .06 per pound, java coffee for .30 per pound. Fine cut chewing tobacco was priced at about .75 per pound. Even more expensive was oolong tea at .77 per pound; whole figs were about .18. All sorts of spices were included in the transaction, with ground ginger .20 and, most expensive of all, whole nutmeg .99 per pound. Shoppers expected to pay more for tea, coffee, and spices because they were imported from distant lands. Flour on the other hand could very well have been milled right here in town, possibly at Seth Chandler's establishment on the corner of Main and West Hollis Streets.

Nashua boasted many fine hotels. The Indian Head Coffee House, the Tremont House, the Washington House, and the Laton House were probably the four largest and best-known. Only the Laton House continues at the present day. The history of the Laton House goes back to a hotel called the Central House that was originally built on the oval in Railroad Square. Later it was moved to the present location and renamed the Merrimac House. This burned down in the late 1870s and, when rebuilt by Thomas Laton, was opened in 1881 as the Laton House.

By 1880 the business district was firmly planted along Main Street, which was starting to lose some of its magnificent shade trees and many of the fine homes which had added an air of charm and grace to the center of town. This busy commercial area offered shoppers a large variety of goods and services. Many new businesses sprang up alongside the older ones. With the advent of coal stoves, the local coal dealer, S. Churchill and Sons, figured prominently in the lives of many Nashuans. The city dwell-

er could also obtain baled hay for his horses from this same dealer. Since grazing areas within the city had become almost non-existent, the availability of baled hay had become a necessity.

In her journal entry for January 13, 1880, Almy Wilder described in detail the last moments of her mother's life. Her diary notes: "Henry goes to Nashua to see about funeral arrangements." Another note: "Henry and I select Mother's casket and robe." On the next morning she wrote: "Soon Mr. Rockwood comes and the earthly house of Mother's dear spirit is put into the casket." This highlights the fact that the undertaking business had now become an accepted business institution. In earlier years a local carpenter, as a sideline and as the need arose, had built caskets. By the 1880s the services of a special mortician or funeral director were readily available. A.J. Rockwood was one of these for many years, offering complete services at his Water Street location where he sold ready-made coffins, mourning cloaks, robes, etc. The hearse was a horse-drawn vehicle with a glass compartment in which the casket was placed. The horses were usually draped in black and decorated with black plumes. The funeral procession received every courtesy from townspeople as it made its way to the cemetery, a tradition which has survived to the present. Another mortician whose name still survives was A.A. Davis, son of Moses Davis, whose establishment was directly behind the Greeley Building. Albert Davis, the last member of the family to operate this undertaking business, was a prominent member of the Nashua Historical Society until his death in 1973.

A final note on unusual types of businesses which sprang up as needs became apparent should men-

Merrimac House with the town pump at the right.

tion that around the middle of the century establishments were set up where both men and women could go for cleansing and refreshing baths. These came into being because home conditions in the way of sanitary facilities were still quite primitive and afforded little privacy. The motto over the entrance to C.T. Gill's Water Street Bath House read, "Go Wash and Be Clean."

After her husband's death Mrs. John Bly decided to run Bly's Dining Room on West Pearl Street with the help of her son Waldo. In the year 1900 how much did a meal at Bly's cost the consumer? Twenty-five cents or twenty cents on a weekly meal ticket system.

Women in Business

As indicated by the several examples already cited, the role of women in nineteenth century business should not be underestimated. Their enterprises were numerous enough to make their presence felt as a prominent thread running through the fabric of commercial life, especially in the service industries. There was for example Mrs. Catherine Sullivan who, from her grocery store at Washington and High Streets, also carried on activities as the sole agent for the Cunard Steamship Lines.

Women were also book store owners, boarding house keepers, music teachers, artists, and teachers of art. In 1885 one woman was listed as a shoemaker and three as "clairvoyants." One Hannah Dow advertised that she was a botanic physician. In 1896 three women were listed as saloon keepers (out of a total of fifty-three), probably reflecting the fact that widows often chose to continue a lucrative means of family support built up by their husbands. In the same year two women were listed as chiropodists, one as a masseur, and only one as a hairdresser, since beauty shops as we now know them had not yet become a popular service. The single woman who offered this latter service to ladies was Miss Anne Emmott who showed versatility in making full use of the space she rented in the Laton Block. During the day she gave manicures, did chiropodist work and hairstyling, even offered face massage. In the evenings she used the same shop to give elocution lessons. In 1896 there was also a female soap maker, a dancing teacher and, anticipating a whole new area that was just beginning to open up, one "type writer and stenographer." Three ladies by the name of Moore—Mrs. Marietta S., Mrs. Sophia M., and Miss M. Etta—were listed at various times as piano teachers. Because of the great interest in music there was a steady demand for this type of instruction and women with musical talent could develop excellent professional careers in the field.

Growth of Retail Business

Nelson's 5 and 10 Cent Store was part of a small chain started by F.E. Nelson, the Nashua store going into operation in June, 1900. Norwell's Department Store, on the other hand, was started by Henry Norwell, a man who came to Nashua at the close of the Civil War. The store was in the block at 97-109 Main Street and by 1900 had become a very large establishment, the most extensive retail business in Nashua and one of the largest in the state.

In 1912 Sceva Speare bought out the Norwell store and changed the name to Speare's Dry Goods Store. Several generations of Nashuans were familiar with this establishment in its quarters on the ground floor of the Odd Fellows Building, until it finally was closed in August, 1973. This store, therefore, had a direct link to one of the great retail department stores of Nashua's nineteenth century period. One store that has remained in business steadily is C.H. Avery Co. on Factory Street where furniture has been sold ever since 1889.

In 1889 a Board of Trade was formed with eighty-five members, the beginning of a Chamber of Commerce.

Role of the Banks

Along with the great growth in retail services as well as industries, banks proliferated to control the increasing cash flow. Until 1835 Dunstable residents had no local banks, but had to go to Amherst for all their banking business and even this was not available continuously. In 1806 the first bank in Hillsborough County had been established in that town. This Hillsborough County Bank, however, had failed in 1809 and another, the Farmers' Bank, was not started until 1825. The Nashua Bank opened in 1835 with John M. Hunt as cashier and continued as an orderly and respected business until 1865, at which time it gracefully closed its doors when the National Banking Act went into

effect. The directors chose not to go national.

Another bank that was in operation during this period was the Pennichuck Bank, opened in 1855. This was a one-man operation for much of the ten-year period that it was in business. Harrison Hobson was the cashier and office worker, assisted part of the time by a daughter, whose name is not known. This institution's management did not want to reorganize under the National Banking Act either and the directors voted to discontinue it.

The First National Bank was organized in 1863 and put up its own building in 1867 on the Main Street lot it had purchased from Colonel Leonard W. Noyes. A newspaper article describing the new building gave particular attention to the Corliss safe which was considered one of the most impregnable in New Hampshire. Thomas Chase was the first President and others were E.H. Spaulding, E.P. Emerson, and George A. Ramsdell. In 1907 this bank merged with the Second National Bank, the resulting organization continuing under the latter name. The Second National had been formed in 1875, with headquarters in the Merchants' Exchange. In 1922 it bought the Tremont House at Main and West Pearl Streets, tore down the hotel, and erected the present bank building. In 1970 the Second National Bank became the Bank of New Hampshire.

Bill of Old Nashua Bank.

By 1897 there were also, in addition to these banks, six other institutions that had come into being in response to the great need for savings banks. The Nashua Savings Bank, chartered in 1854 with many leading citizens on its board of directors, was a move toward replacing the very simple arrangements made by the cotton manufacturing companies to offer savings accounts to their employees at 5 percent interest. (Under the company system no employee could have a larger balance than five hundred dollars.) During its lifetime until it closed in 1895 the bank occupied quarters at

three locations—the Merchants' Exchange, the Telegraph Block, and the Odd Fellows Building.

Solomon Spalding, the gentleman who built the first brick house at 39 Orange Street in 1834, was President of one of the small banks, the N.H. Banking Company, which was a "Guaranty" type of bank. This type offered customers a paid up guaranty of stock. The N.H. Banking Company operated from 1879 until 1895.

The Indian Head Bank was incorporated in 1851 with Joseph Greeley as its first President and Albert McKean as cashier. It was a Nashville enterprise, started because citizens of the area north of the river felt the need for such an institution in their bailiwick. Since that time the bank has had several locations. It started out in the Central House, from which it moved into the depot building when more space was required. From 1893 to 1909 it was quartered in the Whiting Block, then it moved south of the river into the Telegraph Block at Main and Temple Streets. The fire of March, 1922, which destroyed this famous old building, burned out the banking rooms. The bank carried on its operations in temporary quarters until the beautiful new building that has occupied that corner ever since was

erected. In April, 1924, the Indian Head Bank was back in business at this location.

The Nashua Trust Company is a relative latecomer; it was incorporated in 1890, with its banking rooms in the McQuesten Block. In 1900 it moved into its present location in the Masonic Building. The McQuesten Block was approximately where the Slawsby Building is located today. The directors of the new bank were especially proud of the appearance of their quarters; the main feature was a mahogany counter twenty-five feet long. Although it started later in the century than some of the other banks, the Nashua Trust has played a prominent role in the great events of the city's history since that time. Among its presidents have been George B. French, George W. Currier, and William D. Swart.

Three building and loan associations were established in the last decade of the century—the Nashua Building and Loan Association, the Home Building and Loan Association, and the People's Building and Loan Association.

It seems amazing today that these nineteenth century banks often issued their own paper money. Sometimes the engraved plates were ready-made and the bank merely printed its name at the top.

Although the papers often reported instances of banks in other parts of the state experiencing financial difficulties in times of economic crisis, the Nashua banks seemed to have successfully weathered all such periods.

Advent of the Iron Horse

Just as banks were important to an industrialized town to control the great volume of money that changed hands daily, the railroad was an improved means of transportation that kept goods and services flowing smoothly. The New Hampshire Historical Society in its documents collection owns the original copies of the petitions signed by Dunstable people who wanted the Boston and Lowell Railroad extended to this town. The date of three petitions found in the collection is June 1, 1835. They were addressed to "the Honorable Senate and the House of Representatives in General Court convened." One, signed by ninety-five citizens, pointed out that:

The petitioners of the undersigned, inhabitants of Dunstable and vicinity, respectfully represent that on the route from Nashua Village to Lowell and thence to Boston, there is a great amount of travel and transportation–that said route is the natural and easiest channel of communication with the seaboard for the middle and northern portion of N.H. and Vermont; that the expenses of transportation to and from the interior are very great and burdensome, being taken from the hard earnings of the people by lessening the value of produce, and that in consequence of these burdensome expenses the inhabitants residing at a distance from the seaboard are deprived of many of the advantages of a good and ready market; that if the facilities for conveyance were increased, the expenses would be lessened and the advantages of a market secured more equally to all, whereby a great saving to the people would be effected, all of which would conduce to the welfare and prosperity of the state and augment its wealth and resources.

The other two petitions were signed by leaders such as Daniel Abbot, Jesse Bowers, and two of the Greeleys, some of whom would become directors of the railroad company that was soon to be formed.

The coming of the railroad was second in importance only to the establishment of the cotton mills in changing Dunstable/Nashua from a rural village to a full-fledged and densely populated city. Most of the French-Canadian emigres came by train from Montreal. By 1890 so many railroad lines criss-crossed Nashua that travel in almost any direction became a simple matter of boarding the right train. Trade and commerce up and down the Merrimack Valley as well as east and west flourished by means of this network of tracks.

In the *Nashua Daily Telegraph* for October 25, 1902, a quaint story was published in which an elderly resident, Noah Roby, talked about a walk through the southern part of town taken by himself and his brother, Luther, seventy-five years before. Since one of the sites visited by the two youngsters was the new Taylor Falls Bridge, then under construction, the actual date must have been November, 1826. A curious note in this article is the following:

The boys crossed the road just near Indian Head and were taken to see the first railroad ever put in operation in the world, some historians say. The railroad was a small affair, double-tracked, and was run upon an incline so that the full car, rushing down, would pull the empty one up. Today it would have been called a very primitive road, but then it was thought wonderful. The tracks had no flanges. The Quincy Granite Railway of Quincy, Mass., was built that same year, but I think ours was the first.

The Quincy railway was built in 1826 to carry granite from the quarry to tide water. W.W. Bailey, in his chapter on railroads in *Parker's History* makes no mention of a similar railway ever being built in Dunstable. Yet the memory of the elderly Mr. Roby seems clear and lucid on all other details concerning the Dunstable of his youth.

An article on early railroading in the *Weekly Telegraph* for January 4, 1881, throws more light on this question. Speaking of the Quincy experiment, it says: "This paper has heretofore shown, however, that a railway was in use a year or two earlier at the construction of the Indian Head mills in this city." *The History of the Nashua Manufacturing Company* by MacGill, in describing the building of these mills, makes this comment: "There was a 'railroad' built from the ledge to the Merrimack River, to carry the loaded vehicles."

Steam locomotion as a means of transportation advanced very rapidly once the efficiency of the idea became apparent. Starting in England in the late 1820s with the building of the Liverpool and Manchester Railroad, the first freight and passenger railroad in the United States was completed

in South Carolina in 1830, using an American-built locomotive. That same year, 1830, the Boston and Lowell Railroad was incorporated, the first trains running on June 26, 1835. The cost, with only one track, was one million dollars. The Dunstable people who petitioned the New Hampshire Legislature for an extension of this line were fully convinced of the practicality and need for this extension, therefore, even before the Boston to Lowell line was operational. The legislature also was apparently quickly convinced because just three weeks after the petitions were submitted it authorized construction of a railroad line from Nashua Village to the state line. The following spring the Massachusetts Legislature authorized construction of a connecting line from Lowell to the state line. The two corporations were merged immediately into one and thus was born the Nashua and Lowell Railroad. Construction was started in the fall of 1837 and one

year later the first trains ran, coming at first to a temporary station at Temple and Amory Streets. After the Nashua River was bridged, the trains as of December 23 came all the way to the end of the line on Main Street at what is still called Railroad Square.

Further extension of the line came with building of the Concord Railroad in 1842. These very first railroads were one-track affairs and the laying of a second track was an obvious necessity to make full use of the economic possibilities. By 1845 this second track had been laid and in 1848 the passenger station at Main and Canal Streets was built, with a second floor auditorium that served Nashville as a town hall and later was a popular gathering place known as Franklin Hall. This historic railroad building burned down in 1930.

One of the controversies that had to be ironed out legally before railroads could be developed fully was the question of right-of-way through privately owned lands. The New Hampshire Supreme Court decided that the great public benefit of a railroad justified its taking property wherever necessary to place its tracks.

A man who has been called "Nashua's railroad pioneer" was Peter Clark who according to some authorities was more responsible for getting railroad service into Nashua than anyone else. Clark came to Nashua from Francestown in 1835. He was interested in the Concord Railroad as well as the Nashua and Lowell. His philosophy of transportation service was very much along populist lines—that is, he favored keeping passenger fares and freight charges as low as possible. Some cost statistics that were compiled in 1881 proved that the coming of the railroads dramatically reduced the general expense of travel and transportation of goods. The faith of far-sighted persons such as Peter Clark was more than justified by the advantages to the public of this means of travel.

Many railroad lines sprang up in southern New Hampshire in the course of the nineteenth century. By 1887 the mighty Boston and Maine Railroad Company had begun to swallow up these smaller lines, including the Nashua and Lowell and the Concord Railroads, usually by the process of leasing the lines.

One of the most famous failures in Nashua railroad history was the ill-fated Nashua, Acton, and Boston Railroad which opened operations in 1873. A great deal of Nashua money was invested in this enterprise which was eventually taken over by the Concord Railroad on a mortgage foreclosure and finally abandoned. Until recent years the rusting tracks, overgrown with weeds and grass, could still be followed in Nashua's South End.

In 1880 the Concord Railroad built the passenger station off West Hollis Street that was a familiar landmark until it was torn down in 1965. Arch McDonnell, the well-known painter of old railroad scenes, included this station among his subjects.

For the cotton mills and the many other industries the railroad provided the necessary lifeline that brought in raw materials and took out finished products for distribution. Several years before the Civil War, the age of the horse-drawn freight wagons and sledges, the stagecoaches, and the river and canal boats had passed forever into transportation history. Railroads, going from woodburning to coalburning engines and finally to diesels, dominated the landscape with their interlacings of lines.

Many older persons undoubtedly remember with a pang of nostalgia the "Peanut," the train that left Boston late every weekday afternoon and made its way up the line to Lowell, to Nashua, to Manchester, to Concord, then on by a northwesterly route across New Hampshire to White River Junction, Vermont. In towns all along the route its whistle was listened for as the sun set and the twilight deepened each evening. Mothers set bedtime for their children as "after the Peanut has gone by." Farmers as well as villagers would hear its thundering approach and remark, "He's running three minutes late tonight"

Antique toy train . . . symbolic of the Age of Steam.

or "Here it comes—right on time." It was the train on which company often arrived, especially on Friday or Saturday nights, and a family went down to the station to greet them. Visitors and commuters descended from the coaches, baggage was taken off with a great show of bustle and efficiency, then the bell clanged, the conductor called "A-a-all A-b-o-o-ard," and the "Peanut" was once more thrashing the rails and had disappeared around a bend. This particular train was popular because it was a "Local," stopping at many places along the way. Other trains were faster because they were "express," stopping only at the large cities, but most of them slowed down when approaching certain towns so that newspapers and mail could be thrown off.

What went up to White River Junction had to come back down again, of course, but this train was called the "Peanut" only on the famous evening trip. For most people along that line, the word that it would no longer run signified in a very personal way that a revolution in transportation methods was once more under way.

The larger communities such as Nashua where several railroad lines met became centers where people changed trains in their journeying and where all kinds of goods for homes and industries were channeled to various destinations. The railroad at the height of its glory was the pulsing bloodstream of trade and commerce, and Nashua had a full share in the colorful drama of this great age of steam.

13

Cotton and Other Industries

AS THE 6:00 A. M. BELL RANG young Lydia Purington began another day of work on a shop loom at Nashua Manufacturing. Within minutes the noisy clatter of the mill machinery reached a peak and Lydia started the monotonous task of manually retying tangled or broken threads and rethreading the automatic shuttle. Wisps of damp cotton lint soon filled the air and as the hours slowly passed a layer of the white puffs accumulated on everyone and everything inside the shop. Just before nine o'clock a short ten-minute break interrupted the mind-numbing activity which continued until the noon lunch hour. Though most of her co-workers were young ladies like herself, a handful of children scurried about filling bobbins, helping repair machines, and running errands. When the closing bell rang at six the mill gates opened and Lydia and her friends returned to the company-owned boarding house for the evening meal.

Seeking adventure and economic independence, Lydia had left a farm in Weare, New Hampshire, to come to work in the mills in 1831. The life-style of Lydia and her co-workers was controlled by the company in virtually every aspect, from place of residence to education. Almost self-sufficient, the complexes included housing projects, school rooms, dining rooms, and church facilities for their workers. Through this personal and social control the corporations hoped to disseminate an ideology demanding that each employee be both a virtuous and productive member of the closed society. In the early 1800s in various parts of New England numerous examples of such mill town settlements were being built on the fringes of the vanishing wilderness.

Before leaving to marry Isaiah Bailey in 1835 Lydia had encouraged her friends at the mills to pen verses of remembrance in her autograph book, including the name, home town, and date of the writing. The sentimental and often romantic messages reflect the very special need the writers felt for companionship and trust from fellow workers. One example in Lydia's book makes this feeling very clear:

> Afar, to woo in distant lands
> The smiles that fate denies you here
> You fly and burst the silken bonds
> That absence will but more endear;
> But though no more at evening's close

You sit beneath th'accustomed tree,
To watch the twilight shut the rose—
At that calm hour—Remember me—

The numerous pages of warm remembrances from men and women reflect a life-style of strict morality and idealistic virtue. The devoutly moral and spiritual values promoted in the "mill girls" are exemplified in Lydia's book. These beliefs, closely guarded and encouraged in the early years of industrialization, reflected the sincere conviction that the factory offered the finest and widest opportunities for young ladies and gentlemen. Epitomizing the faith and reverence in the factory was the "Factory Song" by C. Upham:

While in the sable shades of night,
With curtains round our head,
The watchman calls, the lamp is brought,
To light us from our bed.

Then we arise and all prepare,
To receive corporal food,
And some complain while others say,
That theirs is rich and good.

The Factory bell begins to ring,
And we must all obey,
And each their own employment mind,

Or else be turned away.

This corporation now is good
Its rising with some others,
May friendship reign throughout the whole,
And all unite as brothers.

Rise of the Textile Mills

Such optimism may be put in some perspective by considering the period in America's growth when the factory towns were rising. The twenty or so years of uncertainty and sectional dissensions following the Revolution were brought under some control by the end of the War of 1812. America it seemed had come to the threshold of nationhood and faced a future that was almost dazzling. Nearby Boston had survived the revolutionary crisis and prospered with the ruin of so many of its rivals. The port community was attracting more and more adventurous merchants who had taken advantage of the decline of shipping during the war years and the boycott of English goods following the war to build up a manufacturing system and supply the American people with native products.

Factory-towns were rising on every hand, in eastern Mas-

sachusetts and New Hampshire—Lawrence, Lowell, Fitchburg, Manchester, Lynn. Every village with a waterfall set up a textile-mill or a paper-mill, a shoe factory or an iron-foundry; and as Boston remained the financial center, for manufacturing as well as for shipping, the mercantile fortunes of the inland counties were joined with those of the magnates of the seaboard.

Thus Van Wyck Brooks, in writing of the literary flowering which later followed, traces the social and cultural influence the coastal center had on the hinterland during this transitional period.

Also of great importance to the opening of the uplands north of Boston was the elaborate Middlesex Canal system which has been discussed in Chapter 10. The intricate series of locks and channels which linked Boston with what is now Lowell proved to be a major engineering achievement of the time. The route further up the Merrimack to Concord, with the numerous falls and rapids, posed added problems but by 1814 Superintendent John Sullivan proudly completed the necessary series of detours, thus making the route from Boston to Concord navigable. Once completed, the

Middlesex Canal system became a busy waterway providing a slow but definite route for transporting produce, materials, and goods into and out of the interior. Rafts of lumber and a steady stream of heavily-laden barges slowly moved along the Merrimack.

It has already been noted that Dunstable took advantage of the new waterway by launching its own canal boat on the Fourth of July, 1803. In the years that followed a whole fleet of boats was built, some owned by Nashua people and others by people of Concord, Piscataquog, and Litchfield. Until the coming of the railway, the waterway provided the main means of transportation of large quantities of heavy goods. By the 1840s the trend was clear that many who had utilized the canal boats transferred their business to the faster, more efficient railroads which developed. However, in the early decades of the 1800s the role of canal boats in the industrial development of the area north of Boston was clear. From the diaries of men such as John Sullivan the slow, lazy pace of life on the river is revealed. On June 18, 1819, the steamboat *Mer-*

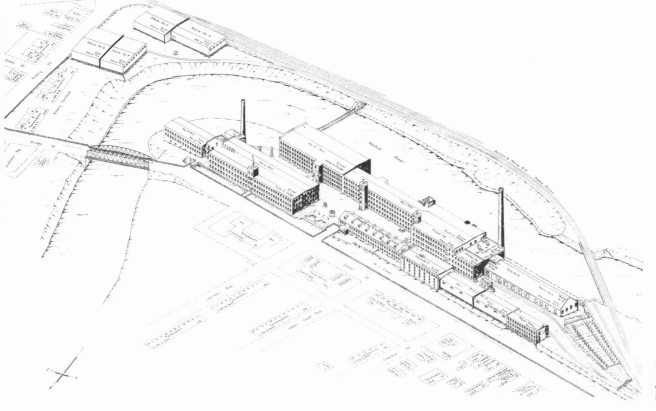

Survey perspective of the cotton mill of the Jackson Co., made by H.C. Starbird in 1912.

rimack, with 157 passengers and music from a private band on board, made its way up past Concord, having traveled on the Middlesex Canal from Medford to Lowell, then up the Merrimack to Concord. Moving at between four and seven miles per hour the slow and scenic trip was typical of travel at that time.

In 1810 Francis Cabot Lowell of Newburyport traveled to England to inspect the Lancashire cotton mills. In 1813 he returned and with Paul Moody designed spinning and weaving machinery which proved to be superior to the best in England. Convinced that a successful cotton industry could be set up here in America, he and an old friend, Patrick Tracy Jackson, with Nathan Appleton, began a venture which would alter the future of New England. In 1814 at Waltham, Massachusetts, he established the first cotton mill in the United States in which the whole process of manufacturing from spinning to weaving was carried on by power. Though he died in 1817 his ideas survived and were carried out by others who continued the concept that the manufacture of cotton goods could be done from raw material to finished product, all under one roof. It was further believed that the mills should provide everything for the welfare of their employees, from housing to schools and churches. Thus the Lowell system, or Waltham Pattern, came into existence. The success of Waltham led to additional ventures such as that in Lowell. In each the mill girls were considered the best labor source available. The infant industry was helped further by the Protective Tariff of 1816 which put a 25 percent duty on imported cotton and woolen goods. The effect was to exclude the cheap cottons from India and help remove a major threat to the mills. The devastating Panic of 1819 which disrupted the country's economy raised fears which helped result in the Tariff of 1824.

With the continued success of the new mills Boston investors began branching out in search of new sites. In 1821 Charles H. Atherton of Amherst convinced Nathan Appleton of Boston that he should examine the falls on the Souhegan as a site for a factory. The wealthy industrialist led a party of investigators to the spot but concluded that the water power there would not be sufficient. Returning through Dunstable they apparently were not concerned with Mine Falls and proceeded to Chelmsford, near the Pawtucket Falls, and decided to locate their new venture there. By the winter of 1821 news of the new cotton mill further south provided lengthy stories and gossip for those lounging in the country stores of Dunstable.

In 1822 a few townsmen banded together with Boston and Salem investors to embark on a daring project which proved to be a milestone in the industrial development of the tiny settlement.

The Nashua Manufacturing Company

The association, which included Daniel Abbot, Joseph Greeley, Moses Tyler, and others, purchased all lands between Mine Falls and Main Street. Very shortly the group applied for a charter from the State of New Hampshire to organize a corporation. On June 18, 1823, the charter was signed by Governor Levi Woodbury and enacted, permitting the Nashua Manufacturing Company to manufacture cotton, woolen, and iron goods, and conduct other business and trade as could be conveniently managed, on and near the Nashua River in Dunstable. The capital stock was set at one million dollars but at the first meeting at Moses Tyler's tavern it was decided that only three hundred thousand dollars of the sum would be issued. The initial division of 300 shares included: 30 for Daniel Abbot; 30 for Benjamin F. French; 30 shares jointly for the Greeleys; 30 for partners John Foster and Stephen Kendrick; 15 shares for John Kendrick of Boston; 75 for Augustus Peabody; 30 for Moses Tyler; and 60 shares for Daniel Webster, who was represented by Augustus Peabody. Though Webster never paid for his shares they were carried along on the company books for several years, chiefly on notes signed by Daniel Abbot, until they were finally sold. It seems that on more than one occasion Webster was paid a retaining fee for legal services but Augustus Peabody apparently did all the work. Undoubtedly the stockholders were concerned mainly with keeping his prestigious name as an endorsement to the stability of the company since the future of manufacturing firms was relatively insecure. Though the extensive land holdings initially were purchased at quite low valuations, the costs of developing the manufacturing facility required a larger investment and represented a bold commitment to a project of uncertain success. The determination of the corporation to assume the tremendous risks inherent in an infant industry must have been strong and should not be considered lightly. The shareholders were taking a big chance in locating their factory experiment in the tiny village at Dunstable.

The corporation wasted no time in getting the project underway. Noted surveyor John Lund was engaged to survey carefully the entire land holdings. Locating the factory at Mine Falls was considered but the idea was quickly discarded since the adjacent land was unfavorable and the site was much too far from the Merrimack and transportation routes. Consequently the plan of channeling water along a canal to the site in Nashua Village was adopted. The construction work consisted of three major projects: the dam and upper end of the canal at Mine Falls; the lower end of the canal including the penstock and millwheel; and finally the actual buildings and machinery. The first part was placed under supervision of James F. Baldwin whose father, Loammi Baldwin, had been instrumental in the engineering and building of the Middlesex Canal. Soon digging crews got underway and the three-mile canal began to take shape. Descending over thirty feet in elevation from the falls down to the village, it was approximately thirty-five feet wide and six feet deep. Referred to by some as a "miserable ditch," the original canal was improved and repaired as problems arose. William Boardman who had worked on bridge and highway projects in the town supervised the second phase of work, which progressed more slowly than the first. The water was supposed to be turned on by October 1, 1824, but the installation of the millwheel and gearing was not ready. Ira Gay who was in charge of the third phase became rather impatient since he was eager to build the machinery without delay. Finally on December 5 the water ran through the millwheel but the gearing was incorrect. Eventually the much needed power was made available. Soon Ira and his brother went to work in the newly-constructed machine shop, the first mill building to be completed. Before coming to Nashua early in 1824 Ira and Adin Gay had been building cotton machinery in a small shop in Chelmsford. With his genius and mechanical background Gay impressed the company directors and was employed not only as machinist but also as superintendent of the department of manufacturing.

By fall of 1824 Daniel Abbot was given full authority over affairs in Nashua and John Lemist, a stockholder in Roxbury, was appointed purchasing agent in Boston. To raise further capital additional stock was issued and sold, providing needed dollars for the large-scale building program. Due partly to the delays and early problems with the canal and millwheel it was decided that further expertise was needed and the noted Boston architect, Asher Benjamin, was employed as mill agent. Now four key individuals—Ira Gay, Daniel Abbot, Asher Benjamin, and Augustus Peabody—served as executives in the project. The latter three held regular meetings to discuss planning, laying out of streets and lots, and pricing and selling house lots on the property on the south side of the Nashua River. In addition a school and church were tentatively scheduled for construction.

By spring, 1825, Mill No. 1 was well underway. The five-story structure, erected on a foundation 45 by 155 feet, was capped by a steeply-sloped roof. Once completed it proved to be a rather imposing brick edifice in tiny Nashua Village. That same spring proved to be disastrous to the new canal when flooding washed away part of the bank, requiring heavy repairs. Huge slabs of granite from a newly-discovered ledge near the canal were used to help shore up the bank. The granite quarry ultimately proved to be a valuable asset to the company and provided cut blocks for many future projects. To help in moving the granite a "railroad" of some sort was built upon which loaded sledges were dragged down to the Merrimack for further transporting. Wagon-loads of fill were hauled from the top of the hill on the east of Main Street where Asher Benjamin planned to build the company church. Washouts and periodic flooding necessitated raising the new roadbed still higher.

Earlier, in 1824, the Nashua Manufacturing Company had obtained a charter from the State of New Hampshire permitting it to build additional canals between the Nashua River and the Merrimack. Construction started on a canal beginning on the north side of the Nashua below Main Street, along Canal Street, eastward to the end of Lock Street, and on to the Merrimack. Work on this "lower canal" was begun early in 1825. At this time, a large logging operation was underway on the Nashua, chiefly by an English company. As a result plans for the waterway included the building of a basin to hold the floating logs which would then be loaded on barges for shipment. The work on the locks in the new canal was done by Moses Barrett, with James

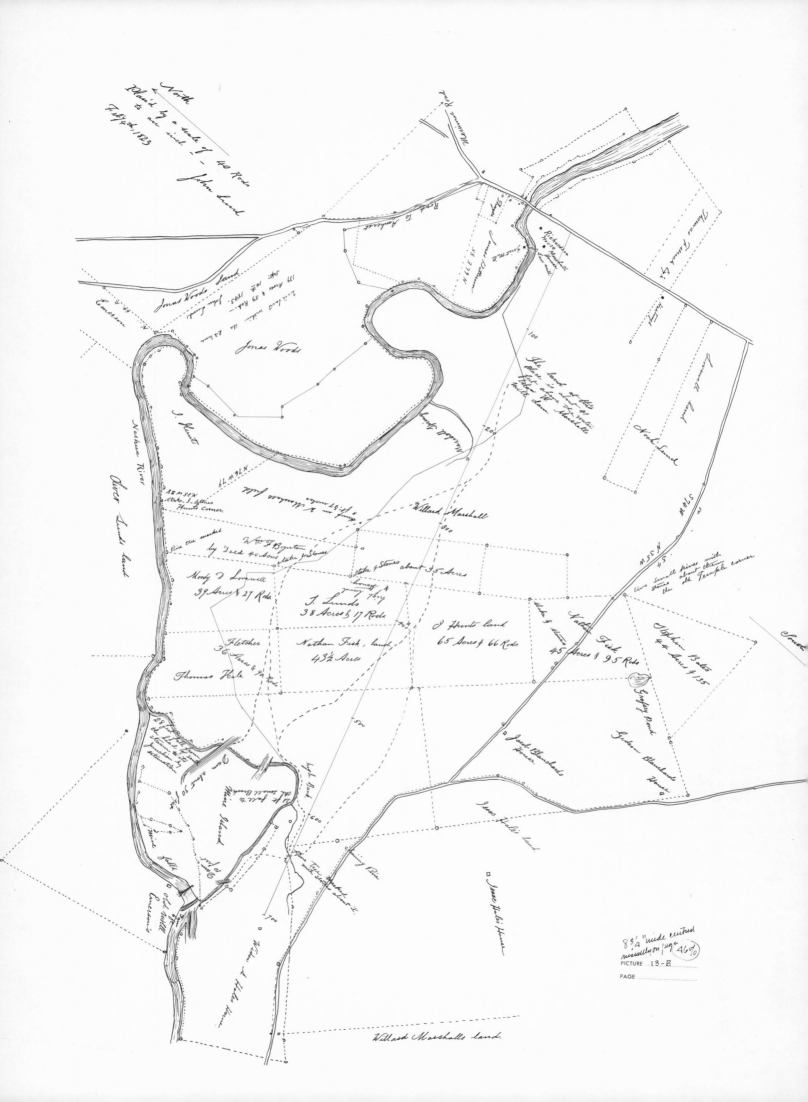

F. Baldwin in charge of the whole canal project.

Activity at Nashua Manufacturing had progressed rapidly since Mill No. 1 was begun. The Boston representatives of the company, John Lemist, Joseph Adams of Adams and Amory, Joseph Russell of the China trade firm, and apparently George and Thomas Searle, all were busy surveying potential markets. It appears the original intention was to produce a coarse cotton cloth for the markets in China, including Shanghai. However the company also decided to produce a finer grade of printed cloth intended for trade in South America. All stages of manufacture were to be carried on in Nashua except for bleaching which—if required—would be done elsewhere, such as in Lowell. With water power readily at hand, the machine shop in operation, and the first mill under construction, the chances for success seemed favorable. By the end of 1825 actual production was in sight.

Though the exact date is uncertain the first cotton cloth was manufactured early in 1826. Unfortunately no brisk sale followed its introduction into the marketplace. John Lemist was in financial difficulty in Boston and soon sold his stock. In February, 1826, George and Thomas Searle then became sole buying and selling agents. Also about the same time Joseph Russell, active in the China trade, became director. The changes came at a critical time since the South American markets were complicated by numerous wars within and among the Latin republics. Strained relations between England and China over opium soon hampered the China trade.

Technical Developments

By 1826 Mill No. 2 at Nashua Manufacturing was still under construction and Mill No. 3 was begun. The second mill was opened in 1827 and produced finer cloth including 28-30-inch-wide shirting and some 42-inch-wide sheeting of No. 16 thread. The technical success of the entire operation was due mainly to the skill of Ira Gay and his associates. His ability to devise and assemble machinery utilizing homemade and borrowed parts was uncanny. Technical problems were dealt with and solved as problems arose. Yankee ingenuity in these early years of the industrial revolution before interchangeable parts was a significant factor in getting a new device working properly.

As always technology was forever changing and processes and equipment came and went, being replaced by something which was hopefully better. By 1830 the New England mills were manufacturing cloth faster and often cheaper than people could make at home. As a result hand looms gradually disappeared from some farm houses. Small carding mills and spinning mills soon felt the competition of mass production. The "cottage" industries were in decline as the industrial revolution swept New England, though they did not disappear.

Whether made at home or in a factory certain procedures were necessary for making cloth. Using cotton cloth as an example, the manufacturing processes may be considered more closely. The whole procedure begins with raw cotton which is divided into three classes. The first is Sea Island or long-staple type which is noted for the length and beauty of its fiber, and the delicacy of the thread made from it. It is generally used for the warp of the cloth, comprising its lengthwise threads. The second class is the medium-staple cotton commonly raised in the United States. Besides being shorter, softer, and silkier, it fills up the cloth better and is used for the filling or weft, which are the crosswise threads of the cloth. Finally there is the short-staple cotton which usually comes from India and consists of harder fibers used only when mixed with medium staple.

Since the mills were located so far from the cotton fields it was necessary to ship bales of cotton over great distances. The baling and packing were done under great pressure to compress as much fiber as possible into a small shipping space. When a bale arrived and was opened at the mill it was extremely tangled and matted. Consequently the cotton was cleaned and picked apart in a device called an opener or spreader. Generally the machinery devised for these processes included pulling apart the cotton by toothed cylinders or beating it with blunt knives while a current of air blew through it. It emerged from the spreader in the form of a lap, or thick, fluffy sheet of fiber, cleaned and now ready for carding. The lap was carefully wound around a large roller as it emerged from the spreader.

The next operation involved the carding of the cotton lap. The term card referred to a broad cylinder which was covered with wire teeth and revolved in contact with two smaller cards. The lap was carefully fed onto the large cylinder and slowly combed out, between it and the small cylinders, into a gauzy film which was then combed from the card by the action of the doffer. Leaving the card in a roll the cotton then passed to a pair of rollers which pressed and stretched it slightly and let it drop into a tin can. At this point the form of the cotton is called a "sliver." In some mills the cotton was run through the carding machine more than once, as was the common practice in England. Most of the carding machines used here were of American make, lighter built and able to run faster and cheaper than their English counterparts. Quality machinery and careful processing were essential in order to make smooth level thread. The tufts or knots of the cotton must be perfectly teased out or the fibers exhibit inequalities and are "clouded."

When the slivers came from the cards they were taken to the drawing frames. Several slivers were fed through a series of rollers, each revolving faster than its predecessor. The fibers were stretched and united into a new sliver with the cotton strands parallel with each other. By repeating the process many times a more perfect thread could be made. The elongated sliver resulting from this continued stretching was taken to a roving frame and given a slight twist. Once in this slightly spun form it was called a roving, and was wound around a bobbin ready for spinning.

The speed and efficiency of spinning increased rapidly after the invention of the spinning jenny in 1767. Instead of merely eight spindles the improved spinning machines carried three hundred and sixty. The rows of spindles were mounted upon frames called mules and the cotton roving was systematically twisted and wound around the bobbins. Several variations in spinning machinery were developed, one example being called a self-acting jenny. Ira Gay and brother Adin of Nashua developed a self-acting mule which they claimed would make the spinning process faster and more efficient. Run by water instead of manpower, the device was patented but it apparently was not very popular outside Nashua.

It became possible for one girl to tend thirteen hundred spindles. The thread when spun was reeled off from the bobbins into hanks of 840 yards. It was then numbered according to the number of hanks to the pound, No. 2 being very coarse and No. 300 very fine. Thread for the weft of the cloth was wound upon bobbins for placing in the shuttles of the looms, while the warp was stiffened with sizing, using a device called a dressing machine, and then wound upon beams for the loom.

The weaving of the cloth was done on power looms mostly of American manufacture. The earliest looms were designed to make a simple, plain cloth and operated at 105-120 picks, or throws of the shuttle, per minute. Newer printlooms operated much faster at 180-200 picks a minute while fancy looms making such cloth as ginghams made 135 to 140. In Nashua simple sheetings and prints were the only cloths made in the early years. The average production per loom was 30-45 yards for a ten and a half hour day. Generally a mill girl operated three or maybe four looms. Pride was taken in the designing and perfecting of power looms, and rivalry between inventors developed.

The Indian Head Company

The bustling activity in Nashua was heightened further with the founding of a new company located on the lower canal and incorporated July 4, 1825. Charles C. Haven of Amherst with a group of Boston capitalists organized and started the Indian Head Company for the manufacture of woolen cloth. The group of investors included Haven, Augustus Peabody, and even the Nashua Manufacturing Company which put up $12,500 which was to be paid to Indian Head in the form of land and water power. The corporate stock was originally divided into 150 shares, with Ebenezer Appleton elected president, Thomas C. Amory as treasurer, and Charles Haven, agent. With Mr. Haven in charge, planning and layout of buildings were begun, with installation of machinery tentatively set for the spring of 1826. The first factory building was 155 feet long by 48 feet wide. The two-story dye house was 150 feet by 48 feet and a large building with a "bell frey" over it was 250 feet long. Besides a blacksmith shop, granary, and barn there were numerous houses on Bridge Street and four on Prospect Street for renting to employees. Machinery to be built by the company machinist—Mr. Winslow—would include carding machines, spinning jennies, and Stimpson-designed looms.

After considerable problems and delay the water was turned into the canal late in June, 1826, celebrated by a grand ball in the new factory. Some of the woolen cloth produced by the mill was displayed by Haven at the Hillsborough County Fair in 1828. A special prize was awarded for the samples of black, blue, and brown broadcloth. Chances of increasing production were severely dampened, however, by a heavy storm on September 29, 1827, which gouged one hundred feet of bank, changing the course of the river and sweeping away a new small bridge over the Nashua River behind the mill. The damage proved to be another factor in the eventual failure of the company. Only a small amount of cloth was produced afterward but it was sufficient in 1829 to enable the stockholders to pay all debts and escape bankruptcy. In November, 1830, the property was sold to a new firm called the Jackson Company. The incorporators were David Sears who was elected president; Amos Lawrence, treasurer; Ebenezer Francis, and Benjamin F. French, elected clerk.

In agreements with Nashua Manufacturing, Ira Gay with machine shop tools was made available to aid in reorganizing the machinery for manufacturing cotton cloth. Amos Lawrence was authorized to sell the old machinery at auction and to fit the mills with equipment adapted to shirtings, sheetings, and printed cloth. The dye house became Mill No. 1 and the original mill became Mill No. 2. Among the machinery specified by new mill agent Benjamin F. French was equipment to be copied by the Elliot Company from that in operation at the Appleton Mill No. 2 at Lowell. Unfortunately the Appleton Mills refused to allow representatives of the Elliot Company to do so. The machinery was to be inspected by a group including Ira Gay, Paul Moody, agent of the Waltham Mills, and Moses Paul before final building would begin. Eventually the contract with the Elliot Company was canceled, and Ira Gay and Otis Pettee proceeded to build the machines, using some parts ordered from other firms. After minor delays in fitting together parts of different origin, the machinery was finally assembled and production began. In 1831 management was reorganized and by December the first cloth was manufactured.

Almost from the beginning, the cloth made bore the Indian Head stamp. The first known sample with the symbol was a cut of yard-wide cloth made in 1833. The very first sheetings were sold under the name of Jackson but their sale was hampered by the unfavorable association of the name with the unpopular President Jackson. However,

the Indian Head trademark soon became known as a standard of quality in the newly-revived South American trade and in China. The cloth was sold unbleached in foreign and American markets.

The Indian Head has been a Nashua symbol for two hundred and fifty years. In 1724, after the Thornton's Ferry incident, a second fight supposedly took place near the mouth of the Nashua River. After the Indians had departed, a representation of an Indian's head was found carved on one of the trees. It was apparently intended as a taunt, as a reminder to the white settlers that the Indians were still a threat.

Laying Out the Town

With the administrative, marketing, and technical phases of manufacturing under reasonable control, Nashua Manufacturing began the task of literally planning the layout of the town. Asher Benjamin in scrupulous detail laid out streets and planned extensive housing for families and boarding houses for the mill girls. By 1826 there were thirty-five tenements for boarding houses costing $28,530. These, plus an additional five small houses, were expected to bring in rent of $2,491 a year. Nine larger houses costing $8,484.40 were expected to yield $885 in rent. Actually the company established rents lower than Mr. Benjamin's plans.

The map completed by John Lund in 1825 shows less than a dozen streets with several roads leading to nearby towns. Once Asher Benjamin arrived early that year he began plans for improving and adding streets, planting trees, and constructing needed buildings. Under the supervision of Ira Gay some work already had been done, such as the erection of the machine shop and some rental dwellings to help house the workers who began pouring into the village after hearing about the future factory.

The rest of the town including the town government soon felt the sudden growth and activity. In June, 1825, Temple Street was laid out from East Hollis Street to Main Street. In April, 1827, part of East Hollis Street was laid out from the Taylor Falls bridge site west to the Joshua Pierce house, which stood opposite the foot of what is now Arlington Street. In August, 1828, sections of Canal Street were laid out from Main Street to the land owned by the Jackson Company near the foot of Chandler Street. By December, 1828, West Hollis Street from

Chestnut west to the junction of the Dunstable and Hollis Roads was completed. In January, 1829, Bridge Street from the Taylor Falls bridge west to Charles Haven's land was laid out, and by February remaining parts of Canal and Bridge Streets were added. In June, 1830, West Hollis Street from Main to Chestnut Street was officially laid out through land owned by Nashua Manufacturing and Joseph Greeley. In 1832 Nashua Manufacturing laid out East Pearl Street. With the impetus of the company a network of roads and streets sprang up within only a few years.

Religious and Cultural Developments

In the summer of 1827 Reverend Nott began services in the new Olive Street church, built by Nashua Manufacturing with the help of Indian Head Company. Once completed it was turned over to the First Congregational Society. Earlier, in 1825, a dispute between the "Orthodox" and Unitarian Congregationalists led to the forming of the American Unitarian Association. The "New Light" Unitarian leadership championed the cause of providing education for the hundreds of mill girls who soon flocked to Nashua. Local leader of the "New Lights" was the Reverend Andrew E. Thayer, a friend of Patrick Tracy Jackson and like him an ardent Whig. As minister of the Congregational Church when the split occurred, he championed the Unitarian cause and gained the support of Ira Gay, Benjamin French, Daniel Abbot, and other influential citizens. Later, in 1829, he became the owner and proprietor of William A. Brown's bookstore and published the Whig weekly, the *Nashua Constellation*. Stressing wholesome literature for the mill girls he established a circulating library which reached about two thousand volumes, each of which could be borrowed at $1.50 or $3.00 per year depending on whether new or old. Between 1827 and 1830 four bookstores and circulating libraries were opened.

Industrial paternalism soon spread to encompass all aspects of life for the mill girls. Besides providing boarding houses and a church, the company provisioned a store and brought in a storekeeper, Leonard Noyes. A Sabbath School superintended by John A. Baldwin was started in the Unitarian Church. The company also built a small brick schoolhouse. As an inducement to help the mill girls and other employees save some of their wages a company savings bank was instituted in 1826. An evening school and singing school with quarters provided in a company building were offered. An ambitious student for a tuition fee of a dollar a month could study geography, English grammar, Latin and Greek Literature, and public speaking. As early as 1826 there was a library in the Nashua Manufacturing counting house, started originally by mechanics. In April, 1827, they organized as the Nashua Mechanics Institution with William A. Brown as secretary.

Importance of Women Workers

The lure of the factory life remained into the 1850s. The mills were the pathway for the upward mobility of hundreds of young farm girls. They provided the means for earning and saving money, gaining an education and possible career, and perhaps marrying into a successful family. Some ultimately became teachers and traveled to other parts of the country.

For those interested in creative writing there was some opportunity for having poems and stories published in the *New Hampshire Telegraph*, established in 1833 in the back of Thayer's bookstore. Edited by Alfred Beard, who was sympathetic to the young writers, the paper printed numerous short entries usually signed by a "Clarissa," "Susan," or simply "A Factory Girl." The most famous of these writers was Mary Grace Halpin, an operative in the mills in the 1840s. One particularly good contribution was sent by Beard to *Godey's Lady's Book*, which subsequently published it and launched Mary Grace on a writing career. By 1853 she left the mills to devote her time to writing. She became a frequent contributor to *Godey's* and similar periodicals. Her fame reached a culminating point when she became editor of the *Mother's Assistant and Young Ladies Friend*, published in Boston.

During the Civil War mill girls became involved with war projects after working hours, including making bandages and clothing for soldiers. Though there were growing numbers of Irish and later French Canadians in the labor force, some girls continued to occupy the boarding houses through the 1860s until their numbers gradually dwindled. As wider employment opportunities became available the era of the boarding house lifestyle faded.

Labor and Other Problems

A small segment of the work force was children. According to payroll records the number of boys and girls was not large and generally their duties included only light work. They served as helpers to spinners and weavers and ran errands around the mills. Apparently the only mill in Nashua which ever made a real effort to secure child labor was the Indian Head Factory which advertised for "boys and girls over ten years of age, none to be received who could not read and write, or were not of good moral character." Though the hours were long they were no longer than working time on a farm. The general work ethic at the time had no tolerance for idleness even among children. A child of eight or ten was expected to contribute in some way to the welfare of the family. The mills were but a means for children to earn modest sums of money. Industry and thrift were the standards of the day and good honest work was believed to build stamina and endurance in men, women, and children. Though working in the mills was never a picnic, no evidence suggests that any child labor atrocities occurred in Nashua.

Throughout the decades prior to the Civil War the mills underwent changes and growth interrupted periodically by the economic difficulties which affected the nation. The Panic of 1835-1837 caused an industrial catastrophe and sent prices zooming downward. Early in 1835 a new treasurer, superintendent, and agent were installed. In addition two hundred new shares of stock were sold to provide money for finally finishing Mill No. 3. However, the great Panic of 1837 brought on the temporary closing of Mill No. 3 and partial closing of No. 1 and No. 2 as well. Compounding the misery was a smallpox epidemic in the community. A labor shortage immediately followed the economic panic, requiring the mills to send representatives throughout New England to recruit employees.

Labor problems were complicated further by dissatisfaction among some over length of the work day. Eventually on March 3, 1853, the twelve-hour day was reduced to eleven, running from seven to seven with one hour for lunch. Meanwhile the bottom dropped out of the cotton market in 1840. Cloth that had sold for 37½ cents a yard fell to 8 cents. New tariff uncertainties and problems in the China trade added to the calamity. Local wages

were reduced to help survive the rough period. In 1842 another slump occurred and the firm of Upham, Appleton, and Tucker became selling agents for the mill. During the summer Mill No. 4 was started and completed by 1844. In 1843 the Jackson and Nashua Manufacturing Companies were partially united under one management when William Amory resigned as treasurer of Jackson and was replaced by James S. Amory, who now was treasurer of both companies.

Among the notable events during the 1850s were the introduction of gas lights to the mills in March, 1855, and the tragic fire at Mill No. 1 in June, 1856. The origin of the blaze was never determined but an overhead spinning frame was suspected as the cause. It began shortly after noon when a sweeper named Mrs. Burke was the only one in the building. Upon discovering the fire she became panic stricken and ran out upon the roof, leaving the skylight open behind her. Within minutes flames burst through practically every window. Firemen arrived and with workers from the mill set up a bucket brigade, but to no avail. Before rescuers could reach her with tall enough ladders Mrs. Burke leaped to the ground and died from the resulting injuries. The new town water supply received its first real test and though it worked efficiently it did not prevent Mill No. 1 from being destroyed. Firemen and citizens were praised highly for confining the blaze as much as they did, preventing further destruction in the neighborhood. The mill itself was promptly rebuilt.

With the uncertainty of relations between cotton producing and manufacturing states, plus general financial uneasiness, the years leading up to the Civil War were difficult. The company suffered a financial loss in the year 1858 when a ship carrying a cargo of cloth to Liverpool was hit by lightning and sank. When war finally broke out in 1861 the price of raw cotton was sent skyward. Through great foresight the mill treasurer had bought extensive quantities just before the tragic event.

The Period of Expansion

Up to this time the mills produced cloth that consisted of certain coarse grades of sheetings, shirtings, prints, and drills. In recent years the trade with China had been growing while the South American trade was declining. Sheetings and shirtings were sold under different brands according to quality, the best being "Two Storks." Other goods were sold to dealers who put on their own mark. With the war came the chance to bid on a government contract for making cotton flannel underwear for the Army. Nashua Manufacturing was awarded the contract and began immediately to build napping machinery which they installed in the old picker room. Within weeks the cloth was being made and the underwear cut in the cloth room. Very shortly women and girls from the area arrived to pick up work which they took home for sewing. The contract called for 300,000 pairs the first year, 500,000 the second, and 175,000 the third. Eventually 1.9 million pairs were made, thus providing substantial sums of supplemental earnings for housewives and employees. As the contracts increased work which had begun in Mill No. 1 was expanded to the other buildings. Thus, though the mills were temporarily shut down for a time in 1861, they were soon busy again. The napping operation continued to a lesser degree after the war, producing cloth used mainly in underwear.

The boom period immediately following the war was only a hollow promise which soon ended in the Panic of 1873 and beginning a period of industrial and financial depression. Anti-trade feelings were becoming more common in Congress, especially among western delegates. The uncertainties had a dampening effect on the domestic trade as well since companies were reluctant to make any long-term commitments in expanding business. Fortunately by 1879 and 1880 the China trade began to grow again and Indian Head cloth in particular felt a surge in demand. Business improved in 1881 and the Jackson Company had nearly 30,000 spindles and 1,012 looms at work. In 1879 Nashua Manufacturing employed 861 and manufactured 18,087,164 yards of cloth. A new storehouse was built and considerable new machinery was added. The following year 200 new looms were added and an electric clock was installed. In addition the No. 2 penstock and raceway in the canal was rebuilt using iron instead of wood. Beginning in 1881 a new 1,000-horsepower steam engine and boiler were being installed, prompted mainly by an extended drought. Due to another period of low water in the canal in 1883 the directors of the Jackson Company decided to install a 700-horsepower steam power plant capable of running 1,200 looms.

Beginning in 1885 the mills began to feel compe-

tition from goods being made in southern mills. In order to broaden the product line in Nashua the mills began developing flannel cloth in the 1880s. Beginning in 1890 the first cotton blankets were made and sold by Nashua Manufacturing. By 1893 the blanket trade was expanding rapidly. In order to meet the varied demands of the market Nashua Manufacturing now made 122 kinds of cloth. In spite of all the effort the mills experienced several unprofitable years. Periodic labor strikes further hindered production, such as a mule-spinners' strike in 1892, followed by a weavers' strike. At this point the labor force consisted heavily of immigrants who were flocking to Nashua. The last of the boarding houses were converted to tenements to house the many new families. The shift in the labor force came at a time when production was being speeded up and the old paternalism in many ways was a thing of the past.

A Serious Accident

Though the management stressed safety and the accident record was low there were a few unfortunate incidents. The most spectacular occurred one afternoon about 1895 when a huge thirty-five ton flywheel about twenty feet in diameter suddenly shattered. Within seconds it crashed into the mill wall, throwing pieces of metal as far as the canal. It also smashed through the dressing room floor and ruined a slasher. Live steam from the power plant quickly poured into the No. 3 weave room, badly burning a worker named Mrs. Watts who was dragged to safety by a Mr. Hebert. Unconscious and with arms badly burned she undoubtedly would have lost her life without his brave actions. In all two persons were killed and several more injured in what was one of the most serious accidents at Nashua Manufacturing.

Dieudonne DeLacombe at age seventy-two in 1944 completed his fifty-ninth year of continuous service. Coming to work in October, 1885, at age twelve, he spent his entire career in the spinning room oiling spindles. His early duties also included arriving at 5:30 each morning to light the gas lights. He was paid on the last Thursday of the month and his first five weeks' pay totaled $12. At this time a man working for the mill could get "room, board, and wash" for $3.50 a week while a woman would pay $2.75.

Success and Failure

Though the China trade was becoming a thing of the past, the company offered one hundred and forty kinds of cloth in a diversified market. By 1903 the net sales of Nashua Manufacturing reached $3,265,700. In 1908 the first of the famous "Nashua Woolnap Blankets" were sold.

Between April 26 and May 10, 1911, a series of directors' meetings were held for the purpose of uniting Nashua Manufacturing and the Jackson Company. Despite some opposition, on January 3, 1916, the first of the two purchased all the property, franchises, and trademarks of the Jackson Company. In the meantime the Panic of 1907 brought on an unstable economic period which preceded the large-scale labor disputes of 1915, but over the long term the Nashua Manufacturing Company continued to grow and by 1926 it owned the Nashua and Jackson mills in Nashua, the Suffolk mill in Lowell, and the Cordova mill which had been built in 1898 in Alabama. Its extensive textile products were being sold around the world, in Canton and even in Mombasa, East Africa. In spite of a fluctuating economy, changing markets, and labor problems, the mills—as they approached the one hundred year mark—were in solid financial condition.

A third textile factory, which was later called the Vale Mills, began in Nashua in 1845. The original building, located where Main Street crossed Salmon Brook, was called the East Mill and used for making satinette cloth. The original operation did not do as well as planned and a Walter Crane later used the building for making twine. A second building was constructed nearby on Main Street by Thomas W. Gillis for use as a machine shop. In 1852 he and a partner named Taylor moved their sewing machine company there from its original Water Street location. The venture proved unsuccessful and soon failed.

There is no record of the exact dates when Elias Howe worked in a small machine shop at the Harbor, while experimenting with his invention, the sewing machine. It was probably sometime in the early 1840s, since he obtained the patent on the machine in 1846. Strangely enough, there is no reference to his sojourn in Nashua in any biographical writings concerning Howe. This is, however, a tradition that has been mentioned in several local histories.

In 1854 the Harbor Manufacturing Company was formed with Gillis as agent and I.H. Marshall as treasurer and clerk. The new company purchased the East Mill and the machine shop on Main Street, using the first for carding and spinning and the second for weaving.

In 1863 the company was purchased by Benjamin Saunders who modernized the factory and incorporated it as the Vale Mills in 1868. The capacity of the mill was soon doubled, with five hundred ring spindles and one hundred looms in operation. Power for the facility came from water turbines rated at 225-horsepower and a 100-horsepower steam engine.

With the death of Mr. Saunders in 1888 Edward Labrie became manager, with Markham Dexter of Boston as treasurer. The business continued to grow so that by 1895 the number of employees had increased from seventy-five to two hundred and fifty, and the annual output was valued at a half million dollars. In spite of this temporary success, by 1909 the firm went out of business for undetermined reasons.

Heavy Industry in Nashua

With cotton providing a solid economic base, a commercial climate was generated that stimulated other types of manufacturing. A great many diversified industries using a wide variety of raw materials developed in the city in the course of the century.

Heavy industry and manufacturing in metals were well represented. One of the earliest was the Nashua Iron Foundry established in 1845 by two brothers from Easton, Massachusetts, Seth and Charles Williams. Taking over a small existing foundry on Water Street (about which little is known), they started making heavy castings for cotton and woolen machinery. The wooden foundry structure they built on the corner of Temple and Pearl Streets burned down in 1849 but they rebuilt immediately in brick. Later Charles Williams, Mayor of Nashua in 1876-1877, ran the foundry by himself until his retirement in 1892 when it was closed down. The Temple Street site was sold to Roby and Swart, lumber dealers, who used the space for their yard.

Once upon a time, believe it or not, there was actually a foundry in Nashua that was owned and run by its employees. Originally part of the Nashua

Lock Company, it was later owned by a man named Jotham D. Otterson. An article in the *Nashua Weekly Telegraph* in January, 1880 (this paper specialized in reporting on the state of local industrial arts), described the Otterson operation as being in a very prosperous condition in spite of the fact that an advance in the price of raw metal had caused some business problems. Just one year later, January, 1881, the foundry was a center of controversy and speculation. Otterson had died late in 1880 and without his guiding hand the firm was on the brink of bankruptcy, temporarily controlled by one of its creditors; the workmen had gone without wages for several weeks. Out of this desperate situation came the formation of the cooperative by the very workers who depended for their living on the continuation of the business. *Parker's History* in its excellent chapter on "Manufactures" by R.T. Smith makes the following comment regarding this development:

The specialty of the company is, and always has been, small and fine castings, and the company takes pride in both the quality and workmanship of its productions. The success of this cooperative enterprise is a result of two important elements: the company was composed of working men, who knew little of business and who, recognizing the fact, employed a good business man as agent and left him to conduct the department. The workmen also realized that

they were working for themselves, that their faithfulness was to their own personal advantage and no shirk was harbored in the works for one moment.

In 1914 this type of management ended when a Scotch inventor named Charles M. Smith took over controlling interest. In the final stage of the company's history Walter Ellis owned the foundry and George Thurber was the President from 1919 until it finally went out of business in 1946.

The manufacture of stoves was an industry that for greatest efficiency required its own foundry, a hard fact that was faced by James Hartshorn who in 1839 had moved his stove and tinware business from Milford to Nashua. His inventory came from Walpole, Massachusetts, and he found that to be sure of obtaining his stoves he had to do the transporting with his own team. A friend suggested that the only way to continue in business without this inconvenience was to set up his own foundry and manufacture stoves himself. He took as a partner a man with great business acumen, Winslow Ames. The two started their foundry on Water Street, which was fast becoming a central industrial area, in 1851. As often happened the business in its initial stages was marked by close personal attention to all details by the owners themselves. Accounts of the first delivery of their own brand of stove conjure up a comic picture of perseverance as they struggled down Main Street with the stove in a wheelbarrow propelled by Mr. Hartshorn on its way to a customer, Mr. Ames preserving the equilibrium of the freight. The business prospered so fast that they had to move to a larger building on Howard Street. One problem with this type of enterprise, however, was its seasonal nature—nobody bought stoves in the winter, spring, or even summer. Customers suddenly decided they needed new stoves in the fall of the year as winter loomed ahead. Unfortunately the firm was hit hard by the panic of 1857 when a recession in October caught them with $100,000 on their books and no customers who could afford to pay for the stoves in their warehouse.

The most famous products made by Nashua Iron and Steel Works were the stoppers for the ports in the turret of the S.S. *Monitor* which was sunk off Hampton Roads, Virginia, in a battle with the Confederate battleship, the *Merrimack,* during the Civil War. The company made many other iron and steel items such as tires for driving-wheels of locomotives, steamer shafts, and all kinds of forgings. In 1880 they made the largest steel shaft ever forged in this country up to that time. Smith observed, "Its furnace was the first of its kind built in America and marks an era in the steel manufacture of this country." The firm was started in 1838 as the Nashua Manufacturers and Mechanics Association but in 1845 the name was changed to Nashua Iron Works, and in 1872 to Nashua Iron and Steel Company. A plaque in front of the present Osgood's Hardware Store on East Hollis Street marks the site of what was familiarly called "the Old Black Forge Shop." The works occupied fifteen acres of land at this location extending all the way back to Tyler Street. Their biggest trip hammer, the largest in the world for its times, was a ten-tonner, the foundation castings for which weighed one hundred tons.

In good times the Nashua Iron and Steel Company employed more than three hundred men. The political arguments of these workmen sometimes became almost as heated as the iron they were forging. Between "heats" they had time to engage in conversation and with an election coming up this often took the form of wagers on the outcome. A Republican and a Democrat once made the following bet: the one whose candidate lost would travel on all fours from the railroad station to the Post Office, carrying the victorious bettor on his back. It is regrettable that no photograph of the paying off

The American Shearer Co. plant, present site of Simoneau Plaza.

of this wager has been preserved!

It was at their plant, in the bar and plate mill, that the first electric lights in Nashua were installed in January, 1880. A man named Brush in Cleveland, Ohio, had devised electric lights especially intended for street lighting. Two of these Brush lights each having two thousand candle-power were placed in position at the iron and steel works in a cavernous space where a great deal of night work was done. The cost of the generating machine was $550. Everyone in town marveled at the brilliance of the illumination provided by the new wonder of electricity.

Although this company was a pioneering effort in iron and steel making it did not survive the nineteenth century. It was listed in the Nashua Directory for the last time in 1899.

In the famous reference work, *Kane's First Facts,* Nashua is given credit for only one "first"—the first engine lathe ever made in America, built by John H. Gage in the Nashua Manufacturing Company's machine shop on Water Street. Each shop in those days had to make its own tools, as there was no such thing as a source of supply of the ready-made article. Clever and inventive machinists such as Gage were valuable employees. It was inevitable that

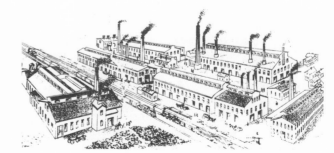

Artist's sketch of Nashua Iron and Steel Co. in the late 1800s.

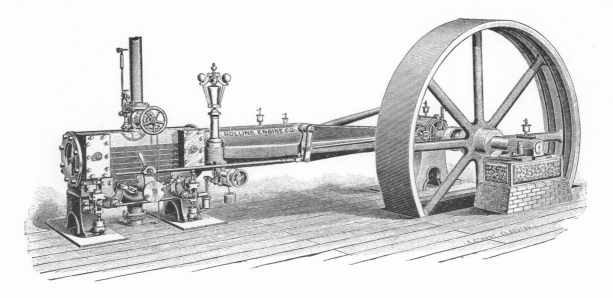

Gage would eventually form his own company where his talents could be put to work for his own profit. He started working for the cotton mill in 1838. By 1851 the firm of Gage, Warner, and Whitney had been formed and the following year the East Hollis Street shop was built. The company actually chalked up another first—that has won less publicity—when it made the first automatic gear-cutter ever offered for sale. Turbine wheels were also among its products. Gage was killed in a hunting accident in 1872 and the firm did not survive his or the deaths of the other partners.

Two real giants of heavy industry were Flather and Company (engine lathes) and the Rollins Engine Company (steam engines). The founders of Flather and Company, Joseph and William Flather, were brothers who originally came from England. In 1867 they came to Nashua, where Joseph had previously worked as a machinist, and set up a machine shop on Water Street. They concentrated mainly on one product, the engine lathe. Because of their belief that the business should remain in the family, passing from father to son to grandson, the concern kept going right up until the retirement of the last owner, Oscar Flather, in 1942. They too had a foundry in connection with their plant.

An article in the *Weekly Telegraph* around 1880 described a square area bounded by Quincy and Foundry Streets and the railroad tracks as "a busy manufacturing place." Besides the Otterson (later

the Cooperative) Foundry, this area included the Cross and Tolles Lumber Company, and the Rollins machine shop. Gun machinery was once made by the company later known as the Rollins Engine Company (it had various names in the course of its history). Their real claim to fame, however, was their excellent steam engine which was patented in 1867. George Rollins was originally associated with Josephus Baldwin (a man who had a finger in every pie) in making iron and woodworking machinery in the early 1850s. After starting to manufacture the steam engine Rollins constantly worked on improvements so that his machine would be as nearly perfect in operation as possible. Proving that perfectionism does pay off, his company endured for a long while, as its last directory listing was in 1957.

Another firm that used metal was the Underhill Edge Tool Company which exported its products all over the world. They made axes for many different uses as well as adzes, hatchets, hammers, chisels, cleavers, and other similar tools. The founder of this highly successful organization was a remarkable man who ranks as one of Nashua's all-time greatest citizens. George W. Underhill was a native of Chester where his ancestors had been very early settlers. Like many other ambitious young men he began his career by making his product with his own hands. Twelve years later he was still finishing the edges of the axes on a common grindstone. In 1852 a more sophisticated organization of the business took place and the company was formally incorporated. Its shop was near the railroad tracks at the mouth of Salmon Brook. The firm grew so rapidly that in 1879 it was able to buy up the Amoskeag Axe Company of Manchester and before the end of the century it was making almost 150,000 axes a year. Virgil Gilman at one time was the President of this company and William H. Beasom was its Treasurer for many years. The Underhill firm moved away from Nashua in spite of bitter protests from citizens. Before 1900 it was bought up by the American Axe Company.

George Underhill himself died in 1882. He could well be called "the father of Crown Hill"—he bought this large tract in the 1840s, built his own home there and, thirty years later, divided it into house lots. His widow, Mary Gale Underhill, was one of several women who contributed generously to the building of the First Congregational Church.

The Nashua Lock Company was another well-known firm that used metal. It arose out of an idea conceived in the imaginative brain of the inimitable Samuel Shepard. He had come to Nashua as an associate of Asher Benjamin. Realizing that the population of Nashua was mushrooming and that homes must be constructed, he understood well his value to the community. Shepard was truly an inventive man. Faced with the building boom he invented new and improved cabinet-making machinery. He devised a method to manufacture pre-built doors and windows. While engaged in the making of doors, sashes, and blinds—in partnership with David Baldwin—Shepard decided that there had to be a better way to put a lock on a door than attaching it to the outside. In 1834 he proceeded to design a method of placing the lock in a mortise so that it could be enclosed within the wood of the door itself. Leonard Noyes bought out Shepard's interest in the resultant lock company in 1835—as a businessman Shepard was somewhat less than a genius.

The lock company changed hands again after the panic of 1857 and in 1860 a plant known for many years as the "Lock Shop" was built on Spring Street. Although this was a highly respected company, it too eventually passed out of the control of Nashua people. Smith comments on this development in its affairs: " . . . the hold obtained by competitors was too strong, and it was found necessary for Nashua to surrender her own child to others, because others had nourished the child Nashua had neglected."

R.T. Smith himself, author of the Parker chapter, was a bookstore owner, a mechanical engineer, an inventor. He played an important part in the formation of at least one metal-using industry that survived well into the twentieth century—the American Shearer Company of which he was President for many years. While visiting a farm in Vermont, Smith had noted the need for a sheep-shearing machine. On his return to Nashua he persuaded J.K. Priest, a skillful mechanic, to experiment with inventing such a shearer. After a year of work by Priest and Smith, the invention was in working prototype so that it could shear a single sheep in two minutes. It was displayed at an exhibition in London where it was highly praised for its novelty. The company, which was formed in 1865, then turned to making horse clippers. It did not make sheep shearers again until 1900, in response to a demand from Australia, which became one of the best markets for this type of clipper. This extremely successful firm, which was run by three generations of the Priest family, also made barbers' clippers and similar tools until 1950. Its plant on Main Street, long known as the "clipper shop," was finally razed in August, 1972, when Simoneau Plaza was expanded.

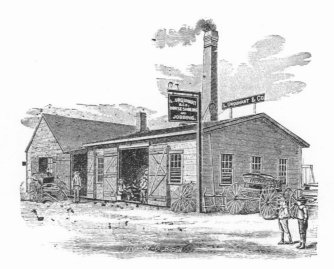

Typical blacksmith shop of the late 1800s.

Two other firms working in metal were the Nashua Saddlery Hardware Company and William Highton and Sons. Incorporated in 1889, Saddlery Hardware expanded by the purchase of a plant in Rome, New York, which was moved to Nashua. In 1923 the demand for the original product having

Staff of Proctor Brothers, makers of barrels and kegs, pose in 1899.

somewhat diminished, a new corporation was formed, now known as the Nashua Brass Company.

William Highton and Sons came to Nashua from Boston in 1889 and built a plant at Pond and Otterson Streets to manufacture registers and ventilators. The city government encouraged the move by exempting the company from taxation for ten years and the Indian Head Bank extended financing to help them.

Millwork Companies

The list of industries that used wood or its by-products as a basic material is almost as long as the list of metal forgers and fabricators. The great importance of sawmills in the economy of Ancient Dunstable and Dunstable, New Hampshire, has already been noted. A familiar sight in the Nashua River many years ago was the log boom of the sawmill of the Sargent and Cross Company on the south bank at the Jackson Company dam. This firm was later known as Cross and Tolles, under whose management the mill was moved to Quincy Street. The twentieth century name of this firm was the Tolles-Bickford Lumber Company which operated until the mid-fifties.

The manufacture of doors, windows, sashes, and frames was a tradition that had of course started with Samuel Shepard and David Baldwin in their shop at the north end of the Jackson Company dam where they used the water power for their machines. J. and A.J. Rockwood, better known later on as the town undertakers, began business as manufacturers of this type of house fittings and then branched out into making caskets. In 1870 David and Daniel Gregg moved their small sash and blind plant from Goffstown to Nashua, attracted by the fact that here they had the advantage of excellent shipping facilities. The Nashua firm was one of the first national manufacturers of doors, windows, and other types of millwork. Successive generations of sons and sons-in-law were involved in management so that the company remained on the Nashua scene until the early 1960s.

In 1881 Ira H. and Nathaniel H. Proctor of Hollis expanded their business and built a cooperage factory at Marshall and Hollis Streets in Nashua. A year later they acquired further property on Tyler Street. They owned thousands of acres of timber from which they cut about eight million feet of lumber each year. The firm manufactured a wide line of kegs, barrels, and pails, plus building supplies. The firm flourished until the mid-fifties of the present century, rebuilding completely after total destruction in the 1930 Crown Hill fire.

Another firm that did millwork was Roby and Swart whose manufacturing plant was in Edgeville along Salmon Brook (which provided some of their power) where they started their business in 1890. Charles A. Roby was the son of Luther A. Roby who had originally owned the Sargent and Cross sawmill. William D. Swart was married to Luther Roby's daughter, Lizzie. They made wooden boxes as well as a wide variety of other millwork products. In 1902 the company was incorporated under the name of the American Box and Lumber Company which continued in business until 1937.

Other Wood Products

Nashua was too far from the sea to become a shipbuilding center but the ship timber yard of Luther A. Roby contributed thousands of feet of timbers to the construction of some of the greatest clipper ships. Most of the timbers in the *Great Republic,* the largest clipper ship ever built in this country, came from the Roby yard. Roby himself was an outstanding Nashua citizen. A native born here in 1814, his early career was in canal boating. When the railroad displaced this means of transporting freight he went into the lumber business and specialized in timbers for ships, wharves, and piling until the early 1890s.

The Sanders Box and Furniture Factory located at the mouth of the Nashua River, was considered inaccessible for shipping but George Sanders, a native of Hudson, solved this problem by putting in a railroad track to connect with the Concord Railroad line. He made pine and spruce boxes at the plant, which was destroyed by fire in 1889; a second fire destroyed the rebuilt plant in 1890.

Another box-making firm moved to Nashua from Tyngsborough in 1890, operated by E.O. Fifield. He built a large shop on the corner of Taylor Road and the street that was subsequently named for him. This company later moved to Milford.

The Baldwin Bobbin and Shuttle Works and its successor, Eaton and Ayre, represented a wood industry that was closely related to textile manufacture. It was one of the largest plants in the old Water

Street industrial complex. It developed from humble beginnings around 1835 when two young brothers started making bobbins in a small shop behind their father's farmhouse on the Highland Farm in South Nashua. After setting up shop on Water Street the business run by Edwin and Josephus Baldwin was twice disrupted by fire. When his brother Edwin died in 1848 Josephus carried on alone. Nashua's first mayor had interests in several other businesses and often ran into financial difficulties, so by 1862 he had sold the business to Eaton and Ayre, another bobbin maker. In time this firm became known as the Nashua Bobbin and Shuttle Company which by 1891 had been in Smith's words "gobbled up by a trust." Eaton and Ayre in its heyday employed as many as two hundred and fifty workers, and orders came from as far away as England. To the average Nashuan their shop was always known as the "bobbin shop."

Other products made from wood included churns, pencils, toys, wooden ware, cradles, cabinets, picture frames, and considerable furniture. John Coggin was apparently the first furniture maker, possibly as early as 1825. The first of many partners was a Mr. B. Blanchard. Coggin made furniture in Nashua for sixty years. In the early days of his enterprise he was often seen trundling pieces of furniture in a hand-cart from his mill at the Harbor to the retail outlets in Nashua Village. There were several other men who made furniture but E.G. Sears, around 1850, was the first one who shipped his products to outside markets. His specialty was bedsteads. In 1857 the business was sold and guess who took it over: None other than Josephus Baldwin!

Another well-known furniture maker was Fletcher and Webster, the name under which the firm was incorporated in 1868, although it had several names as various partners came and went. What-nots (typical Victorian bric-a-brac holders) were among the small pieces they turned out, as well as such items as folding cribs and music racks.

The Crosby invalid bed won prizes at national expositions and was used by the government in veterans' hospitals. This famous adjustable bed was invented by Dr. Josiah Crosby in 1873 and patented in 1876; the company was incorporated in 1886. The first plant of the Crosby Invalid Bed Company was on Lowell Street. Later it was moved to Water Street. The bed was originally made of wood but eventually an iron model was turned out, the factory operating its own machine shop for this purpose. This was a viable Nashua industry until 1921.

Paper Products

Paper products were and still are well represented by a company that has had a very long history—the Nashua Corporation as it is known today. Its nickname for many years was "the card shop." The 130-year-old story of this Nashua firm, tracing its numerous changes of name, management, and technological progress, would require a rather large book in itself. A chronology of its nineteenth century events will have to suffice:

1848: Charles T. Gill, popular Nashua book store owner and bookbinder, was chatting one day with his good friend O.D. Murray, publisher of "The Oasis." He commented that he wished he could figure out a fast way to make playing cards because there was a big demand for them in the gold rush camps of California. Murray, who had experimented with printing wallpaper, demonstrated that simultaneous printing of several colors could be done just as quickly on playing cards. The machinist John H. Gage was approached for technical help. Never a man to pass up a chance to turn a profit, Gage insisted on going into the business with them. The first partners of the company thus formed were Gill, Gage, and Murray; the first name of the company was Gill and Company.

1849: A building was erected for the new business on the north side of Water Street. Ironically, they never did make playing cards. The only New England supplier of cardboard in rolls was a clergyman who recoiled in horror at the use to which Gill and Company intended to put any supply of cardboard they bought. He refused to sell any to them and the partners decided they would have to make their own. Soon after this, Charles Gill died and with him died the playing card project. The equipment purchased for the project rusted away but the company kept on making cardboard and other paper products.

1851: Gage sold his interest in the company to Virgil C. Gilman (another man with a finger in every pie) and the name was changed to Gage, Murray & Co. The making of cardboard and glazed paper continued and met with success as improvements were introduced into the manufacturing process.

1857: Virgil Gilman's brother, Horace W. Gilman, bought a quarter interest in the company.

1861: The company bought the old Washington House headquarters of the Nashua Watch Company on Main Street between Bowers and Prospect Streets.

1866: The firm was entirely bought out by the Gilman Brothers—Virgil, Horace, and O.B. Gilman—and the name was changed to Gilman Brothers.

1869: The Nashua Card and Glazed Paper Company was formed by a consolidation of Gilman Brothers and the Nashua Glazed Paper Company, and was incorporated the same year. The entire company was then moved to the building on Pearson Avenue where the Nashua Glazed Paper Company had its factory. Later the Eagle Card Company, another competitor, was bought out.

1872: Virgil Gilman sold his stock and retired from the business.

1883: Orlando Dana Murray (O.D. Murray), President of the company, retired after thirty-three years of active interest.

1889: H.G. Bixby secured control of the business and built the plant on Franklin Street. Bixby was the leader of what the Parker history calls "outside capitalists" who took control of the Nashua Lock Co. Bixby, described in a 1937 newspaper article as an "outstanding millionaire of the day," owned a home on the Main Street plot that later became the site of the St. Joseph orphanage.

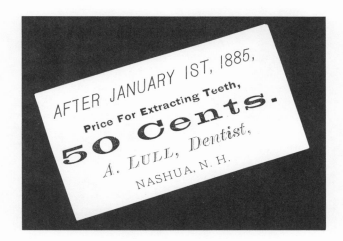

Soapstone and Spring Water

There were two companies that successfully exploited natural resources easily available in the local area: Francestown Soapstone Company and the Londonderry Lithia Spring Water Company. One of the finest soapstone quarries in the country was located in nearby Francestown. Francestown

Soapstone Company, incorporated in 1865 to make useful items from the stone taken from a local quarry, was located first in Milford, then it moved to Nashua.

Soapstone has excellent heat-retaining qualities and one of its most popular uses was as a bed warmer, a great comfort in the days when bedrooms were unheated in winter. A piece of soapstone was thoroughly heated in the kitchen stove oven, wrapped in flannel, and placed between the icy sheets before bedtime. In this way energy from the wood or coal stove was transferred to where it was temporarily needed and the body heat of sleepers was conserved for a restful night under coverlets and quilts, even though the temperature of the bedroom might be near zero. (It was an old-fashioned custom, but one that may make a comeback if the energy crisis of our time becomes acute!)

Soapstone was also used to make flatiron bases, one of which was recently dug up in a Nashua field. Since soapstone can be ground to a very smooth finish it was as suitable for ironing as metal; the wooden handle was attached with a bolt sunk well beneath the surface. Laundry tubs and sinks, as well as ovens in bakeries, were also made from this hard and durable stone. The Francestown quarry was worked out when it had gone down to a level of 134 feet around 1891.

The Londonderry Lithia Spring Water Company bottled and distributed a fabulous medicinal water that came from a source only six miles from Nashua. There is a legend that the Indians knew about the magic properties of this sparkling water and held a yearly dance around the spring in honor of it. The spring was discovered anew in 1882 on a farm in Londonderry. A son of the farmer, knowing that the family needed water, had decided to try dowsing. While walking all over the farm holding a forked stick he accidentally fell into a hole that turned out to be the outlet for the spring water that had trickled down through the granite of the hill above. A Nashua man first became interested in bottling this water. Then some Nashua doctors' tests found that it had a large amount of lithia which was considered beneficial for health problems caused by uric acid. Two of the doctors formed a stock company to bottle and market the water. It was sold in plain or carbonated form and the amount spent for advertising was unusually high for the time. The trademark was a big green bottle, with stopper flying through the air and several brownies riding the stopper. The company marketed the water all over the country until about

1920. The Food and Drug Administration did not agree that the amount of lithia was sufficient for the medical benefits claimed and forced the dropping of the word "lithia" from the label. Without the magic word, sales dropped disastrously. Since the water had also been widely used in carbonated form as a mixer for drinks Prohibition completed the demise of the company.

A firm that has supplied Nashua with just plain water for one hundred and twenty-five years is of course the Pennichuck Water Works. A full and detailed history of this private corporation up to 1937 can be found in the WPA volume entitled *A List of Active Industries*. The company has also published its own short history of its operations. Its lifetime almost equals that of Nashua as a city, as it was in June, 1852, that a charter was issued to the "Nashville Aquaduct," which about a year later changed its name to Pennichuck Water Works. The first storage reservoir was set up by building a dam across Pennichuck Brook at the head of the old Ayer's Mill Pond where in Ancient Dunstable times a man named Ayer had set up a "spice mill."

An important figure in the management of the Water Works was John F. Stark, son of George Stark, who studied the example set by the city of Lowell in order to improve on the Nashua water system. Among the men associated with the Works when it started were Albert McKean, William D. Beasom, D.H. Dearborn, Israel Hunt, Leonard Noyes, George W. Underhill, Thomas Chase, and the Greeleys—Alfred and Joseph.

Light Industry

Clay suitable for pottery is not available in the area so very little has been made commercially. The only pottery-making business of which there is any record was that of a man named Martin Crafts who, for six years, 1838 to 1844, ran a kiln at a cottage at Bowers and Main Streets. In 1919 when a Buick salesroom was built on the site his cottage was finally torn down.

Light industry included a few products that bordered on the frivolous, to add a touch of gaiety and color to the workaday scene. Josiah M. Fletcher, who later went into the furniture-making business with Amos Webster, started a valentine business in 1850 and apparently did well enough to keep it going for ten years. This same Mr. Fletcher was also

a partner in the Nashua Novelty Works with L.C. Farwell. This company started out by making bird cages in 1856; Fletcher invented the machinery to make these metal cages. The line of products was expanded to include a variety of toys and souvenirs. Another "first" can be chalked up for Nashua in the manufacture of carpet sweepers, that boon to the housewife in the days before the invention of the vacuum cleaner. Fletcher and Farwell made the very first sweepers in the world although they are not credited with the actual invention.

Josiah Fletcher was a lively person who seems to have combined a touch of whimsy with mechanical aptitude and business ability. As a youth he worked in the Nashua cotton mills as a bobbin boy and was a

Jug made by Martin Crafts; circa 1840.

product of the night school run for mill operatives. In 1848 he was caught up in the Gold Rush fever and took off for California. He was a magazine publisher in New York for a while before returning to Nashua to spend the rest of his life. He was the first person in town to use coal for heating and the first purchaser of a typewriter. In many ways Josiah Fletcher sounds as if he might have enjoyed living in the late twentieth century! In addition to his other facets he was also a poet who published a volume of verse, *A Thousand Songs of Life, Love, Home and Heaven*.

Other local light industry products were hoop skirts, India rubber combs, spectacles with real

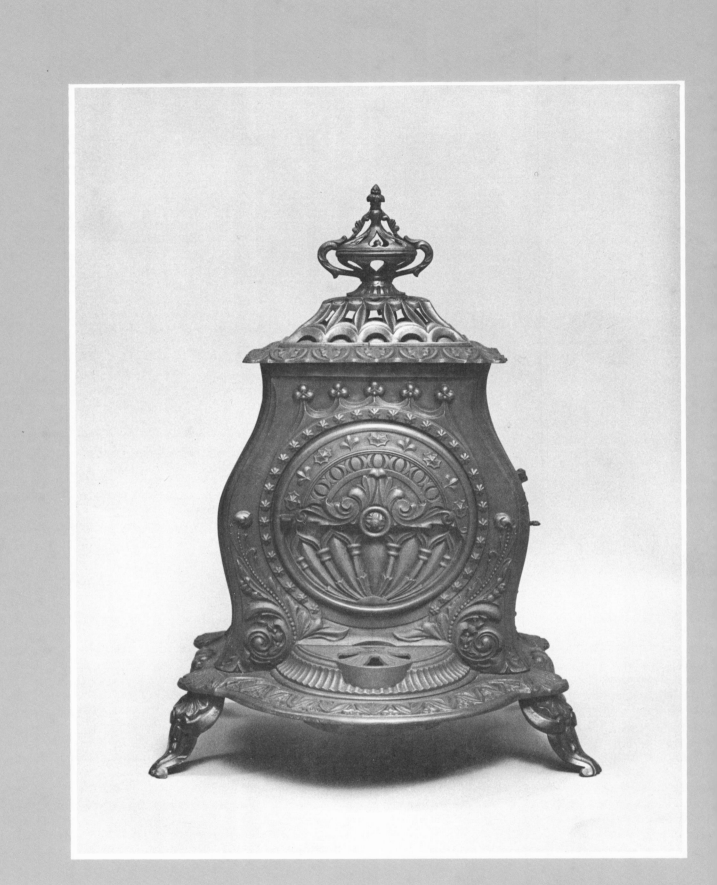

Bedroom stove made in Nashua by Hartshorn and Ames;
circa 1855.

silver bows, wallpaper, palm leaf hats, soap, and cigars. The cigar makers, who came and went in rather quick succession, few staying in business very long, seem to have been a closely knit breed of workers. There were at least twenty of these small shops over a period of many years where the favorite tobacco product of gentlemen of all classes was prepared. At one time there was even a cigar-making shop on the first floor of the Universalist Church.

Since the ingredients were a trade secret we will probably never know the chemical formula for one of the most unusual Nashua products—Hall's Hair Renewer. R.P. Hall started off in Amherst peddling door-to-door a mixture he had concocted that was guaranteed to grow hair. In 1861 the burgeoning business was moved to High Street in Nashua. Ex-

humility. Roswell T. Smith comes through as a man of great gifts who never "kidded" himself that he was invincible. Actually what defeated the fan business was a fire plus stiff competition from Japanese fans.

A good example of an industry run entirely by a woman was the Lucy R. Baker knitting firm. This was started by still another woman, Mrs. J.P. Barker, in 1870. Mrs. Baker was in sole charge after 1877. Mittens, gloves, hosiery, children's underwear were among the clothing items made by a work force of as many as one hundred persons, most of them women. The business had a rather large building at 111 Lock Street and was listed in the directories up until 1905.

tensive advertising was effective in tapping a rather large market that apparently existed among the balding. There are no reports available on the efficacy of the concoction.

Fans were made in Nashua for about three years in the late 1860s. The American Fan Company was the brainchild of R.T. Smith, under the stimulus of Virgil Gilman who wanted an additional product for his card company. Smith invented a folding machine to use in the process. *Parker's History* says concerning this effort: "... the members of the card company induced Mr. R.T. Smith to take charge of such a shop. This was a great mistake ... Mr. Smith did not have the right qualities to manage such a business." When it is remembered that this very same Mr. Smith was the man who wrote this statement, we cannot help but admire his candor and .

Ingenious Inventors

No story of former Nashua industries would be complete without mention of the Nashua Till Company. A Nashua man, Edwin White, invented an alarm money drawer which was patented in 1859. By 1880 Egbert O. Wood had become the sole owner of the Nashua Till Company which had been formed to manufacture the money drawers. Wood also was an inventor who devised an alarm till of his own, one combining the features of a cashier's desk machine and a till, in many ways the forerunner of the cash register. These were manufactured at a shop on Quincy Street until 1921.

Another unusual Nashua product was the melodeon, a popular home musical instrument of the period. The firm of C. and E. Sawyer made these at the rate of about four a week for a few years after 1853. J.D. Nutter was a builder of church organs and installed some of the first pipe organs in Nashua churches. Neither one of these companies stayed here long, both moving to Vermont.

Refrigerators and ice cream freezers that combined many materials including wood, metal, slate, tin, and porcelain were also made in Nashua. The Maine Manufacturing Company is, of course, an important part of the modern industrial scene. Originally this company was a woodworking firm in Fairfield, Maine, where it produced many types of light furniture. In 1894 I. Frank Stevens and John E. Cotton moved the firm to Nashua. Within a short time they had built an extensive plant on Bridge Street where they concentrated on making refrigerators. Until 1930 all of these were ice boxes; the electric refrigerator made for a few years after that date was given the brand name of "White Mountain." This has always been very much a family-managed firm under the steady leadership of the Stevens family.

As has already been mentioned in Chapter 11, Thomas Sands was the inventor of the ice cream freezer, which he started making in Laconia. The first Nashua plant of the White Mountain Freezer Co. was on East Hollis Street. After complete destruction in the 1930 fire it was moved to Broad Street. The company owned its own stands of pine trees from which the tubs were made. The inside of the ice cream container was made of pure tin and the company had its own foundry for the cast iron parts. The early freezers were, of course, cranked by hand, a pleasant chore for the children in a household since anticipation of the delicious results of the cranking lightened the tedium. Home-made ice cream for Sunday dinner in the hot summer months was a tradition in many homes. These freezers, by the way, are still manufactured at the present time but not in Nashua. In 1963 the company was sold to the Alaska Freezer Company of Winchendon.

Lost Industries

There were two companies whose names were often linked together as prime examples of industries that were started in Nashua and allowed to move away because of indifference and lack of local financial support. An article in the *Daily Press* for April 16, 1898, expressed in rather bitter terms the feelings that many Nashuans had about the loss of such companies. The author cited these two companies, the Nashua Watch Company and the Weed Sewing Machine Company, as especially great losses and made the following statement:

Why have they not stayed? Because the rich men of this town did not care a rap for its business or its prosperity. They sent their money to Boston and when these firms wanted a few thousand dollars to get a good start or to pull them through a bad year, they couldn't get it here and had to go elsewhere. This town has been built up by the labouring people; the moneyed men have done nothing for Nashua.

The Weed Sewing Machine Company was one of several abortive attempts to develop this type of industry. Since Elias Howe started tinkering during the two years he lived here, it would have been appropriate if a solid business based on the perfected sewing machine had taken hold. One such firm was run by J. and S. Chase who started producing the brand known as the Weed machine in 1856. Financial problems caused removal of the business to Hartford, Connecticut, but in 1866 it came back to Nashua using the name Weed Sewing Machine Company. The firm soon moved to Boston, however, where it ended up making bicycles. The sewing machine was one of the most revolutionary inventions of the entire century, creating the ready-made garment industry and lightening the chore of home sewing. It would have been, without a doubt, a great boost to Nashua if a large and prosperous business based on this machine had been built up here. Fate ruled otherwise but many persons never ceased lamenting the fact.

The Nashua Watch Company was regarded as a particularly sad loss because it had made such a brilliant technological start in Nashua. Many people felt that the fame and prestige acquired by the Waltham Watch Company could have been the Nashua Watch Company's. Leonard Noyes, who made the Nashua Lock Company a resounding success, helped to finance the watch company when it was first established in 1859 by raising $100,000 in capital. Noyes had been proprietor of a small clock-making factory which was in operation during the 1830s. Among those making clocks for Noyes was a man named Belding Dart Bingham, who later ran a watch and clock shop in the Long Block on Main Street. To learn more about the trade of watchmaking Bingham spent some time working for the American Watch Company in Waltham, Massachusetts. He and the Assistant Superintendent, Nelson P. Stratton, decided to start their own watch company, Bingham suggesting Nashua as an excellent location. Five other watchmakers were lured away from the American Watch Company to work in the new venture. Because these men were especially skilled craftsmen, the new company was able to place on the market a really fine watch. The company bought the Washington House, which in 1852 had been moved to Bowers and Main Street, to use as their factory. Unfortunately the Civil War created a demand for cheaper pocket watches for the soldiers in the field. The company was also handicapped by one technical problem involving the escapement in the watch. After the firm started to run out of money the stockholders refused to invest any more funds and it was purchased for $53,000 by the American Watch Company which moved it to Waltham in 1862. The "Nashua Department" of the company was maintained as a separate operation because the watch developed in Nashua was considered an especially fine product. After 1906 the American Watch Company became known as the Waltham Watch Company.

Still Other Enterprises

From the tanned hides of animals came leather, the basic material for another important Nashua product—shoes. This industry was developed in the last quarter of the century, starting with Crain, Leland and Moody in 1874. The Washington House building was their first headquarters where they made about 1,200 pairs of shoes daily and employed two hundred people. In 1879 three officers of this company, Frank E. Anderson, George E. Anderson, and F.W. Estabrook, formed a partnership to set up their own shoe company, Estabrook and Anderson. The Second National Bank assisted them in financing their enterprise. A factory building between Palm and Pine Streets off West Hollis Street was built in 1885 when the firm required more space for its very successful business. Toward the end of the century the firm was making ten thousand pairs of shoes a day and employed as

Roswell T. Smith, book store owner, prolific inventor, and author of the chapter on "Manufactures" in Parker's "History."

many as one thousand workers, but it ceased operations in 1900. Other shoe factories included Brackett & Co. on East Hollis Street and the Nashua Boot and Shoe Manufacturing Company on Allds Street.

Food industries included crackers and confectionary. The earliest cracker maker in the 1820s had a simple but effective system for getting his dough rolled out and baked. After he had prepared the mixture Stephen Bates blew a horn and the housewives in the neighborhood converged on the bakery to finish the production. The Seth Chandler flour and grain business was founded on profits from the bakery business. Chandler (Mayor in 1873) owned a bakery from 1855 to 1860 on Mulberry Street. This same bakery was later owned by Nahum W. Burke

Advertising postcard of 1850 promoting Nashua-made sewing machines.

The Washington House had a versatile career. It served as a
hotel until 1852 when it was moved down Main St. to the corner
of Bowers, and subsequently housed several Nashua   industries.

and his son Charles H. Burke (Mayor in 1889 and 1890). The Burke bakery was famous throughout the Greater Nashua area, as they made a specialty of home deliveries.

Seth Chandler went on to make a fortune in the grain business. In 1866 he bought a flour and grain store that had been started in 1845 by Thomas Chase. Chase was another poor young man from out of town (he was born and reared in Dunbarton) who contributed to Nashua's nineteenth century industrial growth and ended up a very rich man. His first job when he arrived here in 1823 was to clear the trees from the lands bought up by the Nashua Manufacturing Company. Next he went into the hotel business, helping to build the Washington House when it stood on the corner of Factory and Main Streets. (As the genial landlord and host of this hotel, he entertained President Andrew Jackson on a visit to Nashua in 1833.) Chase was in the carriage business for a while and then got interested in railroads, becoming a director of the Nashua and Worcester Railroad. He crowned this amazing career by heading the Nashua Iron and Steel Works.

To go back to Seth Chandler and his flour and grain enterprise: In 1877 he built a grain elevator and installed three runs of mill stones at the northwest corner of Main and West Hollis Streets. His elevator was a prominent feature of the Main Street landscape until it burned down in 1925. He also made cement sewer pipe, another business he bought from Chase.

In 1898 large ads were placed in the local newspapers announcing the auctioning off of part of the Water Street industrial area. The street plans featured in the ads give a good idea of the layout of buildings along the street. The property sold was owned by the American Bobbin, Spool & Shuttle Co. As the century neared its end this sale of property, where a bustling industry had once flourished, seemed to mark the passing of an industrial era of a style that would never be seen again.

The complete list of inventions by Nashuans during this period is far too long to include here. A comprehensive list of patents from 1881 to 1936 is included in the WPA Historical Project volume, *A List of Active Industries*. Roswell T. Smith wins the prize for the most inventions with seventeen to his credit, including an embroidery machine, a music perforator, and an automobile piano.

If one were to summarize trends noted in this industrial era, three stand out significantly:

(1) Many of the industries were run by family groups—brothers or fathers/sons or a combination of these relationships. Daughters played an indirect role in some cases by bringing into the family husbands who became part of the management team of the business. (Researchers were unable to verify a report that there was at one time a lady who was the boss of one of the foundries.)

(2) Certain key figures crop up repeatedly as playing a directing role in several different businesses, sometimes in succession, more often simultaneously. Since these same men are listed as directors of the banks, railroads, and other commercial organizations, it is obvious that there was an elite group of brilliant (as well as very busy) persons who controlled Nashua business and industry.

(3) There was a tendency to keep industrial operations on a small-town, strictly local basis. Roswell T. Smith, that astute observer of the scene who would have undoubtedly called himself only a "book store owner and tinkerer," made an observation to this effect:

When we see the position Nashua assumed as the mother of new enterprises, we wonder at results. Nashua shook the bush and other towns gathered the fruit. Why was this? It was because our business men were provincial and not cosmopolitan; it was because Nashua was simply an expansion of Dunstable; its views did not extend to the far

Thomas Chase, builder of the Washington House.

west; its centre was Boston instead of New York.

As in other areas of Nashua history, reference is made to the research materials gathered by the WPA Historical Project during the 1930s. Readers will find a wealth of information on many of the smaller companies not covered here, as well as fuller detail on industry in general, in *A List of Active Industries* and *Discontinued Industries*.

14

The Civil War

The opening of the War of the Rebellion found me a schoolboy in Nashua, sixteen years of age and in the second year at the High School. I remember clearly the morning of April 12, 1861. I was standing at one of the counters of the store, folding the morning papers, when telegraph wires flashed the news of the firing upon Fort Sumter . . . Several customers were in the store and all, as by a flash of lightning, were stirred to the highest pitch of excitement. I was scarcely able to continue my work and, with a feeling incident to youth, I inwardly rejoiced and was at once filled with a determination to have a part in it.

THIS IS what one Nashuan, Elbridge J. Copp, was doing on the day the Civil War began. Another was much closer to the scene of action, for Lieutenant John G. Foster was on duty at Fort Sumter itself. For several months, from the wall of the fort, in the entrance to Charlestown Harbor, Foster had observed and noted all movements of the South Carolina Militia. His dispatches to the Chief Engineer's office in Washington reported on the progress of his work, strengthening the fortifications at Sumter, and on the movements of the troops outside the fort. Although mail was delivered regularly, provisions and reinforcements only trickled into the fort. It was, in fact, the focal point of a blockade by the local militia. In a dispatch directed to the Chief Engineer of the Army, Foster suggested that reinforcements should not be sent to the fort, as such an attempt would meet with minimal success. In the same month he advised a landing operating on nearby Sullivan Islands instead. Foster realized the perilous position of both the fort and the Union. In his dispatch he stated: "But if the whole south is to secede from the Union, a conflict here and a Civil War can only be avoided by giving up this fort sooner or later. We are, however, all prepared to go all lengths in its defense if the government requires it."

In one of his last recorded dispatches, dated April 6, 1861, Foster expressed concerned skepticism regarding the fort's ability to withstand an outright attack or bombardment. His feelings were based on personal knowledge, since he was the officer who had complete control of the rebuilding of the fortifications. On April 9 he wrote, "I am very busy and am doing all that can be done with the means dispensable." On April 12 the South Carolina forces opened fire and by April 14 the fort had surrendered. As Foster had feared four months earlier, the fort was given up and a Civil War had finally become a reality.

On Saturday, July 27, 1861, Elbridge J. Copp, the sixteen-year-old schoolboy who had been working at his part-time job in a store when the news was flashed that the conflict had broken out, read in the *New Hampshire Telegraph* that Captain James F. Randlett had been appointed the recruiting officer to aid in filling the ranks of the Third Regiment of Volunteers. The article noted that "he has twenty or thirty young men of the best class ready to go as a company." Copp later recalled his resolution and determination to become actively involved in the war, and related the following adventure:

James F. Randlett was commissioned to raise a company for the Third Regiment and had opened a recruiting office in the attic of the City Hall Building, and to Captain Randlett I made known my purpose to enlist in his company, if I could get the consent of my father. He thought I was rather small for a soldier, not quite up to the standard in age, nor feet and inches. This did not faze me, however; I was fully determined to go and was not long in persuading Captain Randlett that I could be of service to him in the capacity of clerk, if not in the ranks. I was then in a position to approach my father to secure his consent to the enlistment. At first it was a flat refusal, to him it was absurd that a boy of my age should go into the army. He finally gave his consent, however, upon the condition that I should go as a clerk to the Captain of the Company and with the understanding that I was not to be in the ranks in the event of a battle. I do not know what pledges were made, but I remember well the promise of the Captain to my father that he would be my friend and protector. In the formalities required for the enlistment, I cannot say whether I stood on tip-toes to reach the required height or the Captain used his discretion in making the entry. Under the law, 18 years was the age limit and here again I suppose the Captain used his discretion. It was fixed up, however, in some way, and I became a private in the ranks of Company F, 3rd Regiment, N.H. Volunteers and we were soon off to the seat of the war.

Elbridge Copp, who thus managed to enlist at age sixteen, received a commission as Lieutenant at age eighteen in 1863, one of the youngest commissioned officers to rise from the ranks. Though his commission was unique, his story was not, as many thousands of other boys across the country enlisted in the Army, leaving their friends and family to join their comrades-in-arms.

The Hour of Need

The events leading up to the outbreak of the Civil War occupied the thoughts of most Nashuans for several months in 1860 and 1861. The public rooms of the Indian Head Coffee House, the Tremont House, and other taverns in town resounded with the din of discussion and debate of the issues— slavery and states' rights. With the help of the local newspapers, people eagerly followed the fast-moving developments. When the crisis was finally

Colonel Elbridge J. Copp.

reached, they received the news with a sense of grim resolution, as they faced the stark fact that problems insoluble in Congress would now have to be decided on the battlefield.

When President Abraham Lincoln made his plea for an army to put down the rebellion, the response was expressed in a popular saying, "We are coming, Father Abraham, fifty thousand strong." The quota for New Hampshire was one regiment and this initial call was for a three-month term of enlistment. Since New Hampshire had no organized standing militia, the process of enlistment prevented the immediate dispatch of troops to Washington. When this delay was criticized in some Massachusetts newspapers, the Nashua *New Hampshire Telegraph* responded with an editorial entitled, "To Our Friends in Massachusetts." It assured them ". . . that New Hampshire had never failed her country in its hour of need and would not do so now." During the course of the war, fourteen regiments were raised in the state and Nashuans filled the ranks of every one. According to the records, Nashua provided 1,348 men for the war, including only thirty-four substitutes.

And so it was that the men of Nashua kept their word, as groups volunteered for duty in the First New Hampshire Regiment. The Niagara Fire Engine Company enlisted seventy-eight men and the Granite State Cadets voted to render their services

Fort Sumter S.C.
February 5th 1861

Genl Jos. G. Totten
Chief Engineer U.S.A
Washington D.C.

General   The sketch upon the margin below gives a pretty
correct idea of the position of the works on Cummings Point thrown
up by the South Carolinians. Of course it is subject to errors
arising from the distance at which I am obliged to obtain the
information by means of the spy-glass alone.
The lines of the work are
not yet complete. The main
effort having been directed
to getting ready those guns
that are intended to fire
upon this work. All the
guns that I have indicated
by a + are (or appear to be)
in position, and covered
by bomb proof roofs. Those
as a.a. are covered by heavy
timbers laid horizontally
upon firm timber supports,
Similar to the marginal
sketch. The revetment of
the cheeks of the embrasures
appear to be formed of palmetto
logs, as also the revetment
of the interior slope, near
the guns. The horizontal
timbers are large
12" raft sticks.

Fort Morris

Bomb proof No 1 at a.a

covered, apparently by a lighter timber or planking running at
right angles to the timbers. The guns at a.a. were then
mounted upon their carriages. The guns (which I suspect from their
using a gin in the operation, are some of the barbette carriage
from Castle Pinckney or Fort Moultrie) at the time I arrived
this morning. Subsequently the rough opening of the cheeks of the
embrasures was made and the revetment of the cheeks
commenced. The second bomb proof battery is built different
The timbers on top are sloped at an angle of 45° about as
in the sketch. They
rest upon two horizontal
supports parallel to the direction
of the battery, one higher than
the other, and these
are supported

Bomb proof Battery No 2

Page from General John G. Foster's "Letter Book."
This letter was sent from Fort Sumter in February,
1861 when Foster was a Captain of Engineers.

to the Governor in order to release other men for duty. Within a few weeks, Nashua had provided enough men to fill both Company E and Company F of the First New Hampshire Regiment. The records of these companies indicate that there were no substitutes or deserters in either of them.

As more and more regiments were raised, newspaper notices requesting enlistees were common. On April 27, 1861, Nashuans read that "active measures are now also afoot for another rifle company so that Nashua stands ready to furnish three hundred men if required." As the war continued from three months to a year and even longer, it became increasingly difficult to recruit enlistments to fill the ranks of new and existing regiments. To provide an incentive for enlistments, many communities began to offer cash bounties for new recruits. Nashua city records indicate that bounties were not offered here until 1862, when the City voted to pay one hundred dollars for each enlistee who volunteered for service. Over the next two years the enlistment bounty climbed as high as six hundred dollars per man. During the course of the entire four years of the war, Nashua appropriated $27,000 to pay enlistment bounties.

While the men of Nashua were prompt in answering the call to arms, so too was the City in allocating monies to aid the families of soldiers. On April 20, 1861, just five days after the surrender of Fort Sumter, the Common Council proposed and passed a soldiers' aid resolution. It became effective in September of 1861, providing one dollar per week for the wife of an enlistee, and one dollar per week for each child and dependent parent. A twelve dollar monthly limit per family was the only restriction. The initial allocation of five thousand dollars must have been inadequate for in March of 1862 another ten thousand dollars was expended for the soldiers' family relief fund. Later that year another twenty thousand dollars was again allocated for the same purpose. The city fathers made a very strong positive commitment toward the war effort, not only with bounties for recruits but also with aid for as many as 310 families.

Sometimes patriotic fervor got out of hand. *The New Hampshire Telegraph* of April 27, 1861, told the story of the South Carolina man who was seized in Nashua for having expressed disunion sentiments. Leading citizens barely managed to rescue him from hanging at the hands of certain locals, and he was required to leave town in half an hour.

How the Women Contributed

While the men were busy enlisting in the Army or running Southern sympathizers out of town, the women of Nashua were making their own substantial contributions. The ladies were deeply concerned for the well-being of the troops, as many of their husbands, fathers, and sons were in the military ranks. Their first major undertaking was organization of a levee for the departing enlistees of the First Regiment in the spring of 1861. (A levee was an evening of dancing, entertainment, and refreshments, for which an admission charge was paid. It was a favorite fund-raising occasion at that time.) This provided the departing soldiers, who were guests of honor, with a gala evening and furnished the hostesses with funds to buy and make needed articles for them. The proceeds totaled $315.51, enough to purchase cloth to make 222 shirts and 28 handkerchiefs and towels for the men of Companies C and F of the First Regiment.

With feelings of concern and urgency the women dedicated themselves to the war effort, as they graciously accepted the responsibility of caring for the men's personal needs. Unfortunately, however, they could not always agree on the priority need. The newspapers carried many suggestions on this subject. On May 18, 1861, one noted that Dr. Crosby, the surgeon of the First Regiment, was seeking bandages made of unbleached muslin, in strips from one inch to four inches wide. Specific directions for making and packing the bandages were given. The paper also noted a letter from a New Hampshire lady who wrote: "Our volunteer soldiers now in Washington are suffering from the sun upon their exposed heads and necks, because of the small caps and short hair." She suggested havelocks as a badly needed item and included the offer of a pattern to anyone who wished to make some.

Although the Army provided each enlistee with a uniform and with equipment that included a rifle, some rather necessary items were not part of the general issue in addition to their army rifles. The controversy in Nashua revolved around the question of which was more beneficial to a man in the field, a revolver or an extra blanket. The local *New Hampshire Telegraph* took a strong stand on the issue when, on April 27, 1861, it stated: "The idea that every soldier for the war be armed with a revolver is giving place to one that an extra blanket is worth a good deal to a soldier . . . An extra blanket, stockings and clothing will save more lives than revolvers."

This position was confirmed in a letter from a member of the Niagara Rifle Company, who described life at Camp Union in Concord prior to leaving for Washington. He pointed out, "Both Companies grumble a little about revolvers since they are the only ones on the field that have not been presented with them, but the thing that we most need now is a rubber blanket." Eventually the problem was resolved when the ladies decided to use their time, energy, and money to make clothing for the soldiers.

Groups of women and girls met for sewing sessions in various private homes throughout the city. In order to organize and coordinate this city-wide effort, Miss Lucy Thayer and her sister, Kate, in February, 1863, founded the Young Ladies Soldiers Aid Society, dedicated to raising funds and providing articles of clothing for the troops. The organization was not a weekly gab-fest for fashionable young single ladies who had nothing better to do now that all the eligible young men had gone off to war. On the contrary, the seriousness of their purpose is evident in a notice of an upcoming work session where they requested that " . . . children unable to donate money or talent had better leave the room for others." The supplies and clothing they made and sent to the front were primarily functional articles like shirts, stockings, blankets, and bandages. In October of 1861, faced with the imminent approach of winter, they sent out a plea for mittens, made with a thumb and forefinger, so that rifles could still be used.

The directors of this hard-working group were Lucy Thayer, Julia Gilman, Laura Bowers, Lucy Beard, Mary Crombie, Atelia Slater, and Mary Baldwin. Their membership included forty young women, all unmarried. Among them were Harriet Crombie and Maria Laton, both of whom later served as city librarians, Clara Bowers who became Mrs. Frank McKean, Mary Hunt, an heiress who never married, and daughters of the Kendrick, Nutt, Richardson, Shepherd, and Gillis families.

Nurse Adelaide Stevens

While most women were content to work at home to help ease the soldiers' conditions, it was not uncommon for some of the more tenacious females to bring their aid and comfort to the front lines. One such Nashua woman was Mrs. Adelaide Johnson Stevens. At the outbreak of the war Adelaide Johnson was just one of many young girls growing up in Nashua. Aaron Stevens had built up a successful law practice in Nashua when the war broke out in 1861. At the first call for a Union Army, Stevens immediately volunteered for service in the 1st New Hampshire Regiment. He was commissioned a Major for the term of three months. Some time before the outbreak of the war, Aaron and Adelaide had met and become engaged, despite considerable difference in age. At that time Adelaide was barely twenty while Aaron was forty-one. Their plans for a comfortable future together in Nashua were interrupted by the war, and after Stevens enlisted things moved rapidly for the two Nashuans.

On May 19, 1861, they were married, only seventeen days after Stevens was mustered into the army and barely ten days before he was scheduled to leave for Camp Union in Concord. Not content to live a comfortable, yet worrisome, life in Nashua, while her husband faced unknown dangers in the field, Adelaide resolved to do more than sit home and knit socks for the troops.

Shortly after the departure of the 1st New Hampshire Regiment from Concord, Adelaide left the security and comfort of her home in Nashua for the uncertainty and rigors of life as a volunteer nurse. She worked both in hospitals and in the field, bringing comfort and assistance to those who had fallen. In this capacity she was always able to be near her husband. Despite the dangers she was even seen on the battlefield, still in close proximity to her husband. Throughout the war she followed her husband wherever his duty took him.

In 1864 during the assault on Fort Harrison Stevens was wounded and later taken to a field hospital to recuperate. Mrs. Stevens was notified and immediately came to nurse him back to health.

Elbridge Copp was also recuperating from wounds at the same hospital. Before the war Copp had known neither Stevens nor his wife but, upon learning of his presence in the hospital, Copp found him and introduced himself to the colonel. The two Nashuans passed many pleasant hours together, talking of family and friends they left behind in Nashua. While in the hospital Copp had the occasion to meet Mrs. Stevens who evidently made quite an impression on the young soldier. He described their meeting:

I had not known her before the war. I met her here in the hospital, a bright and beautiful young woman but two or three years out of her teens. She stayed there until October when they both returned to Nashua.

The "Copperheads"

While the majority of Nashua men and women went all-out to support the war, there were those who were ardently pro-South in their loyalties. Although few in number, they were quite vocal in their sentiments. Throughout the North, these Southern sympathizers were known as "Copperheads." The Copperheads in Nashua found support and leadership in one of the local newspapers, the *Nashua Gazette*. Its editor was B.B. Whittemore and the offices where it was published were located in the Hunt Building at the southwest corner of Main and Factory Streets. The position of the paper in regard to the war was obvious from some of its editorials and news stories. Early in the conflict the paper published its view regarding the reason for it, citing slavery as the only possible issue. The *New Hampshire Telegraph* responded on May 18, 1861, with an article entitled "Political Concern Over Why We Are Fighting." It emphatically pointed out that:

Some of our friends insist that the Republicans are pushing it [the war] for the abolition of slavery . . . That some men who acted with the Republican party desire its abolition may be true, and some may be anxious to push the war for that purpose. But that such is not the idea of the Republican Party is perfectly apparent . . . The war is for the support of the Union and the Constitution, the enforcement of the laws and the protector of the national flag and for nothing else.

The other paper continued to publish its unorthodox views of the war. In March of 1862 the *Gazette* dedicated its entire front page to the text of Jefferson Davis's inaugural speech. Its editorials called for and supported a policy of total reconciliation with the South, including the restoration of all the rights and privileges of the Confederate States. The mere presence of Copperheads in Nashua proved to be a source of irritation, but the leadership, sympathy, and encouragement they received from the *Nashua Gazette* were more than the townspeople could take. As the paper continued to print flagrant pro-South sentiments, public indig-

nation rose to such a state as to cause a mob scene outside the *Gazette* office.

The size and state of excitement of the mob grew rapidly. They were prepared to tear down the building and hang the editor. They might have succeeded in one, if not the other, had it not been for the intervention of General Israel Hunt. From an upper story window Hunt was able to calm the crowd enough to make them listen to reason. He prevented any wanton destruction by reminding the mob that he owned the building and begging it to spare his property. But the crowd still wanted to see the end of B.B. Whittemore, the editor. Hunt again assured them that the editor would refrain from printing pro-South sentiments. The crowd, still not satisfied, called for the editor to put out an American flag. He eventually complied with this demand, whereupon the crowd responded with a cheer for the Union and dispersed.

This stifling of the press did not, however, lessen the feelings of other Copperheads in town. Elbridge Copp recalls an incident of Copperheadism on Main Street after one of the battles in which the Union lost. Several Copperheads gathered on the sidewalk at the south end of the Main Street Bridge and raised a cheer in praise of the Rebel victory. Their noise and continued cheers attracted a large crowd and, although many men were present among the spectators, none of them made any at-

General A.F. Stevens.

tempt to quiet them. Across the street a jeweler, C.E. Richardson, witnessed the entire affair. Being moved by loyalty to his country and contempt for his neighbors, he took his revolver, ran across the street, and fired above the heads of the crowd. He then ordered them all to "shut up and disperse."

Still another incident of anti-Union sentiment caused almost as much commotion. According to Copp, at the conclusion of a particular weekly church service, the minister called for a prayer for the Union. At that point a man in the congregation demanded that the choir immediately sing "Dixie." The congregation was so evenly split in their loyalties between North and South that this seemingly insignificant confrontation caused a permanent rift in the church body. The church disbanded, never to meet again. As far as can be determined, this congregation was the Free Will Baptist Church, since after 1861 it was no longer listed in the Nashua directory.

Wartime Diversions and Amusements

Despite the prolonged uncertainty about the outcome of the war, coupled with the possibility of impending violence at the hands of Southern sympathizers, the folks in Nashua managed to find a few diversions and amusements to brighten their austere lives.

Civic celebrations, although few in number, were far from extinct. One such celebration which was eagerly awaited was the return of the 1st New Hampshire Regiment upon the completion of their three-month enlistment. Evidently there was no apparent plan for a welcoming home celebration since shortly before their anticipated arrival the *New Hampshire Telegraph* stated:

. . . in the course of a week or two the 1st Regiment will return from the war. Whether they shall have been exposed to deadly peril in the imminent breach and come home with their ranks thinned or decimated or whether they shall have escaped such peril they will be equally entitled to an honorable reception and we trust that the citizens will if the city authorities do not see that a fitting "wecome home" is given them.

This public notice evidently spurred the city fathers to action for on August 3, 1861, just a few days from the regiment's arrival the paper printed a notice

that a reception for homecoming soldiers was being planned. The city fathers were to participate and they extended an invitation to the Governors Horse Guards, Granite State Cadets, Fire Department, and citizens to participate.

The *Nashua Gazette* reported on March 29, 1862, that the first Saint Patrick's Day celebration in the history of Nashua was a brilliant success. A festive supper was followed by dancing at the Indian Head House, where numerous toasts were offered.

Reports From the Front

Even though there were many local diversions to occupy the thoughts of Nashuans no one was at a loss for information regarding the progress of the war. From the first news of Sumter to the surrender at Appomattox the weekly *New Hampshire Telegraph* kept its readers informed.

On occasion a notice would appear to announce that a local soldier, home from the war, would be telling of his experiences to any interested listener. Many people flocked to these sessions in an effort to learn all they could about the well-being of fathers, husbands, and sons. On July 27, 1861, shortly before the return of the 1st New Hampshire Regiment from their three-month term of enlistment, the *New Hampshire Telegraph* ran a notice that "Dr. L.F. Locke of this city, who was at the Battle of Bull Run, will relate what he saw at the City Hall on Monday Evening at 8." One could only imagine the horrifying tales of suffering and death that this doctor could relate. For many Nashuans these sessions with returning soldiers gave them a picture of the war which they found neither in the *New Hampshire Telegraph* nor in the tavern dialogues.

The only other sources of information for many folks were the long-awaited letters from the front. Although comforting due to the fact that their men-folk were still alive, these letters brought little if any good news. Many simply described the condition of their camps and lives in the army.

One such letter written by Charles Harris of Company B, 4th New Hampshire Regiment, was received by his cousin in Nashua. The letter, dated May 18, 1864, stated:

I set myself down to write you a few lines to let you know I still live and enjoy good health in this God forsaken country . . . Our camp is close to the beach . . . we have a good sea breeze all the time. That's what keeps us alive. The water is very poor here but we get along some way the best we can. We get whiskey twice a day, that helps the water you know. We have plenty of old salt horse and pork and have cracked corn. I must tell you we had Baked Beans for breakfast this morning. They were nice, I can tell you I hated them worse than I did the devil when I was to home. The army will bring the boys to their appetites.

He also described the location of the camp as being just across the creek from the

'Rebs,' when tide is out we talk across to the Rebs when we are out on picket. We send them papers almost every day. They don't trouble us at all, what I mean they don't fire on our pickets. They could shell us off the island if they was a mind to.

Through his facade of courage and optimism can be detected a glint of homesickness, not uncommon among the ranks.

Have you heard from Levi lately. I should like to see him or hear from him. I suppose Ned is farming this summer. I wish I was with him for all being on this island . . . please send me a paper I am getting short of reading. When we get a paper it seems like seeing the people to home.

Another letter, from Thomas Coffee of the 3rd Regiment, dated August 3, 1863, sought information from home:

I should be very glad to have you write to me and send me all the news. I should like to know if [Willard], lives in the old house yet and how he gets along with the farm, and if he will have good crops this year. If I ever get home I hope I shall work with him again . . .

That hope never materialized, for Thomas Coffee, like thousands of others, gave his life on the battlefield. He was killed on May 13, 1864.

One Nashuan mentioned earlier who figures prominently in discussions of the Civil War was Brevet Major General John G. Foster. Having come to Nashua in 1833, he was educated locally, then went on to graduate fourth in his class at West Point in 1846. Although not gaining recognition until the Civil War, his active military career began with numerous battles during the Mexican War where he was severely wounded. His non-combat accomplishments are often overshadowed by his other noteworthy deeds which warrant mention as they point up the fact that Foster was indeed a talented and intelligent military officer.

Originally commissioned as an engineer, it was in this field that he excelled. After the Mexican War he returned to West Point for a two-year term as assistant professor of engineering. He was later commissioned Captain of Engineers and was placed in charge of fortifications in Charleston Harbor. During the war he saw active duty on the lines and proved to be as adept at military strategy as at constructing fortifications.

In 1867 he received a commission as Lieutenant Colonel in the Corps of Engineers and in this capacity he returned to the business of fortifications, undertaking surveying and construction operations along the New England Coast. Later in 1869 he published a treatise entitled, *Submarine Blasting in Boston Harbor Mass.: Removal of Tower and Corwin Rocks.* Upon retirement he returned to Nashua where he died in 1874.

It took a long while to complete putting up the statue to General Foster in Foster Square. It was on Memorial Day, 1922, that the statue itself was unveiled with appropriate ceremonies. The cor-

Colonel George Bowers.

Two Nashua ladies of the Civil War period . . . possibly the
Crombie sisters, one of whom, Harriet, was
librarian from 1889 to 1915.

nerstone and pedestal had been installed at the semicentennial celebration in 1903.

"Lee Has Surrendered!"

In the spring of 1865 Elbridge Copp was home on leave recuperating from wounds received earlier. While here he worked in his uncle's book store on Main Street, which also sold the local and Boston newspapers. Whenever a big story broke, the Boston paper would wire the headline and ask how many extra papers they should send.

On the afternoon of April 9, 1865, the wire ticked out the news that Lee had surrendered followed by the usual question. Copp received the wire, read it carefully to be certain, then resolved to make the news known. Much to the astonishment of some customers in the store he took a small cannon usu-ally used on July Fourth celebrations from under the counter, loaded it, and brought it out into the street. Without a word of explanation he heated the steam poker and touched off the cannon.

The ensuing explosion broke all the windows in the store and attracted quite a crowd. When the smoke cleared he began to shout "Lee has surrendered! Lee has surrendered!" He quickly reloaded and refired the cannon whereupon the crowd took up the cheer, "Lee has surrendered!"

After four years of hardship, suffering, and anguish, the war was finally over. Some took comfort in the fact that their men were returning. Many found comfort in the fact that they no longer had to live under the cloud of uncertainty regarding the whereabouts of their men. In any event reunited couples and widows alike at last could celebrate the end of the war and the beginning of a new era in Nashua.

15

New Blood
Enters the Stream

NASHUA
———

Etrangère à l'orgueil des vastes métropoles,
Elle a pour gratte-ciel des cheminées d'usines
Et des clochers nombreux, et pour fier acropole
Des maisons de negoce ou le veau d'or rumine.

Quelques ètangs visqueux et deux cours d'eau ravinent
La glebe de ciment de ses rues bénévoles.
Provinciale et terne elle a la sombre mine
D'un homme resigne qu'un faux destin cajole.

Mais la vie et la mort conspirèrent un jour
Pour y fixer mon temps avec des clous solides—
Car mon pere et ma mère y dorment pour toujours,

J'y ai connu mon fils; ici l'amour candide
D'une épouse et de l'Art a su m'illuminer,
–Dites-moi quels pays seraient plus fortunés.

–Leo Levesque

ONE DAY in 1825 a poor Irishman named John Donahoe left Montreal and headed for a small village he had heard about, now called Nashua, in hopes of making a new and better home. Arriving here late in the day, he began searching for a place to stay but was shocked to find that the townspeople would not give him the time of day, let alone a bed for the night. Deeply prejudiced against Catholics, and not particularly fond of foreigners, most gave Donahoe a bitterly cool reception. Unlike the rest, Colonel Mark Gillis kindly offered a resting place in a basement to the weary newcomer. Thus, according to local legend, the first Roman Catholic came to Nashua. Whether or not the story is true, it seems certain that by the 1830s a few Irish stayed at least temporarily. Among the first known arrivals were Michael Earley and John and Patrick Donahue, the latter two residing at the building called the Old Tontine. Michael Earley was the first naturalized citizen in Hillsborough County. He cooked and served meals to the Irish railroad workers and acquired a large piece of property on Kinsley Street which was bought by the Catholic Diocese as the site for St. Joseph's Hospital.

The Irish Arrive

In the early 1800s there was such a rush of Irish and other emigrants reaching Boston that a law was enacted temporarily prohibiting the landing of anyone without visible means of support. Consequently many Irish emigrants who wanted to come to New England cities, such as Lowell or Nashua, were shipped to Montreal. Then, lugging as much of their belongings as they could, they began traveling on foot the long distance southward. Men, women, and children were seen trudging along, often begging for food along the way.

In 1845 with the start in construction of the Wilton Railroad the influx of immigrant laborers grew significantly. That same year the crops failed in Ireland, resulting in a widespread famine which sent thousands of emigrants fleeing to the United States. Upon arriving they scattered in all directions, many traveling to industrial areas. By 1850 about one hundred had found their way to Nashua. Their first employment was as laborers on railroad, roadbuilding, and ditchdigging crews.

By 1855 an estimated four hundred Irish lived in Nashua, necessitating the sending of a permanent pastor to serve Mass. Soon Father John O'Donnell came and began holding services in the Franklin Hall, which was later called the Franklin Opera House. In 1856 a church was begun on Temple Street and upon completion it was dedicated and named the Immaculate Conception parish by the Bishop of Portland, Maine, in November, 1857.

On a gray November day in 1855, shortly after Father O'Donnell arrived, an incident occurred involving two old workmen who were moving his furnishings into his newly-rented house. Everything was going smoothly until the workers began struggling to carry a large bedstead, with a massive headboard such as they had never seen before, up a flight of stairs to the bedroom. When the bed was finally set up, one of the men cautiously inquired if it was true that the huge device was really a torture rack on which the priest punished Protestants, as had been rumored before his arrival. Father O'Donnell, displaying a quick flash of his Irish wit, pretended to go along with the story, solemnly assuring the man that he had guessed the real purpose of the strange-looking piece of furniture. Suddenly, both of the movers rushed from the house in terror, convinced that the Devil himself had taken up residence in Nashua at last! However, such was not the case, since the Father was a kindly man who quickly earned the respect and admiration of parishioners and non-Catholics alike. His warmth and understanding was greatly appreciated by both immigrant and longtime resident.

As the 1850s progressed there was a large increase of Irish immigrants to the city. Of the approximate ten thousand population in 1856, about two thousand were newly arrived Irish. Many settled in a small area around High Street, popularly called "High Rock." However, as the years passed, most migrated outward to other areas including Crown Hill, Kinsley Street, and Lake Street.

In January, 1882, Father O'Donnell died, having served a long career helping his parish and the community as a whole. Besides building the first Catholic church in Nashua and further expanding the parish, he was a valuable member of the School Board for many years. Through periods of both financial depression and prosperity Nashuans came to respect and rely upon this prodigious worker who contributed so much to the city.

The Reverend Father Houlihan succeeded Father O'Donnell and began immediately to make further changes. In 1884 he purchased the old Indian Head House on Concord Street. It was altered, rebuilt, and reopened in September, 1885, as a parochial school named St. Rose's Academy. At his request a small group of nuns led by the Reverend Mother M. Francis of the Sisters of Mercy was placed in charge of teaching at the school.

After several years of impaired health Father Houlihan died in March, 1891, and was followed by the Reverend Edmund E. Buckle. Soon he began a series of improvements, beginning with the building of the Sacred Heart School on the corner of Spring and Eldredge Streets in 1892. This central location was acquired by first selling the St. Rose's Academy property and then purchasing the Hosmer estate on Spring Street. The next major project was the building of a new church, needed because of the increasing number of parishioners. In June, 1901, Father Buckle began plans for the new structure to be located on Spring Street, on the site of an old cement house which recently had served as the home of the local Sisters of Mercy. On Easter Sunday in April, 1909, he proudly opened the partially-completed church to visitors. Unfortunately Father Buckle died on June 25, 1909, his new church unfinished. Bishop Guertin appointed the energetic Reverend Matthew Creamer to finish the task, and three months later, on Christmas Day, 1909, the new priest offered Mass in the completed church named St. Patrick's in honor of the patron saint of the Irish people. Soon after, the old church was sold to the Lithuanian parish and Father Creamer industriously proceeded to improve the parish until his death on October 1, 1936.

Throughout the years the Irish population remained devoted to their faith and their community. By the 1930s there were an estimated 4,620 Irish-Americans in Nashua out of a population of about thirty-two thousand. This 14.4 percent continued to play an active part in community life, in business, education, government, and dozens of other valuable pursuits. Among the notable Nashuans of the early 1900s from Irish families were James B. Crowley who started an insurance agency and William F. Sullivan. Both served terms as mayor. Another notable individual was Judge Frank B. Clancy whose sisters Sadie and Bessie served long careers as Nashua teachers. Other prominent families included: Haggerty, McGlynn, O'Grady, and Shea. Two of the earliest Irish Catholic organizations in the city were the Ancient Order of Hibernians, established in 1868, and the local Knights of Columbus, founded in 1895.

From a modest transient beginning on railroad construction crews in the 1840s the Irish grew to become a permanent group in Nashua and as the 1800s closed they had gradually assimilated and merged into the mainstream of society.

Arrival of the French

Though inconclusive, it appears that the first French residents in Nashua were an Acadian family consisting of Peter Landeree, his wife Sarah, and a son Peter. They supposedly arrived in August, 1760, but little is known about them and no further trace of this family is evident in the years that followed.

In 1839 a John Landry came here from Canada, a descendant of French emigrants. Employed by George Underhill, the two gained a reputation as very skillful axe makers. Once established in his trade, Landry brought his wife and family to join him. His descendants living in Nashua in the 1850s were Napoleon and Joseph Landry.

On November 18, 1852, a Lambert family arrived from East Douglas, Massachusetts. The father was a blacksmith by trade and became employed with the Underhill Edge Tool Company until 1861 when he enlisted in Company E, Eighth New Hampshire Regiment. Working his way up from private to sergeant, he served in the Civil War until 1863 when he was wounded at the siege of Port Hudson.

In 1853 there were an estimated sixteen French families living in Nashua. After arriving from Canada most settled in the area called Edgeville and began working at various trades. One woman ran a boarding house for the Jackson Mill. The occupations of the men included laborer, bobbin maker, toolmaker, shoemaker, woodchopper, and machinist.

Following the Civil War the number of French Canadian immigrants swelled to about fifteen hundred by 1870 and had increased greatly by 1872. This first great wave of Canadian immigration came at a time when the textile mills were rapidly expanding and in need of more help. Not surprisingly other people also took jobs related to the mills, though at first the trend was gradual. Still others were interested only in seasonal work in lumbering, farming, and construction. Many settlers lived in the tenement district just south of Nashua Manufacturing and west of "High Rock." Popularly called "French Village," this area expanded to Hollis Street and west to Ledge Street. Then suddenly in 1873 came a nation-wide economic collapse which slowed the lumber industry drastically and affected railroad construction, banking, and textiles. Hours and wages were cut and many plants simply shut down, thus curbing the demand for workers and ending large-scale immigration.

Most of the French attended Father O'Donnell's church during the 1860s until on June 25, 1871, a Father Girard arrived and conducted Mass for a short time in the old Episcopal Church of St. Luke's which stood at the fork of Temple and East Pearl Streets. In November, 1871, he was replaced by Father Jean-Baptiste Henri Victor Milette from Montreal. Almost immediately work began on the first Franco-American church in Nashua. With its completion and dedication June 8, 1873, the structure on Hollis Street was welcomed by more than twenty-two hundred parishioners. Named in honor of the patron saint of Catholic youth, St. Aloysius, born Luigi Gonzaga, the new church came to be called Saint Louis de Gonzague. Through many decades it served generations of faithful parishioners until it was severely damaged by a tragic fire on July 20, 1976. By mid-August, 1977, all except one tower of the structure was torn down in preparation for the building of a new and smaller church.

By 1879 the economy was improving rapidly and mill production once again expanded, requiring more workers. The economic recovery encouraged the second wave of French Canadian migration to New England. From 1879 to the early 1880s thousands left rural Quebec and New Brunswick, to the dismay of the Canadian government. In 1870 Nashua's foreign born population had been 2,325, and predominantly Irish; whereas by 1880 it was 3,565, with most of it French Canadian.

In 1883 St. Louis de Gonzague had 3,360 parishioners and it became apparent that a new church was needed. In 1885 Father Milette requested a division of his parish to accommodate the growing number of churchgoers living in the section north of the Nashua River called "Indian Head" and later "French Hill." By November, 1885, services were being conducted in the basement of a temporary building next to the site of the new church. On Sunday, July 18, 1896, the cornerstone of the new blue Vermont marble structure was laid. Finally in May, 1898, Saint Francis Xavier was dedicated. Meanwhile the parish membership grew to almost 1,700 by 1890. In addition the St. Louis parish had grown to well over 3,200. This was a total of about 25 percent of Nashua's 19,300 population in 1890. In the early 1890s the influx of French Canadians increased sharply again, reflecting a third major wave of immigration.

By 1910 there were 8,962 foreign born Nashuans, of whom 4,830 were French Canadian. In 1936 Nashuans of Franco-American families totaled 14,560, or 45 percent of the total population, and by 1950 they comprised 50 percent of the 34,669 population. Thus this ethnic group became the predominant one in the city, with the labor force in the mills consisting heavily of Franco-Americans.

Among those active in business were Victor Lussier who established a drug store on West Pearl Street in 1886; P.L. Robichaud who began an undertaking business in 1880; Elie W. Labombarde who founded the International Paper Box Machine Co. in 1903, and Alphonse Chagnon, contractor and builder of St. Francis Xavier in 1896. Other prominent individuals from Nashua included Bishop George A. Guertin, Superior Court Judge Henri A. Burque, Mayor Alvin Lucier, City Clerk Irenee D. Ravenelle, and the Board of Health chairman, Dr. Oswald S. Maynard. Most notable of all was Leo Levesque, born in Nashua, November 26, 1900. After attending St. Aloysius parochial school he studied at St. Charles Seminary in Sherbrooke, Nashua Business College, and the Sorbonne in Paris. Under the name Rosaire-Dion Levesque he had published five books by 1939 and earned recognition from the French Academy in France and the Royal Society of Canada. His most critically acclaimed collections of poetry are, *Les Oasis,* 1930, and *Et L'Amour est Venu,* 1931. The famed poet, journalist, and historian enjoyed a long career and until his death in 1974 epitomized the vitality and humanism of Franco-American culture.

Among the factors lending solidarity to the Franco-American community were the Catholic faith, the parochial schools, the common homeland, and of course the French language. More than anything else, the language became the symbol of the

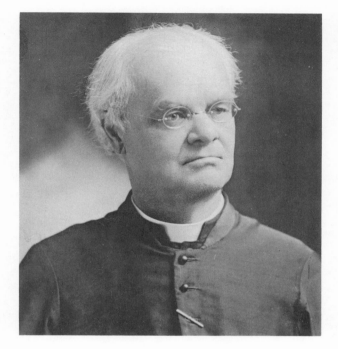

Father Jean-Baptiste Henri Victor Milette, beloved first pastor of St. Louis de Gonzague Church.

survival of the culture here in Nashua. With much pride and emotion many continued to cling to the one feature which demonstrated a clear identity amidst the larger society. Thus a multitude of cultural institutions came to exemplify what has been called "la Survivance."

Leo Levesque (at right) with his literary friend, Louis Dantin.

Helping to disseminate Franco-American news was a local newspaper, *L'Impartial,* which was published from 1898 to 1964. In 1951 the paper changed from two issues a week to one with a decline in subscribers. By 1964 readers had dwindled to the hundreds rather than thousands as in earlier days. Group identification no longer remained the important force. Inter-marriage, with social and economic mobility, plus time, took their toll. More and more individuals, though proud of their heritage, became less affected by it in their daily lives. The eventual decline in the parochial school system further demonstrated the change and gradual acculturation of many in the Franco-American community but their contribution to the community has been important and both examples and reminders of their culture remain.

The Lithuanians

Although there are stories about earlier arrivals the first known Lithuanian to come to Nashua was Peter Kashulines in 1886, followed soon by his brother Joseph in 1889. In the 1890s the number grew steadily. Among the earliest to settle were William Corosa, Anthony (Galinas) Darling, Felexa (Kabashinki) Oakman, Simon Meskinis, Leonard Traynovich, William Backanouska, who served in the Spanish-American War, Katherine Zelanute, Bladis Miskinis, Mike (Bartes) Marshall, Tom (Backanauskas) Backer, and Peter Rusas. The small group came to include individuals of differing interests and trades. Some established restaurants, bakeries, grocery stores, and boarding-houses which catered to their newly arrived countrymen. The first to go into business were Charles Zaelatskas and Felexa Oakman who opened a bar on Tolles Street in 1890. Between 1907-1908 William Corosa operated a grocery store on School Street. Since most did not speak English they tended to live close to each other while becoming oriented in their new home. Many were men who had left their families behind temporarily while they searched for work. Many lived in the Tolles Street area and went to work at Nashua Manufacturing.

In 1904 the Lithuanians had grown in number, necessitating the request for a permanent priest and the formation of their own parish. In 1907 Bishop Guertin sent the Reverend Father Leo Tyllo to be assistant to Father Buckle of the Immaculate Conception Church and serve the Lithuanian community. Then in 1909 when St. Patrick's was opened on Spring Street plans were made to sell the Immaculate Conception church building and rectory on Temple Street to the Lithuanians. In 1910 the transaction was completed and the parish became known as St. Casimir's with the Reverend Leo Tyllo as the first pastor. Soon many improvements were made, including the purchase of cemetery property in Hudson and the formation of organizations to encourage friendship within the new parish. By 1920 the Lithuanian population had reached almost six hundred, with families living in various parts of the city and the breadwinners engaged in a wide variety of occupations, businesses, and professions.

The Polish Group

In 1892 the first of still another nationality settled in Nashua when Mr. and Mrs. Samuel Ross came from Poland. A year later they were running a boarding and rooming house on Temple Street which provided a home for two newcomers, Frank Klaczynski and John Tarnowski who arrived in the fall of 1893. Unable to find work in his trade as a carpenter, Klaczynski worked a short time in a shoe shop before opening a meat and grocery store on Factory Street. This was the first Polish-owned business. It soon became popular with newcomers who also relied on Mr. Klaczynski as interpreter, letter writer, and adviser. Many families found work and new homes with his help.

Within a few years the Polish community grew to several hundred, with many living at "High Rock." As their numbers continued to increase after 1905 the need for unification resulted on March 3, 1907, in the founding of the Jan Sobieski III Organization. Of immediate concern was the need for their own priest, church, and school. Like some other early immigrant groups the Poles attended the Immaculate Conception Church at that time. A special meeting was called and a committee was delegated to request permission from the Bishop to establish a Polish parish. A petition with more than five hundred signatures was gathered and on April 19, 1908, Bishop Guertin granted permission for the founding of the St. Stanislaus parish. Soon the first pastor, the Reverend John Mard, arrived—in April, 1908—but because of poor health he stayed only

until July. His young, energetic successor was the Reverend Francis Taborski who soon bought property on Franklin Street where a new church was built. Construction of the wooden building began in the spring of 1909 and was completed by fall. In September, 1910, the Reverend Louis Wojtys was appointed successor to Father Taborski. Soon a hall was built which was used as a school as well as a meeting place, and in 1914 land was purchased on Pine Hill Road to be used as a cemetery. Then in December, 1915, Father Wojtys left and six months later in 1916 was replaced by the Reverend Peter Kuglawski, who served for five years.

Through the efforts of men such as Frank Klaczynski and Kazimiez Lewkowicz the Polish community founded a parish and continued to grow steadily. By 1920 they exceeded 500 and by 1936 they were approximately 3 percent of the population or about 960 in number. Many owned their own homes and some ran successful businesses. The first child of a Polish family to graduate from Nashua High School was Mary Klaczynski, an honor student in the class of 1917. Others soon followed and went into trades and professions as teachers, nurses, engineers, machinists, and a host of other occupations. One notable individual, Dr. Walter Wroblewski, was a successful physician.

Other Ethnic Groups

By the early twentieth century Nashua's population was becoming more cosmopolitan in character as numerous other nationalities were added. Included were several Italians who came in the 1890s and early 1900s. Stories of several Italian fruit peddlers settling here at an earlier date have not been verified, so this latter group is generally accepted as being first. Among them were Ferdinando Fossa who founded the Fossa Laundry, Peter Mastricola, G. Pederzani, Antonio Rochelle, J. Pedazi, and A. Bacigalupo. Many worked in the fruit business in these early years.

A larger group to settle here were the Armenians. The first to come was Crikos Arigasian who arrived in 1888 bringing several countrymen. Speaking several languages he provided valuable assistance in finding jobs for others, such as in the Moody and Anderson Shoe Shop and the Nashua Lock Co. In 1889 Marshall Markarian arrived and was soon followed by Varto Injan and George Markarian. This small group established the Armenian community in Nashua. In 1897 the Reverend Santigian came to conduct special services at the Pilgrim Church and later the Church of the Good Shepherd. In June, 1898, an account in one of the newspapers told of the deep concern of the Armenian colony over the safety of five fellow countrymen who had gone to the gold fields of the Yukon. A dispatch had been received that a large number of men had been drowned and it was feared that the Nashua Armenians were among them. They had lived in Sullivan's Block on High Street and worked in the shoe shops. By 1936 the Armenian population was estimated at 128.

Early in 1892 a group of Jewish settlers decided to gather for regular services, the first of which were held at the home of Aaron Borofsky on Ferryalls Court. Later in 1895 the group of about fifteen families established the Agudas Achim Lodge with Mark Mandelson as president. In 1899 the name was changed to the Beth Abraham Society and Simon W. Cohen, the first Jewish immigrant to settle in the city, was made president. Meanwhile, property was purchased at the corner of Lock and Cross Streets, and a permanent synagogue was constructed with Rabbi J. Silverman as first Rabbi.

Located on the lower floor of the building was a school for the Jewish children. In 1903 a total of thirty-four families comprised the membership at the synagogue. The officers were: Samuel Blume, President; Samuel Sharpe, Vice President; Mark Mandelson, Secretary; and J. Mirsky, Treasurer. Many wives and daughters were members of the Young Women's Hebrew Association, which was especially active in projects to aid the poor and disadvantaged.

Modernization of the synagogue was completed in 1927 with dedication ceremonies on February 13. By 1936 the Jewish community was estimated at about fifty families totaling about two hundred and fifty persons. Family names included Finn, Mandelson, Sharpe, Pastor, Silber, Willens, Stein, Rudnick, Lovett, and Marcus, among others. Several organizations related to Temple Beth Abraham were established involving men, women, and children in religious and community activities. In 1960 a new synagogue was constructed on Raymond Street and by 1977 membership grew to about 175 families.

In 1906 the first Turks settled in the city including Salis Alicos, Norris Bacu, and Emir Sali Tarus. By 1912 an estimated forty were in Nashua, many working at Nashua Manufacturing and the old Estabrook and Anderson Shoe Co. Several groups lived at 10 Eaton Street for a few years until the majority of them moved west.

In 1908 a society of Roumanians named "Vulture" was founded, consisting of an estimated one hundred members. Among them was Nasi Tamposi who later served as president of the group. By the 1930s many families had left Nashua and the group became inactive. A few who remained were the Daukas and Cassana families. There was also Mrs. Despo Tamposi, born in Macedonia in 1870, who came to Nashua in 1916 and died here July 4, 1935. Her husband Nicholas had been killed earlier in the Turkish-Greek wars. Descendants of Despo and her husband include three sons—Nasi, Spirodon, and George. Earlier in 1907 Nasi came to Nashua at age sixteen and in 1920 he and wife Aspasia ran a farm on Pine Hill Road. Their children include Samuel Tamposi, presently a successful real estate developer, and Nicholas, famed aviator. Spirodon remained in Roumania but George arrived here in 1916. With his wife Sultana, George operated a farm on North Hollis Road.

Still another group who came to Nashua in the early 1900s were several Hungarians who worked mainly as laborers in area farms. Little is known about the few families that settled here in the years that followed.

A small number of Bulgarians and Albanians also came and in 1920 about thirty were living in Nashua. In addition, in the early 1900s numerous Russians temporarily resided here.

Growth of the Greek Community

In 1895 Vasilios Ioannou and his wife came to Nashua from Greece. Within the year a son was born to the young couple. Changing his name to William John he opened the first confectionery store of homemade candies in Nashua. Located in the old Montcalm building, the successful small business continued for nine years until 1904 when it was sold to the Niarchos brothers, newly arrived from Greece. Shortly afterward, William John and his family returned to his homeland.

Until about 1902 the majority of Greeks in Nashua were men either single or married men who had left their relatives behind in Greece. They came to America hoping to earn enough money to send back to their families, and eventually to save enough to pay their own way home. To economize many lived in groups of five to ten per apartment, which quite often was only two or three rooms at most. A

considerable number of these "bachelor" groups lived on Myrtle, Ledge, and Eaton Streets. For a short while the Brackett Shoe Company ran a boarding house on Denton Street which proved unprofitable and was closed. The early Greek immigrant, or "Metanasti," ate, slept, and lived in these very cramped quarters.

In 1902 entire families began arriving. Along with them came a growing number of single girls who soon became the brides of the single men who had come earlier. In addition, wives and children joined husbands as some abandoned all thought of returning to Greece.

An estimated 350 Greeks lived in the city by 1903 with 225 of them Macedonians. The local Greek enclave centered in the area from Pine Street east to Chestnut between Myrtle, West Pearl, and West Hollis Streets. Most were young men living in groups but by now there were about a half dozen entire families. About seventy-five workers were employed in the textile mills with most of the remainder in the shoe shops.

Even though the Greek population suffered a slight setback in late 1903 when numbers of single men headed west to work on the railroad, many felt the need to organize. Beginning earlier in January, 1903, plans had begun for organizing a society aimed at encouraging Greeks to become citizens. On January 19 John Demaras addressed the Greek population assembled in Cercle Montcalm Hall. At a later meeting in February at St. Jean Baptiste Hall the society was formed and named Parthenon with Demaras elected as president. The organization became instrumental in assisting the many new arrivals, some coming to Nashua from Lowell hoping to find jobs in the mills.

The first recorded Greek wedding in Nashua took place on June 12, 1904, when Nicholas J. Surlis, a peddler, married Paraskene Niarhous. Several months later on August 28 Panagiotes Houpis married fellow mill operative Demetra Antiari. Both services were performed by the Reverend George from Lowell. The Houpis wedding was remembered years afterward with great pride as being a true "old country" wedding with all the embellishments and merrymaking typical of such occasions, including music, games, and an elaborate array of foods.

Adjustment Problems

Like their ethnic predecessors the Greek and Balkan groups arriving in Nashua faced the long struggle to gain acceptance and earn a livelihood in a new environment. Their coming was not celebrated with fanfare by the Irish, French, and many others who held jobs in the mills but were still competing elbow to elbow in the limited job market. Each added migration raised fears that the new ethnic group would underbid the wages of the earlier workers. The Greeks soon proved themselves to be steady and reliable. Furthermore their traditional passion for the "coffeehouse" and general aversion to heavy drinking meant that they were relatively free from the Monday morning hangover which habitually retarded mill operations. Favored by the mill overseers but scorned by many of their fellow workers, the Greeks found it necessary to band together and travel in groups to and from work.

Open confrontation occurred periodically such as on June 5, 1901, when the Brackett Shoe Co. attempted to employ a group of Greek workers to replace a work force which was out on strike. As Greeks tried to enter the shop a large and excited crowd swarmed about them, blocking the street. Amid the shouting, pushing, and shoving, knives and guns appeared, and the Greeks fled to a West Pearl Street house for refuge.

Once employed, the newcomers had to cope with some less than cordial fellow workers. The usual disagreements and arguments of factory life sometimes took on ethnic overtones. On one occasion in December, 1903, a young Greek girl at Nashua Manufacturing was badly injured in an argument with another girl over the use of a bobbin truck.

The many minor incidents seem trivial compared to the one on the evening of May 11, 1909, which began when a group of French Canadians were teasing some Greeks who were boarding the seven o'clock trolley in what was called the Belvidere district. The heckling and stone-throwing was interrupted when a patrolman appeared and tried to halt the disturbance, but not before a French boy

grabbed one of the Greeks. Enraged, the Greek allegedly chased him, cornered him in nearby "Pins and Needles" alley off High Street, and stabbed and killed him with a knife. Subsequently charged with manslaughter, he was sentenced to four years in prison. Many people felt he had acted in self-defense and after serving part of his sentence he was released. His countrymen collected a small sum of money and sent him home to Greece. The unfortunate incident further aggravated the tension between the ethnic groups and reinforced their tendency to cluster in their own neighborhoods.

This ethnic population reached a sizable level, encouraging formal plans for organizing a Greek community. A committee was appointed with A. Bacalopoulos as president and about eight members.

Up to that time the Greeks went to church in Lowell or rented the St. Jean Baptiste Hall and invited a visiting priest such as the Reverend George to conduct liturgy. Following a general meeting of the population the Greek Orthodox Church of Annunciation of the Virgin Mary was organized on February 1, 1907. About eleven months later a small cottage was purchased at 50 Ash Street, converted to a church, and used temporarily until it was replaced by a new and larger structure in 1913.

Throughout this early period the members of the Greek community kept especially close ties with their homeland. Many had parents, brothers and sisters, and immediate families in the fatherland where political and social affairs exerted influence here. Of particular concern was the continual political and economic strife caused by warfare between Turkey and Greece and involving other Balkan peoples. With great anxiety they followed news reports of the Balkan War which erupted in October, 1912, between Bulgaria, Serbia, Greece, and others on one side, and Turkey on the other. On October 10, 1912, a contingent of 1,050 Greek-American soldiers, of whom 165 were from Nashua, sailed from Providence on the ship *Patria*. Many were members of military companies organized throughout New England named "Hieros Lohos" or Sacred Company. The Nashua group was commanded by D. Baras, M. Kolkonas, and P. Stergiou. As the weeks passed, news reports of the war prompted additional men to leave for battle so that eventually almost four hundred men departed from Nashua.

An intricate stream of political events precipitated a whirlwind of shocks and changes which affected Nashua's Greek community. Like their countrymen abroad, they disagreed over political issues, particularly over loyalties to either King Constantine or Venizelos. The Greek newspapers, some organizations and societies, and even some leaders in the church took sides. Many in Nashua engaged in heated arguments concerning the political dilemma. Unfortunately church dignitaries in New York and Boston chose to support either side and soon church members in Nashua also split. In 1922 the St. Nicholas community on Palm Street was organized, composed mainly of members faithful to church leaders who supported King Constantine and the Royalist cause. Pressure from the unfortunate chain of events was eased when some of the troublesome bishops were recalled but the schism left marks in the Greek community which required years to heal.

In spite of the politically clouded religious scene many worthwhile projects were completed. Especially active was the Aphrodite Society which in 1923 was reorganized under the name Elpis. Throughout the years this group organized activities and raised money which was used to help the poor, to make needed church repairs, and to assist improvements in Greek community facilities.

The foreign-born Greek population reached about one thousand by 1920 then declined and stabilized at about six hundred by 1930. In addition families of American-born offspring approached and reached adulthood, and began families of their

own. By 1936 about nine restaurants, six grocery stores, five candy stores, two trucking companies, four coffeehouses, and a number of other businesses were Greek-owned.

After fifty years of separation the two churches, the Annunciation and Saint Nicholas, merged into the United Greek Community of Nashua under clergy leadership of the Reverend George Tsoukalas and the Reverend Nicholas Marinos and the lay leadership of presidents George Pappademas and Peter Scontsas. The united congregation decided to build a new House of God and about the beginning of 1973 construction of the new church began at West Hollis Street, directed by Architectural Chairman Zacharias Mandravelis. Early in 1973 the Greek Archdiocese appointed a new priest, the Reverend Soterios Alexopoulos from Holy Trinity Greek Church in Lewiston, Maine, to minister to the faithful in Nashua.

In the summer of 1973 the two old churches were sold—the Annunciation to the Nashua Baptist and Saint Nicholas to the Church of God.

On Sunday, October 28, 1973, the new Greek church at 500 West Hollis Street opened its doors.

On Sunday, October 13, 1974, the church was named Saint Philip after one of the twelve apostles. It is the only church with that name in the Greek Archdiocese of North and South America.

One of the beloved pastors of the Greek Orthodox Community was the Reverend Michael A. Papadopoulos. Father Papadopoulos was the longest resident clergyman of the Nashua Greek

Parish. He served the St. Nicholas Church from October, 1943, until his death in August of 1966.

Although by 1940 large-scale immigration into Nashua had declined, it by no means ceased. French-Canadian workers continued to move here, if only temporarily to earn money to send home to relatives. Following World War II several "war brides" returned with GI's who had been stationed in Europe and elsewhere. A sizable group which has increased recently consists of more than two hundred fifty with Spanish as their main language. In addition there are about 120 persons of Puerto Rican birth or parentage. In all, people from more than two dozen countries are represented in Nashua's population as recorded by the 1970 U.S. Census, including Italy, Russia, Austria, Norway, and Japan. The most recent arrivals include a number of Vietnamese individuals who have come since 1970. Thus Nashua since the last half of the nineteenth century has been and in many ways remains an ethnic community. Though acculturation and assimilation have played an active role, the various ethnic cultures continue to make their valuable heterogeneous mark.

16

Municipal Government and How It Grew

DURING the nineteenth century all municipal operations grew in cost and complexity, as a steadily rising population demanded more services. During the fifty-year period from 1837 to 1887, for example, the budget went from $13,000 to $350,000. In 1837 the cost of town services was less than $3.00 per capita; in 1887 it was roughly $17.00. The simple one page report of 1837, reproduced here, shows that education was on a basis of one child/one dollar, taking less than 10 percent of the total. Other ratios were: 10 percent for regular maintenance of highways and bridges; 40 percent as a separate account for major repairs on the ever-costly Main Street Bridge; 10 percent for "support of paupers," 19 percent to build a new schoolhouse. The town debt at the time was less than $4,000.

Town Finances in the 1840s

Two years later, in the report for the fiscal year that ran from March, 1839, to February, 1840 (from one town meeting to the next), thirty pages were required to explain how the Selectmen had spent $20,000. Schools, including the building of still another schoolhouse, took 25 percent; pauper costs took only 4 percent because very few persons outside the Poor Farm required assistance; highways accounted for 15 percent and the troublesome bridge 22 percent; interest and payment on debt, 12 percent. Police expense was negligible and the only cost of fire protection was payment of a $14 printing bill for the firewards. Miscellaneous items included $8 paid out on bounties on foxes.

In 1840 the population was almost six thousand and the town was on the brink of the civic crisis that was to tear it apart. By 1842 the split between the two sections was an accomplished fact and Nashua itself, limited to the area south of the Nashua River, was thrown entirely on its own resources. Its financial situation was complicated by the need to borrow money to build a twenty-three thousand dollar Town House, since pride dictated that plans to put this building up on its designated site should proceed on schedule. As a result the town now had over eighteen thousand dollars out in notes held by the Nashua bank and fifteen private citizens. Incidentally, several of the lenders were women who regarded loans to the town as a good investment, as well as a way of showing loyalty to their community.

The Town Report for 1844 reveals that out of a total budget of $8,600, 13 percent went for highways and bridges, 23 percent for schools, 10 percent for welfare, 25 percent for old bills and interest on debt, 12 percent for a special appropriation to finish the Town House.

Meanwhile, on the other side of the river, Nashville neatly balanced its budgets from year to year and seems to have had no really pressing financial problems. In 1848 it took the lead in education by including a high school in plans for a new school at the Mount Pleasant location. Not to be outdone, Nashua started a high school in 1851 in rather makeshift quarters in the "Old Brick" on West Pearl Street. A committee appointed to study the high school problem advised that a special building for these upper grades should be erected immediately. The subsequent building on Main Street, not far from the present Church of the Good Shepherd, was built in 1853. By that time, with a reconciliation between Nashua and Nashville, the City of Nashua had been established.

Benefits of the Union

When Nashua and Nashville came together to form a single city total cash assets in the "kitty," to which each town contributed its unexpended balance from the previous year, was $1,976.06. The debt assumed was that of the Town of Nashua, $27,500. The city charter had been issued by the State of New Hampshire and signed by Governor Noah Martin on June 27, 1853. On September 17 of that year both towns voted separately on whether to accept this charter. In Nashua the vote was slightly more than four to three in favor of acceptance; in Nashville it was slightly more than two to one.

Although reunion was by no means a unanimous decision, when the results were announced a spirit of jubilation spread throughout the new city on both sides of the river. Rockets were fired off that evening and a torchlight parade led the way to Franklin Hall, where a huge crowd had gathered for celebration. Albin Beard, the great editor of the *New Hampshire Telegraph,* commented editorially:

. . . we can say in truthfulness and sincerity that it was the happiest day of our whole life. . . . it brought us back to our old position again; it restored us to our friends . . . and beat down the partition wall which separated the community whose interests and sympathies were really one and which could not be sundered.

He then went on to call for a non-partisan election of city officers, since men of all parties on both sides of the river had worked hard together to bring about the reunion.

The New City Administration

Even before the first election, public opinion expressed a preference for Josephus Baldwin, the popular South End bobbin manufacturer, as Mayor. Daniel Abbot was old and ailing and Charles G. Atherton was busy in the United States Senate, so neither was available as a candidate. On October 8 Baldwin was elected Nashua's first Mayor, along with a Board of Aldermen and a Common Council as stipulated in the Charter. On October 15, 1853, these duly elected officials met at the Town House, now called the City Hall, and were sworn into office, with Senator Atherton administering the oath to the Mayor.

The original City Charter divided the city into eight wards, considered little towns in their own right. "Section 4. Each of the city wards shall be a town for the purpose of the election of governor, councillors, senators, etc." A ward elected three selectmen, a moderator, and a town clerk, and held its own town meeting on the second Tuesday of every March. Each ward was entitled to be represented by one alderman and two members of the Common Council. Every March the entire city elected a new Mayor as well as Aldermen and Councillors for the next year by ballots marked at the ward town meetings. The Aldermen, with the Mayor as Chairman, constituted the main executive body. The lawmaking duties of the Common Council were spelled out in the Charter which specified twenty-six subjects on which the Council was to "make, establish, publish, alter, modify, amend or repeal ordinances."

The first administration was a short one because the following March another election was scheduled to take place. A description has been preserved of the enthusiastic scene that took place when Baldwin was first nominated as a candidate. As he came down the aisle of the City Hall auditorium, he gave his stovepipe hat a toss before ascending the platform. "A baseball expert . . .

ANNUAL REPORT
OF THE
SELECTMEN
OF NASHUA,
FOR 1837.

The Selectmen for the year 1836, ask leave to make the following Report :——

That they have assessed and ordered into the Town Treasury, the sum of — $12903,63

This sum, with our proportion of the Literary fund, received from the State, — 159,66

Eleazer Fiske's Pension, — 29,90

Cash rec'd of County for support of Paupers — 174,90

For licences of Show-men, — 60,00

For Taverners' licence, — 29,00

For military exemptions, — 20,00

From Dorchester, for support of Town Pauper, &c. — 47,50

Amounting in the whole to — 13,424,59

Which sum has been reduced by abatements of taxes in Samuel Merrill's list, — 241,01

Which deducted from the above, leaves a ballance for the use of the town, amounting in the whole to — 13,183,58
Which sum has been reduced as follows—

For State tax, — 659,45

For County tax, — 87,06

For schools, including Literary Fund. — 1256,00

For School-house Order for building school house in District No. 9. — 2500,00

For collection of Taxes, — 254,09

Which deducted from the above sum leaves, — 8426,98
which sum has been expended for the current expenses of the Town as follows—

For Poor establishment—support of paupers, including County paupers & paupers belonging to other towns, and prosecutions under Police laws, — 1378,96

For repairing highways and bridges — 1843,18

Horse and carriage hire, — 1,62

Room hire, — 21,50

Postage, — 1,75

Soldiers' rations, including powder. — 99,49

Sexton's bill, — 11,75

Sealer of weights and measures bill, — 6,69

Dr. Eldredge's bill for doctoring town and county paup's 80,00

Services of Selectmen, Town clerk, Treasurer, Committee's, Constables, and all other town officers, — 516,79

Stationery, books, printing and advertising, — 62,37

Cash paid for damage done in consequence of bad roads, 12,00

For materials and labor on the Nashua river Bridge, 5,547,63

For Engine house, — 154,16

To cash paid for old bills due last year — 79,50

Amounting in the whole to — 9,797,39

Being thirteen hundred and seventy dollars and 41 cents above the available sum raised for the use of the town for the past year—seven hundred and forty one dollars and eight cents having been expended in cancelling old town orders of last year.

The Selectmen have drawn orders upon the Town treasurer during the year for the sum of $17,207,50, which orders include the payment of a note held by Moses Hunt, against the town, the principal and interest of which amounted to $1172,20—which order is still in his hands and on interest at six per cent per ann.

The amount of town orders now outstanding is $3,819,19, which sum may be estimated as very nearly what the town is now in debt.

So far as the knowledge of the undersigned extends, there are very few outstanding bills against the town. The outstanding orders are all bearing interest at the rate of six per cent per ann. There is now a balance of cash in the Treasury amounting to $236,87, and debts due the town amounting to $300, which being deducted from the above sum of 3,819,19 leaves the sum of $3,282,32, to be provided for by future appropriations.

PURSUANT to a Vote of the Town at the last annual town meeting, the undersigned took a Census of the inhabitants, which shewed the following result. Whole number of Males 2105—Whole number of Females 2960. Total population 5065. There being no additional expense in taking a Census, in connection with the taking of the invoice by the selectmen, the undersigned would recommend that a similar vote be passed, in order that the comparative increase or decrease of the population of the town may be accurately ascertained.

At the last session of the Legislature, an Act was passed providing for the deposit of a large amount of the Surplus Revenue of the United States among the several towns of the State. By this act, our proportion of the deposite money for the present year will be $21,359,40. But as this money belongs to the General Government, and is liable to be called for upon any emergency, and as the aforesaid act of the Legislature contains a provision prohibiting the several towns from expending any part of the principal, the undersigned would respectfully suggest the expediency of still continuing to raise such sums of money by taxation, as will be sufficient to defray the ordinary expenses of the town.

The sum of money which the town is by law compelled to appropriate for the support of common schools, has heretofore been extremely limited in comparison to the number of scholars who are entirely dependent upon the common school system for their improvement in the various branches of education.—The wise and judicious manner of division, adopted by the town in apportioning the school money to the several school districts according to the number of scholars in each, has operated favorably to the smaller ones, while it has not wronged the larger ones nor deprived them of their just rights. But the whole amount of money being inadequate, it has accomplished little more, in some of the districts, than to commence the schools and get them into successful operation.

The total number of scholars in all the school districts in the town, as reported by the committee raised for the purpose of numbering them, the past year, was 1256, and the whole amount of money appropriated for schools was $1256—being only one dollar per annum to each scholar.

By the increase of our proportion in the scale for raising all future public taxes, as adjusted by the Legislature at their last session, we shall now raise for the use of schools $1627,10, which, with our proportion of the Literary Fund, annually received from the tax upon Banks, will probably amount to $3000. This sum it is thought, will be amply sufficient, under a fair distribution, and proper management, to place our primary schools in a flourishing condition, without raising any sum in addition to what the law requires, or encroaching upon our proportion of the public revenue.

The undersigned would again call the attention of the town to the subject of enlarging and improving the condition of the buildings upon the Poor Farm. The number of the inmates of that Institution is now very large—has been constantly increasing for the past year, and unless some measures are speedily taken to insure a corresponding increase in the accommodations of the establishment, a resort must be had to the ancient and more expensive mode of quartering the paupers upon the inhabitants at large.

Respectfully submitted by

JOHN M. HUNT,
JOHN EAYRS,   Selectmen
PERLEY FOSTER,   of
MOSES T. D. GREELEY,   Nashua.
ELEAZER BARRETT.

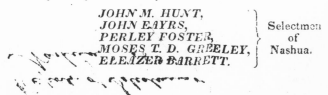

caught onto his curve, caught the chapeau and elevated it high in the air, amid uproarious cheering . . .

A well-known singer sang the comic song, "When the Old Hat was New." In March, 1854, Josephus Baldwin tossed his hat once more and was reelected.

The reason for two legislative bodies was balance of power; each was intended to act as a check upon the other. It soon became evident that the more heavily populated wards felt poorly represented and an amendment to the Charter was passed providing for the same number of Councillors as there were Representatives to the State Legislature with one Alderman for every two Councillors. This resulted in Wards 5 and 6 each having two Aldermen and four Councillors in 1857. Near the end of the century all wards except two were so represented. Eventually there were nine wards instead of eight, as the city spread geographically. In 1901 there was a total of sixty members on the two boards, but it was not until a new Charter was written in 1913 that this cumbersome system was changed to our present single Board of Aldermen in which some of the members are Aldermen-at-Large.

The Board of Health

The Board of Health is a good example of a municipal department that grew in scope and importance during the nineteenth century, although its budgetary requirements were very modest compared to other services. Even in 1900 it spent less than five hundred dollars a year, operating out of the office of one of its physician-members. A Board of Health was stipulated in the original Charter and this requirement was carried out in 1855 in a resolution that a "Board of Health, consisting of three persons, of which the City Marshall shall be Chairman, shall be appointed by the Board of Mayor and Aldermen." It was not until the early 1870s that at least one doctor was appointed to serve on this board. By 1886 there were two doctors on the Board and by 1896 three.

A typical report of the Board of Health, revealing the real importance of this under-financed department, ("T.G. Banks and others, Health Officers, $20.") dated February 29, 1868, read in part:

There was much less ready compliance with the orders and suggestions from the Board, on account of less apprehension of Cholera, than in the previous year, but a reasonable compliance was obtained; and it should be remembered that a good sanitary condition of the city is as much a public benefit in warding off or mitigating the common diseases that usually prevail, as it is in guarding against the more malignant and less frequent diseases . . . There was but one case of Cholera that came to the knowledge of the Board . . . The rigid rules in relation to small pox have been continued, and but one case of varioloid has been known to exist in the city for the past year . . . It will be seen that that much dreaded disease, under proper regulation and management, will be shorn of its terrors.

Smallpox, that terrible pestilence that was only finally eradicated within our own century, was not "shorn of its terrors" by any means. Three years before, in the spring of 1865, Nashua had had a close call in the form of a near-epidemic. There had been fifty-one cases of "real small pox" and forty-eight cases of the milder form commonly called varioloid. Seven deaths had occurred.

A typical nineteenth century municipal institution was the "pest house" for the isolation and care of victims of contagious diseases. In Nashua this was the earliest approach to anything resembling a hospital. There is mention of the first facility of this type in Dr. Edward Spalding's story of how he happened to settle in Nashua. In 1837 he and his father, also a physician, were riding around the countryside. When they came to Nashua they were asked to examine a very sick child whose illness the local doctors could not diagnose. To their horror, Spalding and his father realized that the child had contracted smallpox, traced to a beggar woman who had asked for food at the home. The child died and young Spalding was asked by the frantic town officials to stay until the resulting epidemic was over. He says in his account: "We organized a hospital, now known as the pest house." The location was near the present Water Street ramp. Spalding stayed on and became a prominent Nashua citizen.

The "pest house" was often an empty tenement that the city rented, moving in some cots and medical supplies and fumigating the premises when the emergency had passed. In 1867 the city built a small building near the Poor Farm, on Taylor Road, as an isolation ward for contagious disease cases. In 1873 the Board of Health made the following suggestion concerning this facility: "The small pox hospital was built during an epidemic and in warm weather, therefore no rooms were plastered. We would recommend that part of the lower rooms be plastered,

that it may be comfortable for those who are there in winter."

In the winter of 1879-1880, smallpox caused another bad scare. Two families were involved, with one death. The pest house had now been dignified by the term "City Hospital" and a complete inventory of its furnishings, down to "3 chambers, 1 bed pan," was given in the City Report. There were ten beds, as compared to eight in 1876 when the furnishings were inventoried under the heading, "Invoice of goods and chattels at Pest House in City of Nashua."

The report of the Board of Health for 1886 stated that the year past had been an unusually healthy one: "There have been no epidemics of any kind and the efforts of the health board have been chiefly directed to the improvement of the sanitary condition of the city." An example of the type of health hazard they had been working to eradicate was piping from kitchen sinks that led directly into a nearby cesspool. Describing one house, the report says: "There was nothing to prevent the free circulation of the noxious gases of the cesspool into the kitchen and sitting room, thus thoroughly contaminating the air . . . where the family lived." The result had been the death of two children from diptheria.

By 1886 the city budget provided one hundred and seventy-five dollars for this department. The Board's report for 1887 was remarkable for its con-

ciseness, the entire text reading:

Three hundred nuisances reported.
Minor duties attended to requiring from one to three hours daily during the summer months.
Inventory of Hospital furniture taken.
Hospital needs repairing.
Several cases of Typhoid Fever from the deadly dumps. A few deaths ditto.
All attempts of this Board to remedy the evil "tabled for further investigation."
Duties of Board increased by Legislature.
Salary the same.
More Sanitary Science and Fewer Doctors the only recommendation of this Board.

By 1894 three hundred dollars in salaries was paid to the three members of the Board and the "Incidentals" account itemized several expenses connected with health services, such as supplies, clerical help, and "Lund Cafe, dinner, board of health—$2.50." Their report for that year was quite lengthy and reflected the fact that the department exercised considerably more muscle than in previous years and even had ambitions for expansion, as shown in the recommendation for "the constant employment of a duly appointed health officer, and that the city councils should take an annual appropriation placing the board of health in a firm position to do its legitimate work." There is also mention of the solid waste disposal problem, which even then was considered serious:

In 1896 the three members, Doctors Nutter, Woodward, and Moran, reported that the city was in fairly good sanitary condition except for certain perennial knotty problems: "the dumps, the disposal of garbage, some badly constructed sewers and the disposition of nightsoil." The death rate was given as 17.30 per thousand. In 1900 the death rate in Nashua was 21.86; the rate for the United States as a whole for that year was 17.20 per thousand and for the State of New Hampshire 18.50.

The Poor Farm

The Nashua equivalent of going "over the hill to the poorhouse" was going "down Taylor Road to the Poor Farm." This institution, sometimes referred to as the Almshouse or the City Farm, served a dual purpose as it was also the local House of Correction. It was both the depository for paupers no longer able to maintain homes of their own and the jail for prisoners serving short terms for minor offenses. The Poor Farm officially took on this latter function around 1858 when the City Report first referred to it as "City Farm and House of Correction."

No recorded description of daily life at the Poor Farm is available, but it must have been at any one time an interesting mixture of persons from the lower socio-economic levels of Nashua society. The house itself had a capacity of fifty persons and in 1868 had to be rebuilt after a fire at a cost of three times as much as the insurance collected. Inmates were expected to perform chores on the farm and in the household, and able-bodied males were used as part of the work force on the city roads. The Nashua City Farm was extremely well run, compared to most facilities of this type in nineteenth century America. Two writers of the period who made a study of poorhouses were Edward Eggleston and Sarah Orne Jewett. The horrors of the living conditions they described make our local example look almost, if not quite, like the country club that it

later became. Reports on the annual inspection and taking of inventory by city officials always stress that it was neat, clean, and in good order. Nashua authorities took pains to select experienced and hardworking men as Superintendents; they also insisted on a businesslike operation. In some years the City Farm almost made a profit for the city, but most of the time an appropriation had to be made to cover the difference between income and expenses.

After Nashua and Nashville became separate towns, the Town of Nashville bought the old City Farm which had been operated since 1829. In 1844 Nashua purchased the property of Jacob Parkhurst for $3,100, and this remained the Poor Farm for the entire city after 1853.

The matron of the City Farm was the only woman listed in city reports as a member of the municipal government. A Department of Labor monograph on Poor Farms in the United States pointed out that: "the matron of a small almshouse is a public official by marriage. Socially her responsibility is greater [than her husband], for she has the direct care of the inmates and the management and direction of the household." She had to care for the inmates when they were ill and even delivered babies occasionally, although the services of the City Physician were available to the people at the Farm. A good husband and wife team was the key to successful and efficient operation of such a facility and Nashua appears to have attracted several such couples. In one case, the widow of a Superintendent married her husband's successor in the job.

Inventories of foodstuffs and household supplies at the Farm provide evidence that the inmates were supplied with a fairly nutritious diet and minimum comforts. There were plenty of vegetables, barrels of pork and beef, a good supply of hams, cheeses,

"The Pest House" on Taylor Road . . . for those with infectious diseases.

butter, dry apples, and cod fish. It is interesting to note that a supply of tobacco was made available to inmates. Pastors of Nashua churches regularly held church services at the Farm. In later years the Farm provided stabling for the city teams of horses. One very useful service performed by the institution was garbage collection, especially at the numerous hotels.

Towards the end of the century, the City Farm came under fire from citizens who felt that it was becoming a burdensome agency. Remarks were heard around town to the effect that it would be cheaper to put the indigent up in hotels than to maintain a working farm for their support. Yet the Farm was only part of the solution to the welfare problem. The city budget account headed "Paupers not at the Almshouse" shows the varying amounts of money spent for a dole to provide temporary relief. As in most New England towns, compassion for the unfortunate was mingled with suspicion of malingering. The Overseers of the Poor always had difficult decisions to make in differentiating between the deserving and those willing to take advantage of the system. By 1891, Mayor Beasom in his inaugural speech was endorsing a suggestion made by the outgoing mayor, Charles Burke, that a full-time clerk, with office space in City Hall, should be hired to handle requests for city aid.

This system of welfare was certainly a more humane approach than the oldtime "warning out" or the infamous auctioning of the poor. Under this latter system, the lowest bidder took the indigent person into his home and supplied board and room. It was a good way to get cheap labor for farm and household tasks, while at the same time collecting regular sums from the town for support. After 1885 welfare expenses for all towns and cities increased tremendously because of the state law requiring communities to give direct aid to veterans and their families if they were unable to support themselves. By 1896 relief was costing the city six thousand dollars a year. Mayor Tolles took pains to praise the numerous local charitable organizations for helping to keep the cost to the city from going even higher.

In July, 1908, the City Farm and House of Corrections was finally closed down and the tools, equipment, and furnishings were auctioned off. In phasing out the facility, the indigent inmates had been the first to go, as it was, by that time, cheaper to board them out in private homes, or make other arrangements such as sending them to the County Farm. The property was bought in 1915 by the Nashua Development Corporation which turned the former fields and pastures on the 160-acre tract into an eighteen-hole golf course. The city received ten thousand dollars in the sale, a windfall which it had a hard time deciding how to spend. In August, 1916, the Nashua Country Club was formally opened with the former poorhouse remodelled into a clubhouse. By 1925 there were only ten poorhouses left in all of New Hampshire.

The Police Department

The Nashua Police Department is compiling its own history, so little needs to be said here about this important agency which stands guard over a community that in recent years was declared high on a list of the fifty safest cities in the United States. In 1826 three constables had been appointed, marking the beginning of a Police Department. It is a long way back to the 1830s and 1840s when citizens felt the necessity of forming a Society for the Detection of Thieves and Midnight Marauders. All through the middle of the nineteenth century the night watch patrolled the streets after dark, their lanterns swinging as the members of the watch checked on suspicious activities. This watch, consisting of several men, was considered such an important force that its account in the city budget was kept separate from the regular police operations. By 1879 it cost over $3,800 to pay six regular watchmen and more than twenty on occasional duty. In the same year the Police Department itself cost only $882 for a staff consisting of the City Marshall and his Assistant. The reorganization of the early 1890s eliminated the Night Watch which was replaced by a special force within the department known as Night Patrolmen.

In 1891, the State Legislature enacted legislation setting up a Board of Police Commissioners as well as a Board of Fire Commissioners for the City of Nashua. The Governor of New Hampshire appointed the three Police Commissioners to serve staggered terms of six years each, thus taking out of the hands of the Mayor and Aldermen power to appoint and remove police officers. A rule was made that no more than two of these commissioners should be of the same political party. This solved a problem that had developed because of the annual turnover in municipal administration, resulting in too frequent changes of key personnel.

Alvin C. Eaton, appointed City Marshal in 1890.

The Fire Department

The Fire Commission, set up about the same time, consisted likewise of three Commissioners, each to serve three years, again staggered so that only one was chosen annually. Unlike the Police Commission, these members were appointed by the Mayor, subject to the approval and confirmation of

Nashua's Police Department in the late 1890s.

the Board of Aldermen. All finances of the Fire Department were placed in the hands of this Fire Commission, as were all appointments and removals of personnel. This guaranteed tenure of appointments as long as individuals proved competent to discharge duties, removing jobs from the political arena.

As in most American towns and cities, a certain aura of romantic excitement surrounded the Fire Department. In Nashua it was definitely the glamor service among municipal operations. Contemporary news stories as well as nostalgic reminiscences appearing later convey a legendary tone. "Yarns" about famous fires and the men who fought them were told with a special zest and a relish for the humorous aspects. Even the names of the various fire companies, some of them originating in names given pieces of apparatus by the manufacturers, convey this aura: *Niagara, Lafayette, Protector, Torrent.*

The first end-stroke fire engine in Dunstable was bought by the Nashua Manufacturing Company in 1824. Dubbed the *T. W. Gillis,* in honor of the famous company agent, Thomas W. Gillis, Mayor of Nashua in 1857, this relic is now on exhibition at the Nashua Historical Society. In 1826 there is the first record of the appointment of fire wards, citizens who were given the responsibility of setting up orderly procedures and preparations beforehand, as

well as giving leadership in the actual crisis. One newspaper account mentions a standardized fire bucket that was designed by the Dunstable fire wards.

A news item in the *Nashua Gazette* of April 15, 1836, reads: "The Nashua Fire Club and the Lafayette Engine Company No. 3 celebrated their anniversary by a supper on Thursday evening last, at the Washington House." On July 1, 1836, the following announcement appeared

FIRE! FIRE! A meeting of the Citizens of Nashua will be holden at the Washington House on Sat. evening, July 2, at 8 o'clock, to see whether anything will be done by them to sustain Engine Company No. 3; or in other words, to see whether they will do anything for the payment of the Engine and for the erection of the Engine House. A full attendance is desired. Nashua, June 30, 1836.

Sometime in the early 1830s, therefore, a Fire Club had been formed to promote organized fire protection. About the same time, the Jackson Company had also bought an engine, called *Torreni No. 2.* McGill's history of NMC mentions plans for firefighting. Between July, 1836, when the meeting noted above had been held, and the following spring, the engine known as *Lafayette No. 3,* made by the Thayer Company of Boston, had been purchased by subscriptions from townspeople. It was described as "a most excellent Suction Hose

Engine, with hose and apparatus complete," in an editorial in the *Gazette* in June, 1837, which praised the "liberality and promptness of the citizens." The editorial went on to say:

This, with the two others, owned by the Manufacturing establishments, will, under a properly organized, efficient and well disciplined Fire Department, render our buildings tolerably secure from the ravages of the devouring element . . . Those who profess to be judges of the article . . . are unanimous in the opinion that the Lafayette is a first-rate piece of mechanism, and if well manned at the brake, will . . . be a powerful extinguisher.

By September 1, 1837, this organization of a municipal Fire Department was complete and was celebrated with a

grand display of our whole department, with their engines, hose carriages, with torches and other apparatus, accompanied by the Fire Wards and an excellent band of music. After parading through our principal streets they exhibited a specimen of their skill by deluging several of our edifices. The Fire Wards and the several Fire Companies are deserving of great credit for the spirit manifested by them on this occasion and we trust they will be fully sustained by the public.

The quotation here is from another editorial in the *Nashua Gazette*.

The Fire Wards continued to have supervision of fire-fighting operations right into the 1840s. The town government had few financial demands made on it because the engines had been bought by the two cotton companies and a citizens' group, and personnel was on a volunteer basis. In the first year of the Nashua-Nashville split, 1842, the Selectmen allocated only $20.21 under a *Miscellaneous* heading for "Repairs of Engine and Hose, oil, etc." and $12 to two men for services as firewards. For 1844-1845, a regular account appears in the Selectmen's Report, headed "Fire Department." *Lafayette No. 3* had had to be taken back to Boston for a repair job that year, accounting for over $150 in expense. The list of town officers includes nine firewards. In 1845 the account required over five hundred dollars, mostly to pay for seven hundred feet of hose. Banks and Franklin Monroe had been busy that year examining buildings in town for violations of safety factors. The roster of town officers lists Banks as Chief Engineer, with eight assistant engineers. The power of the firewards appears to have been dis-

solved finally as there is no further mention of them. By 1847 nine engine stations had been set up and a start made on bringing water from the mill canal to reservoirs on Main Street, so that a ready source would be available in the center of town.

In 1848 a real catastrophe, as often happens, brought home the need for even more protection against fire. The population was still growing rapidly and additional houses, industrial buildings, and businesses were being erected. On October 13 an early morning fire broke out in the Central Building next to the bridge on the Nashville side. The business building was destroyed, along with the Baptist Church and one house. It was a disaster that shook up both towns and caused a public outcry. At a special town meeting in Nashua money was raised immediately to buy another engine, more hose, hooks and ladders, along with provision for another engine house. This added expense was reflected dramatically in the budget for fiscal year 1848-1849, in which over three thousand dollars was allotted to build Engine House No. 2 on High Street to house Niagara Engine No. 2. The regular Fire Department account now totalled over six hundred dollars, about a third of which was earmarked to pay members of five fire companies for their time on duty. The Volunteer Fire Department, like the fire wards, was on its way out.

The following year the Chief Engineer of the greatly enlarged Nashua Fire Department, Josephus Baldwin, turned in the first report that was printed as part of the annual town report. There were now three engine companies, one hose company, and one hook and ladder company (Union). Personnel numbered almost one hundred and fifty men. Although two reservoirs had been set up, some parts of the town were not accessible to a good water supply and it was recommended that pipe should be laid to various parts of the village.

Nashville had its own Fire Department, having purchased in 1843 a Hunneman engine that was called *Nashville No. 1;* this became known as *Protector No. 4* after the two towns were reunited. In 1850 the Jackson Company replaced the old engine it had owned for many years. The two fire departments were, of course, consolidated in 1853, after which the Nashua Fire Department developed into a truly efficient organization that was a source of great pride to Nashuans in the latter part of the century. It became increasingly professionalized as

ABOVE
Weathervane from Amherst Street Fire Station was stolen in 1973, recovered, and placed on exhibition at the Nashua Historical Society.
RIGHT
1. Nashua fire buckets of the 1800s. Before the 1820s, the bucket brigade system was the only fire fighting method and each household, by law, had to have one or more buckets handy to the front door.
2. Typical 19th century fireman's helmet.
3. Detail of weathervane.
4. Complimentary ticket to 1859 Fireman's Ball of Niagara Engine Company No. 5.

1.

2.

3.

4.

Pre 1870 photo of Nashua Fire Department with Olive Street Church in background.

far as equipment was concerned, but various leading citizens were much involved on a part-time basis in its direction and management. All of the officers had regular businesses or occupations of their own, as participation in Fire Department activities appealed to many men who were prominent in business and politics.

The biggest step forward for the Fire Department was the building of Central Fire Station in 1870. Until the end of the century the fire stations were: Amherst Street, Arlington Street, Quincy Street, and Olive Street or Central. There was also a fire station for a few years on High Street. After the Lake Street station was built in 1901, the Quincy Street Station was abandoned. By 1900 the Fire Department required an annual appropriation of thirty thousand dollars.

The lists of citizen-firemen, in the days before this duty became a fulltime job, show a wide range of occupations. The cotton mills apparently did not encourage their operatives to join this force, probably because their system could not tolerate interruptions of work. Workers in the support industries for the mills, such as bobbin and shuttle shops, were well represented in the lists of firemen. When an alarm sounded, the self-employed, or those working in places of business that did not object to sudden absences, dropped their aprons or tools and rushed to their respective engine houses. It was the blacksmiths, the cabinet makers, the grocers, the masons, the machinists, the paper hangers, the carpenters, the tinsmiths, and the boarding house keepers who fought the fires of Nashua. As they were paid for the hours required for this duty, little or no loss of income was usually incurred.

The Board of Public Works

The Board of Public Works was created in 1901 by an act of the State Legislature. This reform brought about a long-overdue organization—a single agency of several municipal functions, principally the Department of Highways and Bridges and that of Sewers and Drains. The legislative act was not, however, implemented until 1903. The Board of Public Works at that time was given an annual appropriation of forty thousand dollars, out of which it took care of repairs of bridges, street maintenance, the laying of edgestone for sidewalks, snow removal (in 1903 this cost $1,875), collection of city waste (not including garbage), construction of sewers, and street cleaning. A typical sight in the early part of the twentieth century was the street cleaner, one of four assigned to this duty, pushing his two-wheeled barrow as he swept and shovelled debris, including the horse droppings, from the main business district.

Nashua's thirty-year gaslight era came to an end in 1886 when electric street lights were tried on an experimental basis. The city was rather reluctantly persuaded by the electric company to permit lamps to be put up in a cost-free trial. The improvement in illumination was so evident that, needless to say, a contract for permanent lights was signed at the end of the trial period. Another familiar sight that would be seen no more was the corps of lamplighters making their rounds as dusk approached each day!

The Park Commissions

No separate department to maintain parks and recreation areas was really needed during most of the nineteenth century, because there were only two such areas, North Common and South Common, where the main task seems to have been cutting the hay in the summer; planting shade trees and keeping up walkways did not require large sums of money. In 1896 three Park Commissioners were designated, marking the birth of the Park and Recreation Department as we know it today.

In 1881 Joseph Thornton Greeley had bequeathed his entire farm property on Concord Street to the City of Nashua, designating it as a future public recreational space. Greeley was a descendant on the female side of his family of Matthew Thornton, the Merrimack resident who signed the Declaration of Independence. An amendment to the city charter, dated September, 1883, acknowledged this new responsibility: "The Joseph Thornton Greeley farm, devised by said Greeley to the city, shall hereafter be under the sole management and control of a board of three trustees . . ." The mayor was one of the members of this board and the other two, chosen by the aldermen, had to be persons outside the city government. The trustees were given five hundred dollars in 1884 to spend on care of the farm but even this appropriation was not regularly repeated. Because of lack of funds in the large amount needed to turn a farm

into a public park, very little progress was actually made in developing the property. For many years its value was routinely listed as four thousand five hundred dollars. In 1897 a joint resolution was passed appointing a special committee to "examine the conditions upon which the city holds the Greeley farm and make such recommendations as to the future management or control of same as may seem advisable." But no constructive action was to be taken until almost thirty years after the original bequest of the property. This is one more instance of a project beneficial to the city being delayed in execution until a civic-minded donor came forth with the gift of money really needed to do the job.

Cemetery upkeep appears to have been a housekeeping expense that the city fathers were always very glad to pay. Great pride was taken in landscaping the various burial grounds. The beauty and dignity of these areas today is a heritage from the care and planning devoted to them in the nineteenth century.

The Public Library

The Public Library, although highly praised by all administrations as a culturally beneficial institution and a handmaiden of the school system, got along for the first twenty years of its existence on the original one thousand dollars a year appropriated for its support. Some members of the town government, while visiting other cities, had observed that an impressive library building was often a main feature in the civic landscape. They suggested that such a building was just what Nashua needed and began hinting out loud that it would be quite fitting for some wealthy citizen to donate funds with which to finance it. In 1893, the need for extra space for the library was temporarily met by moving it from the County Records Building to the Odd Fellows Building, with an entrance on the Temple Street side. By 1900 the library budget was five thousand dollars, the book collection had grown to twenty thousand and the circulation was sixty-two thousand a year. Virgil C. Gilman was a Trustee from the opening of the library in 1867 until his death in 1903. Governor George A. Ramsdell was another distinguished Nashua resident who served as a Trustee. A woman member of the Board was Dora Spalding who succeeded her father, Dr. Edward Spalding.

At the Turn of the Century

By 1900 Nashua's municipal government had most of the departments and offices usually associated with any small city of the time. It had appointed the first City Engineer in 1890, and had a City Solicitor (who spent much of his time settling law suits brought by citizens who had taken falls on city sidewalks). It had weathered a controversy with the State of Massachusetts over water taken from the Nashua River. It was also a quarter of a million dollars in debt but with the assistance of a fiscal device known as the "sinking fund" was keeping abreast of its obligations as they fell due. It had many of the same problems encountered in the 1970s, including sewer-building and the need for additional schools to keep up with a rising population.

The tax rate during the last thirty-one years of the nineteenth century fluctuated, possibly reflecting the many changes in administration. The highest tax rate for this period was in 1869 when it was $28 per thousand. It dipped to a low of $15 during the late 1870s, zigzagged between $16 and $24 in the 1880s and early 1890s, and in 1900 was $21.50. Total valuation of real estate for the same period showed a steady upward trend, from five million dollars in 1869 to fourteen million dollars in 1900. In 1900 city property was estimated to be worth $654,000 and twenty school buildings were included in the list.

Since the incorporation of Nashua as a city in 1853, up to and including 1900, twenty-eight different men had served in the office of Mayor. Ten had held the position for only a single one-year term, although one of these, William Cook, had missed out on five months of his term because of a charter change in 1878 which designated November as the date for municipal elections instead of March. Sixteen mayors had served two terms, including George Bowers whose terms were seven years apart. One mayor had served for three years and one for four years.

Some of the ordinances passed by the City Councils were: no riding or driving in the center of the city at a speed faster than five miles an hour (this was changed to eight miles an hour for self-propelled vehicles, after 1903); no bathing or swimming or undressing within view of any house or shop, absolutely no gambling, very strict obser-

vance of the Sabbath with medicine the only item that could be bought or sold, no sheep, swine, horses, mules, asses, oxen, cows or other cattle to be permitted at large in any street or public place, all dogs to be muzzled and collared if running at large, all buildings in the city center to be built of brick or stone, no spitting in public places or on sidewalks. After the state prohibition law was passed in the 1850s taverns and bars were a perpetual problem. The city appropriated money each year to purchase the supply of liquor that could be legally sold for medicinal purposes as well as communion wine for the churches. There was a minor scandal when it was discovered that keeping this supply at City Hall proved altogether too tempting for some city officials.

For very detailed information, with charts and graphs, on the financial aspects of the municipal government, readers are referred to an excellent compilation done by A. E. Brownrigg in the late 1930s, entitled *Financial History of Nashua, N.H.*

On January, 2, 1901, the Honorable Milton J. Taylor, who had been elected Mayor the previous November to succeed Jason Tolles, took the oath of office and delivered his inaugural address. He concluded his summary of the state of city affairs with the following remarks:

Let us as citizens drop all petty strife and quarrels, let there be no north side, no south side, no east and no west, but let us have a united people and work together for the welfare of Nashua. Any enterprise that is for the benefit of a particular section or citizen must help us all indirectly. Again I say be true and loyal to Nashua, and may a kind Providence keep us in health and prosperity.

The Nashua City Seal
in needlepoint.

17

Architecture and Buildings

NASHUA'S PROGRESS from colonial garrison village to today's still-growing industrial city can be traced architecturally through the buildings which still remain as well as through records of those we have lost.

Early New England buildings, of necessity, reflected fashions current in England. They were of square construction with small windows and sometimes an over-hanging second story. As colonists became sufficiently established, they devised their own designs according to the site and the availability of building materials. Eventually a design of unrivaled simplicity originated which combined the English style with the added qualities of American vigor and craftsmanship.

The Tyng House

In our area today there remains one home of faultless design. Although it was built over three hundred years ago, its design is so classic and its interior so spacious that it would be suitable and extremely fashionable for a large family of today.

As Tyngsborough, Massachusetts, is not a part of Nashua, New Hampshire, today, we must remember that both towns were once a part of Dunstable, Massachusetts. Therefore, we would be remiss if the Tyng House were not included in this history.

It seems impossible today that one could find a home from the 1670s, in a fair state of preservation, on its original granite-terraced site overlooking the Merrimack River Valley—a piece of property (originally consisting of 10,800 acres) so historically rich that it not only shelters the remains of one of New England's most famous Indians but also shrouds the ghosts of two victims of a shameful murder.

This is the Tyng House, located on the west side of Middlesex Road about two miles south of the Tyngsborough bridge in Tyngsborough, Massachusetts. In the small cemetery below the house lie many of the Tyng family, including Edward Tyng, the first proprietor, originally from Dunstable, England. Tyng, a Boston merchant and legislator, did not live in this house until the last two years of his life although he had owned the property for some years before his death in 1681.

His son, Jonathan, however, did build the house in the 1670s. It is Jonathan who stood alone against threatened attack during the Indian wars when every other settler had left to find safety in the villages to the south. This made Tyng House the only fortified dwelling between Woburn and Canada; and Jonathan Tyng's perseverance made him the first *permanent* settler in this area.

This mansard-roofed, twelve-room, three-and-one-half-story house has large chimneys at either end which are supported in the cellar by massive brick arches—so large that six men could stand shoulder to shoulder within them. The arches were built with narrow ledges on either side, originally designed to hold racks for smoking meat. A fire pit was fashioned below the arches and a hole in the center of the arch carried the smoke up and out of the house.

The house is constructed of large, hand-hewn pegged beams. In the area under the eaves the cross and supporting beams are marked with matching Roman numerals from I to V, leading one to believe that the framework as well as the beautiful raised paneling had been imported from England for the Tyngs. There are hand-forged square nails visible in the unfinished portions of the house and original hair plaster in the finished rooms. A two-storied portico supported by columns of two different designs runs the width of the front of the house and appears to be a much later addition, as does the small screened enclosure on the second floor. Summer beams with double crown molding are visible in some of the rooms as are gunstock corner posts.

A central hall running from the wide front door to the back door of the house separates the four first-floor rooms and contains an open stairway to the second floor. The front and back rooms on either side of the hall—while having doors that open directly into it—have cleverly concealed connecting doors which form passageways/closets to the room beyond. These doors are made of paneling matching that of the wainscoting around the walls and the fireplaces.

On the second floor, the four rooms are arranged in much the same manner. Each room has its own entrance into the hall as well as the passageway/closet arrangement at either side of the fireplaces. However, in addition to an open stairway leading to the third floor, there is also a small stairway in one of the closets which leads to the third floor.

The third floor rooms appear to have been servants' quarters. A doorway in the northeast corner room reveals a small, cramped stairway to the slave quarters under the roof. It is impossible to stand upright in the area at the top of these stairs. The only light comes from the top three panes of the twelve-over-twelve windows that serve the rooms below. To the right and left of this area are the slave pens. It is only possible to enter them on hands and knees.

As you look around, you realize the air has become stifling—and three-century-old dust motes hang suspended in the slanted light—and then you see it—a remaining ring bolt to which a slave was shackled each night, a silent, poignant reminder of those who lived out their days in service to the Tyng family.

Another curious stairway seems to lead directly to the roof although no hatch or opening is visible today. Past histories of the house mention that there once was a lookout window which was built under the eaves. This window was used as a lookout post during the Indian wars and was so constructed as not to be visible from the outside. Could this stairway which now goes nowhere have been the place where Jonathan Tyng made his lonely stand against the Indians while every other Dunstable settler slept safely in the towns to the south?

When peace came at last between the settlers of the Merrimack Valley and the Indians, Chief Wannalancet, last sachem of the Merrimack Valley Indians, came to live with Jonathan Tyng. Wicasuck Island, the Chief's traditional home, became the property of the General Court and the tribe was scattered. It was from a boulder in front of the Tyng House that Wannalancet spent his last days looking at the Merrimack River and Wicasuck Island. Jonathan Tyng buried Wannalancet beside this boulder as a last act of kindness to his old friend. Hannah Dustin was said to have found shelter and rest at this house after escaping from the Indian camp at Pennacook. George Whitefield, the English Methodist preacher, was also said to have been a guest of the Tyngs.

The Tyngs, due to their great wealth and social standing, were said to have entertained lavishly. They not only had slaves and servants but occasionally called in young women from the neighboring farms to help on special occasions. Judith Thompson, one of these girls, was said to be the most beautiful girl north of Boston. She caught the

eye of Jonathan's son, John, who fell madly in love with her.

The course of true love ran smoothly for John and Judith until a child was born and John discovered the meaning of the word "responsibility." One night John either smothered or strangled Judith and the child as they lay sleeping in the southwest bedroom of Tyng House. John buried Judith and their child in the cellar; and, from that moment, Judith did not allow John to draw a peaceful breath.

Judith haunted John with a determination and perseverance unheard of in the spirit world. John no longer felt comfortable, to say the very least, in the Tyng House. He built a home nearby. As soon as John stepped foot in this house, Judith moved in also. John built another house to which Judith followed him. His days began to be shortened through fear and misery while he lived at this house. During his last illness, many of the neighbors tried to aid him, but they were always met at the door by a ghostly Judith who would tell them that their services were not required.

The night John died, a brave friend, one Captain Butterfield, sat by his bed. Butterfield claimed Judith stayed with John to his very last terrified gasp and proclaimed in a wraith-like voice, "The end of John Tyng is destruction and misery!" Her main goal in death completed, one would expect Judith to return to the spirit world in righteous complaisance. Not so! Judith had apparently gotten her teeth into a starring role and she was not about to give it up.

A tale is told of a young woman, traveling from Chelmsford to Nashua. Caught by a sudden storm, the woman sought shelter in Judith's house, which she thought was abandoned. Her knock at the door was answered by a lady who graciously asked her in, showed her where to put her horse, and invited her to stay for dinner and the night. The traveler was served dinner in a beautifully furnished dining room and was then shown by her hostess to an equally beautiful bedroom where she spent the night. When she awoke in the morning, she dressed leisurely and descended the stairs to the room where she had been entertained the evening before and found it bare, dusty, and shrouded in cobwebs. She ran back to the bedroom and found it in the same condition. Gathering her belongings and her horse she left in wild-eyed haste. A few miles down the road she met a man and asked who lived in the house where she had spent such a pleasant evening. She was told that the house had been empty for years and that it was haunted.

Other travelers had similar experiences. Sometimes they would be met at the door by a beautiful woman holding a baby in her arms. The house would often appear illuminated by a golden glow and music could be heard coming from the building. Sometimes dancers would glide past the windows. Once, Judith, holding her child, beckoned a visitor to follow her—and she disappeared down the cellar steps.

Finally the house was torn down. Judith's golden light was seen for several years afterward around the grounds of Tyng House, but she never entered again the home where she experienced her first and only true love.

The Tyng House today is owned by the Marist Brothers Order and is not open to the public. It is to their credit that they have diligently tried to save this historic treasure.

In September, 1977, it was announced that the Colonel Jonathan Tyng House, 80 Tyng Road, Tyngsboro, nominated for inclusion in the National Register of Historic Places by the Massachusetts Historical Commission, had been accepted by the National Park Service of the United States Department of the Interior. A newspaper announcement stated: "The Tyng Mansion is significant as the home of the region's first European settler, for its architectural quality and for its association with events and personages important in the history of the Merrimack River Valley." It also said: "It is hoped that a future professional preservation plan will accurately record the history of the structure."

The next two buildings in our review of early Dunstable architecture, while not grand in the scale of Tyng House, are nonetheless perfect examples of homes built by the less affluent early settlers. They are the 1700 House and The Haunt.

The 1700 House

The 1700 House, sometimes referred to as the Killicut or Blodgett House, is a delightful center-chimney "Cape." It has not only withstood time itself, but also encroachment by one of Nashua's busiest highways. It still stands on its original site but is now cradled against an entrance ramp to the F.E. Everett Turnpike at 105 Robinson Road. A glance at this home gives one the impression that everything that could possibly be built around it has been; and now it asks only to be left in peace, surrounded by its evergreens and lilacs, to serve its new

owners in the style of the eighteenth century. Although its various owners have remodeled it from time to time, structurally it remains the same as it was when it was built by a Mr. Killicut sometime between 1680 and 1700. The room arrangement has not been altered. The old borning room, although at present a den, is nevertheless still referred to as the borning room. The main fireplace, once plastered over, has been restored to its original appearance complete with its brick oven. Fortunately, this home has been treated with great respect and it remains for us a prime example of early architecture.

"The Haunt"

A nineteenth century jester was responsible for originating the name, "The Haunt," for the Deacon William Cummings home on the east bank of the Nashua River near Runnell's bridge; unfortunately, this misnomer remains to the present day. Excursions on the river from Main Street Wharf or the Nashua Boat Club were popular during the late 1800s. As the Cummings House was unoccupied at the time and in a sad state of repair, a "haunting" was staged for the amusement or fright of those on the evening cruises. Strange noises emanated from the house, flickering lights appeared and disappeared at the deserted windows. What young man in Nashua could resist the opportunity to have the apple of his eye snuggle closer in mock fright? And so the Deacon Cummings House became "The Haunt" for all times, without a genuine ghost, but with a dedicated following among the young people of Nashua!

"The Haunt" on Davis Court when owned by William Spalding.

It is said that William Spalding, enjoying an afternoon cruise, noticed the house and with his discerning eye recognized it for exactly what it was—an attractive 1740 center chimney saltbox. He immediately bought it and had it moved to its present location on Davis Court. He restored the exterior, rejuvenated the interior, and used it as a show place to house his extensive collection of antiques.

The present owners, Mr. and Mrs. Henry Willett, knowledgeable in early eighteenth century architecture, are presently restoring the interior to that period. At the time it was built, the saltbox design had been employed for some years to avoid additional taxes. A saltbox could only be taxed as a one-and-one-half story house rather than as a full two-story house. There are five rooms and five fireplaces. The Keeping Room runs the entire width of the rear of the house. This room has vertical and horizontal sheathing and features a very large fireplace, suitable for cooking and large enough to hold a "back log" of the 1700s.

The rooms have all the original paneling as well as summer beams, gunstock corner posts, Indian shutters, corner cupboards, and nearly all the original hardware. Two large bed chambers up the captain's staircase from the entrance hall have feathered boards—some twenty-seven inches wide. The Deacon not only conserved the family funds by building a one-and-one-half story house, but he was not above using a few illegal twenty-seven inch boards also! At that time all trees which would yield boards of that width were automatically the property of the King's Navy. It seems Deacon Cummings had a sparkle in his personality that is still visible today.

The Lund House

The Lund house on Robinson Road is the oldest two-story dwelling in Nashua. Constructed in 1767 for the Lund family, it is a large, square, center-chimney colonial. The original barn which stood to the west of the house burned some years ago, but the foundation stones are still visible. The saltbox adjunct to the rear as well as the attached rambling sheds appear to be later additions. The Bert Warren family is credited with the restoration and preservation of this home in the early 1900s.

There are two large rooms to either side of the wide front door. The room to the right appears to have originally been two rooms as there is evidence of a partition approximately three quarters of the way to the rear. The smaller portion of this room was probably the original keeping room, indicated by the large fireplace. A small room adjacent to this is known as the well room, as the Lunds were an affluent enough family even in the mid-seventeen hundreds to have nearly had inside plumbing! Each room has its own fireplace, summerbeam, and random-width floor boards.

Each generation of Lunds added to the history of Dunstable/Nashua. Perhaps a little-known story about Oliver Lund will add to the character of the house itself. Oliver owned several canal boats on the Middlesex Canal, was a very successful businessman, and a land owner as were his predecessors. At the time of Oliver's father's death, there was some question as to just what Oliver should call his own, and just what his mother could call her own. Such was the extent of bad feeling between mother and son, that a board of mediation made up of neighbors was appointed to arrive at a solution which would keep both Lunds happy. Eventually it was decided exactly which rooms Mrs. Lund would possess and which could be called Oliver's. One wonders if Mrs. Lund spent her days in that tiny room under the eaves!

The Abbot-Spalding House

No history of Nashua architecture would be complete without mention of the Spalding House on the corner of Nashville and Abbott Streets. Sylvia Spalding, present owner, credits her father, William E. Spalding, with coining the phrase "One Abbott Square" as an address for his home. He felt that Nashville Street, Nashua, was too confusing an address and thus it became what it is today, One Abbott Square, and it is the only building on the square. As we have noted in an earlier chapter, this house was built by John Lund and in 1803 was bought by Daniel Abbot.

There are a library, a receiving parlor, and a living room along the foyer which leads to a large reception hall, with a spacious dining room, kitchen, and pantries beyond. The second floor contains four large bedrooms, two of which have unusual shuttered fireplaces.

In all, there are five fireplaces which are original to the house as are all the paneling and woodwork. According to Miss Spalding, the only changes made by her father at the time of his purchase in 1905 were the removal of a Victorian tower addition around and above the front door and the replacement of all the flooring on the first floor. Here, it is interesting to note, that house-raising parties were the style of the day of Daniel Abbot. Indeed, it must have been quite a party, for the frame of the building was constructed upside-down! Proof of this is in the fact that the upstairs windows are, in fact, taller than the windows on the first floor. Which says a great deal about the refreshments that were offered at the Abbot house raising!

Other Unusual Homes

Number Six Concord Street, whose property abuts that of the Abbot-Spalding Home, is another building in which the size and grandeur of Nashville has been carried to a rather high Victorian degree. Originally built as a residence by Dr. Samuel Dearborn, a Nashua gynecologist, it has changed hands through the years to become an office building.

Beasom House at 176 Main Street.

Built in 1886, it is a massive structure with vast entrance and reception halls. An open stairway is highlighted with a leaded glass panel which reaches to the top of the second floor. It seems obvious that this building reflects the Victorian influence in its size, decoration, and arrangements of rooms within, as well as its size and ornamentation on the exterior. Social functions in the private homes of the city had to be limited to fifty persons, as parlors of that day could accommodate only that number comfortably. How many guests can you entertain comfortably in your living room in 1977? Without using your family room, your playroom, and your patio?

Further up Concord Street, at number twenty-two, is an excellent example of Italian Villa influence in domestic design. This building is known as the Stark House.

This building dates from 1853. It was built for George Stark, grandson of General John Stark, the hero of Bennington. George Stark began his career as a surveyor and engineer by working during school vacations with Uriah A. Boyden, the man who did the preliminary survey of the canal and factory complex in Manchester. Stark was assistant engineer on the Concord Railroad and also worked with the staff of engineers in surveying for the Nashua and Lowell Railroad. He was appointed chief engineer of the Nashua and Wilton and Stony Brook lines (the first lateral roads built as feeders to the trunk lines). Stark became superintendent of the Nashua and Lowell Railroad and its branches; it was during this time that his home was constructed.

The characteristics of Italian Villa design in his home are the picturesque asymetrical massing of the parts of the building featuring the expression of the tower as a distinct element as opposed to the Victorian cupola. This design is emphasized particularly on the front east wing by large flush boards. Special treatment was given to the first floor windows, with a double arch within and a balcony above. In 1928 this home became the First Church of Christ, Scientist, which recently vacated it.

Two other homes with designs of Italianate influence were built in Nashua during the early 1800s. These two homes actually began as neighbors but the encroachment of the business district caused one to be moved and the other to be hidden from view.

The Spalding Homes

The first home, that of Isaac Spalding, is still on its original site, but is completely hidden from Main Street by stores which have been built in front of it. It can be reached today through the arcade near Philbrick's Fish Market and the Transfer Station. Built in 1852, its proportions reflected the wealth of the owner, as Isaac Spalding was the richest man in New Hampshire at that time.

It is a two-story brick residence whose structure shows the beginning of simplified colonial proportions being softened with Italian influences, such as the belvedere and the decorative eaves. At one time this home was surrounded by a large wrought iron fence enclosing a front yard which reached to the street and the building itself was festooned with ivy. This was the first residence in Nashua to have running water.

Isaac's wife, Lucy, left her mark on Nashua as well. Her charities were varied and numerous, always administered with a great deal of foresight and prudence, but with very little fanfare. She gave the site for the First Congregational Church and contributed very generously to its building fund.

The Isaac Spalding Home is now owned by the Methodist Church and is used to house the church offices and school.

The second home to reflect a similar Italianate influence is the Atherton Home on Fairmount Heights. This is a nicely proportioned, two-story residence with gabled roof, large decorative eaves, bracketed details over the windows, and a belvedere. Originally the home of Dr. Edward Spalding, it was built about 1820 on the site of the present Court House on Temple Street. Dr. Spalding was Nashua's first physician-mayor.

The Henry Athertons

In 1902 the heirs of Dr. Spalding sold the home to the Hillsborough County Commissioners who wanted that site for the new Court House. Captain Henry Atherton, a local attorney who retained his Civil War rank, decided it would be scandalous to destroy such a fine building, so he bought it and had it moved to a piece of property he owned on Fairmount Street. The building was cut in two and moved from Temple Street, through Main Street, across the bridge, and up to the Heights. It created such a colossal traffic jam that the aldermen immediately enacted a law prohibiting the moving of large buildings through the business district. The barn at the rear of the Atherton House was also moved from Main Street. This barn originally belonged to Isaac Spalding and once was one of the most magnificent in the city. It is two-storied and completely paneled. The stalls as well as the walls and ceilings are paneled in dark oak. There is a landed stairway of black walnut curving up to the second floor.

Captain Atherton's wife was Dr. Ella Blaylock Atherton, a dedicated gynecologist-obstetrician who was the second woman to receive a medical degree from Queen's University, Kingston, Ontario. The University, however, would not issue her a license to practice medicine as she was a woman!

From the time the Athertons moved into their new home on Fairmount Street, the household was managed by one woman whose devotion to duty was certainly as great as the Doctor's devotion to her patients.

Jessie McLaren, a kindly but very firm Nova Scotian, was the woman who ruled the Atherton household with an iron glove. She referred to her employers as "Captain Henry and Doctor Dear," and caring for the children and running the house were left entirely in her capable hands. No one dared interfere with Jessie, her charges, her household, or her kitchen. And the kitchen remained just as it was when she entered the house—soapstone sink, small drainboard, wood stove and no cabinets or other "modern inconveniences" to clutter her domain!

Homes of Other Prominent Citizens

Residences of other prominent Nashuans of this era affected a grandeur that has never been duplicated. Victorianism was embraced with a fervor! Towers, cupolas, balconies, piazzas, and fretwork were added. The home of James H. Tolles, 65 Concord Street, is one such residence, as is the home of Mayor Albert Shedd, 267 Main Street. The home of Mayor Charles Burke, 1 Prospect Street, certainly is a monument to Victorianism, although its appearance today is not as impressive as it once was.

Homes constructed earlier in the Georgian and/or Federal styles began to disclose changed appearances also by the additions of verandas and much ornamental woodwork. The Solomon Spalding and the Henry Stearns Homes on Orange Street both exhibit these traces or ornamentation.

The Spalding home, built in 1834, was the first brick house north of the river. It was considered to be some distance from town at that time. Solomon Spalding was twenty-three years old when he had this house built.

The home of Mayor W.H. Beasom, built in 1852, is one of the residences we have lost, replaced by the State Theater. It was interesting since it was less ostentatious than the residences built by other mayors who seemed to be outdoing each other in pomp and splendor. The Beasom home started as a rambling two-story wood frame structure. Architectural interest was added by a Greek temple front with flanking pairs of pilasters at the street side. This stretched its proportions to the full two stories and lent a dignified impression to an otherwise modest structure.

The Anderson Home

Another Nashua residence, although of a later date, 1905, deserves to be mentioned here not only for its uniqueness, but for its importance in the city today. It is now Mount St. Mary's Seminary, a girls' high school, conducted by the Sisters of Mercy. It is located at 90 Concord Street, and was the Frank E. Anderson House.

A newspaper account of that time reads:

The residence of Frank E. Anderson, which was recently occupied by Mr. and Mrs. Anderson, is regarded here as the most substantial and imposing in the state of New Hampshire. It is situated on Concord Street near the Greeley Farm, the most fashionable section of Nashua. The grounds are ample, extending back along Bartlett Avenue as far as Webster Street, and although the ornamentation of the lawn has not been completed its features already disclose a generous measure of elegance and novelty.
The house is of dark red brick with ample trimmings of white marble. It is of colonial architecture, with a well proportioned front and a very spacious wing on the rear. Among the interior features are a theater, complete with stage, and an oval dining room. The structure faces the east. At the south entrance is a marquet of corrugated glass top and sides.

Frank Anderson's widow, Ella, was as well known for her charities as Isaac Spalding's Lucy was known for hers. The Anderson Chapel was built in Edgewood Cemetery for Nashuans by Ella Anderson.

Mercantile Buildings

As the railroads brought prosperity and industry to Nashua, and a building boom for private residences, the need developed for more elaborate public, municipal, and mercantile buildings as well as inns and taverns.

The Merchants' Exchange was built originally in the early 1870s. This building replaced the paint shop of William Gaskin and Norman Fuller's harness shop. A fire in 1930 nearly destroyed the north end, so that the south end remains as the only original part of the structure. Its location is on the corner of Main and High Streets, extending southward toward Pearl Street and taking up a large frontal portion of that city block. Although a great deal of gaudy advertising now hides its facade, close examination will reveal the original beauty of the building. The Merchants' Exchange is an excellent example of mercantile buildings of the era. It has a large projecting cornice with paired brackets. Originally, the first floor featured the regular spacing of columns (since removed) at about five-foot intervals

that supported a stone lintel. The second floor features planar brick surfaces accented by decorative semi-circular arches.

Mrs. Emma Manning Huntley, public reader, teacher of elocution and physical culture, had her office in this building. Of her services, Bacon had this to say:

Reading aloud has long been shamefully neglected in our public and private schools, and it is only of late years that the attention of the people has been directed to the deficiency of our educational system in this respect. Not one person in twenty even in the more cultivated class, can read aloud acceptably, and a striking proof of this may be had by attending one of the "Author's Readings," which have lately come into vogue, for, although each author reads from his own works, and hence must know precisely what ideas the writer intended to convey in the vast majority of cases, the subject matter is made obscure rather than simplified by its delivery. Nashua has an earnest and well-equipped, most successful teacher of elocution in the person of Mrs. Emma Manning Huntley, who fills engagements as a public reader, and gives instruction in elocution and physical culture to individuals and to classes. We would most earnestly advise all interested to call and obtain such further information as may be desired, as it will cheerfully be given on application.

A man with many abilities, one J.W. White, occupied Number One, Merchants' Exchange. This was a drug store, and White employed four assistants to run it for him. His other interests included offices he held in other businesses, such as, president of the Second National Bank, treasurer of the Mechanics Savings Bank, also treasurer of the Nashua and Lowell Railroad and president of the White Mountain Freezer Company.

Industrial Development

The advent of the Middlesex Canal in 1803 was instrumental in changing Nashua from pastoral village to a center of trade. Prior to the canal Lowell and Haverhill were the northernmost outposts with easy access to Boston and its harbor. By 1826 Nashua was showing signs of industrialization beyond the hopes and dreams of its first lonely settlers. The Nashua Manufacturing Company became a reality with the Indian Head Company soon to follow.

At this time two men came to Nashua who were to leave their mark on this city and its industrial expansion. They were Asher Benjamin, noted Boston architect who was asked to design and construct the mill building for Nashua Manufacturing; and Samuel Shepard, a student of Benjamin's, who came along to assist. After the construction of the mill buildings Asher Benjamin became the company's first agent. Another building, that of the Olive Street Church, is attributed to him as well as the original mill building.

The first mill of the Nashua Manufacturing Company is interesting due to its siting to make use of water brought from Mines' Falls by canal. From the canal water flowed through the building to turn large water wheels which, in turn, through a belted system powered the machines. In later years the system was easily converted, using the same water power to operate electrical generators. The mill buildings themselves were built into the hillside of the river bank making it possible for water to flow from the canal above, through the buildings, and out into the Nashua River.

The main design features of the first building are the original stair towers. The brick work is corbeled and the design is similar to the Tuscan style of Italy. Later towers in the buildings to the east were more elaborate in their design.

Municipal Buildings

Soon it became apparent that a building to house town government was needed, and Samuel Shepard was asked to design one. Although the site chosen served as a beginning of the ever-widening rift between the north-enders and those who lived on the south side of the river, it was nevertheless constructed on a lot previously owned by Aaron Sawyer, an attorney who retained his home and law office on the north boundary of the site. When the present Nelson Block was built in 1904 the Sawyer home and office were torn down and a right-of-way was granted between the Town House and Nelson's. This right-of-way is still in existence today—many of our readers may have used it as a short cut to Court Street.

Completed in 1843, the architectural lines for this three-story brick and granite structure were standard for its era and were sufficiently classic to be incorporated into the present-day City Hall.

Several of the rooms in the basement of this new Town House were designed and used for specific purposes which may sound strange today. One was a meat market, another a jail, and an extra room really not designated for any particular use was utilized for emergency surgery! The Selectmen and other officials, including the constables and night watch, had their offices on the first floor, the rear of which was a public hall with seating capacity of five hundred. This hall was later to become the Hillsborough County Court Room. Narrow winding stairs led to the second floor auditorium and gallery, with a seating capacity of nearly a thousand. Stairs to the gallery joined a central stairway to a third floor that served as the town's armory until one was constructed on Canal Street. (The new structure housed the militia, as well as the City Guards during the years of their military activity.) Above the third floor was the bell tower which was topped by a golden eagle. The bell was installed to be used to call the court and was also used as a fire alarm.

The halls were in frequent demand for large social gatherings, lectures, concerts, balls, banquets, rallies, and other public meetings. The Hunt lecture courses and the YMCA Star courses were given here as well as concerts by the Nashua Oratorio Society under the talented baton of Eusebius Hood.

Five Presidents of the United States spoke from this building: Franklin Pierce, James Garfield,

Chester Arthur, Benjamin Harrison, and Theodore Roosevelt. One amusing photograph, taken at the time of Teddy Roosevelt's visit, shows the politically elite of the city greeting him in a setting of potted palms, tent-like staging—each man wearing a pith helmet! Nashua has always had astute politicians!

Very little was done to change this building during the ninety-six years it served as a home for Nashua town government—a "public sanitary" was eventually installed and an "iron man" was added on the sidewalk in front of the building to afford citizens a cooling drink during the hot summer days.

Thus the affairs of the city were met with dignity and consideration until one rainy evening in 1926 when the roof began to leak on an aldermanic meeting. Further investigation by the drenched aldermen and mayor revealed a general condition of disrepair. Parts of the building were actually in a dangerous condition. Aldermen of that day did not apparently have to be summoned by the president of the aldermanic board to make up a quorum—they were all present, and bids were opened immediately for general reconstruction and complete updating of the interior.

The Nashua Building Company submitted the lowest bid—$85,869, but the contract was not let and no repairs were made at that time, except perhaps stop-gap measures. The cost of this building in 1843 had been $23,000, so inflation is not new in the twentieth century. The bell had to be removed eventually due to decaying stanchions and it was eventually given to the Greek Church of the Assumption. The eagle was discovered to have an advanced case of terminal molt, so it was removed. The records are not clear as to what happened to it but the eagle now atop the new City Hall, although a very close copy, is not the original.

This building had stood for less than a century, first as Nashua's Town House in 1843, until the divorced townships of Nashua and Nashville buried their hatchet when the city became incorporated in 1853—then as Nashua City Hall from 1853 until the present City Hall was built in 1939. The only remaining items we have of this building in the city today are the bell and the ornamental wrought ironwork which has been incorporated in the Nashua Historical Society building at 5 Abbott Street.

Central Fire Station (now the Nashua Arts and Science Center) was dedicated on February 9, 1871. Newspaper articles of the day describe it:

The architecture is modern Norman with a tendency towards the Gothic in the construction and finish of the gables and towers. The house front on Church Street is built of brick, with rough hewn cornices and window cappings, slated roof and tower.

The Tremont House

By the year 1875 the city was humming with social activity. The Tremont House was built on the corner of Main and Pearl Streets. This four-and-a-half-story building, raised one-half story above the street level to give it prominence, had an imposing entrance marked by a decorated columned porch with pediment. It boasted steam heat, gas and electric lights, baths, 50 well-furnished rooms, a dining room which seated 125, and the food as well as the accommodations were highly recommended. Carriages left the hotel every ten minutes for any station in the city. Make no mistake about it, the Tremont House was the place to be seen!

Years after the Tremont was razed, a Nashua businessman of some repute had occasion to travel to Washington, D.C., and was one of a group of businessmen from around the country who were to meet with President Franklin Roosevelt. The Nashua businessman expected very little in the way of conversation with the President, realizing that perhaps the men from larger, more wealthy states would have the President's ear. Therefore, his surprise was genuine when, after being introduced to the President, Roosevelt smiled up at him and asked, "Tell me, is the Tremont House still going strong in Nashua?" It seems that Roosevelt, while attending nearby Groton School, used to spend his Friday evenings, as he said, "swanking around the Tremont" and he reminisced that some of his happiest boyhood days were spent there!

Harrisonia Manor (now Wayside Furniture—corner of Spit Brook Road and Daniel Webster Highway, South) was also popular although quite a distance from the center of town. It was known far and wide for its Strawberry Festivals.

Late Nineteenth Century Buildings

A Police Station was built in 1890—another proud municipal building adding stature to the still-growing city. The top floor features a rather unique pattern of brick work. The entire building is of brick with stone lintels and very large arches on the first floor. The upper two floors have been integrated into the design by the vertical window alignment terminating in the arches of the top floor. Sound familiar? It is now the American Legion Building on Court Street.

The Masonic Temple built in 1891 stands much as it did initially. The first floor which formerly had large window openings was remodeled after the turn of the century. The main feature of this building is the turret on the corner of East Pearl and Main Streets which was originally supported by a free-standing column. It has a decorative cornice of corbeled brick and its mass is broken up by a grid of horizontal and vertical stone facings. Special elements add interest, such as the projecting bay windows and the roof-top pediment at the south end.

The building's all-day dedication on January 21, 1891, was the social event of that season. There were services in the morning, a banquet in the early evening, and an eight o'clock reception followed by musical entertainment in the lodge room. The Mendelssohn Male Quartette performed. Howard Dow was the organist and Miss L.E. Dow was vocalist. Dancing in the banquet hall went on into the wee hours, and the Masonic Building was well launched.

Not to be outdone, the Odd Fellows laid the cornerstone to their new building on May 14, 1891, with proper pomp and ceremony. However, the dedication of the building on April 26, 1892, outdedicated prior formalities. Parker notes, "Favored by a beautiful day, and at a time of year when all nature was propitious, the beautiful building was consecrated to the work of benevolence and good deeds of the noble order of Odd Fellows."

The building itself may appear not to have mellowed with age, and it seems overly ornate by today's standards, but a closer look will change your mind. It exhibits a fantastic variety of influences. At the time, it was one of the largest buildings downtown, and from its towers Nashuans had their first birds'-eye view of the city. The design of the facade shows it was built in the transition period between planar brick surfaces, such as the Merchants' Exchange, and the new Italianate style. This was a new and fresh approach toward the design of the office building. The bay windows and large glass area of the Main Street side reflect the beginnings of the influence of the Chicago School of Architecture. This style is exemplified by the buildings of Louis Sullivan, an early advocate of functionalism in architecture.

The design shows an attempt to define strongly each corner of the building by giving it a vertical rendition that terminates in a tower with special roof treatment. The motif of the turrets resembles French Chateaux. Details of the facade show extensive use of brick corbeling and rusticated stone that create an endless variety of shadow and texture. The design of arches on the first floor, Temple Street side, reveal a series of three massive brick arches of Romanesque design. In taking your second look at the building, note the Temple Street side at different hours of the day (morning and afternoon). The patterns formed by light and shadow may change your mind about this building.

Ralph Adams Cram, a native New Hampshire man, was the architect chosen for the Hunt Memorial Library. Completed in 1903, it was the gift to this city of Mrs. Mary A. Hunt and Miss Mary E. Hunt. It was called The John M. Hunt Memorial Library, in memory of their husband and father.

The original inspirations for the style that was to make Cram famous came from Copley Square, Boston. On one side was the Romanesque Trinity Church whose architect was Henry Hobson Richardson; facing it across the Square was the classic Boston Public Library, whose architect was Charles Follen McKim. Adding to these two great architectural styles was Henry Vaughn, who started the Gothic trend right here in New Hampshire. His contribution to the emerging Cram style was the chapel of St. Paul's School in Concord. Following Vaughn, Cram realized and appreciated the picturesque qualities effected by the combination of these three styles: Romanesque, Classic, and Gothic. The product of this combination has been called Gothic Revival, and the years between 1880 and 1900 were to be remarkable stepping stones in American architectural history.

Architectural treasures created by Cram are many: Portions of the United States Military Academy at West Point; the Graduate College and Chapel in Princeton, New Jersey; the Academic

The Hunt Memorial Building opened as Nashua's library in
1903 after ten years of bitter controversy over the site.

Building at Phillips Exeter Academy, Exeter, New Hampshire; the chapel for Wheaton College, Norton, Massachusetts; the chapel of St. George's School, Newport, Rhode Island; the Cathedral of St. John the Divine, New York City; the Federal Building, Boston, Massachusetts; and our own Hunt Building.

Cram chose to design the Hunt Library in Elizabethan Gothic style. It is of brick construction with heavy limestone trim. The mixture of Old English and Gothic architecture was carried out in both the interior and the exterior of the building—but it is most predominant in the doorways. The main door (replaced recently) was originally of English oak, very deeply paneled. The ornamental framework of the door is arched to a point and exhibits heavy yet gracefully detailed design. The main portion of the building is low, being of one story, with a large wing extending from the Clinton Street side of the structure. From the center of the building proper rises a tower which heightens the imposing appearance of the building. The windows are long, deep, and narrow. Originally they contained leaded glass which, with the covering growth of ivy, adds to the English appearance.

When the Nashua Public Library on Court Street was completed in 1971, the Hunt Library became the property of the School Department and now houses its offices. In 1973, the Hunt Building became a National Historic Site due to its unique architecture, a living testimony to the creative genius of Ralph Adams Cram.

Churches

As the history of the growth of a city may be traced through the architecture of its municipal buildings and the homes of its citizens, so also can be traced the religious history of the city through its church architecture.

Each of our churches brings to the city its own unique style; and, however glorious and ornate, it cannot deny its humble beginnings. Church architecture through the ages has followed one basic plan. The farmer was the first ecclesiastic architect. Does this seem strange when you consider the grandeur of St. Francis Xavier Church, the First Church and others? Consider again this basic plan which has evolved over the centuries. There are two points of visual affinity between the structure of

barns and the interior of our churches. These are the large end entrances and the division of the interior space. The interior is divided into a wide central corridor with the side areas divided into seating areas. The central aisle corresponds with the threshing floor of the barn, and the seating areas on either side correspond to the cattle stalls. The architectural term used for barns with this interior division is appropriate when one understands the background history of the structure—it is called "basilican."

Nashua's pastoral beginning saw each settler as both producer and consumer. Each homestead was a self-contained unit. The first meeting house/church, completed in 1678, was designed and built with an eye to the availability of materials close at hand; and necessity dictated that it be utilitarian. It was constructed of logs, was barnlike, and was unsteepled. It was used as a meeting house less than ten years. This church of simple but utilitarian construction was the foundation for two of Nashua's largest churches—The First Congregational Church and The Pilgrim Church.

Ecclesiastical construction was scant until the advent of the Middlesex Canal, the Nashua Manufacturing Company, and the Nashua and Lowell Railroad brought wealth to the city as well as a growing population of diverse religious interests.

In 1825, the Olive Street Church was built by the Nashua Manufacturing Company for its employees. The classic design of this church is attributed to Asher Benjamin, architect and first agent of the Nashua Manufacturing Company. The first pastor of the Olive Street Church had the delightful name of Handel Nott. In 1826 it became the Pilgrim Church.

St. Francis Xavier Church, from an old postcard.

St. Luke Episcopal Ch.
Junction E. Pearl & Temple Sts.
1870 - A H Foxhall

In 1835 the Old Chocolate Church was erected near the corner of Park and Main Streets. Following the continuing utilitarian decrees of the era, the first story and basement, constructed of stone and brick, were used to house various business establishments which provided rent for the growing congregation. The second story was of wood and was used as the meeting house. It was surmounted by a heavy cupola. It was referred to as "Old Chocolate" not for its sweet promise of the glorious hereafter, but for the color of its painted exterior. This church was destroyed by fire in 1870.

The Church of the Good Shepherd, dedicated in 1878, stands today on Main Street much as it did originally with few changes to mar its peaceful exterior. Who of us has not traveled and congratulated ourselves upon correctly labeling an Episcopal church in an entirely strange town? Episcopal architecture can be recognized wherever it is placed. The building is Gothic in design. The walls are granite with brick trim. Memorial windows, carrying out the theme of The Good Shepherd, enhance the interior as well as the exterior design of this church.

The second oldest Catholic parish in Nashua is St. Louis de Gonzague. This building was erected on West Hollis Street in 1871. According to the Inventory of Roman Catholic Church Records in New Hampshire, it was of New England meeting house style — red brick with granite trim — of the Christopher Wren style. The interior was Gothic with French adaptations. This church burned in the summer of 1976 and the parishioners are in the process of rebuilding. At present the central tower is the only portion of the original church that has been salvaged and it will be incorporated in the new church.

St. Francis Xavier Church on Chandler Street, built in 1896, is one of the outstanding architectural treasures of Nashua. Built on an elevation it commands views of the entire city, and can be seen on entering the city from any point of the compass.

This is the first marble church to be built in New Hampshire. Built of Southerland Falls blue marble on granite foundations, it is of Norman style with a floor plan of a Latin cross. In the center of the facade rises a main tower flanked by two minor towers. The main entrance, through the central tower, is composed of white Vermont marble enriched by columns and carvings. It has a three-bell carillon and the bells are named Jesus, Mary, and Joseph. At the center of the transept is the "baldachino," a traditional pavilion-type structure within the building that houses a figure of Jesus Christ.

In direct contrast to St. Francis Xavier is its near neighbor, the Unitarian-Universalist Church on Lowell Street. This church is constructed in neoclassic style, suggestive of Greek architecture. Built in 1827, the huge columns that ornament the front are solid, as they are trees, carefully selected and felled in a nearby town. There are no records to reveal the architect, but it is supposed that Asher Benjamin designed the front, if not the entire building.

The First Congregational Church on the corner of Concord and Lowell Streets was built in 1893. It is of Marlboro granite. The chimes occupied space at the Chicago World's Fair in the same year as this church's dedication. The rose windows for which this church is justly famous were dedicated to the memory of departed members of the church.

It is a long way from the rough-hewn log structure of the first meeting house, surrounded by alien forests and unfriendly Indians, to the grandeur of the churches chosen for their distinctive architecture to be included in this history. However, the floor plans remain basically the same; the embellishments to the interior and the ornateness of the exterior are due to the needs and wishes of each congregation. Each group brings its own special charm to its house of worship.

Unitarian Church, believed to have been designed by Asher Benjamin.

St. Louis de Gonzague Church stood for over 100 years on West Hollis Street.

18

Cultural, Social and Recreational Life

THE FRENCH TRAVELER Alexis de Tocqueville, in his book *Democracy in America,* observed: "Americans of all ages, all conditions, and all dispositions, constantly form associations. If it is proposed to inculcate some truth or to foster some feeling by the encouragement of a great example, they form a society." This faith in group power ran strong throughout the nineteenth century and Nashua was no exception. In fact, Nashua had more organizations than any other city of its size in New Hampshire.

Early Organizations

On September 25, 1835, the *Nashua Gazette* carried a notice of a new organization that had been formed—the Society for the Detection of Thieves and Midnight Marauders. The town had become metropolitan enough to develop a crime problem, and concerned citizens took emergency action in the only way they knew. We have seen how the Fire Club, formed in the early thirties to promote better techniques for fighting fires, encouraged the town government to purchase equipment and to start the first fire company.

Municipally managed police and fire departments soon took over these protective duties, but there were plenty of other problems left for people who were joiners. In 1836 two groups appeared that were concerned about the social evils caused by alcoholic drinking, the Friends of Temperance and the Nashua Young Man's Temperance Club. These early temperance organizations were succeeded by many others, with women taking a special interest in this subject.

The Woman's Temperance League was established in 1876 to " . . . provide an education to a higher standard of living and in the banishment of saloons and their kindred evils."

The scope of the League's activities went far beyond fighting alcoholic beverage consumption. The members were concerned about many problems involving women and took effective action to solve them. For example the League was successful in placing a matron in the police station to care for unfortunate women confined there. "This was not accomplished without effort on our part, though the city officials now see and acknowledge the wisdom of the movement, and only eternity can reveal the work done by Mrs. Eliza Carey, who was the first police matron." This group in many ways tried to do for young women what the YMCA did for young men.

Gone were the days when a barn-raising or a corn-husking, along with casual visiting, satisfied the social instinct. Organizations serving a wide variety of needs and tastes now played an important part in community life. A shared interest in cultural affairs, for example, inspired the Literary Club and the Young Men's Lyceum, which were started in 1835 and 1837. These earnest groups met regularly to discuss abstract as well as timely topics: "Is war ever justifiable?" "Had our forefathers a right to this country?", "Is conscience an innate principle or the effects of education?"

A group of forty-five gentlemen employed at the Nashua Manufacturing Company met on January 27, 1840, to form a debating club. Its aim was " . . . the improvement of minds by way of debates and declamations on any subject that is not counter to religion or morality." Calvin Stanley was the first leader, and the group met in church halls debating such subjects as, "Ought petitions of females, relative to political affairs, be regarded by legislative bodies?" There is no record of any feminine group being challenged to take the affirmative side of this question! However, the Excelsior Literary Society, formed February, 1869, was a debating group for women as well as men, and one of the topics chosen was: "Women are deprived of their rights by the present public sentiment in New Hampshire."

Organizations in the Late 1800s

The Chautauqua Literary and Scientific Circle, whose members were said to be the most intelligent women in Nashua, organized in October, 1882, and held weekly meetings for readings, essays, and discussions of scientific topics.

Interest in cultural, social, and civic affairs led to the formation of other groups for self-improvement through discussions, reports, debates, and lectures. During the years 1886-1887 there was a growing awareness of the need for combined literary effort among women. Men at that time had clubs where they met for sociability and discussion and could " . . . exercise their garnered wealth of literature in a wide variety of ways, but for the ladies there seemed to be nothing but repression, until the iron band became unbearable. Inter-change of sentiment, the catching of others' ideas, the lift that comes from mutual thought in a given direction looked so desirable—more so, charming, that in 1887 Mrs. Hiram M. Goodrich determined on decisive action." Her friends were in sympathy with the idea and were willing to cooperate with any movement in that direction. Gentlemen as well as ladies caught eagerly at the idea and the Fortnightly Club as it was called quickly became a mixed group. Orren C. Moore, " . . . with his rare literary ability, calm faith, and steadfast will, put all of these qualities into the movement." Joining him were many of the leading professional men of Nashua, the principal newspaper editors, prominent business men and teachers; but, ironically, although the idea of creating the club was a woman's, all of the officers were men! They were Colonel Hiram M. Goodrich—at whose house the first meeting was held—Orren C. Moore, Henry Atherton, the Reverend Cyrus Richardson, and Dr. Royall Prescott, among others.

Charles C. Morgan, a well-known lawyer and a charter member of the Fortnightly Club, published a book based on his talks before the Club. The only piece that might be of interest to people today describes his ascent of Mont Blanc with three English ladies. His style is ponderous but he was obviously a person of great scholarship who was interested in all kinds of subjects.

The most amazing cultural phenomenon in Nashua society was the simultaneous existence of two ladies' clubs for the study of Shakespeare. A course of parlor lectures in 1889 by Miss Kate Hamlin on "Early English Literature" awakened interest in a few ladies " . . . on whose Shakespeare the dust was fast gathering." A meeting was called at the home of one of the ladies and it was decided to form a club, but what to call it? A Shakespeare Club limited to fifteen members had already been organized two years earlier to honor Shakespeare's name. Since no share had been given to Anne Hathaway in the family glory it was named the Hathaway Club, with membership limited to twelve. The Shakespeare Club proved so exclusive that would-be members formed their own separate club! Each club met separately every Friday afternoon from October to May and held separate observances on Shakespeare's birthday, with readings from his plays and sonnets and Elizabethan music.

It is obvious from the topics discussed by the

members of the Fortnightly Club and the debating societies that these were of interest chiefly to the well-to-do classes with leisure to enjoy these pursuits. However, there was a growing concern, particularly among women, for providing other levels of society with practical as well as intellectual sustenance. Many women's groups whose primary interests had been social or intellectual began to turn to social service to the community.

A group of Catholic women met in 1893 and formed the Columbian Club whose purpose was "to furnish mutual entertainment and advancement in literature." Weekly meetings were devoted first to whist, followed by informal discussions. Each of the sixteen members subscribed to a magazine or review shared by the other members. Since this was a period when work was scarce and times were hard, the group soon became involved with those in need, and the club's activities turned to making clothes, mostly for children. Friends of the members were asked to contribute ten cents a month to a fund to help the needy.

A Woman's Suffrage group was organized in September of 1894 with the immediate aim of educating women, especially in government affairs—municipal, state, and national. The ultimate aim was to secure the ballot for women in every department where their interests were concerned, particularly in connection with schools. They had tried to register, but had been told that they could not, although that privilege was enjoyed by women in other parts of the state. A delegation which went to Concord was warmly received and advised to return to Nashua and publish their intention of voting, which was approved by law.

Aware of the importance of having a club with wider interests and exclusively for women, Mrs. E.F. McQuesten invited a limited number of women to her home on May 29, 1896, the result of which was the Nashaway Woman's Club. The women included Mrs. Orren C. Moore, Mrs. Enoch Powell, Mrs. Albert Flinn, Lucy Thayer, Mrs. John F. Stark, Mrs. John H. Barr, Mrs. S. Withed, Mrs. J.A. Spalding, Mrs. Frank McQuesten, and Mrs. Edward Knight. The first general meeting of the club was held at the Nashua Boat Club with twenty-five members present. The membership was increased to fifty at the next meeting, and dues were set at three dollars a year.

The meetings featured lectures by outstanding personalities of the time, including Booker T. Washington, Julia Ward Howe, Anna Peck (the first woman to climb the Matterhorn), Lieutenant Robert E. Peary, and Fannie Farmer, the first dietician at the New Hampshire State Hospital and founder of the Boston Cooking School, who gave lectures and cooking demonstrations.

In addition to regular meetings, the club sponsored classes in art, music, literature, and current events, and was responsible for the introduction of classes in domestic science and manual training in the public schools, for which it paid until the city assumed that responsibility. In 1934 the Nashaway Woman's Club showed its continued interest in this part of the school curriculum by sponsoring a home remodeling project. Domestic Science and Manual Arts students at Nashua High School worked on a dilapidated house and turned it into a livable dwelling at minimum expense.

The Good Cheer Society

The first group to be organized exclusively for service to others was the Good Cheer Society in 1883. It was limited to twenty-five young ladies, at least twenty-one years of age and unmarried at the time of becoming a member. The purpose of the society was:

. . . to visit the sick and comfort those unfortunates by carrying them fruit, flowers, delicacies, and by bringing bright smiles and sympathetic looks and expressions of confidence in their return to good health.

As the scope of their activities widened, and they not only took flowers and other delicacies to the sick, but assumed the responsibility for payment of rent, food, clothes, and medicines, there was a need for funds to provide these services. Money-raising activities included teas, receptions, dances, garden parties, poster exhibitions, minstrel shows, finally settling on an annual revue and the sale of Good Cheer caramels. The society furnished two rooms in the Nashua Emergency Hospital at a cost of $180. Later it developed pre-school clinics and a nursing service, now the Visiting Nurse Association.

On January 1, 1896, the Good Cheer Society took over the entire edition of the *Nashua Telegraph.*

We have tried to open a broad and generous field that there

be no sphere into which the women of Nashua may not enter. We were not confined to the narrow limits of the Woman's Department, which seemed once to be bounded by the pickle jar on one side and the cradle on the other, but having the entire field to ourselves, we have endeavored to show that the women of Nashua can edit a paper.

And show it they did, for it was a lively and entertaining edition. In place of letters to the editor each Good Cheer member offered a paragraph of suggestions to improve Nashua. Here are some of their ideas:

I would clean up the dump around the Amherst Street School, burn the Mt. Pleasant School and all its pestilential contents, and erect a building after the latest in sanitary science. [An incinerator, perhaps?]
I would sell the North Common to the highest bidder and with the money buy Sandy Pond and its beautiful surrounding slopes for a public park. Nature must have intended it for some such purpose, while no one believes that the miry awkward pasture known as North Common will ever amount to anything as a park.
We have a hospital for the sick but no insane asylum, and this, I fear, we shall soon be obliged to have built; for some of our city officials are beginning to show signs of it already, and when they get to where they don't know what they're doing, I think it is time for medical treatment.

Many other needs pointed out included better sidewalks, wider principal streets, an addition to the hospital, and the replacement of unsightly buildings.

An editorial in the *Telegraph* on the day following the special Good Cheer edition read: "They were the jolliest, happiest, most enthusiastic set I have ever seen. They believed in the cause, and they made the Woman's Edition of the *Telegraph* the greatest success in local journalism in all New Hampshire. The members of the Good Cheer Society have reason to be proud." The editor also could not resist mentioning that he had found his desk littered with hairpins, powder puffs, and other evidence of feminine occupation.

The Nashua Protestant Home for Aged Women was founded in June, 1887, by a group of women from the Protestant churches of the city. They were Mrs. A.M. Stevens, Mrs. Fannie W. Sawyer, Mrs. J.N. Beasom, and Sarah Kendall. It received from Belinda Blodgett the gift of a house on Kinsley Street, which in two years became inadequate, so for

twenty-five thousand dollars a home on Walnut Street was purchased where twenty-nine aged women could spend their last days "contentedly and comfortably." The annual Pound Parties which helped to stock the larder were social occasions as well, and that custom is still continued. The present home at 12 Concord Street was opened in 1966 with accommodations for sixteen women and was named in honor of Helen Norwell, a former president and long-time member of the Board of Directors.

The King's Daughters Benevolent Association started the first day nursery for working mothers in 1894. "The institution receives the aid and support of Nashua's best citizens, as it appeals to the hearts of those who are interested in making the lives of unfortunate children happier, and thus aiding them, by their surroundings, to become worthy men and women." It later became a home for boys between the ages of three and ten from broken homes and supported one hundred children during a four-year period for just one to two dollars a week for each one. In 1925 a home was purchased on Arlington Street but by 1963 rising costs made it necessary to close and lease the property to the Nashua Unit for the Retarded, which operates Mount Hope School with financial help from the city.

The Nashua Grange first met in 1878 at the Indian Head House, at that time the social center of this part of the state and now the site of the First Congregational Church. The purpose of the organization was to provide more effective methods of marketing farm products as well as to support legislation for improving local conditions.

A rented house on Mechanic Street became the first home of the Salvation Army in Nashua in 1892 and was occupied until 1921, when the present building on Temple Street was ready for occupancy.

The Nashua YMCA, whose purposes were religious training and social work, was established in Nashua on October 6, 1877, with rooms at 69 Main Street. Work on a gymnasium on Water Street was begun in 1892, and land on Temple Street at the corner of Spring was purchased later. The cornerstone of the latter building was laid by President William Howard Taft. Later, land on Lake Naticook was purchased for a boys' camp.

In the late 1800s a group of women met to establish the Nashua YWCA. They were Ella Wheeler, Harriet Locke, Mrs. A.S. Colburn, Mary Evans, and Mattie Colburn. Their purpose was " . . . the salvation of young women and to provide for their spiritual, intellectual and physical development." The early meetings were held in a Main Street store-front, but were soon moved to a building on

East Pearl Street, later the location of the Hamblett law offices. The next move was to the residence on Temple Street, adjacent to the YMCA, before occupying the joint YWCA-YMCA building on Prospect Street.

Earliest labor-oriented groups were the United Workmen, Nashua Veterans' Firemen's Association, and the Brotherhood of Engineers. Ethnic groups included the Knights of Columbus, whose first Grand Knight was Jeremiah J. Doyle. This organization supported baseball and football, and later donated the steel bleachers for thirty-five hundred spectators to the Holman Stadium.

Groups of French origin were the Circle Montcalm, led by J.B. Phaneuf; les Montagnards, 1896; Les Dames de Charite of St. Louis de Gonzague Church, who were devoted to helping French-speaking people who settled in Nashua; and the Entre Nous Club, later to be the nucleus of the BPOE, which was organized in Nashua in 1901.

Opportunities for physical activities were provided by the bicycle clubs for men and women, since during the late 1800s there were twelve hundred to fifteen hundred bicyclists in Nashua. These were the Nashua Wheel Club, 1881; the Riverside Bicycle Club, 1884; and the Nashua Cycle Club, 1896. Activities ranged from drills, parades, races, and demonstrations of trick riding to meets with other clubs from Lowell, Worcester, Portsmouth, Manchester, and Springfield.

The Nashua Boat Club on the Nashua River adjacent to Franklin Street provided boating and other sports. It had a flotilla of fourteen boats and canoes, and later added a tennis court and croquet grounds. The club started in 1895 on land leased from the Nashua Manufacturing Company.

The dedication of the Boat Club was a gala affair, as reported by the local newspaper:

As one entered the Club grounds, surprise and delight at the brilliance and beauty of the house were the emotions given. Every gas jet in the house was lighted and the piazza hung with innumerable Chinese lanterns. Inside the clubhouse, the brilliancy did not abate in the least. The American Orchestra discoursed sweet music for waltzes, two steps, and quadrilles.

Social activities included a yearly minstrel show performed by members of the Club in the Nashua Theatre—one of the highlights of the social season.

Nashua Boat Club, Nashua, N. H.

Clubhouse of Nashua Boat Club in 1916, from an old postcard.

The Ovum Novum Societas, organized August 18, 1859, by a fun-loving group of young men, enjoyed hilarious picnics each year at Mine Falls Park with games and athletic competitions. Medals with the group's motto, "Ex Nihilo Nihil Expectamus," on one side and the head of a jackass on the other were awarded to the poorest shot and the slowest runner.

Military Organizations

Military organizations attracted many men both young and old in the post-Civil War period. An offshoot of the New Hampshire National Guard, called the Nashua City Guard, was organized under the leadership of Colonel E.J. Copp and was made up of " . . . young men in the front rank socially and in business." Ties were formed in the drill room and

Sketch of fireplace corner of Boat Club interior, from 1897 program.

muster field which the boys were loath to discontinue when the term of enlistment expired in 1883. After several years, because of the demand on the time and strength of the men "... in being compelled to drill in season and out, the interest flagged, so when enlistments expired, but few could be induced to re-enlist; neither did recruits come forward. Under these circumstances, the company became reduced in numbers and was forced to disband."

The former members of the Guards were unwilling to relinquish the enjoyable aspects of their association, however, and met socially once a month.

The John G. Foster Post, Grand Army of the Republic, assisted by two grants of twelve thousand dollars from the city, erected the Soldiers' and Sailors' monument in Abbott Square in 1889. The unit, organized in 1868, had as its first leader Matthew Benton. In the cornerstone of the monument was placed a list of Nashua's soldiers and sailors who served in the War of the Rebellion.

Fraternal Organizations

Fraternal organizations such as the Masonic orders and the IOOF had their origin in the early 1800s, from which auxiliary women's groups were formed, but these were adjuncts and not completely independent groups. The first of these was the Independent Order of Odd Fellows, Granite Lodge, in 1843, followed by other subsidiary lodges: the Nashoonon Encampment, 1844; Pennichuck Lodge, 1859; Olive Branch Daughters of Rebecca, 1886; Patriarchs Militant, 1890.

Early meetings were held in various places in town, and on April 26, 1892—as has been noted in the previous chapter—the Odd Fellows Building at the corner of Main and Temple Streets was dedicated.

The founders of the first Masonic Lodges were the descendants of men who had fought under Sir Francis Drake and William of Orange. They came to the American wilderness to establish free masonry, churches where they could worship as they wished, and schools not dominated by any church. The seven men who organized the Nashua Chapter met in a private home on Main Street south of Salmon Brook on June 13, 1882. They were John Lund, Alfred Greeley, Willard Marshall, Joel Thayer, Thomas French, Joel Nason, and William Cogswell. After meeting in Nashua halls for several years, they built the Masonic Temple at the corner of Main and Pearl Streets, dedicated on January 21, 1891.

The Rising Sun Lodge was followed by other Masonic groups: the Ancient York Lodge, Meridian Sun Royal Arch, St. George Commandery, Knights of Templar Grand Consistory. Subordinate bodies were Oriental Princes of Jerusalem and St. George Chapter of Rose Croix.

Other fraternal groups were the Knights of Pythias, Improved Order of Red Men, Independent Order of Good Templars, Patrons of Husbandry, Ancient Order of Foresters, American Legion of Honor, Daughters of Liberty, Knights and Ladies of Honor, Order of the World, Order of Pilgrim Fathers, and United Order of the Golden Cross.

Musical Opportunities

Music and art played a large part in the lives of the men and women of Nashua in the nineteenth century. Miss Linda Flagg, a talented artist and teacher, had a studio on the second floor of the Exchange Building on Main Street over White's drug store in 1881. She held annual exhibitions of her work and that of her advanced pupils. These included landscapes, oils, flower panels, water colors and charcoal studies. A newspaper announcement of her yearly showing read, "Visitors are expected to pay a small fee of ten cents, which, considering that Miss Flagg is a professional, and, like all people in business, has bills to pay, is little enough." Among her advanced students were Frank Holman, later a member of the staff of the Nashua Library and the donor of the athletic stadium which bears his name, and Frank Ingalls, a professional photographer whose many pictures of early Nashua are valued parts of the collections of the Nashua Historical Society and the Nashua Public Library.

Music was a source of great pleasure to Nashuans, who were enthusiastic both as performers and listeners. The Franklin Opera House, managed by Arthur H. Davis, opened on February 20, 1890, with a performance of *H.M.S. Pinafore* by the Ideal Opera Company under the musical direction of S.L. Studley. In the early days, the Franklin Opera House was the outstanding stage show theatre of

Southern New Hampshire. Many of the leading actors and actresses of the last quarter of that century performed there. Denman Thompson played in *The Old Homestead,* and Julia Marlowe, the noted Shakespearean actress, appeared on that stage. It was also the scene of sporting events such as basketball, wrestling, and roller skating, and the seats could be removed easily for dancing.

The Ladies' Musical Club organized in 1894 had as its President Mrs. James H. Tolles, a talented musician. Members were Mrs. Tolles' daughter Marion, a violinist, who played with the Ladies' Orchestra of Boston, and Anna Melendy Sanderson, a noted concert pianist and teacher.

The Nashua Oratorio Society, established by Eusebius G. Hood in the late 1800s, brought to Nashua such world-renowned artists as Reinald Werrenrath, Paul Althous, Marie Sundelius, Emilio Gargoza, and Anita Rio. The Oratorio Society, augmented by the Boston Festival Orchestra and the Nashua High School choral groups, presented annual three-day music festivals performing such works as *Aida, The Messiah, Elijah, The Seven Last Words of Christ,* and *Samson and Delilah.* The rehearsal pianists were Miriam Dowd and Anna Melendy Sanderson. Mr. Hood was the musical director of Nashua High School which, under his direction, earned the distinction of being the only high school in the country studying masterpieces of musical literature.

The Nashua School of Music and Elocution, the only institution of its kind in New Hampshire, was established in 1897 and directed by Ethel Blood Ingham at 2 Olive Street, at the rear of the Old Post Office. Vocal, instrumental, and dramatic instruction was offered and attracted students both from Nashua and the surrounding area. Yearly recitals were given by students and members of the faculty.

Drama Was Not Neglected

Nashuans enjoyed both amateur and professional theatrical performances. The Gate City Dramatic Club, on June 20, 1866, presented *The Pilgrim's Search for Happiness, or a Lesson in Life* in the City Hall. Admission was twenty-five cents, with reserved seats a dime more. Another production by this group was *Bradford Folks, or Old Yankee Neighbors.*

The Nashua Theatre, located at what is now the parking lot on Elm Street at the rear of the Police Station, opened on February 1, 1900, under the management of Arthur H. Davis, and featured traveling stock companies which remained for a week at a time, presenting such favorites as *East Lynne.* Admission to the Saturday performance was ten cents, and a program note that was the epitome of tact read, "Every lady who removes her hat during a performance shows a grateful consideration for those who occupy a seat behind her."

Other Activities in Nashua

While balls to celebrate Presidential elections were gala affairs, torchlight parades held in the month prior to the election were also an important part of the political scene. They were composed of state regiments, bands, drum corps, and marching units from Nashua and surrounding towns with as many as two thousand marchers carrying torches. Houses and business establishments along the line of march were brilliantly lighted and decorated with flags and bunting. Chinese lanterns, fireworks, and bursting rockets added to the excitement.

In the Tilden-Hendricks campaign of 1876 a full-rigged illuminated steamboat, run by electricity with one hundred windows decorated in red, white, and blue paper, bore the inscription, "We are sailing for Tilden and Hendricks." One of the many banners in the parade proclaimed, "Reform, Reconciliation, Renewed Prosperity." The *Nashua Gazette* reported, "At the conclusion of the parade, divisions were marched to their appointed rendezvous, where a liberal supply of refreshments was provided."

A continuing link between the past and the present is the Nashua Historical Society, founded in 1870. The early meetings were held in the homes of members, and its first officers were Dr. E.F. McQuesten, David Gillis, Frederick Alvord, S.H. McCollester, and Dr. C.A. Eayers. Officers in 1872-1873 were V. Gilman, Frederick Alvord, Henry Atherton, and Dana King; and in 1874-1875, C.C. Moore, Frederick Alvord, Henry Atherton, Dana King, Dr. Amos Abbot, and Joseph Clough.

Early benefactors of the Society were Annie and Adella Goodrich, whose generous gifts of real and personal property formed the nucleus of the Society's collection. Sceva Speare established a trust fund to provide a permanent home for the Society, and in May, 1972, the Florence Speare Memorial Building was dedicated on Abbott Street. Another generous donor was George Melcher, who gave the land and buildings on which the Historical Society's building now stands.

Hannah Eayres Barron

Nashua produced few outstanding authors during this period, as literary achievement generally was not a field into which many local persons ventured. Fox's history, in fact, probably was the nearest thing to a "best seller" that was produced. A manuscript book of letters and miscellaneous writings compiled by Mrs. Hannah Eayres Barron, now owned by the Nashua Public Library, reveals a woman who had some ambitions along this line. Mrs. Barron, who lived from 1809 to 1891, resided during the last years of her life on Granite Street. She seems to have combined a rather humdrum daily life with extraordinary mental activity. In her numerous writings there are many flashes of intellectual ability, unfortunately never quite fulfilled because of lack of formal education and training as well as stimulating contacts. Her only published book was a volume of her poetry put out by the Nashua printing firm of Barker and Bean in 1884. (Incidentally, the quality of the printing and binding in this book was very good, the pages having scarcely yellowed in almost a hundred years.) The literary quality of the poems is uneven; they express a deep religious faith, a playful sense of humor, and an attitude of resignation toward the problems and disappointments of life.

Probably the most valuable contribution of Hannah Barron was her historic writing on Nashua and the surrounding area, published as a series of articles, "Recollections of Long Ago," in the *Nashua Daily Telegraph.* Her description of Dunstable Village in the early part of the nineteenth century bears the imprint of first-hand knowledge. Her childhood home was just over the line in Merrimack, at a place she notes "is now known as Dean-

croft." Once she was taken to the circus in Dunstable, the very first such performance ever given here, which took place in the barn of Tyler's Tavern. In her account, written many years later, we get a glimpse of a wide-eyed child enthralled by wonders not usually seen.

One of Hannah's short essays suggests a personal philosophy that could be applied in any age by anyone:

I recollect when I was young and teaching school, as was the custom in the district, I had to board among the scholars. In one part of the district I had to climb quite a hill before reaching one of my boarding places. The weather was warm and my health not very firm and only a cold lunch for dinner. I would feel tired and weak and sometimes when coming in sight of the hill I would feel as though I could not reach the top. I got in the habit of counting my steps and so learned it was not best to look at the top while standing at the foot of the hill, I considered that one step at a time was all that I could accomplish and by repeating that one step at a time I would soon find a level and pleasant road and shortly a resting place and a warm supper.

So has life been with me for seventy five years and six months. Had I looked forward in my youth to this day of my life I should have said to myself no, I can never reach such a summit, I shall surely fail. Sickness has often obscured my path–that I have often thought I could not proceed much farther, but with only one beat of the heart at a time has kept my life blood flowing and only one tick of the clock at a time has measured the years and days of my life. Only one day at a time has been present for me to look at, but all of my days when numbered amount to twenty seven thousand five hundred and fifty days. One beat of the heart. One tick of the clock.

Hannah Barron typified a female type often found in nineteenth century New England—one who, trapped in the usual commitments to marriage and family, nevertheless had a talent, an urge toward expressing herself in writing. Very often such women referred to this disparagingly as "my scribbling." Only a few exceptionally sturdy characters were able to overcome the smothering of the creative flame by the expediencies of daily life.

19

Education in Nineteenth Century Nashua

O N AN EARLY September morning in 1898, a young girl waited at a street corner for the trolley car that would take her part way to her first job as a teacher in the Nashua schools. She wore her hair in a high pompadour that was the approved style for that year, and her dress consisted of the typical white shirtwaist and long, dark skirt, with a leather belt from which hung the ladies' handbag of the day, the reticule. At the corner of Main and Allds Streets she left the trolley and walked to the school on Harbor Avenue. In the winter she would have to reach the school on snowshoes on mornings when there had been heavy snow and the streets had not been plowed.

The schoolhouse had no lights, and heat was provided by a stove which the janitor stoked each morning with enough wood to last the school day. Toilet facilities were in a separate building in the rear of the school, and the counterpart of the present-day bubbler was a pail of water and a tin dipper on a shelf in the corner of the schoolroom. Children were summoned to school and back from recess by the teacher who stood in the doorway ringing a hand bell.

She received a salary of only three hundred dollars a year, but from the beginning she made teaching a real career. She enjoyed especially helping children learn to read and soon devised her own system of teaching phonics, a method that is still used today and that can be seen in operation on a children's TV show. She felt that children should have more meaningful reading material in the early grades and became co-editor of a series known as the Beacon Readers which were published by Ginn and Company and widely distributed for use in many schools. She eventually became the first Supervisor of Reading in the Nashua school system for the first three grades, that formative period in a child's education that interested her most.

Her pupils loved her because they sensed her deep concern for each of them. The neglected or underprivileged child especially aroused a compassion in her that took the form of extra attention. She continued to help children in the beginning years of their education until her retirement.

She is still living, one of Nashua's remarkably keen elderly people, now looking forward in a very few more years to her one-hundredth birthday, a resident of Greenbriar Terrace. Who is this lady who has contributed so much over a long lifetime to

the education of thousands of children, who brought to her chosen work so much originality and creativity? She is Miss Alice Trow, who witnessed all the changes of the twentieth century, yet stands as a link with the educational system of the late nineteenth century.

Another elderly retired school teacher, whose memories went back almost to the turn of the century, was Miss Sarah Clancy who died in 1977. She taught in a rural school in Hudson and at the Belvidere School on Canal Street, completing her career by teaching for twenty-six years at the Spring Street Junior High School. One of her students was a Nashuan who later became a well-known professional boxer — "Eddie" Record.

The Early Schools

Both private and public schools flourished in Dunstable in the course of the nineteenth century, and in the last part of the century Catholic parochial schools were also part of the educational picture. During the late 1820s and 1830s, that peak period of population growth, several private schools competed for pupils from families that could afford to give their children training beyond the grade level of the schools set up by the town. In the first issue of the very first newspaper published here, December 23, 1826, J. Read advertised that he was opening an evening school that would specialize in English

grammar, arithmetic, Latin and Greek, Geography, and Public Speaking. He mentioned that the room he planned to use "over Goodnow's Store" had been previously occupied as a school room. Even Andrew Thayer, later editor of the paper, had plans to move in on the profitable private school field, as he ran a lengthy ad announcing the academy he would open the following spring. In February, 1835, the Nashua High School for Young Gentlemen and Ladies announced the opening of its spring term in the *Gazette*. The director was G.S. Brown, A.B., and his associate was D. Crosby, A.B., whose name was to become in the next forty years synonymous with quality education in Nashua. In the announcement of this school, Mr. Crosby was described as one "who has been for more than ten years an approved and successful instructor." Two ladies completed the staff of this institution: Miss H.M. Thatcher, who had formerly taught at a female seminary in Claremont, and Miss R. Spaulding, who was in charge of the girl students. The curriculum sounds fairly ambitious; besides the usual high school subjects, French, Latin and Greek, drawing, painting, and piano and vocal music were offered. Tuition varied from three to five dollars a quarter, with board a dollar twenty-five to one seventy-five a week.

The first member of the staff to break away and open her own school was Miss Spaulding, who set up a "School for Young Ladies" in the fall of 1835.

By the following year, several other schools were opened, including the high school of David Crosby. In March, 1836, he advertised his intention to start an institution at the building where the Masonic Hall was located.

David Crosby's Literary Institute

Professor David Crosby and his wife and associate, Louisa Crosby, were gifted teachers. They kept the Nashua Literary Institute going until Crosby was literally on his death bed in 1876. Among his backers and trustees were Zebediah Shattuck, John B. Chapman, and Josiah G. Graves, M.D. Crosby was a graduate of Kimball Union Academy and Dartmouth College and served a term as president of the New Hampshire Education Association.

The school was located at 10 Park Street. Professor Crosby was described as

. . . a man of forbidding exterior, but who was, in fact, kindhearted and sympathetic. His manner, stern and hard toward the delinquent older boys, was always kind toward the smaller children. As he stood on the platform to address us, the flash of eye and ring of voice all indicated a man prompt and decisive of action. We found him to be all this. He opened school with a prayer and ended it with 'Amen, Dodge, what are you up to now?' using amen and Dodge together. This was Dana Dodge, who was always in a scrape.

Mrs. Crosby was described as

. . . a magnificent woman in all that pertains to womanhood. She was dignified and an exacting disciplinarian— even more so than her husband— and when she said our conduct must be thus and so, there was no getting away from it. She was, too, a remarkably successful teacher.

Before 1853 pupils were sent to school when they were three or four years old, but in that year a law was passed making five the required age for entering school. It was advised that slates be allowed for the use of younger children ". . . to enable them to bear the difficult task of sitting still," a sad commentary on the methods of teaching at that time.

Reading aloud and reciting in unison were frowned upon so that the teacher could devote more time individually to the students. "Each pupil was then obliged to answer for himself, and the indolent ones could no longer await the answer of the more industrious, and sluggishly echo it. Scholars were too prone to answer for each other and encouraged the prompting of more backward pupils by whispering."

Professor David Crosby and his wife, Louisa Hunton Crosby.

Miss Alice Trow's class at the Edgeville School in 1901.
Almost old enough to attend is three year old Anne McWeeney,
future high school teacher, standing on a chair next to Miss Trow.

Nashua Schools in the 1840s

Some paragraphs from a report of the Selectmen and Superintending School Committee of Nashua for 1840-1841 shed some interesting light on the schools of that period:

The primary department composed of very young children has been conducted by Mrs. Law and Miss Waite. These leaders have a happy tact of exciting and sustaining great interest in their infant students by a series of simple exercises enlisting the mind, the voice, and limbs, and giving great variety and frequent changes of position; these serve to create a lively relish for school, which is important for pupils so young. A distaste for school, acquired at this age, frequently exerts an influence unfavorable to learning in after years.

The winter term (for older students) began with good promise, but lack of tact in discipline, combined with extreme rudeness on the part of the boys, disturbed the order and usefulness of the school, and it was decided to close it before the allotted time. The master was drawn into a scuffle with an unruly boy; the boy was expelled afterward and the School languished. This scholar has always been a great nuisance to the School and ought to have been expelled; we trust he may see the error of his ways, become a worthy member of the School and society, and abandon a course that must lead to disgrace.

The report also dealt with the general conditions in the schools such as the fluctuating attendance, " . . . many of the larger scholars working part of the time in the mills, and the population that composes the district being very unfixed." This refers to the area around Elm and West Pearl Streets near the Nashua mills. The children in this district attended what was called the "Old Brick" School.

The report continues,

. . . Without saying anything about the dignity of gossip, we would earnestly advise parents against believing and repeating in the presence of their children all the gossip that is brought home from school. Children are very liable to prejudices and bring wrong reports unconsciously, and it is a sad fact that not a few of them will lie outright.
It would be comparatively comfortable if the laws of cleanliness were observed. The free use of pure water would vastly improve the complexions of some of the pupils, and would be a matter of economy in the saving of books which very soon become soiled and so covered with dirt by the constant application of unwashed fingers as to be illegible.

Salaries for teachers were one dollar a week plus board. Bids for board were let out and averaged one dollar to two dollars a week. Women teachers received $10.12 a month and board for a fourteen-week term, while men were paid $26.10 for a nine-week term. The seeds of Women's Lib were, no doubt, sown here.

Discipline was always, in varying degrees, a problem in the early schools. The value of a teacher was measured by her capacity to keep pupils in a "tranquil mood." "Whispering loomed up as an obstacle which the average teacher found difficult to surmount, and which was looked on with disfavor by the superintending committee, which considered this practice taboo."

Of an early teacher at Mount Pleasant School, the parents said,

No other teacher was her equal, a point of view not shared by the pupils until in later years they appreciated the influence this Christian woman who devoted her life to this ill-paid career had on their later success in life.

One of her pupils, Judge Prescott, recorded in his diary,

She licked us around before school for what we were to do in the morning, at noon for what we had done in the forenoon, and in the afternoon as a warning for the next day. Any boy who escaped with only three lickings was lucky.

A teacher when interviewed was asked if she had enough nerve to administer punishment with a ruler, and once when a teacher was in the process of so doing, the culprit withdrew his hand, the teacher hit herself on the knee with such force that she fainted, and was forced to limp for a week. How her pupils must have enjoyed that!

On the teacher's desk at Old Brick an eighteen inch ebony ruler and a two-foot rawhide were placed for maintaining discipline. There were degrees of punishment varying from sitting in absolute silence for five minutes or standing in the corner face to the wall—often all four corners were occupied—to sitting on a stick of wood for fifteen minutes, a punishment enjoyed by the miscreant, who fell off frequently to the amusement of the class. Another punishment was to fasten snap clothespins to the pupils' ears or nose.

Reports were given out for discipline as well as scholastic achievement, and a report card of that period read as follows:
1. Excellent
2. Generally good
3. Partly good
4. More bad than good

The first Spring Street School burned in 1919.

5. Decidedly bad
6. Insufferably bad—subject for rawhide

The conclusions of the Selectmen and School Committee were that,

In discipline it is highly important that mere playfulness of youth should be distinguished from willful perversity, and the punishment should be adapted accordingly. Although much opposed to the frequent use of corporeal punishment, it should be reserved for extreme cases. The passions developed in the large scholars by flogging are productive of anything other than a good moral influence.

High School in Nashville

In 1846, Daniel Abbot gave the town three acres of land on the west side of Manchester Street, where a four-room school was built at a cost of six thousand dollars and was referred to by the proud townspeople as, "The new, costly, and convenient schoolhouse." The school was destroyed by fire in 1869 and was rebuilt in 1870 for forty-five thousand dollars. The new building had ten rooms, an assembly hall, and accommodations for eighty high school pupils, seventy-two grammar school students, and eighty in the elementary department. Samuel Alvord was the first principal. Students paid tuition to attend high school and, like pupils in

the grades, bought their own books and supplies.

The requirements for admission to high school were arithmetic through fractions, grammar as far as prosody and parsing, geography, spelling, and United States history. High school texts used were Greenleaf's Algebra, Harkness' Latin Grammar, Quackenbos' Natural History, and Xenephon's Anabasis.

The Main Street High School, later the location of the Colonial Theatre, was built in 1853.

The first class was graduated from the Main Street School in 1859, and in 1875 the students were moved to the new school on Spring Street with T.W.H. Hussey serving as principal of the combined schools. The Spring Street building was described by Superintendent John H. Goodale as

. . . not only the most costly, but the largest and best constructed edifice in New Hampshire. There will be no need of strengthening floors or increasing supports. It is strongly and neatly constructed. Fill it as you may, there will be no giving way, no weakness, no disaster. The supply of air is pure, not forced from the basement, but taken directly from the open atmosphere. The basement is utilized by furnishing two spacious playrooms, one for girls and one for boys– each distinct and separate.

This building housed the Quarter Bell, rung as a warning to laggards fifteen minutes before the beginning of the morning and afternoon sessions.

Mrs. Anna Noyes presented one thousand dollars to the school, the income to purchase four gold medals annually, two for boys and two for girls, as a memorial to her husband, Colonel Leonard Noyes. The first recipients were Willis Tinker, William Pinkham, Ella Perkins, and Clara J. McKean. Miss McKean later became an excellent teacher of Latin and Greek at Nashua High School.

The present Temple Street Elementary School was originally built as a high school in 1905 and was used for that purpose until 1919. The Spring Street School was built in 1875 and was used as the high school until 1905, at which time it became a grammar school. It burned down in 1917 and the present building, erected on the same site in 1919, was the senior high school until the Elm Street High School was dedicated in 1937. When the new high school at the Mill Pond site was opened in 1975, the Elm

Street building became a third junior high school.

Other early schools were the Country Club, 1863; Harbor Street, 1874; Arlington Street, 1889; Amherst Street, 1892; Palm and Belvidere, 1897; Lake Street, 1898; Mulberry Street, 1905; Shattuck Street, 1908; James B. Crowley, 1924. Suburban schools were Gilboa and Silver Springs in Dunstable and Coburn and Edgeville in Nashua.

In 1845 there was a summer school for teaching writing, and in 1873 at West Pearl and Belvidere there were evening classes for boys and girls who could not attend school in the daytime because they were working in the mills. A teacher-training school was established in 1894 at the Amherst Street School.

In the fall of 1890, the superintendent of schools encouraged the teachers to organize for "the further-ance of professional study." Soon after that the Teachers' Club was formed to "promote teaching power and general culture." The officers were Charles H. Noyes, Selby Shepard, and Ida Wallace.

Drawing and physical culture were introduced in the schools in 1885, and in 1887 General Elbert Wheeler and Jason Tolles conducted classes in military training in the high school. The High School Cadets, in 1887, conducted drills, competitions, and exhibitions under the leadership of Captain E.D. Hoitt.

The first kindergarten opened in September, 1893, at the corner of Quincy and East Pearl Streets with Jennie Farley as principal. Others were established later on Amherst and Kinsley Streets and in Crown Hill.

Schools were closed in 1870 for a considerable time because of smallpox and again in 1884 for scarlet fever, but schools were never closed because of bad weather. The teacher was expected to find some way of getting to school, and fathers of small children carried them piggy-back.

Public schools were considered to be so good that no private elementary schools were opened in Nashua until 1883, when the Reverend Father Milette opened a school in the basement of St.

The first High School on Main Street.

Louis de Gonzague Church on Hollis Street for five hundred pupils who were taught by eight nuns. In 1898 a school for girls was built on Chestnut Street, replaced later by the brick building which now stands.

In 1886, the Reverend Father Lessard opened a school in the basement of Saint Francis Xavier Church on Chandler Street. The Reverend Father O'Donnell, a valued member of the School Board, built a school in that area bearing his name. It was said that " . . . under his benign influence, many matters which might have caused difficulty were made smooth."

As the nineteenth century drew to a close, Nashua's educational needs were being met by an array of public, private, and parochial schools. The growing body of pupils placed a heavy burden on the community. However, the continued awareness of the important role of education sparked continued interest in maintaining a school system that was efficient and progressive.

The Graduates/1859

Members of the first graduating
class of Nashua High School.

20

Nashua in the Gay Nineties

A VISITOR to Nashua in the nineties found a small, pleasant city with wide, tree-lined streets, many large, well-built homes, and some impressive buildings in the downtown area.

In 1892, Mrs. John M. Hunt and Miss Mary Hunt had given fifty thousand dollars to the city to build a new library as a memorial to their husband and father. Their generosity was acclaimed but the selection of the site for the new building became a matter of much bitter dissension. A North End vs South End disagreement took several years to settle. After court action, the location on the Greeley lot was finally decided in 1895. It was not until 1903, however, that the first books were checked out of the John M. Hunt Memorial Library.

Transportation in the Nineties

One of the most important achievements of the nineties was the development of the electric street railway connecting Nashua and Lowell. This was at one time the longest line in the country. A newspaper feature article written a few years later explained how it was possible to go to New York from Nashua by frequent changes of cars. This electric railway was the most economical means of public transportation for many years.

This decade also marked the end of the era known as the "horse and buggy days." Horses were more than a method of transportation, their care and acquisition were of supreme importance. They were discussed, sometimes cussed, raced, paced, bought, sold, and traded.

The Sunday drive to Hollis, Amherst, or Hudson in the family vehicle or a conveyance hired from one of the local livery stables was a popular weekend diversion. There were several livery stables and two blacksmith shops in the city during the nineties, each doing a brisk business. The papers sometimes published descriptions of interesting places to go for a Sunday buggy ride and picnic.

The Nashua Driving Park Association races at the Fairgrounds track drew large crowds. There were also polo matches played here with teams from Massachusetts and other New Hampshire communities. Polo today is considered a game for the wealthy playboy, hardly the sort of sport you associate with a New Hampshire mill town. Here in Nashua the subject of horses was compelling enough for the paper to publish a long descriptive

Miss Fannie Morrison

Mrs. Roswell T. Smith

Mrs. Wingate Bixley

Mrs. Mary P. Greeley

Mrs. N.T. Morrill

Mrs. Walter C. French

Mrs. George Anderson

Mrs. George H. Lessard

Eight ladies of nineteenth century Nashua

census of the equine population of the city, complete with the names of the owners and the wagons or carriages used by them.

For long journeys, one could make railroad connections, starting in Nashua, to just about any part of the country. This was the fastest and most comfortable way to travel, the luxuriously furnished parlor cars making the trip a real pleasure.

Women and Business

The main industry in Nashua in the nineties, as it had been for many years, was textile manufacturing. The mills had been operating for about seventy years. As a result, many other businesses had developed to supply the textile industry. There were several tool companies, bobbin and shuttle shops, and others directly or indirectly concerned with the manufacture of cloth.

The city directory for 1895 lists a wide variety of shops and businesses. C.H. Avery, Gregg & Son, Nashua Corporation (Card Shop), and Maine Manufacturing Company are some that are still in existence today.

An article appeared in the press about this time regarding women in business. It reported, with seeming surprise, on the success of their various enterprises. Women included one physician, two dentists, an architect, a grocer, several milliners, and seventy-nine teachers. Actually, women were involved in many different businesses and professions and, as is the case today, these were often combined with keeping house and raising a family. The fact that the feminine mind was able to comprehend the finances of business was astonishing to the newspaper writer. He pointed out that these women did not typify "the new woman, ludicrous in her reforms who was but a subject for jokes." "Nashua women," it was said, "exemplified the highest standards of New England womanhood." Today's liberated woman would take exception to the somewhat patronizing attitude taken by this writer and would find nothing at all unusual about successful women in any field of endeavor.

Current Fashions

There were over one hundred dressmakers in the city in 1895. This was one career that women could pursue, sometimes at home, that was both profita-

ble and acceptable. From the large number of dressmakers in town, one could safely conclude that Nashua ladies were certainly fashion-minded. Ladies' fashions in those Victorian days were very fancy. The vogue was for tight-waisted dresses with leg-o-mutton sleeves. There were ruffles, bows, pleats, ruching, decorative buttons, and lace. All of this must have presented the dressmaker with a real challenge. The shirtwaist was a fashion that American women adored. It was said that Paris designers despised and maligned it; however, American ladies found it comfortable and becoming. Worn with a long skirt, usually black, the shirtwaist remained in fashion for many years. Skirts generally were floor-length. However, Sears' catalogue showed two models of bicycle suits consisting of a jacket, skirt, bloomers, leggings, and a hat—all for three seventy-five. These skirts were short, about calf-length. Bloomers, also known as bifurcated garments, were being worn by some of the more daring of the younger set. Supposedly, these were worn for warmth under long skirts enabling the wearer to eliminate one or more petticoats which were cumbersome and heavy to lift when walking outdoors in winter or on rough terrain.

Hats, especially, enabled a girl to indulge her fancy for ornamentation. Frills, feathers, bows, birds, berries, and flowers were all used as trimmings and sometimes all on the same hat! Feathers were so fashionable that even in those pre-conservation days, the Audubon Society was upset by the ever-increasing use of egret feathers. The

Mrs. Ira Harris and her mother set out for afternoon calls.

Home of Ira F. Harris on Orange Street
in the late 1890s. Mr. Harris is at the right and his father-in-law,
Joseph B. Proctor, is at the left.

Gibson Girl as drawn by Charles Dana Gibson was the glamour girl of the day. Her patrician beauty served as a model for American girls everywhere. His drawings appeared in the humor magazine *Life*. Gentlemen of the day aped the escorts of the Gibson Girl, shaved their mustaches and bought clothing similar to that in the pictures.

For Nashua gentlemen there were twelve tailor shops and four stores listed as "Gents' Furnishings." Men's suits were usually black or dark blue wool. The trousers were narrow and cuffless; vests, preferably worn with a gold watch chain, were required. The shirts had stiffly starched collars and the whole was topped off with a derby hat. Summer clothing was a little lighter weight and most men wore a straw "skimmer" with it. These were worn only from Memorial Day to Labor Day. For professional men, the Prince Albert suit was indicated. These had a rather long frock coat, sometimes with a velvet collar. They were either black or dark grey and were very elegant looking. Sometimes a tall, silk hat completed this costume, giving the wearer a truly distinguished appearance.

Children's clothing was incredibly fussy. Small boys were often dressed in sailor suits with a middy blouse complete with bo'sun's whistle in the pocket, knee-length pants, black stockings, and high buttoned shoes. Also shown for boys in sizes up to thirteen were ruffled blouses. These were very fancy with many tiny buttons, pleats, lace cuffs, and tucks. Such a blouse would take an expert laundress about a half hour to iron and the average boy about five minutes to reduce to a mass of limp wrinkles, unless, of course, he was tied to a chair.

Girls were dressed in several layers of clothing, not today's "layered look," but rather for warmth and, in those Victorian days, for modesty. Long underwear, three petticoats, long stockings and high shoes, a woolen dress, and a pinafore were required. Several people who wore such clothing in their youth have attested to its extreme discomfort. It seems, in retrospect, that the clothing was either too large or too small, too itchy or chafed or bound in some way or other. Certainly it was a far cry from the unisex costume worn by today's young, the ubiquitous blue jeans, T-shirt, and sneakers.

Nashua Homes in the 1890s

Home furnishings of the period also were very ornate. Much of the furniture was lavishly carved. Upholstery might be of plush, velvet, or slippery horsehair. The well-furnished parlor would have marble-topped tables, lace curtains, velvet drapes, and perhaps portieres made of silk cord. Many people discarded the traditional furniture such as Chippendale, Sheraton, or Hepplewhite to make room for the heavy ornate Victorian pieces.

Fireplaces were sometimes blocked off to accommodate the parlor stove. These were small with a great deal of nickel trim and had windows through which one could watch the flames. The stoves may not have been as picturesque as the fireplaces but they provided more warmth, which was more important in the days before central heating.

The parlor in the average family home was the room for guests only, while the kitchen was the most important room where the family really lived. Here, the large black stove dominated, providing for both heating and cooking. It required almost constant attention, as the good housekeeper kept it blackened and polished the trim frequently. Keeping the wood box filled was a chore that usually fell to the boys in a family. The stoves also burned coal which would last longer and provide steady heat. Chances are that the ice box in the kitchen of the nineties was made by the Maine Manufacturing Company. The boxes were well made of fine oak and came in many different sizes.

The food that emerged from these kitchens is still fondly remembered by some people. Others try to recreate it by means of the old family recipes. No one seemed to worry about dieting or even knew about cholesterol then, so meals were rich and heavy.

There were seventy-two grocers in town in 1895. In those times shopping was a daily chore, as primitive refrigeration did not allow food to be stored for very long. For convenience it was necessary to have food stores in just about every neighborhood. Some of yesterday's advertised prices would bring a nostalgic tear to the eye of today's housewife fighting the battle of inflation. For example:

Bacon	12 Cts. a lb.
Coffee	15 Cts. a lb.
Beef	10 Cts. a lb.
Sugar	$5.80 per 100 lbs.
Spring Chicken	7 Cts. a lb.
Potatoes	35 Cts. a bushel

Nashua Postmen . . . June 12, 1894.

For a gourmet dining experience, one went to the Tremont House. The menu for one dinner was as follows:

Blue Points	Bouillon	Celery Hearts
	Cold Meats	
Roast Beef	Tongue Turkey	Ham
	Apple Jelly	
Chicken Salad		Lobster Salad
Spiced Peaches		Tomato Catsup
	Bread Sandwiches	
	Vanilla Ice Cream	
	Assorted Cakes	
Bananas	Pears	Grapes
Assorted Nuts		Raisins
American Cheese		Edam Cheese
	Crackers Coffee	

Judging by the menu, this must have been a memorable evening, gastronomically.

Recreation in Nashua

Other diversions for an evening out might be a play at the Franklin Opera House or the Nashua Theatre. A program dated 1893 at the Opera House featured Charlotte Thompson in *The New Jane Eyre*. For music lovers, W.A. Cummings' Orchestra performed at the Opera House much to the enjoyment of the audiences of the day. Mr. Cummings' daughter, Velma Cummings Cole, was a noted Nashua violinist who played with the Women's Symphony Orchestra in Boston.

During the winter, sleigh rides and ice-skating provided diversion and entertainment. For those who preferred to stay home by the parlor stove, stereoscopic slides were a popular form of entertainment. Children's games and recreation, both indoors and out, were not arranged by parents as they often are today. The children were expected to entertain themselves, but to be quiet, polite and undemanding—in short, to be "seen and not heard." In spite of these regulations, several authors reminiscing about small-town childhood comment on the relative freedom of the young. This freedom came, however, after all chores were satisfactorily performed. Duties involving the woodbox, the kerosene lamps, carrying water, as well as the care and feeding of the family livestock, were assigned to boys. Daughters started young to learn the intricacies of home making, cooking, sewing, canning, washing dishes and clothes. They also served as surrogate mothers to younger brothers and sisters. All this was intended to prepare her for her future—that of wife and mother, actually the only career thought really suitable for a girl.

Boys had considerably more freedom to roam than their sisters and in typical boy fashion investigated the mysteries of Mother Nature in the woods, fields, and streams surrounding Nashua. They also could be found observing the foibles of human nature on Main Street.

Holidays were occasions beloved by children then as now. However, some methods of celebration have changed with the times. Christmas was a truly joyous time. The anticipation of a new pair of ice skates or a doll—perhaps one with pierced ears adorned with tiny earrings—to be found under the candlelit tree could make the most mischievous child behave in saintly fashion just prior to the holiday. After all no one wanted to receive a stocking full of coal, a fate that might befall one who had misbehaved. Oranges were a real treat at this time and could be found in many a Christmas stocking, though seldom seen at any other time of year.

Hallowe'en was the time for fiendish mischief. The distracted police force would find a buggy on a barn roof, many an overturned privy, Smith's horse in Jones' barn, and other such pranks. Peashooters were essential equipment and were used to pepper windows and anyone foolish enough to be abroad on such a night. The customs of costumes and Trick-or-Treat came along quite a few years later.

The Fourth of July was the occasion for picnics, the famous Horribles Parade down Main Street and, of course, patriotic addresses by prominent citizens. The Horribles Parade attracted large crowds and those participating showed great ingenuity in designing both costumes and the floats.

Tremont House, from an old postcard.

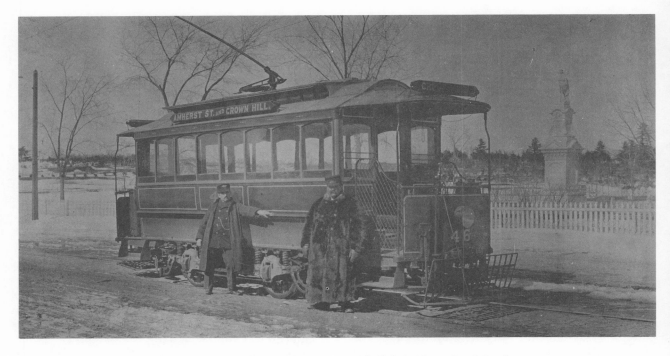

Dear to the hearts of the young were firecrackers, which were manufactured in great quantity and variety. There were two-inch salutes, torpedos, sparklers, Roman candles, pinwheels, and many others. These popped, banged, sputtered, and boomed from dawn until long after dark.

Sports of That Day

Sports activities in the schools at this time were limited to boys. There were baseball, football, and basketball teams in high school. An 1897-1898 photograph shows the Nashua High Basketball team looking, at least, like winners. The YMCA offered a variety of sports to the young men of the area. On a less organized level, boys engaged in many of the same activities of today's youth—fishing, swimming, sand-lot baseball, and ice-skating were some of them.

Girls were considered too delicate for strenuous exercise but they did engage in some recreational sports outside of school, such as tennis, croquet, horseback riding, bicycling, and rowing. Swimming was permissible if the young lady was properly clad. The bathing costume of the day left everything to the imagination, though critics thought them very daring.

Child Labor in Nashua

Not all children in the nineties had the opportunity to enjoy the carefree fun and freedom of youth. Many from low income families began working in the mills when they were very young. The mill owners hired children because of their speed, agility, and nimble fingers, very important in the manufacture of textiles and other goods as well. Also, the children worked at low wages and made no labor demands. Many of them would lie about their ages in order to secure employment.

Child labor legislation was enacted in Massachusetts as early as 1836 but it was not until many years later that meaningful laws were passed in other states. In Massachusetts the law stated that children under fifteen could work if they had attended school for at least three months in the preceding year.

Here in Nashua Superintendent of Schools James Fassett made periodic visits to the mills looking for under-age workers. It seemed customary for children to attend school until graduating from the ninth grade at about age fourteen. Not all attended high school and even fewer in the average family were able to go on to college. Large families were common so that the income from children's labor was essential. A family whose children were healthy and able to work was considered very fortunate.

Health Problems

At the turn of the century life expectancy was only about forty-six years. Since many children had a very brief life span, few families were able to raise all to adulthood. Infectious diseases such as scarlet fever, diphtheria, measles, pneumonia, and many others took their toll. Infancy was particularly perilous. Even if mother and baby survived the trauma of birth, there were still many dangers to the child's health. Premature infants seldom lived as there were no incubators and oxygen therapy was unknown. Once the babies were weaned, many died of cholera infantum, a disease caused by impure milk. In 1895 alone more than two hundred Nashua babies died, with doctors powerless to help in many cases because there were no remedies for the various diseases.

There were thirty-eight physicians in the city in 1895, dedicated people who devoted their lives to healing the sick. Their fees were low and the help they got from scientific equipment was really minimal. There were no X-rays so fractures were set the best way possible by manipulation. If, for instance, the patient limped afterward, he did not sue the doctor but was grateful to be able to walk at all. Infection was a common complication of injury as antibiotics were not discovered for many years after this period. Smallpox vaccinations were required by law but immunization for other diseases was not available.

Tuberculosis was a dreaded and a sometimes mysterious killer for many years. Some victims seemed to benefit from the "fresh air" treatment and would recover after time spent in a mountain sanitorium.

It was early in the decade of the nineties that the shortage of hospital facilities in Nashua became really urgent. There was one room in the police station that was sparsely outfitted for some emergencies but the city doctors needed more efficient and sanitary surroundings for their patients. The doctors with the cooperation of the city government formed an organization called the Nashua Hospital Association and then in 1893 leased the Collins House on Spring Street as the Emergency Hospital. The equipment was simple—a wash boiler as a sterilizer and a few surgical instruments. Eight patients could be cared for under the supervision of two nurses, a matron, and a steward.

In 1899 expanded facilities were needed so the Hall Estate on the corner of Dearborn and Prospect Streets was purchased. These new quarters of Nashua Emergency Hospital were opened on October 9, 1899. Here there was room for twenty-five patients, and a training school for nurses was established. Until this time nurses were trained by the doctors they assisted.

Some of those people who helped establish the hospital were: President, Williams Hall; Treasurer, F.E. Kittredge, M.D.; Secretary, E.H. Wason, Esq. Eventually, with generous funds from the will of Dr. George F. Wilber plus generous gifts from many citizens, a larger building was constructed and completed in 1915, named Memorial Hospital.

In several Nashua families medicine was a family affair. The Smith family of Nashua and Hudson included six physicians. There were the Hammonds, the McQuestens, the Wallaces, and Dr. B.G. Moran, whose son, Edward, is a prominent physician in the city today. Dr. Moran, Sr., was the first Nashua surgeon to perform an appendectomy—done under the uncertain light of an oil lamp in a house on Granite Street. Later he performed the first major operation at St. Joseph's Hospital.

Ed and Willie Gilman, agents for Columbia bicycles.

Nashuans were fortunate to have so many dedicated persons in health services. Some of today's physicians, when talking of the way that medicine was practiced during the nineties, note that their predecessors often performed what amounted to miracles of healing with a minimum of scientific aids. One such Nashua physician, Dr. James T. Greeley, gained the respect and devotion of both colleagues and patients for his untiring work as Regimental Surgeon with the Third New Hampshire Regiment during the Spanish-American War. Later he invented a hypodermic kit which was widely used during World War I.

The Spanish-American War

It was in 1898 when the United States had enjoyed the blessings of peace for over thirty years that war was once again in the news. For some time Americans had been hearing reports of the troubles of Cuban peasants being oppressed by the Spanish government. Some American newspapers began a campaign for American military intervention.

In order to protect Americans living in Cuba, the battleship *Maine* was sent to patrol Havana harbor. In February, 1898, the ship blew up with the loss of two hundred sixty personnel. The American public was truly incensed by this tragedy and the slogan,

"Remember the *Maine*," became the watchword for an angry America. It was never really proven that the Spanish were responsible for the explosion but the assumption was that they were. In spite of President McKinley's efforts to avoid it, war was declared in April, 1898. This was to be the first test for the United States as a world power. Fortunately, the war lasted only four months, for if it had been a prolonged affair the country would have been hard-pressed for both trained servicemen and military supplies. The war, though short-lived, resulted in the acquisition of Puerto Rico, the Philippines, and Guam. Cuba was given her independence.

The Asiatic Fleet under the command of Commodore George Dewey destroyed the Spanish Fleet without the loss of a single American life. It also blockaded Manila harbor until the American troops arrived. Dewey became a popular hero of the war and Nashua especially took a personal interest in him for he had been a frequent visitor to the city when his sister, Mrs. George Greeley, lived at the corner of Abbott and Amherst Streets. The local newspaper advertised lithographs of Admiral Dewey and also a spoon engraved with his likeness as a commemorative item. For navy buffs there was a parlor game available called "Naval Battles."

Between the time of the sinking of the *Maine* and

the declaration of war there were many different opinions on which course the country should take. One Nashua newspaper interviewed many local citizens as to their feelings on the subject and published their varying views. Some agreed with President McKinley's pacificist attitude while others were in agreement with Teddy Roosevelt who was eager for a military solution to the problem.

Nashua men in the National Guard under the command of Captain Woods and Lieutenant Poff were ready for service. When their company was not summoned in the first call to arms, they were very much disappointed. However, shortly afterward they volunteered to make up vacancies in the Third Regiment commanded by Colonel Tolles. In May, 1898, they were sent to Concord to Camp Ramsdell for further training. The local troops were sent off at Union Station by a large crowd, after a parade down Main Street.

The people of Nashua showed a great interest in the activities of the local soldiers, consequently the papers sent their correspondents to Concord to cover the various aspects of life in a military camp. Many interested citizens would travel to Concord on Sundays to visit the troops. Later in the summer the New Hampshire contingent left for the South for further training. Some were sent to Tennessee and some to Georgia. As the war and the summer progressed the soldiers became discouraged by not going into any action. Food was poor, the weather hot, wet, and miserable, and the men longed to be back in "God's country." Many fell victim to malaria and other fevers. The war came to an end in August, 1898, when so many soldiers had become ill that Governor Ramsdell sent a special hospital train to bring them home. Mayor Tolles, who had been promoted to General, made a special trip to the South to expedite evacuation of the sickest men. Even so, several soldiers died and many others arrived home in an emaciated state. The Governor, other officials, and the families were shocked at the appearance of the troops who had left the city less than four months before in perfect health. Dr. Greeley had worked himself into almost total exhaustion in his attempts to treat the desperately sick men.

Into the Twentieth Century

Instead of ushering in the New Year with cham-

pagne and dancing, Nashua citizens celebrated the arrival of the Twentieth Century with Watch Night observances in their churches. There were prayers of gratitude for past blessings and of hope and peace for the future. The accounts of this occasion even mention people taking temperance pledges to welcome in the New Year 1901.

The spirit of the gay nineties, including an indication that women in this decade were achieving a small measure of liberation, seems summed up in a delightful article in the *Daily Press* concerning the sport of bicycling. The "wheelmen" (and "wheel-women") gathered on the Lowell Road on summer evenings to display their speed and skill. The ladies apparently often outshone the men in daring deeds on their two-wheelers. (This sport of riding furiously up and down a road was known as "scorching.") There is just a hint of females breaking out of the conventional Victorian mold in this description of one lady enthusiast: "She was a large stately woman with the most fetching Alpine hat. This woman who easily weighed 200 pounds was the most graceful and the most sensible rider of all the passing show."

Soldiers' and Sailors' Monument at Abbot Square.

Twentieth
Century
Nashua

21

The Peaceful Edwardian Era

WITH THE Spanish-American War over, the United States began a period of booming prosperity. After campaigning to the cry of "a full dinner-pail for four years more," William McKinley was elected to a second term as President in 1900. A high protective tariff, a gold monetary standard, and an imperialist foreign policy marked the transition of this country to the ranks of a world power. The nineteenth century burdens of the Civil War and its aftermath were left behind with the dawning of the twentieth century which was to thrust America through periods of incredible progress, hardship, and change. The relative tranquility of the early 1900s was a fleeting pause in which most Americans were preoccupied with interests at home.

Nashua in the Early 1900s

Nashua, with a population in 1900 of 23,898, was growing steadily. Municipal projects included improved paving of streets, a better sewage system, and—with the help of generous private gifts— several new buildings. The Hunt Home for the aged was begun in the spring of 1898 and dedicated October 13, 1899; it was built with funds provided by Mrs. Mary A. and Miss Mary E. Hunt, wife and daughter of the late John M. Hunt. The home was soon filled to capacity and a long waiting list developed as many elderly citizens were in need of such shelter. With no Social Security and meager savings, many elderly people faced a dire future.

For many in Nashua, life was marked by hard work and long hours of drudgery. Local industry provided employment for workers who still poured in from surrounding areas, but wages were barely adequate for those who tried to raise families and avoid falling deeply into debt. Every family member was acutely aware of the severity of hard work and poverty. Upon women, especially, often fell the heaviest burden. Without the right to vote or express opinions in a male-dominated world, many stoically endured years of hardship. Appealing to their anxieties and weariness were countless medicines and remedies advertised to relieve depression and fatigue. Wonder tonics were available for endless miseries including debility, dyspepsia, and rheumatism. Most contained primarily a heavy dose of alcohol disguised with various herbal concoctions.

Poverty was often acute among the factory workers who were sometimes left without a job. Death, illness, or other misfortunes often left whole families destitute. A growing number of children became orphans. In 1901 Father Milette opened the Saint Joseph's Orphanage on Main Street near Otterson Street. On April 9, 1901, the Grey Nuns took over the facility which housed fifteen children. By 1903 eighty-six children were being cared for and in 1912 the building was enlarged to accommodate more than two hundred children.

There were other citizens for whom Nashua offered relative affluence. Businessmen found plentiful opportunities for investment and development. Professionals, including doctors and lawyers, also found life agreeable. By 1900 there had developed a population with great diversity of income, education, and interests. Nashua seemingly offered something for everyone, from saloon to opera house. One could even consult a clairvoyant, Mrs. Julia Matthews, who claimed to be able to tell the past, present, and future, with office hours from two until nine p.m. The majority seemed, on the surface at least, to be content with life in Nashua. Everyone apparently knew his place, guided by social custom, trial and error.

A general feeling of well-being provided a superficial blanket of security through the spring of 1901. The Pan-American Exposition was opened in Buffalo, New York, exhibiting new discoveries and inventions, signs of incredible progress that sparked the curiosity of nearly everyone. During the summer the *Nashua Telegraph* ran a contest offering a free excursion to the Exposition to the person voted most popular clerk and to the one voted most popular teacher. The two winners would be sent via the scenic Hoosac Tunnel route of the Fitchburg Division of the Boston and Maine Railroad to Buffalo. There they would stay one week at the Hotel Columbia while visiting the Exposition. Hundreds of readers clipped the coupons and voted. The winners were Albert G. Hutchins, general delivery

Chicken salad at 20 cents was the top of the bill of fare at the Y.W.C.A. lunchroom in 1900.

clerk at the Nashua Post Office, and Miss Grace E. Smith, teacher at Mount Pleasant School.

Liquor Problems

The general festive local spirit was disrupted when the sale of liquor became a volatile issue in the community. Charges of discrimination in the enforcement of regulations controlling liquor traffic created hot debate in and out of court. Some liquor dealers claimed that they were fined more frequently than others in the city. Opinions varied as the controversy widened through the summer of 1901. One group of ministers and citizens wanted the sale of liquor banned totally. At the other extreme were the liquor dealers and the masses of their patrons who indulged heavily in alcoholic beverages in establishments all across town. The issue reached a compromising conclusion when City Marshal Eaton made it clear that he would keep Nashua "dry" on Sundays and enforce the laws impartially. The list of offenders subsequently brought to court for violations indicated he meant what he said.

As local affairs continued to interest most Nashuans, national prosperity seemed certain. Then, on September 6, 1901, President McKinley was shot while delivering a speech in Buffalo at the Exposi-

tion, and died eight days later. On Sunday, September 15, Nashua churches conducted memorial services and on Monday store windows were draped in black and white. An overflowing crowd gathered in the Nashua Theatre on Thursday to pay final tribute to a fallen President.

Soon after McKinley's death President Roosevelt acquired the Panama Canal Zone in 1903 by direct and effective, if questionable, action. The growing nation made an attempt to capitalize on its new status as a world power. In Latin America and other parts of the world American investments, with government action, gave rise to the unpopular label of "dollar diplomacy."

In June, 1903, an elaborate celebration was held to mark the semicentennial anniversary of the city. The enthusiasm of the speeches and the heartiness of the participation in the various events on the program reflected the pervading self-congratulatory spirit of the period. Generally everyone was quite satisfied with the progress that had been made in the fifty years since 1853.

Two Prominent Women

A woman who reached prominence at this time was Corona L. Bourgoin who served as acting City Clerk in April, 1904, due to the illness of George B.

Bowler, former Deputy Sheriff and three term City Clerk. While Mr. Bowler was convalescing at home the very capable Miss Bourgoin, who had been the City Stenographer, was on duty in his place at City Hall. Possessing intellectual ability, a warm personality, and stunning beauty—frequently called "the Gibson girl"—she was a striking city official. In spite of all her qualities, she never served an official term, and was succeeded by a man.

Another notable woman of the time was M. Jennie Kendall, who was Deputy Sheriff. On February 10, 1907, she was presented with a solid gold badge inscribed: "Deputy Sheriff M. Jennie Kendall, Nashua, N.H. From Friends of the Cause She Represents." The presentation took place in the Probate Court Room just as she was about to call to order a meeting of the Woman's Humane Society, of which she was a member. A short speech followed by Colonel Dana W. King, Register of Deeds.

New Public Facilities

During Mayor Andros B. Jones' administration, 1905-1906, a new Post Office on the lot next to the old Central Fire Station on Court Street was completed. In 1909 under Mayor Albert Shedd, 1907-1910, the Shattuck Street School was completed to relieve overcrowding. An addition was also made to the Spring Street High School. The City Council authorized construction of the concrete Taylor Falls Bridge across the Merrimack in 1909; the project was finally completed in October, 1912.

On May 1, 1908, Saint Joseph's Hospital was dedicated by the Most Reverend Georges Albert Guertin, Bishop of Manchester. Monsignor Jean-Baptiste Henri Victor Milette, Pastor of Saint Louis de Gonzague Parish, had purchased the land on Kinsley Street in 1906 from the family of Colonel Michael Earley. The entire project involved the work and dedication of many Nashuans. The long list of benefactors included many local donors and the Nashua and Jackson Manufacturing Companies.

The Sisters of Charity, Grey Nuns of Montreal, founded in 1747, accepted the invitation of Monsignor Milette to administer and staff the new hospital. Nine sisters were sent from the Order in Canada to begin their duties which included running the new School of Nursing at Saint Joseph's.

The surgical and medical staff quickly gained a reputation for skill and dedication. The demand for services grew steadily, so that an addition was soon needed and finally built in 1915. Meanwhile, technical improvements had been made in 1913 with new X-ray apparatus and a new Pathological Laboratory.

Other Advances

Industrial growth in the city included the building of a new dam by the Jackson Company in 1907. Also that year Johns Manville Corporation took over the old Asbestos Wood Company on Bridge Street. The Wonalancet Company purchased land for a cotton plant in 1908. Roby and Swart bought the Campbell Paper Box Company and the W.H. McElwain Shoe Company came to Nashua in 1909, building a shop at 51 Lake Street.

In 1908 considerable progress was made in the Greeley Park project, thanks to a generous gift of five thousand dollars by John E. Cotton, with the City providing matching funds. Consequently the plans announced by the Board of Park Commissioners in 1898 for converting the Greeley Farm to a public park received a much-needed burst of momentum. In addition, three valuable strips of land were given by Mrs. Clara R. Wheeler, Mrs. Anna S. Colburn, and the Highland Spring Sanatorium. This land with the strip purchased from Mrs. Nannie E. Watson made it possible to make an entry from Manchester Street. By 1908 the Greeley buildings had been removed, much grading and seeding was done, and many evergreens and maples were planted, with more to follow. By 1909 the work was progressing and the first flower

beds of cultivated plants were added. In 1911 Mr. Cotton provided an additional gift by having the stone and cement Rest House constructed. Installed midway between the building and Concord Street were a fountain and shallow pond, along with a gravel walk and flower beds. By 1914 a caretaker on duty from May to October provided routine maintenance and care for the many trees and shrubs of the park. Hundreds of visitors enjoyed the quiet beauty and winding walkways in the years that followed. Additional plantings and proper care made Greeley Park a continuing popular recreation area.

The Trolley Era

Beginning in 1902 an extensive network of electric railways was being expanded to link Nashua with easterly communities such as Salem, New Hampshire, and Haverhill, Massachusetts. The building of the trolley system was no small achievement, requiring construction of carhouses, power stations, and miles of roadbed. During 1902 many small companies were consolidated and became subsidiaries of the New Hampshire Traction Company, Western Division, among them the Hudson, Pelham, and Salem Company and the Nashua Street Railway.

American Express Company at Railroad Square . . .
complete with small boy and proud mascot.

By prior agreement H.P. & S. cars were allowed to run over Nashua Street Railway tracks, across the Taylor Falls Bridge, down East Hollis, Temple, and East Pearl Streets to Tremont Square on Main Street in Nashua. The first car from Salem ran on September 8, 1902, with regular service beginning two days later. Early in the summer of 1903 brochures were distributed which glowingly described the routes of the Western Division. Many tourists were drawn to Nashua to take a ride over this part of the system, which had a reputation for its splendid scenic beauty. A further attraction was Canobie Lake Park, opened August 23, 1902. Each summer hundreds boarded a car in Nashua and made the trip which took about sixty minutes.

Unfortunately the operation of the electric railways was not trouble-free. On Sunday morning, September 6, 1903, Car 125, with fifty-four passengers aboard, was en route from Nashua to Canobie Lake, while Car 137, carrying thirty, was coming from Canobie Lake to Nashua on the same track. On a blind curve about a half mile northwest of Pelham Center the two collided head-on. Six persons were killed, about a dozen maimed, and another sixty sustained lesser injuries. In addition to this tragedy, occasional mishaps occurred, sometimes involving confrontations between trolleys and horse-drawn wagons.

On January 1, 1907, the system expanded further when the Manchester and Nashua Street Railway opened the 12.5 mile route between Hudson and Manchester. The relatively flat stretch of track provided a connecting link between Concord, New Hampshire, and Boston, Massachusetts. Just who made the first trip from Boston to Concord is not known, but among the first was an elderly lady who proudly described her trip in a letter to her

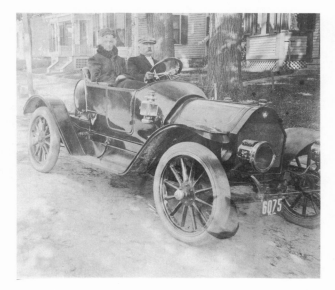

Miss Patterson and Willis Dodge in a Reo, September, 1911.

Shop at 64 Main Street owned by George E. Bagley, at rear in doorway. Frank M. Ingalls is at the extreme right.

daughter in Waltham. In great detail she carefully recalled the exciting six-and-a-half-hour trip which cost $1.05. She particularly noted the kindness of the conductors and fellow travelers who helped her transfer to the proper cars in Lowell, Nashua, and finally, Manchester. On her way from Lowell to Nashua she decidedly asserted that "the New Hampshire air is different from that of Massachusetts. Perhaps it's just an old woman's notion, but it seems so to me . . . It's so good to see so much of the real country . . . whole stretches of woods and fields, and no houses for miles and miles." Stopping in Nashua was particularly memorable for she notes, "I walked down the street not far from where the Manchester car would be, and saw some of the cutest little dresses in the window. When they were bought it was nearly time for my car." She, like many others, found the electric cars an inexpensive means of transportation to and from the outside world. The epoch of the electric railways gradually ended as the private automobile gained popularity and ultimately glutted the roadways. But in the blissful days around 1910 the electric cars played an important part in the developing community.

The Automobile and Airplane Arrive

The love affair with the motor car was attracting ever-increasing numbers. In the early years of development, steam and electric powered vehicles were especially popular. One Nashuan, Frank Anderson, drove a Stanley Steamer. Later, Dr. Henry H. Jewell on Pearl Street also owned one. Some still recall Dr. Jewell getting up very early in the morning to start the vehicle, which required a rather lengthy warm-up period to build up pressure and operate properly.

A few citizens owned electric autos, including Seth Chandler and Albert Wheeler. Mary Ellen Tolles of 65 Concord Street owned an electric car made by Detroit Electric, and her smooth-running vehicle was often seen breezing silently about town. However, as gasoline-powered autos gained popularity, fewer and fewer steam or electric autos were seen.

The 1904 *Nashua Directory* lists forty-one car owners, including: Seth Chandler of 257 Main Street who owned a Rambler; Frank A. Davis of 59 Walnut Street who owned a Grout; Dr. Auguste Guertin of 220 Main Street, owner of a Crest; Ralph W. Holt of 42 Kinsley Street, owner of an Olds; Herbert C. Lintott of 12 Prospect Street who owned an Orient; and John Whitney of 18 Chestnut Street, owner of a Pierce, to mention a few. By 1908 the list of auto owners had grown to well over one hundred, and the assortment of makes and models was incredible, including many exotic vintage names. Improvements in newer models helped attract new buyers. By 1913 the new Cadillac boasted a quiet engine, an electric system of automatic cranking, a silent chain-driven camshaft, and enclosed valves. Available at H.C. Lintott, Incorporated, on Main Street, this make was rapidly gaining the reputation of quality and prestige.

On June 20, 1911, "birdman" Harry Atwood of Roxbury, Massachusetts, flew his Burgess-Wright biplane from Waltham to Concord, stopping for a short visit at Nashua. Following the Merrimack River up from Lowell, he approached the city, crossed it diagonally, and dipped his wings to the right as he dropped toward a field at Fairmount Heights. A large crowd, which included Mayor Barry, warmly greeted the aviator on the historic occasion—the first landing of an airplane in Nashua. A short while later, the curious onlookers watched in amazement as the plane sputtered and roared down the field, climbed skyward, and headed toward Manchester.

A New Government for Nashua

In June, 1912, a thirteen-member Charter Commission was chosen under the provisions of a Resolution passed by the City Councils. Following public hearings and much discussion, a majority of the Commission presented a Charter to the Legislature known as Plan One. The minority presented a Charter known as Plan Two. The entire issue was presented to the voters of Nashua at a special election held June 10, 1913. The people voted to change the present charter and adopt Plan One. On June 12, 1913, at a special meeting of the City Councils, the old charter was declared repealed and Plan One was declared the Charter of the City of Nashua. Among the major features of the new plan were: the Common Council was abolished, superseded by a single body consisting of six Aldermen-at-Large and one Alderman from each Ward; no party designations would be made; the Fire Com-

mission and Board of Public Works to be elected by the people. Especially noteworthy was the change allowing women to vote for Board of Education only. Additional revisions and ramifications included separating the City Elections from the State Elections; nomination by petition; the electing of City officers by viva voce vote. Had Plan Two been adopted the City would have been run by a Dual Board system with partisan affiliation at elections. Thus the voters were deciding a very important issue which was to affect City Government in the years ahead. The new charter also provided for the election of the mayor every two years, a provision which remained in effect until the change was made to a mayoralty election every four years, in 1971.

Changing Mores and Fashions

The desire to accumulate material goods was rewarded with the readily available gadgets, appliances, and clothing goods. The ever-changing fashions were continually teasing and tempting the fickle tastes of the ladies. The parasol was the rage

in 1913; new shapes, domed, pagoda, canopy, or fringed, were offered—the variety was almost endless. Every city was a potential mass market of consumers and Nashua was no exception. In the *Telegraph,* February 22, 1913, the latest fashion tips inform us that

parasol handles are longer and more slender than ever. The modish woman knows how to stand in the "new pose" with the knees relaxed and the figure making a series of natural, curved lines and the hands being crossed carelessly over the top of the tall parasol handle. It is an exceptionally graceful, if craftily artful pose, and one that will likely be seen practiced a great deal this summer on country club piazzas, boardwalks, lawns, or wherever dainty summer costumes are in order.

The curious mixture of popular rationalizations which dominated this era, including the desire for economic gain, the belief in America's prestigious destiny for greatness, and the Christian ethic, all contributed to the style of the beginning years of the twentieth century.

22

Industrial Violence and World War 1

SLOWLY THE ENGINEER guided the shifting engine along the spur track which led into the mill yard. As he rounded a curve he suddenly saw a group of women, some with babies in their arms, sitting on the track. The brakeman on the roof of the first car saw them too; both acting quickly brought the train of several empty freight cars to a halt. The women remained passive as a dense crowd of men, women, and children emerged from the Pine Street neighborhood and stood along the track at the rear of the Nashua Manufacturing Company.

There had been trouble in the neighborhood earlier that morning of October 18, 1915, when two milkmen, Thomas G. McKay and Leon R. Moss, a fruit man, Fred Rochelle, and a baker were driven away by an angry crowd while trying to make deliveries at the mill gate. Also that morning two Nashua Building Company workers were chased away from the gate adjacent to Factory Street.

Now at around 11:00 A.M. as the crowd watched the stalled freight train a group of policemen proceeded down Pine Street and along the railroad spur, approaching from the rear. Ordered to disperse, the crowd erupted in noisy excitement; remained densely packed; and did not budge. Soon stones were being hurled at the police who kept relatively calm under the circumstances. Within minutes word was sent for reinforcements. The police chief notified Mayor James B. Crowley who in turn ordered the Militia commander at the mill to send out a detachment to aid the police.

As the Militia emerged from the rear mill gate, coming along the railroad track with fixed bayonets, the police wielding clubs closed in on the crowd from behind. Lieutenant Alfred F. Gravelle, at the head of the advancing detachment, was waving an automatic pistol. Many of the crowd fell back while others, when ordered to move, stood firm. Suddenly there was a shot and a spectator standing beside the track fell. A young woman rushed to his side, taking his head in her lap, sobbing hysterically. She was his bride. The two had been married the Saturday before at Saint Casimir's Church.

With bayonets flashing on one side and clubs swinging on the other, the unarmed crowd quickly fell back, but not before a second and third shot rang out. Both men and women fell in the onslaught. Shouts and cries were heard over the roar of the rushing crowd as the injured sustained bloody wounds. Soon ambulances arrived and rushed the injured to Saint Joseph's Hospital. Within minutes the incident was over. The stunned crowd dispersed. Small groups disappeared back into the neighborhood for the noon meal.

At Saint Joseph's the wounded were being treated. The first to fall, Adam Rasavitch, suffered a critical bullet wound. Most of the others received deep gashes, bruises, and broken bones on head, neck, or back from the bayonets and clubs. Some of the injured received aid in homes of friends in the area where the incident occurred. Besides civilians, one policeman and two militiamen were hurt, resulting in the arrest of half a dozen rioters for assault.

The unfortunate violence was part of a struggle between labor and management which was to disrupt the coming months and continue through the years ahead. It was a painful period in Nashua, marked by severe social, economic, and political upheaval, from which no segment of society would escape.

The 1915 Strike

The turbulent events of 1915 began on Monday morning, October 4, when about one hundred and fifty workers in the dye house at Nashua Manufacturing Company walked out of the mill. On Tuesday the number of strikers had mushroomed to an estimated six hundred. At noon the crowd clustered about the gates. Meanwhile mill officials decided to close indefinitely until conditions improved. A notice was posted throughout the departments signed by mill agent Roscoe S. Milliken.

When the six o'clock closing whistle blew, a large group of police contained the strikers who hurled insults and occasionally handfuls of mud at the workers who filed out.

From the strikers' point of view the timing for the strike was unfortunate, since the company storehouses were well filled with finished goods to supply orders for an extended period.

Shortly after the strike at Nashua Manufacturing Company began, workers at the Jackson Manufacturing Company walked out in sympathy and officials closed that mill also.

On Thursday morning, October 7, a serious confrontation between strikers and police occurred on Myrtle Street. Four patrolmen were stoned and beaten while trying to quell a disturbance. That evening the Nashua companies of the New Hampshire Militia were quietly called to the armory on Canal Street. On Friday a detachment was moved to a mill storehouse at Nashua Manufacturing to be ready to back up the small police force if necessary. Meanwhile noisy skirmishes between police and strikers occurred near the two closed mills.

On Monday, October 11, Governor Rolland H. Spaulding came to Nashua to confer with city and mill officials concerning the strike and to inspect the troops. That afternoon Mayor James B. Crowley announced that it was decided the Militia would remain at the mill for as long as needed.

The strike that had started only a week before had suddenly burst into the most serious labor conflict in the history of the city. The dye house workers who had protested low wages and a short lunch period sparked a seemingly uncontrollable chain of events. Their complaint stemmed from the fact that the dye house was at the west end of the mill yard, remote from the boarding and tenement district. They were unable to make the trip out for dinner and return in the allotted time. This, plus the desire for a two dollar a week raise, was about the extent of their complaints.

Within a week the mushrooming number of strikers had organized at a headquarters, Hamlin Hall, on West Pearl Street. Former Mayor William H. Barry served as their legal counsel. On Wednesday evening and again on Saturday parades were held. Arranged in divisions as before, the one on Saturday drew large, cheering crowds. Most notable was the large division of women strikers which was just behind the Saint Stanislaus band. American flags and banners were carried at intervals in the column as it proceeded to march, circling the monument on Abbott Square and turning down Main Street. Many were surprised by the large number of women strikers and their staunch determination.

In the days that led to the violent confrontation and use of militia on October 18, negotiations were attempted between strikers and mill officials to end the work stoppage in an orderly fashion. The strikers formulated a list of demands on October 6: Men in the dye house would receive a minimum wage of ten dollars and a half and in the bleachery eleven dollars per week. Men in the napping room would be raised from six forty-five to eight twenty-five a week. Other departments would receive a 15 percent raise. No mention of women's wages is made, although undoubtedly they were a good deal lower than the men's. In addition the hours of the men in the dye house would become 7:00 A.M. to 6:00 P.M., with one hour for lunch from noon to one o'clock. Agent Milliken of Nashua Manufacturing was reluctant to enter negotiations, feeling the mill had nothing to gain by compromising. The storehouses were filled with goods awaiting shipment so the shutdown in manufacturing was of little immediate concern to the finances of the mill. In fact with the payroll at rock bottom, expenses were cut. Thus a stalemate seemed certain as the violence of October 18 drew nearer.

The frustration and desperation of the strikers increased with each passing day of idleness. In the neighborhoods around the mills, such as near the Pine Street crossing, the tension became acute. The despairing men and women realized that the company would still ship goods and function while they huddled in their homes becoming penniless. Seeing the freight cars going into the mill yard to load shipments under their very noses was more than they could endure. The tragedy of October 18 marked a culminating point in their desperate struggle. That Monday morning mothers clutching babies in their arms rushed from their homes to sit on the tracks, defying authority they felt was unjust.

The tragedy which shocked the community on the eighteenth was followed by the senseless death of a young man as a result of an attack occurring at five thirty Tuesday evening, October 19. Jim Stivie, born Demetrios Karadimos, and a companion Costas Dinele were on their way home when they were attacked and beaten by three men near the corner of Tolles and Canal Streets following a disturbance at the Jackson mill. Two shots were fired during the attack, but both missed. When police arrived the two were found standing in the midst of a crowd of onlookers, bleeding badly from head injuries. Within minutes they were rushed to Saint Joseph's Hospital for treatment. The following morning Jim Stivie died.

The murder aggravated the tension between some of the ethnic groups which comprised the labor force at the mills. Some Polish strikers had accused some Greek strikers, such as Stivie, of trying to go back to work. In retaliation against these accusations and the murder, some members of the

Hon. David A. Gregg, businessman, banker and philanthropist.

Greek population threatened to defy the strike.

An investigation into the murder followed, in which two men were held for trial. Several others were arrested on charges relating to the attack. This incident, with the dozens of other assault and disorderly conduct cases, overburdened police authorities who carried on painstaking investigations. As cases reached local court Judge Clancy faced the difficult task of hearing the lengthy details of the almost endless number of crimes. Throughout the trying months of late 1915, fair and impartial justice in court prevailed despite the turmoil in the world outside.

Elmer E. Roundy in his cobbler shop about 1915.

The same evening Stivie was attacked, other violence had occurred. Shots were fired and missiles thrown in street fighting near the Indian Head mill of the Jackson Manufacturing Company when strike sympathizers massed outside the mill gate attacked strike-breakers. A charge by police into the crowd broke up the riot; Mayor Crowley was there directing them to do their duty.

Following the incident, at a mass meeting in Hamlin Hall, about thirty women and girls signed a statement charging that Mayor Crowley had struck a woman striker on the head at the beginning of the riot. They claimed he tore an American flag from a girl's hand, grasped a club from a policeman, and while shouting orders to the police hit the woman on the head. Mayor Crowley subsequently admitted being at the scene and through an interpreter ordering the women to disperse, but he emphatically denied having struck anyone. The sensational charge made headlines for several days but soon quietly died out.

As time passed it became apparent that there was to be no quick settlement to the strike. Many idle workers became impoverished as the weeks dragged on. An estimated five hundred workers left the city to search for jobs in other areas, including Lowell and Lawrence. For those who stayed there seemed little to look forward to as rent and household bills went unpaid. Many had little or no savings to rely on, since even in the best of times wages had been meager.

In an effort to reach a settlement, strike negotiators went to Boston to discuss issues with mill executives who resisted compromise. Company officials remained firm in asserting that wages in Nashua mills were not lower than those in other cities as was charged, but as high or higher. William Barry and the strikers felt otherwise and remained unconvinced.

The Strike Ends

With little chance of gaining demands from mill officials, Barry and strike leaders cautiously looked at labor unions which were developing. Among them was the Industrial Workers of the World, a controversial group of militants who crusaded across the country for causes ranging from free speech and unionism to socialism.

William Barry knew all too well the background

of the IWW. Not surprisingly the initial overtures from the IWW were soundly rejected by most but not all of the workers. Told they would be thrown out of town if they caused trouble, the minority group lost all chance of leading the strike though some joined its ranks. The strikers were weary of the weeks of frustration and violence and wanted only to return to work, perhaps with better wages.

Hoping for a peaceful solution, Barry went to New York to consult officials of the American Federation of Labor. Shortly after his return to Nashua, organizers of the Textile Workers' Union of the AFL arrived to address the strikers and try to convince them to join. By October 26 it seemed likely that up to half the strikers would sign up. However, many were fearful of reprisals by the mills if the workers unionized. After so many weeks of idleness many were afraid and willing to abandon all hope of gaining their demands. Consequently, unionizing was to be a slow and painful process.

Unfortunately the strikers seemed partially divided along ethnic lines, with the Poles and Lithuanians very vocal about demands, claiming that some of the Greek and French workers were more willing to compromise and return to work. Some others went so far as to claim it was a Polish strike to begin with. However, there were examples of every opinion within each ethnic group. Thus, there was wide disagreement as to what should be done next. By early November mill officials repeated their offers to reopen with no wage increase to be granted. Since time had weakened the determination of the strikers to persist with their cause the strike finally ended. The mills resumed work and no wage increase was granted.

Throughout the entire ordeal many Nashuans had remained shocked and bewildered, unable to understand how or why the events could have even occurred. The concept of the pleasant factory with happy, peaceful workers diligently toiling from dawn to dusk was shattered. The community was painfully aware of the disparities between the myth and reality of industrial life.

World War I and The Flu Epidemic

While labor strife shocked and jolted American communities, countries in Europe began taking sides in what was to be a global war. Resisting involvement as long as possible and finding it hard to choose sides, the United States nevertheless came to admit it had a stake in the struggle, and on April 6, 1917, President Wilson signed a joint resolution of Congress proclaiming a state of war with Germany. Beginning May 18 all men between twenty-one and thirty years of age were required to register for the draft. By June in Nashua 3,174 were signed up waiting to be called. By June 26 the first American troops arrived in France. The country mobilized for war and in the coming months Nashua and the nation were reminded daily of the grim events by the press. The Aisne-Marne offensive of July 18 to August 6, 1918, which proved to be the turning point, made the headlines. By October Germany wanted to accept Wilson's conditions for peace negotiations. On November 11 the Armistice was declared.

While the end of the war came into sight, the nation suffered through an influenza epidemic. The disease first appeared in early September, 1918, in Boston, New York, and Philadelphia. It spread over about forty-six states and ultimately claimed from four hundred thousand to five hundred thousand American lives.

In Nashua the outbreak struck on September 13, 1918. On September 16 health officials recorded 794 cases and by Tuesday, September 24, 2,053 cases. One week later the figure reached 3,747. By Sunday, October 6, the epidemic was reaching a peak with 7,644 persons reported ill. Hospitals were filled to overflowing. Early in October Dr. Kittredge issued a call for nurse volunteers to aid at both hospitals. Meanwhile, volunteers were busy making gauze masks for the Red Cross, located in the Beasom block. Mrs. Charles Nutter headed a committee in charge of training nurse volunteers. In daily classes at Memorial Hospital she trained a total of about seventy-five persons. Automobiles were needed to transport nurses around the city to visit and aid the hundreds of people ill in their homes, and soon three Nashuans volunteered their vehicles.

On Saturday, October 12, local stores and banks were ordered closed, as were certain other public places such as schools, churches, and pool halls.

Throughout the tragic period, the courage and devotion of the women and young girls of the city were clearly shown. Hundreds of families were aided in their homes by volunteers, mostly women,

who cooked, cleaned, and aided the sick. Members of the Good Cheer Society were especially helpful. Mrs. Elmer W. Eaton and Miss Mary Pillsbury set up a soup kitchen with the help of friends. In addition, some ladies of St. Louis de Gonzague, with members of the Catholic Charity Club, established another.

Fortunately, only a relatively small percentage of cases ended in death. By October 15, one hundred and seventy-six deaths were attributed to influenza, and by October 22, two hundred and eight deaths. The daily paper listed deaths and funeral services. As a result of sudden demand, there soon developed a shortage of flowers and floral arrangements. Finally, the worst was over and health officials decided that as of October 28, 1918, schools, pool halls, and other public places would be allowed to open for business.

One year after the Armistice Nashua cheered the end of World War I. A three-and-a-half-mile parade of eight divisions marched from Abbott Square across town to a Victory Arch constructed across Main Street, and halted in front of City Hall where the soldiers of the war were solemnly honored. It was a time of cheering and celebrating; and mourning and loss.

On November 11, 1920, the people of Nashua paused on the second anniversary of the end of World War I to dedicate Deschenes' Oval at Railroad Square in honor of Nashua's veterans of the recent war. The bronze oval was named after Private Amedee Deschenes who posthumously received the Croix de Guerre medal for bravery in a battle fought in the French town of Xivray, June 16, 1918.

Born and reared in Nashua, Deschenes enlisted in the National Guard on March 26, 1917. Soon afterward, at the Massachusetts Mobilization Camp, he was assigned to Company I, 103rd Infantry, and went overseas with the 26th Division on September 27, 1917, to serve in the trenches in France. Following his heroism at Xivray, he served at Saint Mihiel September 12-27, 1918. Suddenly he was caught in a deadly gas attack and died four days later, October 1, 1918, in the base hospital near Saint Mihiel and was buried in France. He was one of many who served and died in a struggle which to many Americans seemed so very far from home.

During this period of local and worldwide strife and violence, two events occurred in Nashua that were in sharp contrast to the general feeling of turmoil. On September 18, 1916, a monument was placed in position at Greeley Park, on a knoll east of the highway, commemorating the settlers of the north end who had been buried in an ancient graveyard at that spot. This graveyard, estimated to have contained about ninety graves, had completely disappeared in the course of the years, mainly as the result of road-building. Ira Harris, a cashier of the Indian Head Bank and a very popular Nashua personality, arranged for an appropriate boulder, with a bronze inscription plate, to be set in place. The inscription reads:

This knoll was the burial ground of the first white settlers locating near here north of the Nashua River. In grateful recognition of the blessings which have come to us through their sacrifices, this memorial is placed here by one of their posterity.

The other peaceful event, a gay and festive happening, was the dedication of the Nashua Country Club on August 3, also in 1916. The former Poor Farm house had been extensively remodelled and beyond it lay a golf course that was the fulfillment of a dream for sports-minded Nashuans of the day. Ira Harris, incidentally, was the speaker for the ceremonies which opened the club, stressing the historic significance of the location.

23

Thirty Years of Progress and Another World War

ON THE EVENING of January 2, 1920, a group of policemen in plain clothes inconspicuously filed through the doors along with dozens of Nashuans who had come to hear the speeches of the evening's meeting at Saint Jean Baptiste Hall. Meanwhile outside the entire Nashua police force, which was quite small, was quietly gathering under the supervision of Chief Goodwin and a U.S. Justice Department agent. Within minutes the small raiding party descended. Some of those attending, hearing last minute rumors of the raid, ran out the back door of the hall and scattered in all directions. The rest seated inside to hear the speeches were not so fortunate. Suddenly at 8:30 P.M. as planned the police seated in the crowd rose up while the raiding party covered the doors. Within seconds a noisy scuffle erupted as the peaceful citizens were handcuffed and led two-by-two to a line of cars outside. Hopelessly outnumbered, the small police force frantically scurried about trying to place the entire crowd under arrest. Meanwhile the hundreds of people pushed and shoved in a desperate effort to get away. Finally, 160 men and 23 women were arrested and transported to the police station. Since only a few police cars were available many persons were jammed into private automobiles and rushed across town. Upon arrival the group was herded into the station, the men into the guard room and the women into the commissioners' room. As the Friday evening continued each prisoner was interrogated concerning his or her affiliation with "radical" or "communist" causes. While the questioning progressed, many in the group laughed and chattered, wondering what all the fuss was about. Some had gone to the hall because of curiosity and had absolutely no idea what was going on. Soon a group of women, thinking the whole affair ridiculous, began singing loudly, their voices echoing through the halls. Late in the evening the repertoire concluded with an emotional rendition of "My Country 'Tis of Thee." By the following noon twenty-four men and five women were detained, the rest having been released. Most of those detained were aliens without proper papers. Several days later on the afternoon of January 4, six more were arrested, and all thirty-five persons were taken to Union Station to be sent by train to Deer Island, Boston, for trial and possible deportation.

The Friday meeting was sponsored by the Rengia L.K.S. 192 Society. A.A. Karalius, an alleged communist organizer from Chicago, was to have been the guest speaker. However, he never made it, having been arrested in Gardner, Massachusetts, after federal and local authorities had heard rumors of bomb plots planned for Nashua.

The raid in Nashua was one of many in January, 1920, ordered by President Wilson's Attorney General, A. Mitchell Palmer, in a nation-wide campaign in which thousands of so-called anarchists and communists were jailed with little regard for their constitutional rights.

The Era of Reform

One of several reforms put into effect after years of hard struggle was woman suffrage. Nashua women registered for the Presidential Primary of September, 1920, and voted on November 2. Mrs. Sarah Balcom, age ninety, was believed to have been the oldest woman in the city to cast a vote.

Another reform put into effect was prohibition. During the war public opinion supported the belief that soldier and factory worker alike should keep a clear head and remain sober at all times. A wartime "dry" act was passed, to go into effect July 1, 1919; the Eighteenth Amendment providing permanent prohibition was ratified, going into effect on January 20, 1920.

If anyone really thought the nation would actually go dry, they were soon proved wrong. Federal and local authorities began the impossible task of enforcing the law. Organized crime muscled into the now illegal liquor business. Rumrunning of bootleg liquor continued unabated on rivers and bays up and down the coast. Many citizens experimented in home brewing, making "bathtub gin" and other concoctions in cellars and woodsheds. Local bootleggers occasionally ran into problems with the law, but more often with hijackers looking for quick and easy profit. Needless to say the bootleggers who were robbed got little or no aid from the police though the incidents were occasionally reported in the press. Despite the zeal and good intentions of the reformers, bootlegging was rampant throughout the 1920s.

Violation of prohibition laws was only part of a general defiance of old standards, especially by many of the young. Manners, morals, and even fashions were affected by the new permissiveness. Gone were the ankle-length skirts, so that by 1927

hemlines hovered at the knee or slightly above. The knock-kneed, furious, foot twisting of the Charleston dominated the dance floor, followed shortly after by the Black Bottom. Changes were everywhere, to the shock and dismay of many. Old values seemed lost as some women even smoked cigarettes and openly and unashamedly discussed topics from divorce to sex. It was the era of "Coolidge Prosperity" with government in Washington saying and doing as little as possible to cool the frenzy of having a good time.

Labor Unrest Again

However, not all were impressed, since some old nagging problems remained unresolved. Labor strikes hit the country in rapid succession. More and more workers saw the walkout as the most productive means of showing their dissatisfaction.

On Monday, February 13, 1922, the Nashua mills and Jackson mills of Nashua Manufacturing Company shut down for an indefinite period when most of the four thousand employees failed to report for work. Crowds gathered near mill gates on Factory and Canal Streets, watched closely by police.

The strike was to protest lengthening of the work week from forty-eight to fifty-four hours with a twenty percent wage cut. All across the Northeast textile workers walked out, rallying behind strike organizers of the American Federation of Labor's United Textile Workers of America. On March 13, 1922, AFL President Samuel Gompers spoke to a mass meeting of strikers in Manchester, declaring "This America of ours is too big to permit the overlords of industry to break the hearts and crush the spirits of the people." But no amount of rhetoric could ease the hardships in the weeks that followed. Strikers picketed and demonstrated. On April 10 police used clubs to quell a disturbance on Factory Street. Other small skirmishes occurred as the weeks of bitterness continued. When it was finally over and the mills reopened, the weary workers returned, beaten once again.

The strikes in 1922 were the direct result of problems beginning in 1921 when high cotton prices caused a buyer's strike, preventing the marketing of any cotton. Subsequently, companies declined to cut prices and labor refused to accept a wage cut. Finally, commodity prices were forced down and wage cuts imposed, triggering the strikes and clos-

ing of the mills for several months in the Merrimack Valley and Rhode Island.

Peace and Prosperity

At noon on May 16, 1922, thousands helped celebrate the dedication of the two-hundred-mile Daniel Webster Highway. A lengthy parade with exuberant band concerts was culminated by a special ceremony at the state line where two granite markers were unveiled. Throughout the day people from the area, including neighboring Massachusetts, joined in the festivities.

As the 1920s progressed Nashua slowly settled into a period of development and relative calm. In 1923 the cornerstone of the Indian Head Bank building on Main Street was laid. Also that year construction of the James B. Crowley School was begun. In 1925 the Mount Pleasant School was built. Civic as well as business projects were numerous and marked the steady growth of the city. In 1926 the Chamber of Commerce was organized with William F. Sullivan as President and Horace E. Osgood, Vice-President.

In 1923 a group of men formed the J.F. McElwain Company on Temple Street. Initially employing 350 workers, the firm grew to 2,200 workers by 1928 and turned out five and a half million shoes a year.

J. Franklin McElwain, Seward M. Paterson, and Francis P. Murphy were the three founders of "J.F." Another prominent individual was Robert C. Erb who later became president of the new firm and its parent, Melville Shoe. These four had been members of the predecessor, W.H. McElwain Company, which had factories at Claremont and Newport, besides the one in Nashua. Before coming to Nashua Francis P. Murphy had earned a reputation for his outspoken wit and managerial abilities while running the facilities at the first two locations. He provided the spark and drive which motivated the workers and helped the new J.F. McElwain Company get off to a prosperous start. Partially as a morale factor, he sponsored baseball teams which gained a semi-pro reputation, due partly to the crack college players who were given summer jobs at the factory. The Nashua Millionaires were especially popular, including an early bat boy named "Birdie" Tebbetts who went on to play professional baseball.

In 1936 and again in 1938, the highly respected F.P. Murphy was elected governor of the state. The victory was noteworthy since he was the first Catholic Republican governor of New Hampshire and his success came while the Democrats under Roosevelt were sweeping most of the country.

In 1904 the Nashua Gummed & Coated Paper Company (now Nashua Corp.) was formed to take

John G. Foster Post 7 of the Grand Army of the Republic on
Memorial Day, 1927.

John G. Foster Post 7 of the Grand Army of the Republic on Memorial Day, 1927.

over the coating business of the Nashua Card and Glazed Paper Company which was commonly called the "Card Shop." In 1908 the company began manufacturing waxed paper, and was the first to make bread wrappers, plus many specialty gummed and coated products. The rapidly expanding company soon added assorted subsidiaries around the world. Officers in 1928 were: Winthrop L. Carter, President and General Manager; Vasco E. Nunez, Vice-President; Eliot A. Carter, Treasurer.

In the fall of 1909 the National Wrapping Paper Co. moved to Nashua from Boston so as to be nearer their supplier, Nashua Gummed & Coated. The manager, Henri A. Sevigne, devised a bread wrapping machine which would revolutionize the storage of food products. The first power machine was made in 1913, with further developments of the Sevigne Wrapping Machine under the name of Carter Rice & Co., Machine Division. In 1920 the business was merged and incorporated as the National Bread Wrapping Machine Co.

In the fall of 1903 the International Paper Box Machinery Company began operating in Nashua. Its water-powered plant was located on the site where the first sewing machine was made by Elias Howe. On April 1, 1904, it delivered its first Rotary Folding and Gluing Machine, an innovative device which could quickly and accurately fold and glue any kind of carton. Further development included

machines for making envelopes, and boxes for tobacconist and druggist uses.

The first official work day of the Improved Paper Machinery Co. in Nashua was November 12, 1901. Its property in what was commonly referred to as the Edgeville section of Nashua had been occupied earlier in 1896 by the Bates Machine Company, followed shortly after by the American Motor Company which produced horseless carriages for only a short time there. The tract remained temporarily idle until the founding of Improved. The new company grew in fits and starts in the early years. For example, in 1907 business dropped drastically due to a nationwide economic slowdown. In 1912-1913 Charles and Walter Morey sold the company to Arthur J. Connors of Exeter. In 1917 the original building was expanded as the company again began to grow. Later, in September, 1930, Walter L. Barker bought out Connors' interest just as the country began struggling with the depression. Keeping the company alive was further complicated by the flood of 1936 which swamped the basement and rose into the first story of the building. By 1941 Improved was retooling for the war effort and soon was expanding rapidly. In 1953 the name became Improved Machinery, Inc. (IMPCO), to reflect the broadening product line. In the years that followed, the success of the company grew and IMPCO became a subsidiary of Ingersoll-Rand.

One recurring problem was finally settled on the night of December 11, 1924, when a spectacular fire destroyed the old wooden Main Street bridge and sent it crashing into the Nashua River. Years of floods and heavy use had weakened the structure, necessitating regular repairs. Immediately after the fire the Boston and Maine Railroad bridge building crew constructed a temporary wooden replacement which was still in use a year later when work began on a more permanent cement and steel span. By early May, 1926, the western lane of the bridge was opened to traffic but the whole project was plagued with obstacles and setbacks, including serious underwater construction problems.

Finally the work was finished and on June 18, 1927, the bridge was formally accepted by the Board of Public Works, the widest span for its length in the world.

On Monday, July 2, 1928, the city prepared for a three-day celebration of its seventy-fifth anniversary. With a population of thirty thousand, the community was prospering; local banking institutions held assets totaling over twenty million dollars, and local business and industry were also doing quite well.

The festival began on Tuesday, July 3, with the opening of the Bernardi Greater Shows carnival at South Common, followed by a midnight bonfire. On Wednesday a Civic Parade featuring five divisions of colorful floats was staged.

Prosperity, however, rested upon precarious footings. Finance and industry were built largely around the textile mills, the city's largest employers. Operating for one hundred years, the mills had been the main force in the transformation of the community from a town to a small city. Security rested heavily on the success or failure of a single commodity in a fluctuating market.

The Depression

Then as things were going rather smoothly, on Tuesday, October 29, 1929, sixteen million shares of stock were liquidated on the New York Stock Exchange in an avalanche which marked the point of no return for a faulty national economy. The panic climaxed the collapse of a system flawed by an unsound credit structure, wild speculation, and a complexity of excesses. A dazed nation waited for the effects of the shocking debacle. Thirty-five billion dollars of paper wealth had suddenly vanished from the economy.

Luxury items were the first to be affected; soon the curb in buying reached all areas of consumer goods. People's needs were still there, but the pur-

chasing power of the great bulk of the population dwindled. The average wage earner was never able to put aside any substantial savings. An estimated five percent of the population controlled about forty percent of the wealth. Wages had remained relatively constant while huge profits had accumulated and been poured into booming securities speculation.

With the worst of the Depression still to come, many Nashuans were suddenly made homeless by a fire which started on the Sunday afternoon of May 4, 1930. The blaze began in a trestle of the Boston and Maine Railroad, where it spanned the Nashua River off Temple Street. A high wind from the northwest carried embers to the roof of a factory building. Soon the fire spread across Temple Street, down Spruce and across East Hollis Street to the Crown Hill residential area. Within hours flames swept from one building to the next, as frantic residents helped battle the blaze with bucket brigades, shovels of dirt, and even blankets. Fire apparatus came from surrounding towns and as far away as Boston to battle the conflagration. As the day and evening wore on, almost four hundred homes were destroyed. The area was reduced to a wasteland of ashes with only a few chimneys and skeletons of trees left standing. The total loss was set

at well over two million dollars. Most of the homeowners, having little or no insurance, were devastated by the catastrophe. The National Red Cross aided at the scene while temporary shelter was set up in the National Guard Armory. Most victims salvaged only a few belongings and moved in with friends and relatives. Meanwhile, a local committee organized by the Mayor began raising a relief fund which soon totaled about eighty thousand dollars, to provide financial help.

Civic groups such as the Good Cheer Society helped the many homeless people. An untold

City Station being demolished after the 1930 fire.

number helped directly with clearing the ashes and debris, and relocating and sheltering hundreds. The local relief effort demonstrated once again the fortitude and generosity of the community in helping one another overcome sudden calamity.

On May 4, 1931, one year after the fire, more than four hundred families had rebuilt their homes. With newer zoning laws, streets were made wider with safer intersections. Many small stores, including a drug store, were rebuilt. In addition, a new Infant Jesus Church was constructed. On Marshall Street the Proctor Brothers Co. was back in business. In all, a commendable job of rebuilding Crown Hill had been accomplished.

Despite the reassurances of government and industry leaders, the Depression grew worse. With demand and buying down, unemployment grew with alarming momentum. In April, 1930, three million were out of work; by October, 1932, eleven million; and by March, 1933, the figure was between thirteen and fifteen million. Countless others were working at drastic wage cuts. Sadly, some came to accept poverty and despair as a fact of life.

For those needing jobs the City of Nashua, with liberal federal contributions, sponsored many projects including street and sewer repair; park work; fire prevention; writing local history; and a variety of civic-minded tasks. Other needy individuals received direct relief with the state contributing half the cost.

For 1933, the City Paupers Department spent an estimated forty thousand dollars, according to figures reported by then Mayor William F. Sullivan. Prior to the Depression the department had spent an average of nine thousand dollars per year. Also in 1933 general relief assistance by churches, organizations, and individuals, was estimated at fifty-five thousand dollars. Private benefactors included: orphanages, Community Chest, Hunt Home for the Aged, Good Cheer Society, and many religious and charitable societies. An estimated total of five hundred thousand dollars was spent for relief in Nashua in 1933 through public and private sources at the state, county, and local levels.

In 1934 Nashua Police Department installed police radios and claimed the distinction of being the first unit of any community in New Hampshire to use this innovation.

On March 13, 1934, the Board of Aldermen authorized the Mayor to acquire property situated between Pine Hill Road and the Keene Branch of the Boston and Maine Railroad, owned by Joseph Therrien and the Cotton heirs. Additional land was to be acquired, all to be developed as a CWA Project for an airport.

In July, 1934, a parcel located at the southwest corner of the airport was designated for use as a transient relief shelter as directed by the Federal Emergency Relief Administration.

During 1934 the city thus acquired land and with CWA and FERA assistance developed an airport. Even at this stage of completion it was a so-called "flag stop" for U.S. mail and passengers on the Boston to Montreal air route. It was large enough to accommodate regular transport planes but it lacked a hangar. Shortly thereafter, on March 12, 1935, plans for a brick and steel structure for use as a hangar and administration building were prepared under the direction of Fred L. Clark, city engineer, and approved by New Hampshire ERA officials. Construction began immediately utilizing ERA labor. Other improvements at the airport completed in 1935 with ERA assistance were: additional clearing and widening of the landing field; a new entrance from Amherst Street, and removal of hazards on adjoining properties. In addition, studies were completed for later improvements such as hard surfacing of runways and proper lighting.

Thus by the mid-1930s the Roosevelt Administration made available millions of dollars for communities to use for larger scale projects. By January, 1937, groundwork was laid for the new Nashua City Hall, forty-five percent of the cost to be paid by the federal government. The building was finally completed in 1939. On September 2, 1937, the new Elm Street High School on the South Common was dedicated. The funding of the six hundred thousand dollar project was discussed late in March, 1935, when Mayor Alvin Lucier sought approval for federal PWA funds to underwrite forty-five percent of the costs. After several weeks of delays approval was finally obtained for the largest PWA grant made to New Hampshire towns. Construction of the foundation began by December, 1935; the structure itself was begun in the spring of 1936. One final project which benefited partially from federal funds was the building of Holman Stadium and fieldhouse. However, the project was made possible mainly through the generosity of Charles Frank Holman who left fifty-five thousand dollars. The fieldhouse was to be dedicated to the youth and people of Nashua in memory of his parents. His wishes were fulfilled on September 23, 1937, when the new facilities were officially dedicated.

Natural Disasters

In March of 1936 while Nashuans struggled with the Depression, a natural calamity was developing far up the Merrimack River. Heavy snow which had fallen during the winter months suddenly liquified during a warm spell in mid-March instead of melting gradually in a series of thaws. Heavy rains followed, so that within days torrents of water were rushing into the Merrimack Valley. The flow crested in Nashua on the nineteenth. The old Taylor Falls bridge was under water and as much as twelve feet of water covered a large area around Union Station near Johns-Manville, including warehouse buildings and side streets. For several weeks the clean-up operations continued.

Nature conspired against the community once again on September 1, 1938, when a severe hurricane blasted across the city toppling hundreds of trees and causing an estimated half-million dollars damage. Thus by the late 1930s it seemed that every disaster, natural or man-made, had occurred. However, throughout the period the stamina and community spirit quietly endured.

World War II

Criticism and debate over the success or failure of

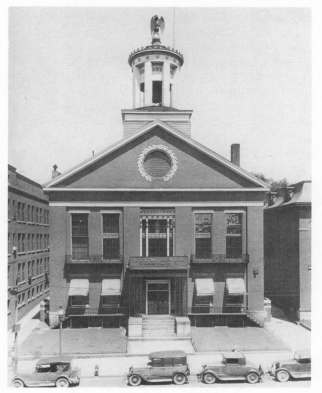

Old City Hall in the thirties.

the New Deal soon became academic. In September, 1939, Germany invaded Poland, and Europe was at war. As the conflict became worldwide, American industry began to tool up for the gathering storm. In 1940 unemployment was cut in half; by 1941 it was practically eliminated. America had hemmed and hawed until December, 1941, when Pearl Harbor jolted the country into action. Apparently war had done in a few years what six years of programs failed to accomplish. However, it seemed a terrible price to pay for economic recovery.

During the difficult years of World War II stringent anti-inflation measures were put into effect, including wage, rent, and price controls. On May 4-8, 1942, registration for sugar rationing began in Nashua, followed on May 12 with the rationing of gasoline and, on October 24, fuel oil. As the war dragged on, shortages in consumer goods developed. In January, 1943, fuel oil was in short supply; by February canned goods were getting scarce and many meat cases were empty. Butter all

but disappeared, being replaced by newly developed substitutes. Capsules of yellow coloring had to be mixed, at home, with the whitish margarine to produce a lard-like substance that bore little resemblance to real butter. The sacrifices seemed almost endless as families skimped and in many cases went without. However, most remained united in their firm determination to support the war effort in every way possible.

Many tried growing their own vegetables in tiny plots in their back yards. Dubbed the "Victory Garden" the vegetable patch became a common sight and did help ease the food shortage. Beginning in 1942 Nashua Manufacturing set aside land for more than two hundred and fifty individual plots. In 1945 the yield of these gardens was estimated at ten to fifteen tons of produce per acre. An annual Harvest Show was held in mid-September at the mill's Recreational Building.

During the war many Nashuans served in all branches of the military service. Hundreds of men and women enlisted or were inducted to be trained and sent to Europe and various parts of the globe. In mid-March, 1942, a large group of Nashua men arrived in Australia for duty in the Pacific. For some, the incredible demands of war proved to be overwhelming, while others endured the holocaust and performed feats of heroism. An unfortunate number would never return, being killed or reported missing in obscure places from Bataan to North Africa.

On September 22, 1943, the Selective Service Board reported that 13 percent of all Nashuans, or about 4,160, had gone to war. Groups of men and women regularly left Nashua for training and war assignments. More than twenty young men left high school, went into the service, and later earned diplomas when the war was over. Many families suffered the agonizing loss of a father, mother, son, or other close relative.

Finally after almost six years of war Germany unconditionally surrendered to the Allies on May 7, 1945. On August 15, 1945, V-J Day marked the end of the war in the Pacific. The official surrender document was signed by Japan on September 2, aboard the *U.S.S. Missouri.*

On Sunday, September 9, 1945, the Nashua Airport was officially renamed and dedicated Boire Field in honor of Paul Boire whose parents resided at 108 Tolles Street. The young Navy bomber pilot was killed March 23, 1943, off Trinidad, the first Nashua pilot to give his life in World War II. Chairman Alvin A. Lucier of the Municipal Airport Commission presided at the solemn occasion which was heavily attended by various civilian and military groups. Through the years the airport continued to grow and develop, utilizing ever more modern equipment and facilities.

Several years later on November 11, 1953, an impressive stone monument at Railroad Square was dedicated which lists the one hundred and twenty men and women from the community who gave their lives in the struggle. With the demands and sacrifices of the war finally in the past, a weary people faced the hopes and frustrations of peace.

Crest of the flood on the Nashua River at the Jackson power station in 1936.

24

Textron Pulls Out and Nashua Recovers

FOLLOWING WORLD WAR II the country began the shift back to a peacetime economy. Serious problems including ruinous inflation, bitter labor disputes, and an acute housing shortage threatened the prosperity which seemed so long overdue after the deprivations of war. All across the country unions called strikes for higher wages. By 1947 food, clothing, rent, and other necessities rose drastically in price, causing further unrest among a populace struggling with the bittersweet fruits of victory.

Post-War Developments

On Saturday, August 31, 1946, the first forty units on Rancourt Street of the eighty-unit Veterans Housing Project were officially turned over to the city. The Emergency Housing Office at City Hall quickly filled the converted Camp Myles Standish barracks with waiting Nashua war veterans and their families. More than two hundred applied for veterans' assistance in locating housing.

One memorable year for sports enthusiasts just after the war was 1946. Edward Dobrowolski, a junior at Nashua High School, was the football hero for the year. Under Coach Charles "Buzz" Harvey the NHS football team won the 1946 State Championship. They also won the East Coast Championship in Jacksonville, Florida, that same year. It was also a memorable year for baseball fans when the Brooklyn Dodgers ran a Class-B club in Nashua as part of the New England League. From early spring to August, hundreds of jubilant fans enjoyed the season's games, and especially players like Roy Campanella.

A graduate in the NHS Class of 1930 who resided in Nashua to the early 1960s was George "Birdie" Tebbetts, famed baseball player. For many years he lived at 68 East Pearl Street, and was a long-time associate of the Paul Sadler Insurance Agency. His illustrious career included playing for the Detroit Tigers—1936-1942, 1946-1947; Boston Red Sox, 1947-1950, and the Cleveland Indians, 1951-1952. In addition, he managed the Cincinnati Reds, 1954-1958; Milwaukee Braves, 1961-1962, and the Cleveland Indians, 1963-1966. By 1973 he was scouting for the New York Mets.

Among the young Nashuans who had already finished high school was Dennis Sullivan (later Mayor), a graduate in the NHS Class of 1937. In the

Class of 1941 were Samuel Tamposi, a future real estate developer, and Walter Peterson, who later served as Governor, 1969-1973. Another Nashuan who became Governor was Hugh Gregg who graduated from Phillips Exeter Academy in 1935. He went on to earn degrees at Yale and Harvard, plus honorary degrees from UNH and Dartmouth. Beginning in 1942 he became an attorney with Sullivan, Gregg, and Horton. He also served as Treasurer and President of Gregg and Son, Incorporated, and Chairman of the Board of the Indian Head National Bank in Nashua. He was an Alderman-at-large, 1948-1950, and from January to December, 1950, he served only part of a term as Mayor before being called to active military duty. Later he served as Governor, 1953-1955. Through the years he has been very active in social and community affairs and projects. His recent positions include being on the Board of Directors of the Crotched Mountain Foundation, Director of Wildcat Mountain Corp., and President and Treasurer of Gregg Cabinets, Ltd.

The first radio station in the city granted a license by the Federal Communications Commission was WOTW-AM which went on the air September 13, 1947, followed in March of 1948 by WOTW-FM. Ten years later in 1958 WSMN broadcasting station began operating at 1590 on the dial, offering Nashuans a choice for local radio listening. In addition, WSMN began publishing the weekly 1590 Broadcaster featuring news and comment. The local stations have provided entertainment programming and national news, and have been particularly valuable in supplying local news. With radio newscasts and articles in the daily *Nashua Telegraph,* residents have been informed concerning local issues and events of importance to the community.

Instrumental in the development of local communications media is Mr. D. Alan Rock, a graduate of Boston University School of Public Relations and Communications. As general manager of WSMN and publisher of the 1590 Broadcaster, he has become active in the social and political development of the community. After serving as a state Representative in Concord, he was elected to his first term as a state Senator in elections held in November, 1974. In addition to these legislative duties, he was elected to the board of trustees of the University of New Hampshire. Throughout the

years he has been involved in local organizations and served in a variety of positions, including president of the United Fund of Greater Nashua and Hudson, and member of the St. Joseph Hospital Advisory Board.

Nashua Industry Falters

In the midst of the post-war struggle Nashua soon found itself confronted with economic crisis. By 1948 Nashua had an industrial base which was dangerously dependent upon the textile mills of the Nashua Manufacturing Company.

For several years prior to the war the textile industry began a phase of changes in which mills were being closed in the North and reopened in the South. A variety of factors have been cited to explain the trend, including the fact that industry was now being fueled by coal instead of water power, so moving nearer the supply of coal could lower costs. Another factor was the outdated condition of many of the industrial machines in northern mills, some of which were over a hundred years old. But perhaps most important of all was the fact that the South offered an untapped reservoir of cheap labor which as yet had not been unionized. Thus a critical collection of ailments threatened the old textile industry. The temporary demands of the war had been merely a postponement of the inevitable. All over New England—especially in Lowell, Lawrence, and Manchester—mills were quietly closing.

Textron Closes!

In 1945 Textron, a new company founded by Royal Little of Providence, Rhode Island, bought Nashua Manufacturing, including the former Indian Head and Jackson holdings. The financial manipulations and speculations of Royal Little helped Textron to rise very rapidly, with companies in thirteen states. However, by July, 1947, Little claimed that things were not going very well in Nashua and that a series of changes would have to be made if the mills were to stay open. Lay-offs regardless of seniority, lower wages, higher workloads, and demands for lower taxes were included in the series of cutbacks, all commonly referred to as the "Nashua Plan."

Then suddenly on September 13, 1948, Textron announced that the Nashua Mills, after 125 years of

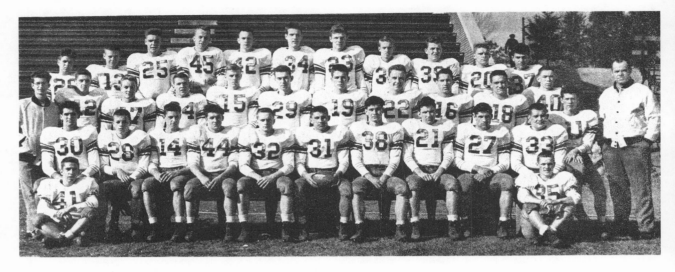

operation, would be closed. The *Nashua Telegraph* prepared the headlines for the evening paper. In bold type the editor set "TEXTRON CLOSING." A phone call at one o'clock urgently requested that a meeting of community and business leaders, including the Chamber of Commerce, be held in the editor's office to discuss press reports of the tragic news. When the daily paper reached the streets, the headline read, "CITY SWINGS INTO ACTION," and in smaller type, "Textron Announces Plant Closing Here."

It seemed to some that the "Nashua Plan" hardly had a chance to work. Others were not convinced of the claim that the mills were not making a profit. Many were openly bitter. They felt that Textron had pulled "a fast one." A full-scale investigation followed. Local and state officials protested and arranged for an inquiry by the Senate Small Business Committee. Hearings were held on September 22-23 in the Nashua High School Auditorium by a subcommittee of the Committee on Interstate and Foreign Commerce. For two days an emotional, packed crowd witnessed the exchange of charges and counter-charges which echoed back and forth between company and Textile Workers Union officials. The tactics and maneuvers of Royal Little were presented and examined by union officials who depicted him as a ruthless capitalist in the not-so-grand tradition, who had exploited Nashua in his aggressive attempts to amass an empire in textiles.

Royal Little vigorously defended the action taken in Nashua. Although admitting that the Nashua Mills were operating at a profit, he claimed that the closing was necessary if Textron was to survive. He cited low output per man-hour, high taxes, and high power costs as key problems in Nashua as opposed to southern operations. He conceded that wage differentials between mills in the North and South were not great, and therefore not a factor. In the coming years it seemed to him that the Nashua operation would become less and less efficient and less profitable, justifying his decision to close. It remained unclear which side was right, but there was no doubt in anyone's mind about which side the working people of Nashua were on.

In a final agreement it was revealed that the blanket operations of the mills would close as of December 31, 1948, putting about one fourth of Nashua's industrial workers out of work. The sheeting operations at the Jackson mills, employing about 1,000, would remain open until December, 1951. Hardest hit were the older workers, unable or reluctant to relocate or retrain to a new job.

In the weeks of uncertainty Nashuans faced the gloomy prospect of seeing the economy of the community collapse. Finally, a local committee was formed to negotiate with Textron to purchase the mill properties of about two and one-half million square feet of floor space. In the final agreement, Textron agreed to a price of a half-million dollars, one hundred thousand in cash, with the remainder to be mortgaged. In order to facilitate the transaction, the Nashua-New Hampshire Foundation was formed with capital from seven main sources: Indian Head National Bank, Second National Bank,

Nashua Trust Company, Improved Machinery Co., Nashua Corporation, Gregg and Son, and J.F. McElwain Co.

The Road Back

During the next three or four years, due largely to capable management, the Foundation brought several new industries to Nashua, making it possible to repay the original underwriters and the mortgage. Also instrumental in the successful recovery was the Chamber of Commerce, which carried on an extensive and capable publicity campaign. Within six years the properties on Canal Street which had been the Jackson Mills were sold, the largest part to an electronics firm, Sanders Associates, which has since grown to be one of the city's largest industries. Thus as the years progressed Nashua rebounded from a potentially catastrophic economic crisis. Eventually over thirty new industries came to the city, occupying virtually all of the floor space of the old mills. The original goal of providing stable employment and industrial growth became a reality. Civic, municipal, and industrial leaders, with the Chamber of Commerce, had salvaged the city's industrial balance. The result was an economy based on a great diversity of industry. Barring national calamity, never again would the total economy of the city be so easily jeopardized.

With economic recovery more certain, Nashua faced other pressing problems, such as housing. The first low income rental housing project, the O.S. Maynard Homes, was completed and dedicated December 13, 1949. The total cost of the hundred-unit project was about eleven thousand five hundred dollars per dwelling unit. Further housing problems were tackled by the newly appointed Nashua Housing Authority.

As the 1950s began, inflation, the internal threat of western communism, and the uncertainty of world peace, were the main concerns of the nation. Very shortly, North Koreans crossed the thirty-eighth parallel into South Korea, and the U.S., as part of a United Nations police force, embarked on a costly military action which lasted until July, 1953.

Meanwhile at home, Nashua held its centennial celebration which included a three-night performance in Holman Stadium of *Drum Beats,* an historical pageant depicting three hundred years of Nashua's growth. The gigantic production opened on Wednesday, June 24, 1953. Comprising seven-

teen scenes, it was created by Donald H. Martin, centennial coordinator, with the pageant script written by Don Moll. Samuel J. O'Neil served as director of the cast of seven hundred and fifty. On Saturday evening, June 27, a band concert and fireworks display was held at Holman Stadium. Also featured was colorful international dancing. Finally on Sunday, June 28, a huge parade culminated the week of celebrating. Twenty-seven bands and hundreds of marchers were in the procession. About one hundred thousand spectators stood in ninety-one degree heat to watch the display, which included many floats. Most striking was a twenty-foot balloon shaped as a pirate. The coolest spot during the entire affair undoubtedly was the Kiwanis Club float which included a swimming pool filled with a swarm of happy children. Nashuans were justifiably proud of one hundred years of achievement as a city.

However, not all was joyful celebrating elsewhere in the country, for earlier, Senator Joseph McCarthy had leveled charges of communist activity within the State Department, and a special investigation was launched in 1950.

The long arm of McCarthyism reached the city in 1954 when a number of Nashua residents were called before the State Attorney General in Concord for lengthy interrogation concerning their views on communism. All took the Fifth Amendment against self-incrimination, and some cited the New Hampshire Fifteenth Amendment which protects an individual from testifying against himself. Working with the Attorney General was a former FBI agent from Nashua. In January, 1954, Joe McCarthy's investigating committee was in Boston, presumably to rout the communists from Yankee territory. One Nashua resident appeared, but took the Fifth Amendment.

The Post-War Baby Boom

While the media kept Nashuans aware of national developments, the community continued its slow but steady progress. New homes sprouted along side streets and back roads, many of them built by newly-wed veterans and financed with G.I. loans. The infants of the post-war baby boom approached and attained school age, placing heavy demands on educational facilities. Due to the low birth rate during the Depression school enrollment had been de-

Looking north over Main Street in the early 1950s. Library Hill and the Hunt Building are in upper center, the Pilgrim Congregationalist Church is still visible on Temple Street, and the Sanders parking lot between the Nashua River and Canal Street is yet to be built.

clining, from 7,369 in 1936 to a low of 5,915 in 1948. Then by the late forties the birth rate was double that of the thirties. By 1950 the school population reached 6,231 and continued to climb rapidly. The fluctuating birth rate tended to frustrate school planning and complicated efforts to provide adequate school facilities.

By 1948 Nashua had four parochial schools in operation: St. Louis de Gonzague, begun in 1883 by Father Milette; St. Francis Xavier, started in 1886; St. Patrick's, begun in 1884; and Enfant Jesus, begun in 1909. These four formed the core of the Roman Catholic elementary school system. By 1936 parochial school enrollment reached 2,755 while public schools had 4,614. By 1948 parochial schools enrolled 2,519 and public schools 3,396. Thus, parochial schools provided education for a substantial portion of Nashua children. The main problem was the uncertainty of planning several years ahead. No one was certain of the number of pupils who would go to parochial schools or to public schools and neither school system clearly understood what the other was doing. Further complicating matters were the changes going on within the Catholic Church. There had never been perfect harmony between the Irish and French officials within the Church concerning the role of the French language in the parochial schools. Old animosities rippled through the Church hierarchy, affecting decisions on school policies.

For Nashua's French community its language remained the focal point of their pride and unity, the symbol of their survival as a group. Thus it was with great pride that they used and spoke French at home, in their church, and in their school. It seemed logical that French children would attend parochial school and learn French culture in its own language. In the early years of the parochial schools this seemed to be true. However as time passed many became less convinced that it was desirable to have their children instructed totally in French. As more years went by, many slowly became acculturated and questioned the desirability of the use of French at all. Thus controversy over the parochial schools and their policies remained an open question, not only for the community as a whole but within the Church membership.

Disaster

The relative tranquility of the mid-1950s was suddenly interrupted on Tuesday, August 31, 1954, when hurricane Carol roared through the city, smashing plate glass windows on Main Street, toppling hundreds of trees, breaking utility wires, flooding cellars, and causing general havoc. Damage was estimated at one million dollars. Work crews cleared the debris for days following the severe storm.

On the morning of November 12, 1954, a Boston and Maine passenger train derailed as it approached Union Station. The seven-car train powered by twin diesel engines ripped up sections of track as wreckage was twisted and scattered across the freight yard near Johns-Manville. Several nearby buildings were damaged by flying debris. While hundreds of spectators came to the scene, causing traffic jams and confusion, emergency crews with cutting torches and heavy equipment began untangling the wreckage. One woman was killed and several other persons injured. It was believed that the derailment was caused mainly by excess speed as the train neared the station.

Another spectacular incident occurred on February 3, 1957, when fire destroyed the National Guard Armory on Canal Street. This required the construction of a new facility on the east side of South Main Street.

In November, 1959, two men were found guilty of the murder of a Rhode Island man found in a Nashua parking lot. The trial and appeals would drag on for months, involving the legality of New Hampshire's laws for carrying out the death penalty. Ultimately, the two would serve a prison term and then go free.

The Late 1950s

An important improvement in downtown Nashua was completed in 1959 when Main Street was widened from the Nashua River bridge to F.W. Woolworth to eliminate a "bottleneck" which hindered traffic flow on the roadway. Plans were begun in 1956 when property owners were approached concerning the action.

Earlier, in January of 1959, Miss Mabel Chandler died and left her property on the corner of Kinsley and Main Streets to be used as the Chandler Memorial Library in memory of her family. Her generous gift provided the grounds, building, and funds to maintain the property through the years.

As the 1950s closed national foreign policy was dominated by the Cold War and the work of John Foster Dulles. Competition with the Russians erupted in 1957 when Sputnik launched the space race which was to dominate the next decade. The recurring recessions, such as in 1952 and 1958, affected the otherwise steady growth and prosperity. The pace of living was quickening; material goods, in short supply during the war, took on new importance with consumers who settled into cozy family living. Many believed in absolutes, and public tolerance of any deviation from the norm was slim. Memories of the tragedies and upheavals of the war were still all too real for many adults who now wanted a quiet world of harmony and conformity.

25

Growth in the Sixties and Seventies

DURING THE TURBULENT DECADE of the 1960s Nashua underwent an extensive surge of growth and development. The population rose from 39,096 in 1960 to 55,820 in 1970. This was an increase of 42.8 percent. By contrast the previous decade had witnessed a mere 11 percent increase. Even during the decade from 1940 to 1950, which included the post-war baby boom, population rose only about five percent. Thus the sixties saw an exceptional increase which was to affect all aspects of community life. This rapid expansion carried a certain price. Gone once and for all was the reassuring small-town atmosphere which many had cherished for so long. By 1970 Nashua was decidedly a medium-sized city with many of the mixed blessings of urban living. Cultural and educational opportunities were increasing but traffic congestion, a shortage of housing, and an occasional lag in providing civic and social services for the growing population plagued the sudden success story. In spite of these problems the city that in 1948 hovered at the brink of economic collapse had risen from imminent despair to seemingly boundless expansion and optimism.

Advantages for Business in Nashua

In the early 1950s it quickly became apparent that geography was to be a decided asset. Situated within an hour's drive from Boston and linked by a network of interstate highways with the industrialized northeast, Nashua found itself in a favorable location. The sudden surge in technology-related industries in a federally supported industrial complex along the Route 128 area of Massachusetts, spurred partly by the expanding space program, made Nashua a likely neighbor for locating supportive industries, such as electronics. A readily available labor force, suitable land, and a general welcoming invitation from civic leaders were added features. Even more alluring was the lack of a relatively oppressive and complicated tax structure as compared with Massachusetts.

Initially many hoped our suburbia would offer the best of several worlds including urban and rural. Broad educational and cultural opportunities were within commuting distance in Cambridge and Boston, while scenic and natural resources were readily at hand. Gradually developing was a growing pool of technically skilled and well educated individuals who sought to raise the quality of life for themselves and their families. Many of this segment of the community worked in Massachusetts in high-salaried professional or skilled jobs but lived in Nashua's quieter surroundings. At first the growing number of commuters contributed to the ignominious reference to Nashua in some circles as a bedroom town for Boston. Though all expectations could not be filled as readily as many newcomers hoped, Nashua was earning a reputation as a progressive city with an identity all its own.

The welcome mat image was not without some tarnish, however. On November 20, 1962, an open hearing conducted by the State Advisory Committee on Civil Rights produced evidence of discriminatory practices in Nashua housing. About twenty-four Nashuans testified as to individuals being refused housing because of race or color. Particular reference was made to multi-family dwellings in the Myrtle Street area, and some expressed deep concern over alleged practices of discouraging and preventing blacks from purchasing homes in other neighborhoods. Fortunately these latter cases were relatively few.

The Industrial Mix

A major project that focused attention on the city was the Federal Aviation Administration's new Air Traffic Control Center. Costing about nine million dollars including equipment, its groundbreaking ceremonies were held June 3, 1961, and it was dedicated on May 4, 1963. The installation was located on a 19.5-acre site just west of the turnpike. It represented a relocation of a center from Boston's Logan Airport which is responsible for the routing of flight paths of all civil and military aircraft operating on instrument type flight plans.

By the 1960s the economy supporting the community rested upon a truly diversified base. New industries had been introduced and some old ones expanded. The Nashua-New Hampshire Foundation and Chamber of Commerce continued their valuable efforts. Among the more successful firms was the Sprague Electric Co., which employed about 1,050 in 1962. It came to Nashua in 1948 and produced a variety of products including ceramic capacitors, printed circuits, and resistors.

Another electronics firm, Sanders Associates, employed three thousand workers by 1962 and was growing steadily. Since coming to Nashua in 1952 Sanders has become a recognized leader in the electronics world, contributing scientific breakthroughs for industry as well as national defense. Missile guidance systems, radar, microwave components, and wiring for hearing aids and computer circuits were but a few of its early products. The company continued to grow and in 1968 the seven-story facility with modern glassed tower was built on DW Highway South. During the peak year of 1975 the firm employed an estimated seven thousand workers.

Other successful industries included Bronze Craft Corp., organized in 1944 for producing metal parts for defense work during World War II. By 1962 it employed 160 and manufactured a broad line of hardware, machined sand castings, and custom products.

Another fast-growing firm was Edgcomb Steel, begun in 1951 and employing seventy-five persons by 1962. The warehouse facilities stocked an expanding line of steel, aluminum, and brass sheets, plates, bars, and rods, plus a wide variety of fasteners and construction materials.

The growing list of new companies also included Allied Electric founded in 1949; Easton Co., Stanley Elevator, 1951; Lochhead Millwork, 1948; Doehla Inc., 1950; Indian Head Millwork, 1946; and Hampshire Manufacturing, 1952. Many older companies, such as Johns-Manville (started in 1907), continued to flourish and contribute to the general economy.

Industrial Parks and Shopping Malls

Realizing the potential for filling the needs and demands of the community, some enterprising individuals introduced plans for massive shopping centers and malls, away from the inner city, downtown area. One early project at the south end of Main Street was the multi-million dollar shopping center proposed in 1960 by Simoneau Plaza, Inc. on the Harbor Pond site near Salmon Brook. The marshy site was filled and soon the expansive center took shape where months earlier ice skating parties had been held. Opened in February, 1962, Simoneau Plaza quickly became a popular shopping center.

In December, 1963, Samuel Tamposi made his first public announcement for an automotive center to be located on a 34 acre site located on the east side of the DW Highway South. In spite of some local resistance the project began to take shape on the chosen site. The New England Auto Village became a reality and continued to grow to include a wide selection of makes and models of automobiles at one location.

In 1960, with Gerald Nash, Tamposi began one of the first modern industrial parks in Nashua, followed by other parks in the years that followed. His growing list of achievements came to include commercial buildings as well as residential developments and even included the Greenbriar Nursing Home for the elderly. In addition the Nashua-New Hampshire Foundation also clearly saw the potential for growth and organized a large industrial park area.

The development of the industrial parks and shopping malls in Nashua in the 1960s reflected a growing trend across the country. The dependence upon the automobile resulted in vast shopping centers, surrounded by acres of free parking, dotting the landscape. Located on the fringes of urban areas and linked by modern interstate highway systems, the malls reflected a society on wheels.

Simoneau Plaza was only the first in a number of such shopping centers in Nashua. Several years later the Nashua Mall off Broad Street was being constructed by developer Robert Gordon, whose family resided in Nashua for many years. By May, 1969, the completed mall offered a wide array of merchandise in an attractive enclosed setting easily accessible by auto.

Other shopping centers sprang up in the city including the SouthGate Shopping Center, The Turnpike Plaza, and the Royal Ridge Mall. In addition a growing number of fast-food franchises dotted the city in strategic locations. The close scrutiny of marketing surveys pointed the way for further retail saturation. It became apparent that in the hectic world of the market place Nashua had come of age. To the dismay of many the DW South became a seemingly endless stream of businesses. Growing traffic congestion quickly demonstrated the need of planning for future growth.

The older business district in the downtown Main Street area underwent changes as the 1960s progressed. Several of the chain stores closed and relocated to the outlying shopping centers in hopes of

staying with the peak business activity. Some older businesses closed completely, being replaced by a growing number of specialty stores and fast-food shops which cater to a growing clientele of employees from the large number of banking and finance, insurance, municipal, and administrative offices in the downtown area. In 1970 downtown merchants formed the Heart of Nashua Foundation to plan and revitalize the central business district. By 1974, 139 members were working to cope with such concerns as beautification, traffic flow,

and particularly parking. The need for high-rise garages was considered on several occasions as a partial solution to the parking problem. Such facilities were conspicuously absent in Nashua considering the size of the city and the widespread use of these garages elsewhere. In November, 1977, ground was broken on High Street for the construction of such a garage. With the great increase in activity in the community came additional strain on the highways and access routes in and out of the city.

Transportation Problems

One acute problem was the slowly crumbling Taylor Falls bridge leading to Hudson. By 1968 a peculiar dip in the roadway near the Nashua side required closing of the span on September 22, 1968, and reopening October 22, following emergency repairs. In spite of the reduction of the load limit to ten tons, the roadway continued to sink.

Finally in June, 1969, construction began on a new bridge just upstream following ten years of running controversy over location and number of new bridges to be constructed. On September 15, 1970, state and local dignitaries gathered to open the new Veterans Memorial Bridge. Meanwhile, the badly weakened Taylor Falls Bridge was permanently closed to traffic.

The problem of bridges still was not settled. By March, 1973, the Taylor Falls span was being removed to make room for a new one which was opened by November, 1974, thus offering two bridges side by side. Meanwhile a new Nashua-Hudson bridge in the south end near the present state liquor store was constructed and opened July 19, 1973. Plans for a fourth bridge in the north end were discussed and postponed. The entire issue was marked by wrangling and debate. As the 1970s progressed the traffic over the Merrimack continued to mount and the congestion remained somewhat of a problem.

On August 28, 1972, a one-way street system was put into effect after approval by the Board of Aldermen. The changes were recommended by a report in 1969 by traffic engineer consultants at Bruce Campbell Associates of Boston. Since its implementation the plan generally has provided increased safety and traffic flow within the city, although initially drivers faced a real challenge getting where they wanted to go. In the first few weeks one occasionally met a panic-stricken motorist trying to drive head-on into two oncoming lanes of traffic to the dismay of all concerned.

Vietnam War Problems

Throughout the decade of the 1960s the strains and frustrations of the Vietnam War complicated relations between family members and citizens of all ages. The controversial question of anti-war dissension which simmered and stewed after 1965 reached a peak late in May, 1970, when an organization attempted to stage a peace rally at either Greeley Park or Holman Stadium. Park-Recreation commissioners turned down the request after several attempts by the peace coalition which included a number of local residents. Supported by the New Hampshire American Civil Liberties Union the group took the commission to court for infringement of rights of free speech and assembly. The U.S. District Court judge upheld the group's right to use the stadium but imposed a number of safety and maintenance requirements which had to be met. The plans were delayed when the group encountered difficulty raising funds to defray costs and finally were foiled when officials produced a report of February, 1970, by a structural engineering firm which declared the stadium unsafe. The incident became a focal point for the emotional frustration about the war which gradually divided the entire community. More than any other single event the enigma of Vietnam evoked the deepest sense of frustration and despair during a decade of social and political unrest.

An early fatality of the Vietnam War was Sgt. Robert L. Gardner, thirty-nine-year-old resident of Vagge Village, Nashua, who had served nineteen years of a twenty-year army career when he was killed on June 13, 1962. His story was featured on a national TV news program at the time. He was the first of nineteen Nashua men who would give their lives before the end of this conflict.

On September 4, 1969, the 3rd Battalion, 197th Artillery, New Hampshire National Guard, including Nashua Battery B, returned after a year in Vietnam. While in combat Battery B lost one man, Captain Roland Labonte of Hudson.

Solving the Housing Shortage

Providing adequate housing for the rapidly growing population became a critical problem as building costs skyrocketed and demand grew. One of the immediate results was the increased cost of older houses. In some cases the market value was inflated to incredible levels considering the age and condition of some of the dwellings, but new homes were even more expensive and rents equally high. Finding housing for every income bracket proved increasingly difficult.

In 1960 the Nashua Housing Authority, established in 1947, opened bids for Vagge Village, a fifty-unit low-rent project for the elderly located on Burke Street. Federally financed at a cost of about $600,000, the complex of six two-story buildings was finished and dedicated in February, 1962.

Vagge Village was named for Mayor Mario Vagge who served the city as its chief executive from 1958 through 1965. Vagge died on October 15, 1973. He is especially remembered by many citizens because of his great interest in the young people of the city. Another ex-Mayor is Lester H. Burnham who served from 1952 through 1957. Burnham, a businessman, was an Alderman-at-large for ten years and pioneered the central purchasing system for the city government. Known as "the taxpayer's watchdog," Burnham was mayor at the time of the centennial celebration.

On June 12, 1962, the Board of Aldermen authorized the Nashua Housing Authority to prepare surveys and plans for the Myrtle Street and Park Street redevelopment projects. In November the Federal Housing and Home Finance Agency approved $197,752 for the plans and survey. Five years later on September 12, 1967, after debate and controversy, the Aldermen approved the Myrtle Street project but rejected the one for Park Street. Groundbreaking ceremonies were finally held November 7, 1972, and the Myrtle Street project neared completion by late January, 1974.

Meanwhile on June 30, 1966, the Ledge Street low-rent housing project was officially completed four years after its construction was approved by the Aldermen. Controversy over site selection, architectural delays, overbidding, and other technical tie-ups slowed the project.

With the Ledge Street project completed, the NHA then began planning for the construction of a ninety-six-unit low-rent highrise for the elderly on Tyler Street. The federally financed $1.7 million structure, named Sullivan Terrace in honor of Mayor Dennis J. Sullivan, was opened for occupancy in September, 1970. Further projects were tentatively planned.

The majority of the population struggled with the housing problem by buying or renting new and not-so-new dwellings. The building boom of single-family units during the 1960s peaked and then suffered, influenced by the gradual stagnation of the housing industry across the country. Soaring costs, with tighter lending policies, placed home ownership beyond the reach of many. Those able to overcome the obstacle of the large down payment faced the blessings and burdens of property taxes and upkeep, and pride in ownership and high resale value. The gradual development of a flourishing group of real estate businesses by the late 1960s reflected the belief that it was all worthwhile.

However, by 1968 there was emerging a shift in preference of type of dwelling. The number of newly built single-family residences decreased by 77 to 527, while the number of apartments constructed almost doubled the 1967 figure, with 366 being built in 29 multi-family buildings. By choice and necessity residents were turning to rental housing.

In 1969 there were only about 200 apartments in the southern part of the city. By 1974 there were over 2,500, with no end in sight. Royal Crest offered about 1,400 with hundreds of additional units in Brook Village, Louisburg Square, Richelieu Estates, and Mountain View, among others. The apartment boom in the south-end continued into the 1970s, making apartment dwellers a growing segment of the population. The ultimate social and political impact of this trend on the community remains undetermined and worthy of consideration.

In 1967 the consulting firm of Metcalf and Eddy

completed an analysis of the city covering population, economic base, and neighborhood conditions. Some areas suffered from sub-standard housing, detrimental land use mixtures, excessive land coverages, poorly designed and constructed streets, inadequate recreational facilities, and various other ills. Fortunately many neighborhoods were weak in only a few of the areas covered by the study. In spite of some shortcomings the study pointed the way for further planning.

Among those deeply concerned with the rapid growth is the City Planning Board established by ordinance May 13, 1952. Throughout the years the Board has mapped and surveyed the sprawling expanse of streets, developments, open lands, and highways and kept a careful watch on the city's seemingly uncontrollable development. In 1967 it was concluded that Nashua needed a comprehensive land use plan and a transportation plan. As a beginning toward a land use plan the staff began work on careful surveys of the city and its needs, including a study of recreational open space. With Greeley Park the only major area, planners in 1967 eyed the Mine Falls area as a potential park site. Later, in 1969, 315 acres were acquired from the Nashua-New Hampshire Foundation for $350,000, of which $175,000 was a federal grant, thus helping make the Mine Falls Park a reality.

In December, 1967, the Board of Aldermen voted unanimously to incorporate proposed amendments to the Land Subdivision Ordinance, thereby securing stricter control of development and construction. Particular areas of concern were enforcing regulations on home construction, improving the living environment, maintaining streets, and preventing abuse of city agencies and materials by developers. The Board of Aldermen approved a resolution which would establish a Code Enforcement Agency headed by a Code Enforcement Director. The agency became operational in July, 1968, and immediately faced the complicated tasks of enforcement.

Another group active in the planning and discussion of area growth is the Nashua Regional Planning Commission, established by ordinance April 14, 1959. With members from surrounding towns the group is involved in understanding immediate and long-range change in the Nashua area. Of special concern is the desire for careful planning in order to fulfill social and human needs while allow-

ing for industrial expansion. In addition maintaining open land areas for recreational use and attaining ecologically safe use of the environment require careful, determined attention. Most critical of all is the imminent population surge in many towns surrounding Nashua, Merrimack in particular, which is the site selected for a massive Digital Corp. plant. The effects of this rapid growth upon Nashua and the area will greatly influence the ultimate quality of life in this section of New Hampshire.

Environmental Problems

One of the most basic yet demanding necessities confronting the growing community was waste removal, including sewage and refuse. In 1961 the Sewage Treatment Plant was constructed. About two hundred visitors toured the modern facility during Open House in May, 1962. Also begun and completed in 1961 was the Salmon Brook Interceptor which eliminated further piping of sewage into Salmon Brook. Further expansion of the system was made in 1963 with construction of interceptor sewers in the Northwest area, Salmon Brook area, and South Daniel Webster area. Begun in September, 1967, the Hassel's Brook Interceptor was completed in December, 1968. The South Merrimack River Interceptor Extension was completed May 17, 1968. The construction plans for the Nashua River Interceptor, the Merrimack River Interceptor, and the additions to the Sewage Treatment Plant were completed by the consultants (Camp, Dresser, and McKee) in March, 1969. During the period July 1, 1974, to June 30, 1975, the Merrimack River Interceptor Contract No. 1 was completed. In addition the Nashua River Interceptor Contracts No. 1 and No. 2 were completed and placed in service, making possible the draining of several sewer lagoons. Further projects included construction of the North Merrimack River Interceptor and the New Searles Road Interceptor among others. Thus an extensive network of sewer lines was expanding as part of a major antipollution effort. During 1969 alone 965 million gallons of raw sewage were processed at the treatment plant and by 1975 the figure reached 1.6 billion gallons.

Coping with the disposal of tons of refuse is no small achievement either. During 1963 some land was purchased and some leased off West Hollis

Street from the Nashua-New Hampshire Foundation to be used as a dump. A "Wilco Tepee Burner" was erected at the site in December, 1963, in order to burn all combustible rubbish. On July 1, 1968, the incinerator and dump were permanently closed down since a sanitary landfill had been started on June 24 at the Coliseum Avenue sand pit. However, a court injunction restricted and regulated the temporary use of this site as a landfill, and it too was closed by early 1970. Meanwhile in 1969 action was taken to acquire a 295-acre site called the Four Hills Area to be used as a sanitary landfill. Well over fifty-seven thousand tons of refuse are buried here annually, a mountain of trash that is a by-product of community growth.

Maintaining a healthful environment and controlling pollution remain as important issues in the 1970s. Fortunately, major efforts toward these goals were made in the sixties, reversing years of neglect and abuse. Hopefully the Merrimack may be made clean again, as it was before industrialization, and hopefully the day will come when few will remember when the Nashua River was named one of the dirtiest rivers in America.

By the 1970s the National Fish Hatchery off Broad Street had become a modern, efficient facility. In contrast earlier accounts describe the original hatchery consisting of a single pond, with a small house, plus a large area of marshland. Prior to the official founding in 1898 it is believed that a small commercial bait fish and trout raising operation was run by a group of owners headed by Virgil C. Gilman, utilizing a hand-dredged brook and Stark Pond. Further digging was carried out to improve the flow of water. On April 28, 1898, the *Telegraph* reported the official purchase by the U.S. Government of the Stark fish ponds. Construction of the federal hatchery began immediately with the building of a dam on Colraine Brook and the digging of a new well by August, 1898. Very shortly a new superintendent's residence, garages, shops, and an ice house were added. By 1900 a very healthy twenty thousand brook trout were being raised. In 1926 major improvements to the water system were made and newer advances in fish culture were utilized. In 1938 an entirely new and improved system of raceways was built. After a temporary decline in production during World War II the hatchery expanded once again in 1948, with a record trout production year in 1953. Today the hatchery

stresses highly efficient methods and strives for quality fish propagation. It has also become a very popular attraction for school classes and individuals concerned with the environment and ecology.

Cultural Concerns

At present organizations and clubs of a wide variety provide cultural and educational activities and meet an array of interests and needs.

On October 8, 1971, Nashuans mourned the death of Elmer "Pop" Wilson, eighty-five-year-old former music director of the Nashua School Band,

1929-1956. He was also organist and choirmaster of the First Congregational Church for forty-two years until his death. He founded the Nashua Boys Band and the Nashua Symphony in 1929. After his retirement from the Nashua School System in 1956 he was named music director emeritus by the Board of Education. His talents and dedication helped countless Nashuans in cultivating music interests and careers.

The Nashua Symphony, reestablished in 1960, provides an opportunity for area musicians to develop their talents and perform in concerts held during the year. The Nashua Choral Society was formed in 1965 and gives several concerts a year, including joint appearances with the orchestra. Amateur actors and singers may join in the Actor-singers of Nashua begun in 1956 and the Nashua Theater Guild. The Nashua League of Arts and Crafts in cooperation with the League of New Hampshire Arts and Crafts (begun in 1931) provides an opportunity for developing a variety of talents in such areas as pottery, weaving, silk screen, and even jewelry making. Local artists may participate in the activities of the Nashua Artists Association which sponsors an annual art exhibit at Greeley Park. Other organizations include the Nashua Audubon Society, Nashua Mineral Society, Chess Club, Nashua College Club, and dozens of others. With their modern and spacious building on Prospect Street, built in 1964, the YWCA-YMCA also offer an extensive program of sports and activities.

Among the projects underway in 1970 was a new Nashua Public Library on Court Street. The $2 million project was begun in April, culminating several years of controversy over its construction and location. Funding for the project was provided mainly by a generous gift by Eliot A. Carter, a local industrialist. The 57,000-square-foot building offers a wide range of materials and services in spacious, colorful surroundings. Dedication of the new library took place on September 26, 1971.

Also begun in 1970 was the new Nashua Historical Society building on Abbott Street named in memory of Florence H. Speare, wife of a deceased benefactor. The new building was made possible by generous gifts and bequests by numerous individuals. On display are artifacts, pictures, documents, costumes, and materials of historical significance to the community. The attractive structure was occupied in the fall of 1971.

In November, 1973, the Arts and Science Center moved into its new quarters on Court Street. The three-level building includes a renovated part of the old Central Fire Station plus an expansive addition. The lower level includes a meeting room, theater, and art storage areas. On the main level are art galleries, staff offices, and a fascinating Children's Museum. The upper level features facilities for the diverse workshops and courses offered by the Center. A ballet studio, painting and sculpting studios, and classrooms are included. The Center is a focal point in the cultural and social life of the community and is used in cooperation with other groups and organizations.

Some Prominent Citizens

Particularly active in cultural and community affairs is Archie Slawsby, a life-long resident of the city and owner of a well-known insurance company. Among the many positions he has held are: member of the board of directors of Nashua Symphony Association, incorporator of the New Hampshire Charitable Trust, and director and treasurer of Nashua Arts and Science Center since 1959. In 1974 he was named "Citizen of the Year" by the Nashua Chamber of Commerce.

Eliot A. Carter whose great contribution to cultural life in Nashua was the new library building, began his long career in March, 1913, working for Nashua Gummed and Coated which was managed by his brother, Winthrop. A short time later he became Assistant to the Purchasing Agent and then head of the department. With the death of his father in 1923, he became treasurer and Winthrop was made president. In 1943 Eliot began concentrating his attention on the public relations aspects of the business and remained as a director. Following World War II he was made a vice-president and held the position until his retirement at the end of 1954. Throughout the years he was active in the expansion of the Nashua Company, now Nashua Corporation.

Besides his extensive business interests, Eliot Carter became involved in social and political affairs. He served three terms as a state Representative, two terms as a state Senator, and from 1931-1934 was on the staff of Governor Winant. For his service in both World Wars he was awarded the Purple Heart and the Distinguished Service Cross. His successful fund-raising activities helped many citizens at various times during the years. As early as 1930, following the tragic Crown Hill fire, he clearly demonstrated his humanitarian concern for his fellow citizens. Though selected "Citizen of the Year" in 1951 and again in 1969, he shunned public praise and chose to work diligently and quietly on various projects, speaking out on issues about which he felt particular concern. His death in July, 1976, at the age of eighty-nine, marked the loss of an outstanding individual.

His wife, Edith (Gardner) Carter, shares and carries on his humanitarian devotion to the city. For many years she has demonstrated an energetic ability to become deeply involved in worthwhile projects. Many will particularly remember her long hours of physical labor digging holes and planting trees and shrubs to beautify the grounds of the new library and the Arts and Science Center. Though Nashua has many devoted and generous citizens, few have been as gracious and productive as Mrs. Edith Carter.

Among other notable women is Isabelle Hildreth who, on May 10, 1977, received a Brotherhood Award from the New Hampshire Chapter of the National Conference of Christians and Jews. She was selected "Citizen of the Year" by the Greater Nashua Chamber of Commerce for 1970, and in 1976 was the recipient of the Nashua Exchange Club's Book of Golden Deeds. Active in many organizations she has been especially noted for her interest in the New Hampshire Heart Association of which she is Director. Her awards and citations only partly reflect her involvement in an extensive array of services and programs.

Mrs. Margaret Flynn, a well-known lawyer, has served several terms on the Board of Education and has been the President of that Board. In 1976 she received the Distinguished Service Award of the New Hampshire School Board for outstanding contributions to education in her school district. In 1974 Mrs. Flynn became the first woman Police Commissioner.

Growth of Educational Facilities

Also affected by the rapid growth of the community were the educational institutions in the city. Increasing numbers of students necessitated expanding the public school system and most private schools and colleges. In spite of this trend enrollment in parochial schools decreased by 1976 to about twenty-five hundred students as opposed to more than fourteen thousand in the public schools. However, Bishop Guertin High School, originally staffed by the Brothers of the Sacred Heart, still provides quality education as it has since its dedication September 6, 1964.

In 1966 coaches Charles "Buzz" Harvey and Anthony "Tony" Marandos marked their twenty-fifth year at Nashua High. Since coming from Holy Cross in 1941 the two helped NHS maintain an enviable record. In the period 1952-1966 the school won five state basketball championships, three in baseball, and eight in football. On May 23, 1977, more than seven hundred attended a testimonial to "Buzz" who was retiring as NHS Director of Athletics after thirty-six years. Among those present was star quarterback Greg Landry of the Detroit Lions who until graduating in 1964 was quarterback for Nashua High before going on to the University of Massachusetts and subsequently into pro-football. Also present was Edward Dobrowolski, top scorer on Harvey's undefeated 1946 football team, who went on to be lead scorer at Syracuse University. Earlier on August 31, 1973, Anthony Marandos resigned as associate principal of Nashua High.

Thus the passing of an era in Nashua High sports took place as the 1970s continued.

At present the public school system consists of sixteen schools including the new high school which was dedicated October 26, 1975. The impressive structure on the Mill Pond site accommodates three thousand students and provides a broad array of programs. Especially noteworthy are the vocational education areas funded by a $2.6 million grant to Nashua as part of the development of regional vocational education centers throughout the state. With the opening of the new high school the Elm Street building was converted to a junior high school.

The public school system also developed and implemented an Adult Basic Education Program aimed at helping adults earn a diploma or high school equivalency certificate. In 1975, about two hundred were enrolled in the Diploma Program.

Among the colleges in the city is Rivier College, established in Hudson in 1933 as a liberal arts school for women and moving to Nashua in 1941. Since then the forty-four-acre campus has expanded its facilities and programs so that by 1976 it accommodated fifteen hundred students on a full or part-time basis. Traditionally thought of as an undergraduate college for women, its programs serve men and women, including courses at the graduate level.

In the fall of 1970 the New Hampshire Vocational Technical College at Nashua opened its building on Route 101-A. Like its counterparts it offers primarily two-year associate degrees in Applied Science.

Another school is the New England Aeronautical Institute. It offers an Associate in Science degree in Aeronautical Engineering and similar subjects. Daniel Webster Junior College, a division of the Aeronautical Institute, began in Nashua in 1968. Its specialized curriculum leads to an associate degree in Business Administration or Merchandising.

In addition special interest schools include schools for driving, hair styling, and karate. Foreign languages may be learned at Rosetta Stone Associates, a local translating service.

Also filling an essential educational need is the Mount Hope School at 40 Arlington Street, its third location since its founding in 1955. With its dedicated and capable staff and the leadership of the Nashua Association of Retarded Citizens, the school offers programs to aid retarded individuals in living and working in society. Through workshop techniques older pupils are helped and encouraged in making a transition into useful employment.

Nashua Social Services

A wide variety of services and opportunities are available for different ages and interests. Particularly successful is Senior's Place in the former Montgomery Ward building on Main Street. Stressing a casual and friendly atmosphere, it is visited by hundreds of people daily who enjoy the warm surroundings. Besides offering a place for the elderly to dine and meet new friends, the building also houses several social service agencies.

Both local hospitals have found it necessary to expand their facilities. On June 17, 1967, the new St. Joseph's Hospital building was dedicated and opened; a modern intensive care unit was added in September, 1971. On June 13, 1973, the contract was signed for a major expansion of Memorial Hospital. On June 10, 1974, cornerstone laying ceremonies were held and the $4.6 million addition was dedicated October 24, 1974. On June 6, 1975, the third and final stage of construction was begun and it was completed September 5, 1975. Later, on December 27, 1975, the renovated pediatric unit was dedicated. By September 18, 1976, an expansion site study was completed and Memorial Hospital began plans for even further expansion. Meanwhile, in June of 1971, the Matthew Thornton Center on West Hollis Street was being planned, to be partially funded by federal grants. Open house and dedication of the new building was held November 10, 1971. In addition, other medical office buildings were constructed by several groups of doctors. Thus Nashuans were assured adequate medical care at local facilities.

The Judicial System

In an effort to deal fairly with young criminal offenders the Juvenile Court for Nashua has implemented a rehabilitation program. In August, 1971, for the first time, the Nashua District Court set up a fully-staffed Probation Department in an effort to correct antisocial behavior in a constructive manner. Rather than simply sentence an offender to an institution the Court takes steps to counsel juveniles and refer them to community services such as Community Council and New Leaf, which may be beneficial. Many drug offenders have been placed in rehabilitation programs at Odyssey House in Hampton and Marathon House in Dublin. In addition church and civic groups and individuals offer their services in close cooperation with Juvenile Court.

Instrumental in providing effective judicial services is Aaron A. Harkaway, appointed justice of Nashua District Court on June 11, 1973, succeeding the Honorable Kenneth F. McLaughlin, who resigned. Harkaway studied law and earned an LLB degree at Columbia in 1941. He was the first chairman of the Nashua Housing Authority from 1948-1952.

Another important figure in the court system is Judge Edward J. Lampron, justice of the New Hampshire Supreme Court since 1949. A resident of Nashua, he was born here on August 23, 1909. He earned his LLB degree at Harvard in 1934. Admitted to the New Hampshire Bar in 1935, he practiced in Nashua 1935-1947. Posts he has held include president of the advisory board at St. Joseph's Hospital; member of the advisory board of Rivier College, member and former chairman of the board of the Nashua Public Library, and vice president and director of l'Association Canado-Americaine.

Other Nashuans prominent in the state Judiciary Department are Robert F. Griffith, an Associate Justice of the Supreme Court from 1967-1976, and Charles J. Flynn, an Associate Justice of the Superior Court since 1967.

Two former attorneys-general of the State of New Hampshire reside in Nashua. Warren Rudman served from 1970 to 1976 in this post. Previously he was special counsel to former Governor Walter Peterson. As the state's top legal official, he gained a sound reputation and served as President of the National Association of Attorneys-General. George S. Pappagianis served both as Deputy Attorney-General and Attorney-General during the late 1960s and is presently Clerk of the Supreme Court, a position to which he was appointed in 1970.

Representing Nashua and twenty-eight area towns is Executive Councilor Bernard A. Streeter, Jr., who was first elected to his post in 1969. A native of Keene, he now resides in Nashua with his family, and during his five terms has played a leading part in the changes and growth of the region.

City Government

With an efficient Police Department, Nashua continues to be a relatively safe city, unlike many neighboring communities in Massachusetts which have higher crime rates. Other city services such as fire protection, health, and public works have also maintained favorable conditions, in sharp contrast to general declines in many cities despite their expenditures of larger sums which put them on the brink of bankruptcy.

Nashua's continued success in these vital areas thus is a result of a multiplicity of factors, some chosen by design, others occurring quite by accident, all interacting and responding to the growing, changing microcosm that is the city.

More than any other single individual, Mayor Dennis J. Sullivan has been an active participant in the dynamic period of the 1960s and 1970s. An outspoken defender of some projects and changes, and a determined critic of others, Nashua's five-term mayor stressed economy in city government and progress—but controlled—not mere progress at any price. In addition city government was conducted as efficiently as possible and intense concern with cost effectiveness earned him the support of many Nashuans. Unintimidated by controversy, Mayor Sullivan confronted the problems of rapid growth very early in his tenure and willingly faced the ire of some developers when he made it clear that private projects would not be permitted to take undue advantage of city materials and supplies, as had allegedly occurred earlier. Particular concern centered around the installing of streets and utilities in private developments. He gave notice that there would be strict enforcement of city regulations with no favoritism. As a result, Mayor Sullivan earned a reputation as a tough administrator willing to take a stand on an issue regardless of its popularity or controversy. His openly-stated opinions and remarks about local dignitaries and individuals are legendary. This former U.S. Post Office employee maintained a close identity with the working people of the city and shared their immediate concerns with rising taxes and living costs. He was an outspoken opponent of some of the high-cost projects which were built with tax money or were tax supported and his staunch individualism and belief in private initiative raised stormy disagreement on many occasions and issues. After defeating Mario Vagge in November, 1965, Dennis Sullivan maintained an active, outspoken administration with free and open dialogue with the citizenry. Many citizens deeply regretted his resignation due to poor health on August 12, 1977.

On January 9, 1978, ex-Mayor Sullivan died, a victim of the kidney disease that had caused his resignation. In the November election he had been elected a member of the Board of Public Works, an office he was destined never to fill.

On November 8, 1977, Maurice L. Arel, a former administrator at Sanders Associates, was elected Mayor, to complete the slightly more than two years remaining in Sullivan's four-year term. Arel was a graduate of Nashua High School, with a bachelor's degree in chemistry from St. Anselm's College and a master's degree in physical chemistry. Arel had previously been a candidate for Mayor in 1971.

Arel's opponent was Mrs. Alice L. Dube, who was the first woman elected to the Board of Aldermen and the first woman to serve as its president. Despite her well organized campaign, she failed to gain the critical votes needed to win and, before the final tally was in, delivered her concession speech. Congratulating her opponent, she asserted her devotion to the community and continued concern for its development.

One final issue settled in this election was the controversial recall election of Acting Mayor Donald C. Davidson, a professional airline pilot and the owner of a local travel bureau, who had filled the sudden vacancy since August. Receiving more votes than either of his two opponents, he won the recall election to complete his term as Alderman-at-Large.

Davidson became Acting Mayor after a charter change in the mayoralty succession had been decided in a referendum held on July 26, 1977. The 1913 charter provided for mayoral succession, in case of a vacancy in the office, by election of one of the Aldermen-at-Large by the Board itself to fill the unexpired term. The charter change voted upon in the July 26th referendum provided that the President of the Board of Aldermen should act as Acting Mayor. If there were six months or less remaining in the term he would serve for that period. If more than six months remained in the Mayor's term, a special election would take place. If the vacancy occurred within six months or less of the next regular election, the vacancy would be filled in that election.

Late in June of 1977 the filling of two vacancies on the Board of Aldermen had resulted in a shift in the balance of power on the Board, which had been stalemated during much of the previous year and a half. As a result of this shift of power, Mrs. Dube was replaced on July 19th by Donald Davidson as President of the Board. When Mayor Sullivan resigned, Davidson became Acting Mayor under the provisions of the new mayoralty succession law.

The most recent period of rapid change in Nashua continues, and, though many may disapprove of some of the results, few will complain that it has been dull or static. As in the past, Nashuans seem to thrive on discussion and controversy. Few if any major decisions have been made hastily. Most have required the test of time with lengthy public debate. School issues, public works projects, or whatever—all have undergone careful consideration before being implemented. The watchful eye of the press has kept the public informed. The participation in community affairs has been and continues to be strong.

The Bicentennial School was completed for the fall of 1977. In November, 1977, excavations were begun for a new Court House on the Walnut Street oval. A surprising federal grant of more than six million dollars in June, 1977, proved to be the incentive to begin various planned projects—the Court House, a downtown garage, library parking lot, and beautification improvements for the downtown area.

Earlier, on June 13, 1976, thousands of Nashuans and area residents lined Main Street to celebrate the Bicentennial parade. Dozens of floats, bands, and displays were included in the colorful procession sponsored by the local American Revolution Bicentennial Committee which first met informally in July, 1972. A resolution officially establishing the Committee was passed February 13, 1973. A series of programs was held to encourage interest in the Bicentennial, culminating in the parade. Nashua, with the rest of the nation, paused momentarily to celebrate and take a brief glimpse at the past before plunging toward an unknown but promising future.

26

Toward
The Year 2000

NASHUA in the twenty-first century? It may seem far away to most of us but we'll reach it in just twenty-two years. What will it look like? What changes do we want? What changes are likely, whether we want them or not?

These questions and others like them fill our minds when we think about the unforseeable future. However the future is still to some extent a logical extension of the past. So using measurable trends from the past and adjusting them by things we now know or can reasonably predict over the next few years, it is possible to make intelligent forecasts about the future.

An obvious example is Nashua's population: the past is known through 1975 as shown in Figure 1. As to the future, projection A is unlikely without radical change in land use for housing.

Projection B appears feasible of itself, with population leveling out at a little higher level than currently. However industrial growth and housing trends combine to tell us that more growth than B is likely.

As to Projection C, only a calamity—another disaster, such as a bigger Crown Hill fire or something equivalent—could cause such a slow-down projection. What's left is the heavy dotted line—the actual reasoned forecast from 1980 to 2000 of the State Office of Comprehensive Planning in cooperation with the Nashua Regional Planning Commission.

Before discussing futures planning, first a caution. Forecasting or predicting is not a certain process. There are many pitfalls and chances for error or misjudgment. An excellent example is the only known forecast made in the nineteenth century concerning Nashua's future. In his oration of May 14, 1891, at the laying of the cornerstone for the Odd Fellows Building, Orren C. Moore, editor of the *Telegraph,* predicted what Nashua would be like in 1941, fifty years hence. Here are some highlights of his prophecy:

Nashua in 1941 will have a population of 120,000 . . .
Above and below the present Hudson or Taylor Falls Bridge, two stately iron structures now appear, rendered necessary by the rapid suburban growth of Hudson and the multiplication of manufactures on the Nashua side of the Merrimack . . .
Above the old Main Street bridge, the Nashua is spanned by a stately iron structure . . .
The bridge that spans the Nashua at this point connects at

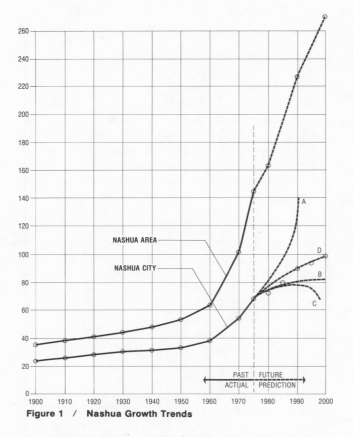

Figure 1 / Nashua Growth Trends

*the south end with the entrance to our "Fairmount Park,"
comprising more than 2000 acres along the river front
and including the picturesque region of Mine Falls . . .
Up Amherst Street the march of improvement has gone as
far as the eye can reach . . .
On Kinsley Street is a people's college, where the useful and
beautiful meet to furnish the truest and best higher education of the twentieth century . . .
A new and beautiful City Hall has risen on the site of the
old City Hall of 1840. A stately public library building,
with a magnificent reading room and gallery . . . keeps
open day and evening and on Sunday. On an open space,
west of the old High School lot, extending through to Main
Street, a splendid Government building is located, and
from the tower the old flag still floats, with fifty stars
instead of forty-four . . .*

His error in forecasting population growth was in
over-emphasizing the impact of Nashua's strategic
railroad and river location and its position in the
center of New England.

Next, with this caution stated, the broader questions are introduced of who is doing futures plan-

ning, what factors must they consider, how is it
done, and what is most likely if we integrate all
responsible available projections.

The answer to who is doing planning would include these public and private professional organizations and more:

The Nashua Regional Planning Commission
(NRPC). It ties together and helps guide the planning activities of the city of Nashua as well as those
of the Planning Boards of the eleven other towns
comprising the NRPC.

The Nashua (city) Planning Board providing
guidelines for orderly growth of the city, and com-
plementing the activities of the eleven town Planning Boards through common membership in the
NRPC.

The Southern New Hampshire Association of
Commerce & Industry—made up of the Chambers
of Commerce of Nashua and of Milford/Amherst,
and of the Nashua Area Personnel Group. This
latter organization promotes the growth and development of business and industry in this regional
area.

Two recently-created bodies: first a State Advisory
Committee on future planning, established by the
Governor; second the Forum for New Hampshire's
Future, a citizen activist group, including two
former Governors. Both groups have an interest in
and commitment to the future development of the
state.

There are other state and regional organizations
promoting the orderly development and growth of
the area. This list would include among others the
Nashua-New Hampshire Foundation which played
a major role in the 1950s and 1960s in developing
the business level and potential of Nashua, and
various quality-of-life oriented groups such as the
Society for the Preservation of New Hampshire
Forests, the Audubon Society, and others.

Stepping outside of New Hampshire for a moment and into the national and even world frame of
reference, there are many national and world-wide
organizations studying and predicting the future
and the trends which are leading us there. The
Hudson Institute near New York City has researched and published futures forecasts. An international society—the Club of Rome—has published several widely-discussed futures studies, the
most famous and controversial being *The Limits To*

Growth which foresees pollution and disaster if world growth trends, generally, continue to follow a rate such as that foreseen for Southern New Hampshire. Its "standard" world model foresees the collapse of world society beginning around the year 2020, safely beyond the shorter range with which this chapter deals.

With this brief summary of organizations involved in planning and forecasting behind us, let us first identify the planning factors considered by such organizations and then finally present the Nashua profile which seems most likely in 2000 A.D.

The major planning factors for projecting the future are a weighted mix of the following, and their interrelationships:

> Current profile—the starting point.
> Past trends leading to starting point.
> Forecast and Trends of key inter-relating factors
>   necessary for projecting beyond the starting
>   point (1977 for us), primarily:
> Total population
> Population mix—age
> Employment
> Land use patterns
> Political considerations
> Socio-economic forces
> Water needs and supplies
> Waste and sewage disposal requirements
> Transportation patterns
> Life-style, quality of life patterns

In interrelating, analyzing, and projecting these various trend factors, certain assumptions must be made covering the period leading to 2000. They would cover such unpredictable events as:

> Major disaster
> Significant energy shortage
> Nuclear war

We assume for our present purpose that these will not occur. After analyzing and projecting the factors above in the light of the preceding assumptions, these planning organizations generate projections which can provide a picture of the probable profile of Nashua and the Nashua area in 2000 A.D.

We will do this in three steps: 1) where we are now, 2) forecastable trends projected from "now," and 3) other futuristic but less objective information which may be relevant.

Figure 2 /
Quality of Life

Comparisons Among Selected Small SMSA's

COMPONENT	NASHUA Rank	MANCHESTER Rank	HIGH		LOW	
Economic	59 C	28 B	Tyler	B	Laredo	E
Political	26 B	25 B	Lacrosse	A	Brownsville	E
Environmental	66 D	14 B	Jackson	B	Lawton	E
Health & Educ.	37 C	70 D	Columbia	B	Fort Smith	E
Social	54 C	11 A	Lacrosse	A	Fort Smith	E
Summary	C	B				

Where We Are Now

Two sources can be cited: First the Southern New Hampshire Association of Commerce and Industry in a recent "Economic Profile" and related studies shows the Nashua area as being the fastest growing area in the state and nation. It leads other areas in New Hampshire as well as New England generally in such socio-economic measures as low costs of government, the youthfulness of its population, the high level of household spendable income, and so on. In economic and demographic terms it is now a healthy area.

The second source of data on "now" is a recent "Quality of Life" study sponsored by the U.S. Environmental Protection Agency. It ranked cities of comparable size throughout the U.S. on these five quality-of-life indicators—economic, political, environmental, health and education, and social. Nashua on a national scale ranked in the middle category "C," compared with Manchester's "B" overall rating. Figure 2 compares the Nashua ranking in the five indicators as well as in total, with other comparable-size cities including Manchester. However in relating such data to the first measure discussed, Nashua has the potential, now, to develop and grow over the next twenty-two years in terms of the five quality-of-life indicators.

For our second step—*what forecastable trends* can tell us where we go from "now"—we have several sources. The first is the population trend of Figure 1, from the OCP/NRPC. It shows the city growing from 63,670 in 1975 to 77,000 in 2000 A.D.; for the Nashua area the comparable figures are 122,560 to 230,400. Most of the growth is absorbed in sur-

Figure 4 / Nashua Area Transportation Study

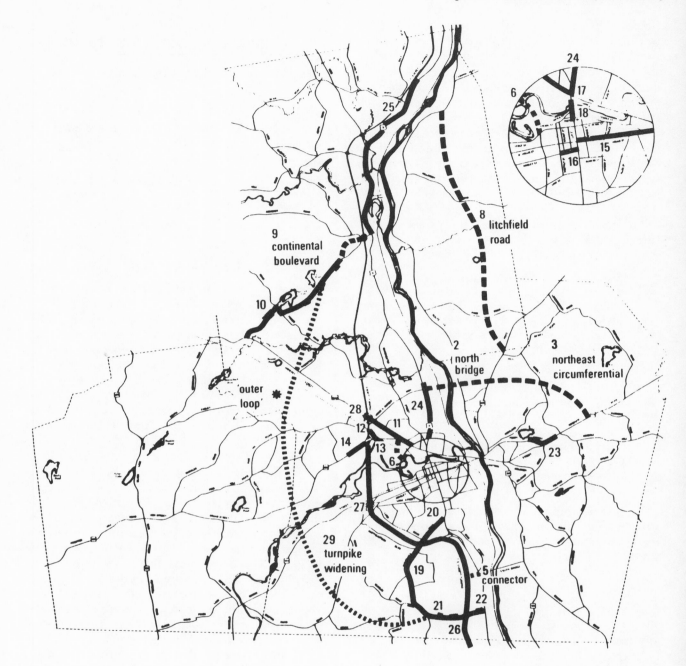

rounding towns, Nashua essentially reaching "capacity" in conventional housing measures.

Secondly, since this growth is expected, the intention of the planning agencies is to direct it to retain essentially the present structure of a core area city, Nashua and the still separate surrounding centers as shown in *Figure 3.* In other words, no continuous "megalopolis" between Nashua and Lowell on the south or Manchester on the north. We must recognize, however, that Nashua already qualifies as an extension of the Northeast megalopolis (Washington to Boston) corridor.

A third point, the trend of highway construction, will be another factor affecting how we look in 2000. *Figure 4* shows the recommended highway plan presented in the Nashua Area Transportation Study of June, 1976. Because it is recommended does not mean it will necessarily materialize, but it pictures new and expanded routes which will help determine the qualitative and quantitative measures of the Nashua area in 2000. Its chief "new" feature is the North Bridge (exact location not yet determined) which should be compatible with the population pattern shown in Figure 3. A fourth and final trend factor is the stated goals for the City of Nashua, at the right, which are partially reflected in Figures 3 and 4.

Finally, step 3, consideration of futuristic forces which may help shape the Nashua area in 2000 A.D. Some futuristic concepts which may be applicable:

> Shopping malls in the central business district, helping to retain the "downtown" environment, even in competition with new and established suburban shopping malls.
>
> More planned unit developments like Coburn Woods—to retain natural areas in combination with singles and multiple dwellings.
>
> Some form of public transportation—probably conventional (not monorails and skycars), particularly if energy shortages begin to limit conventional auto use.
>
> Wind and solar energy applications, already with us, are certain to be more prevalent if not universal. Possibly they will be utility-supplied, but more probably home-owner-applied.
>
> Revitalization of the Nashua River area to include:
> Restaurants
> Housing
> Parks
>
> Millyards development as currently occurring in Manchester and Atlanta, Georgia.

Long Range Objectives

These are defined as the long-range goals which identify the desired essential nature of the city beyond the year 2000:

> Provide sound housing to satisfy a variety of desires and needs.
> Seek a sound commercial base.
> Seek a sound and diverse industrial base.
> Maintain the pre-eminence of the CBD (Central Business District).
> Maintain Nashua as a "small" city with an ultimate population of 100,000 persons.
> Preserve and protect the city's natural and cultural resources.
> Maintain development within the city's ability to provide essential facilities and services.
> Maintain Nashua as a center of regional significance.

The development policies of a community express the means by which the city will seek to implement its long-range planning objectives.

In conclusion, there are many organizations contributing to futures-planning in the state. New Hampshire residents who are interested in the future have the opportunity to help shape it. They can do this by being aware of and contributing to the various organizations and groups working toward those future objectives.

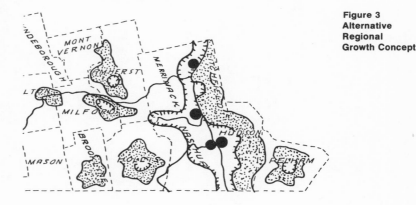

**Figure 3
Alternative
Regional
Growth Concept**

Epilogue

IN CONTRAST to communities that have stayed small, Nashua over the past three hundred years has experienced at all periods an urgent need to accommodate new growth. The required adjustments have almost always been made, despite civic disagreements that, in one instance, caused a division into two legally separate towns. As we survey these conflicts that have arisen all along the way, we might well ask this question: to what extent has the original ideal of "living in love and peace together" survived? Has it been eroded in the inevitable process of history-making or is it still the beacon guiding the eventual resolution of most controversies? Do Nashuans argue with each other as intensely as they often do because they care deeply about the ultimate achievement of community harmony? Are they motivated by a common conviction that somehow Nashua is worth fighting for and the struggles of the moment are all worthwhile? In many instances this seems to have been the way it has worked out in the Nashua experience.

We have seen how the citizens of early Dunstable became embroiled in religious conflict in the middle of the eighteenth century. Around that same time they also found themselves divided over the location of a new meetinghouse, and it is said some of them held services in a barn for several months rather than give in to the faction wanting the church built in a certain part of town. One hundred years later the controversy of the day was whether a town hall should be built on the south side of the Nashua River or in the more recently developed area north of the river. A monument to the veterans of the Civil War was delayed for years because of indecision concerning its proper location. As the nineteenth century waned, the burning question was the site of a library building, with northside/southside polarization erupting once more. Our own century has certainly not been free from differences of opinion over where to place important public buildings. Two examples in recent memory are the new library and the high school.

Change and adaptation to change have always been part of the Nashua story. The very contours of the land have been reshaped in response to the needs of population growth. Library Hill was once much higher as it rose from the banks of the river than it is now. The stagecoach drivers had to urge their horses to make an extra effort to surmount it and they called it the steepest slope between here and Boston. When Asher Benjamin started to build the Olive Street Church he had to remove many tons of earth in grading the site at the top of Temple Street where today a drive-in banking facility has replaced two former church buildings. On the map drawn to outline the grant made to the Ancient and Honorable Artillery Company, a pond or marshy circle is shown, approximately where Holman Stadium and the adjoining recreational area are located today. For many years this body of water, known as Artillery Pond, was part of the landscape until the city filled in the depression over a period of time. In the south end, Harbor Pond was a familiar spot until the land became valuable for commercial purposes when it, too, was filled and leveled. The Salmon Brook itself now flows underground for part of its course before it empties into the Merrimack.

Great changes have undoubtedly taken place in the profile of the downtown business district, but they have not been so rapid nor so complete that all reminders of yesterday's Nashua have disappeared. Beyond the facade of modern Main Street, vestiges of the area as shown in the old photographs can still be discerned. Once there were distinguished private homes and towering shade trees lining the street. Now, once again, we are planting trees in the downtown area. Even in the cynical twentieth century the spirit of man demands beauty for sustenance!

In contrast to many New England mill towns, Nashua can take great pride in the fact that it has preserved its vitality by adroit gear-shifting when the need has arisen. Special resiliency was called forth at the time of the closing of the cotton mills in the late 1940s. Nashuans have reacted with similar gallantry whenever catastrophe has struck. When the Crown Hill fire destroyed a quarter of the city, there was immediate and dramatic mobilization of all community resources to aid the homeless. A few years later a major flood prompted another display of a united front in the face of disaster. In the case of the fire, almost the entire burned-out area had been rebuilt one year after the event.

If a documentary film were made on the Nashua experience, here are some of the scenes that would surely flash before us as we watched it: Jonathan Tyng and his lonely vigil . . . young Samuel Whiting building his homestead . . . Elizabeth Weld dying at too young an age, far from her childhood home . . . the Hassell family falling helpless before the Indian onslaught . . . Captain John Lovewell and his band marching northward on a morning in May . . . Peter Powers hacking a farm out of the Nissitisset wilderness . . . Captain Walker leading his company at Bunker Hill . . . a family gathered around the fire on a winter's night in post-revolutionary Dunstable . . . Daniel Abbot setting up his law office . . . the stagecoaches clattering up to the taverns . . . freight barges moving down the Merrimack on their way to the Middlesex Canal . . . the building of the first mills . . . the excavation of the canal to carry the water power that would move the machines . . . the coming of the railroad . . . Josephus Baldwin exuberantly tossing his tall hat as he announced that he was a candidate for first Mayor of a reunited city . . . the farmers from Quebec crowding in to work in the mills . . . the unbeatable Father Milette building his church and his orphanage and his hospital . . . the owners of the first automobiles proudly driving down Main Street . . . the pathos of the 1915 strike . . . the gayety of the twenties . . . the drabness of the thirties . . . the challenge of the forties . . . the normality of the fifties . . . the dizzying population growth in the sixties . . . the Nashua Symphony Orchestra playing before a hushed audience at the Elm Street Junior High School Auditorium . . . the faces of children exploring the Children's Museum at the Arts and Science Center . . . all part of the Nashua experience in the making of its history.

Nashua, New Hampshire — city with a bright future, where people can still strive to achieve an ancient ideal — "that we may live in love and peace together."

Illustrations and Credits

The illustrations in The Nashua Experience *came from many sources. The majority of photographs, documents and maps depicting Nashua's history of the past were drawn from the archives of the Nashua Public Library and the Nashua Historical Society. These older materials were augmented by photographs from local residents, and the editors are deeply grateful to these institutions and to all those who provided material specifically for this volume. We are indebted also to Frank Ingalls, who collected and preserved hundreds of photographs of old Nashua, many of which appear in this book. The atmospheric photography of Paul Saltmarsh which appears throughout the book was, in the main, specifically commissioned for* The Nashua Experience. *Special thanks are due the Historical Society for its cooperation in permitting Mr. Saltmarsh to photograph the relics of Nashua's past in their extensive collection. All illustrations are listed chronologically as they appear in the book. The abbreviated title of each is followed by the photographer's or delineator's name where such information was available, the source, and the page number on which the illustration appears. In this listing, Nashua Public Library is abbreviated NPL and Nashua Historical Society NHS.*

Bibliography

PUBLISHED BOOKS

Appleton, Nathan and Batchelder, Samuel. *The Early Development of the American Cotton Textile Industry.* New York: Harper and Row, 1969.

Bacon, G.F. *Leading Business Men of Nashua and Vicinity.* Boston: Mercantile, 1890.

Barton-Aschman Associates, Inc. *Nashua Area Transportation Study.* Washington, D.C.: Barton-Aschman, 1976.

Belknap, Jeremy, D.D. *The History of New Hampshire.* Dover: Wadleigh, 1862.

Carter, Eliot Avery. *Lanes of Memory: an Autobiography.* Boston: Todd, 1964.

Clarke, Mary Stetson. *The Old Middlesex Canal.* Melrose, Mass.: Hilltop Press. 1974.

Copp, E.J. *Reminiscences of the War of the Rebellion, 1861-1865.* Nashua: Nashua Telegraph Co., 1911.

Eno, Arthur L., Jr. *Cotton Was King.* Somersworth: New Hampshire Publishing Co., 1976.

Farmer, John. "Note on the Penacook Indians." In *Collections of the New Hampshire Historical Society,* Vol. I. Concord, Moore, 1824.

Fassett, James H. *Early History of Nashua for Fourth Grade Children.* Nashua: Telegraph Publishing Co., 1915.

Fogg, Alonzo J., comp. *The Statistics and Gazetteer of New Hampshire.* Concord: Guernsey, 1874.

Fox, Charles J. *History of the Old Township of Dunstable: including Nashua, Nashville, Hollis, Hudson, Litchfield, and Merrimac, N.H.; Dunstable and Tyngsborough, Mass.* Nashua: Charles T. Gill, 1846.

Gibb, George Sweet, *The Saco-Lowell Shops: Textile Machinery in New England, 1813-1949.* Cambridge: Harvard University Press, 1950.

Green, Samuel A., M.D. *The Boundary Lines of Old Groton.* Cambridge: Harvard University Press, 1885.

Green, Samuel A., M.D. *Certain Grants of Land Made in the Year 1684, Now within the Limits of Nashua, N.H.* Boston: Massachusetts Historical Society, 1894.

Hazen, Rev. Henry A. *History of Billerica, Massachusetts, with a Genealogical Register.* Boston: A. Williams and Co., 1883.

Hill, John B. *Bi-Centennial of Old Dunstable.* Nashua: E.H. Spalding, 1878.

Hills, William Sanford. *Genealogical Data Relating to the Ancestry and Descendants of William Hills.* Boston: Alfred Mudge, 1902.

Hodgdon, Mary Josephine. *Historic Nashua; a Few Notes from Local History.* Nashua: Nashua Telegraph Co., 1902.

Hurd, D. Hamilton. *History of Hillsborough County, New Hampshire.* Philadelphia: J.W. Lewis and Co., 1885.

Indian Head National Bank. *One Hundred Years of Banking Service, 1851-1951.* Nashua: Indian Head Bank, 1951.

International Paper Box Machine Co. *Fifty Years of Progress.* Nashua: International Paper Box Machine Co., 1954.

Kidder, Frederic. *The Expeditions of Captain John Lovewell and his Encounters with the Indians.* Boston: Bartlett and Halliday, 1865.

Kimball, Helen R. *History of the Nashaway Woman's Club, Nashua, N.H., 1896-1971.* Nashua: privately printed, 1971.

Laughlin, Ledlie Irwin. *Pewter in America: its Makers and their Marks.* Boston: Houghton Mifflin, 1940.

Leading Manufacturers and Merchants of New Hampshire. New York: International Publishing Co., 1887.

Lewis, Alonzo and Newhall, James R. *History of Lynn, Essex County, Massachusetts.* Boston: John L. Shorey, 1865.

Lincoln, Waldo. *Genealogy of the Waldo Family: a Record of the Descendants of Cornelius Waldo of Ipswich, Mass., from 1647 to 1900.* Worcester: Hamilton, 1902.

Lui, Ben-Chieh. *Quality of Life Indicators in U.S. Metropolitan Areas, 1970: a Comprehensive Assessment.* U.S. Environmental Protection Agency, 1975.

Lockwood Hardware Manufacturing Co. *Lockwood: the Story of its Past.* Fitchburg: Lockwood Hardware Manufacturing Co., 1953.

McElwain, J.F. Company, *J.F. McElwain Company, Fiftieth Anniversary.* Nashua: J.F. McElwain Co., 1972.

Moore, Charles. *Timing a Century: History of the Waltham Watch Company.* Cambridge: Harvard University Press, 1945.

Moorehead, Warren King. *The Merrimack Archeological Survey.* Salem, Mass.: Peabody Museum, 1931.

Nashua, N.H. *An Account of the Soldiers' and Sailors' Monument Erected in 1889.* Nashua: Barker, 1889.

Nashua, N.H. *Charter and Ordinances of the City of Nashua.* Nashua: N.H. Telegraph Co., 1862.

Nashua, N.H. *Charter of the City of Nashua, adopted June 7, 1913, approved May 21, 1913.*

Nashua, N.H. *Annual Reports.* 1840 to present.

Nashua Centennial: the Story of a Century 1853-1953. Nashua: Cole, 1953.

Nashua City Planning Board Capital Improvements Committee. *Capital Improvements Program, 1976-1981.* Nashua: Planning Board, 1977.

Nashua Regional Planning Commission. *Growth Potential Analysis for the Nashua Planning Region, 1970-1990.* Nashua: Regional Planning Commission, 1971.

Nashua Directories, 1841 to present.

Nashua High School. *Tusitala* (Annual Year Book).

Nashua Telegraph. *Hurricane, the Complete Historical Record of New England's Stricken Area, September 21, 1938.* Nashua: Telegraph, 1938.

Nashua Trust Co. *The Fiftieth Anniversary of the Nashua Trust Company, 1889-1939.* Nashua: privately printed, 1939.

Nashua's 75 Years of Progress, 1853-1928. Nashua: Phaneuf Press, 1928.

Nason, Elias. *A History of the Town of Dunstable, Massachusetts.* Boston: Mudge, 1877.

Nelson's Souvenir of the City of Nashua, New Hampshire. Nashua: Nelson's New Five and Ten Cent Store, 1904.

New Hampshire. *Laws.* Vol. 3. *Province Period, 1745-1774.* Bristol, N.H.: Musgrove, 1915.

New Hampshire. *State Papers.* Vol. 9. *Documents Relating to Towns in New Hampshire.* Concord: Pearson, 1875.

New Hampshire. *State Papers.* Vol. 12. *Documents Relating to Towns in New Hampshire.* Concord: Parsons and Cogswell, 1883.

New Hampshire. *State Papers.* Vol. 24. *Town Charters, Including Grants of Territory within the Present Limits of New Hampshire made by the Government of Massachusetts, and a Portion of the Grants and Charters issued by the Government of New Hampshire.* Concord: Pearson, 1894.

Nichols, Rudge and Poole, Caroline N. *Peter Powers Pioneer.* Concord: Rumford Press, 1930.

Official Report of the Semi-Centennial Celebration of the City of Nashua, New Hampshire, June 28, 29 and 30, 1903. Nashua: Telegraph Publishing Co., 1903.

Parker, Edward E., ed. *History of the City of Nashua, New Hampshire.* Nashua: Telegraph Publishing Co., 1897.

Penhallow, Samuel. "History of the Indian Wars." In *Collections of the N.H. Historical Society,* Vol. I. Concord, Moore, 1824.

Pennichuck Water Works. *Pennichuck Water Works: 100 Years Service to the People of Nashua.* Nashua: privately printed, 1952.

Pratt, Eleazer F. *Phinehas Pratt and Some of his Descendants.* Boston: privately printed, 1897.

Roberts, Christopher. *The Middlesex Canal, 1793-1860.* Cambridge: Harvard University Press, 1938.

Roberts, Oliver Ayer. *History of the Military Company of the Massachusetts now called the Ancient and Honorable Artillery Company of Massachusetts, 1637-1888.* Boston: Mudge, 1898.

Sansouci, L.C. *Le Poete Rosaire-Dion Levesque de Nashua, N.H.* Joliette, Ill.: Le Phare, 1950.

Savage, James. *A Genealogical Dictionary of the First Settlers of New England.* Boston: Little, Brown and Co., 1861.

Schoolcraft, Henry R. "Tribal Organization, History and Government." Chapter V, Part 5 of *Indian Tribes of the United States*. Philadelphia: J.B. Lippincott, 1855.

Sears, Clara Endicott. *The Great Powwow: the Story of the Nashaway Valley in King Philip's War*. Cambridge: Houghton Mifflin, 1934.

Secomb, Daniel F. *History of the Town of Amherst*. Concord: Evans, Sleeper & Woodbury, 1883.

Spaulding, C.S. *An Account of Some of the Early Settlers of West Dunstable, Monson and Hollis, N.H.* Nashua: Nashua Telegraph, 1915.

Stearns, Ezra S. *Early Generations of the Founders of Old Dunstable: Thirty Families*. Boston: George E. Littlefield, 1911.

Stearns, Ezra S. *Genealogical and Family History of the State of New Hampshire*. New York: Lewis Publ. Co., 1908.

Stevens, Philip Ellis. *A History of the Maine Manufacturing Company*. Nashua: n.p., 1975.

Suffolk County, Mass., Registrar of Deeds. *Suffolk Deeds*. Boston: Rockwell and Churchill, 1880.

Sullivan, M.L. *Nashua of Yesteryear, a History of Nashua, New Hampshire, Adapted for Use in the Fourth Grade*. Nashua: n.p., 1953.

Sullivan, W.F. *Nashua Fire of May 4, 1930*. New England Water Works Association, 1932.

Thoreau, Henry David. *A Week on the Concord and Merrimack Rivers*. Reprinted ed. Boston: Houghton Mifflin, 1961.

U.S. Department of Labor. Bureau of Labor Statistics. *The Cost of American Almshouses*. Washington, D.C.: Government Printing Office, 1925.

Waters, Rev. Wilson. *History of Chelmsford, Massachusetts*. Lowell: Courier-Citizen Co., 1917.

Webster, Kimball. *History of Hudson, N.H. 1673-1913*. Manchester, N.H.: Granite State Publishing Co., 1913.

Willoughby, Charles Clark. *Antiquities of the New England Indians*. Cambridge: Harvard University Press, 1973.

Winsor, Justin. *The Memorial History of Boston*. Boston: James R. Osgood, 1885.

Worcester, Samuel T. *Bi-Centennial of Old Dunstable*. Nashua: Spalding, 1878.

Worcester, Samuel T. *History of the Town of Hollis, New Hampshire, from its First Settlement to the Year 1879*. Nashua: Moore, 1879.

UNPUBLISHED MATERIALS

Barron, Hannah Eayres. Manuscript book, "Miscellaneous Writings," owned by Nashua Public Library.

Foster, John G. "Letter Book, Fort Sumter." Books of letters, owned by Nashua Public Library.

Lund, Charles H. "Index to Map of Dunstable-Nashua. Showing points of Interest." Typewritten manuscript with photographs and drawings, copies owned by Nashua Historical Society and Nashua Public Library, 1938.

McCauley, Elfrieda B. Chapter XIII, "Nashua, New Hampshire: the Waltham Pattern," in "The New England Mill Girls: Feminine Influence in the Development of Public Libraries in New England, 1820-1860." DLS thesis, Columbia University, 1971.

MacGill, Caroline E. "The History of the Nashua Manufacturing Company." Manuscript owned by Nashua Historical Society, circ. 1923.

Massachusetts Historical Society Library. Manuscript Collections.

Nashua Historical Society. Manuscript Collections.

Nashua Public Library. Local History File.

New Hampshire Historical Society Library. Manuscript Collections.

"Personal War Sketches Presented to John G. Foster Post No. 7, Nashua, Department of New Hampshire, by Dr. Edward Spalding, 1893." Book owned by Nashua Public Library.

Purington, Lydia. "Autograph Book," owned by Nashua Public Library.

Theriault, George French. "The Franco-Americans in a New England Community: an Experiment in Survival." Ph.D. thesis, Harvard University, 1951.

Wilder, Almy. "Diary." Owned by Nashua Historical Society.

Work Projects Administration. *Ecclesiastical History of Nashua, Discontinued Industries, Financial History of Nashua, N.H., First Settlers, The Flood of 1936, Genealogies (2 volumes), History of Public Schools in Dunstable-Nashua from 1673 to 1936, List of Active Industries, Medical History of Nashua, Military History of Nashua, Nashua, a Story of Progress, Old Houses, Organizations, Reminiscences and Historical Articles, Women's Organizations*.

PERIODICAL ARTICLES

Atherton, Henry B. "Nashua, New Hampshire." *New England Magazine*, June, 1897.

"Courtship of Sally Belknap." *Historical New Hampshire*, February, 1948.

Ingranam, Alec. "An Exacting Study of the Complexities, Obstacles, Successes and Failures Encountered in the Building of the Middlesex Canal." *Towpath Topics*, April and September, 1969.

"Nashua's Famous Indian Head Coffee House." *New Hampshire Profiles*, February, 1952.

New England Historic Genealogical Society. *New England Historical and Genealogical Register*, 1847 to present. (Many articles used.)

Schuster, Richard. "City on the Nashua." *New Hampshire Profiles*, May, 1963.

Selchow, Frederick Mudge. "Nashua Watch Company." *Bulletin of the National Association of Watch and Clock Collectors, Inc.*, December, 1975.

Smith, Norman W. "A Mature Frontier — the New Hampshire Economy, 1780-1850." *Historical New Hampshire*, Fall, 1969.

Spaulding, Charles S. "Pioneers of West Dunstable." *Granite Monthly*, November, 1893.

Spring, Elizabeth C. "The Remarkable Hunts." *New Hampshire Profiles*, August, 1972.

Wiltz, Robert E. "Nashua: New England's Newest Boom Town." *The New Englander*, July, 1974.

Zanes, John. "Nashua Today: a Look at New Hampshire's Booming Southernmost City." *New Hampshire Profiles*, October, 1974.

CHURCH HISTORIES

Burbank, Leonard F. *History of the First Unitarian Society in Dunstable now Nashua, 1826-1926*. Nashua, Cole, 1926.

Church of the Good Shepherd. *A Century of Hope: Centennial Chronicle, 1871-1971*. Nashua, 1971.

Churchill, John Wesley. *History of the First Church in Dunstable-Nashua, N.H.* Boston, Fort Hill, 1918.

Cramer, Martha and Holt, Gladys. *Updated History of the Main Street Methodist Church*. 1968.

Dedication, History, Description of the First Congregational Church, Nashua, N.H., June 2, 1894. 1894.

French, G.M. *250 Years of History of the First Church Congregational, Nashua, N.H.*

Glavin, Leonard. "History of the Roman Catholic Church in Nashua and Hudson, New Hampshire." 1969. (Typewritten manuscript.)

History of the Greek Orthodox Community of the Church of the Annunciation, Nashua, New Hampshire, 1906-1956. No date.

Holley, Eugene E. *St. Christopher Parish, 1950-1975*. 1975.

Mellen, Frank H. *One-hundred and Fiftieth Anniversary, 1822-1972; a History of the First Baptist Church of Nashua, N.H.* Nashua, Accurate Printing, 1972.

St. Casimir Church. *100th Anniversary, 1857-1957*. No date.

Saint Louis De Gonzague Parish, Nashua, N.H. *Centenaire-Centennial, 1871-1971*. 1971.

St. Stanislaus Church, Nashua, N.H. *Fifty Years at St. Stanislaus, 1908-1958*.

A LIST OF NASHUA NEWSPAPERS RESEARCHED IN ORIGINAL COPIES AND ON MICROFILM

Constellation and Nashua Advertiser, Nashua Gazette and Hillsborough County Advertiser, Nashua Gazette (Weekly), *Nashua Daily Gazette, New Hampshire Telegraph, Nashua Daily Telegraph, Nashua Weekly Telegraph, Nashua Daily Press, The Oasis, L'Impartial, Nashua Telegraph,* and *The Broadcaster*.

Subject Index

Province of
Newhampshire

George the Se[cond]
of the

To all to whom these Presents shall come, [greeting]

Antient Boundarys of a Town called Old Dunstable, in our P[rovince]
humbly Petitioned and Requested of us that they may be Erec[ted]
which other Towns within our said Province by Law have an[d]
well as of the said Inhabitants in Particular by maintaining

Know Yee, Therefore, That We of our Especi[al]
Ends aforesaid. By and with the advice of our Tru[sty]
And of our Council for said Province Have Erected Incorporated and Ordai[ned]
tants of the Tract of Land aforesaid (Bounded as follows viz.ᵗ) begining at the Riv[er]
the said River Merrymack North Eighty Degrees West five Miles and forty Rod. to Ne[w]
of Water into Muddy Brook, and down Muddy Brook into Penychuck Pond. then by [some line]
where it first began. and that shall Inhabit the same, be and by these Presents
into a Body Politick and a Corporation to have Continuance for Ever by the Nam[e]
other Towns within our said Province, or any of them by Law have and Enjoy; [unto]
them the said Inhabitants and their Successors for Ever. Always Reserv[ing]
being and that shall hereafter Grow and be on the said Tract of Land fit for the
Successors when it shall appeare necessary or convenient for the benefit of the I[nhabitants]
Inabled and Authorised to Assemble, and by the Majority of Votes to Chuse all S[uch]
Coll Joseph Blanchard to call the first Meeting of the said Inhabitants to be held a[t]
time place and designe of Holding such Meeting. In Testimony whereof we
Wentworth Esqᵈ our Governour and Commander in Chief of our said Prov[ince]
Yeare of our Reigne——

By his Excellency's Command
with Advice of the Council

Theodore Atkinson Secry